Evidence in Contemporary Civil Procedure

Fundamental Issues in a Comparative Perspective

Editors:
C.H. van Rhee
A. Uzelac

Evidence in Contemporary Civil Procedure

Fundamental Issues in a Comparative Perspective

intersentia

METRO

Ius Commune Europaeum

Editors:
C.H. van Rhee
A. Uzelac

Evidence in Contemporary Civil Procedure
Fundamental Issues in a Comparative Perspective

Intersentia Ltd
Sheraton House | Castle Park | Cambridge | CB3 0AX | United Kingdom
Tel.: +44 (0)1223 370 170 | Email: mail@intersentia.co.uk

ISBN 978-1-78068-338-6
D/2015/7849/81
NUR 822

This project has been funded with support from the European Commission. This publication reflects the views only of the authors, and the Commission cannot be held responsible for any use which may be made of the information contained therein.

With the support of
the Civil Justice Programme
of the European Union

British Library Cataloguing in Publication Data. A catalogue record for this book is available from the British Library.

CONTENTS

INTRODUCTION

FUNDAMENTAL AND OTHER PRINCIPLES OF EVIDENCE IN CIVIL LITIGATION

LIST OF AUTHORS

S. Aras Kramar, Assistant Professor of Civil Procedure, Faculty of Law, Zagreb University (Croatia)

P.C.H. Chan, Teaching Fellow, School of Law, City University of Hong Kong (Hong Kong, China); Solicitor (non-practising) England & Wales; Solicitor (non-practising) (Hong Kong)

F. Fernhout, Associate Professor of Civil Procedure, Faculty of Law, University of Maastricht (Netherlands)

A. Galič, Professor of Civil Procedure, Faculty of Law, University of Ljubljana (Slovenia)

V. Harsági, Chair of Civil Procedure, Pázmány Péter Catholic University, Budapest, and lecturer at the Andrássy Gyula German Speaking University in Budapest (Hungary)

F. Hoogers, Bachelor Student of Law, Faculty of Law, University of Maastricht (Netherlands)

T. Ivanc, Assistant Professor at the Department of Civil, Comparative and International Private Law, Faculty of Law, University of Maribor (Slovenia)

H. Jans, Bachelor Student of European Law, Faculty of Law, University of Maastricht (Netherlands)

E. Jeuland, Professor of procedural law and head of the Research Center of Justice and Trial at the Sorbonne Law School, University Paris 1 Panthéon Sorbonne, Legal consultant (France)

B. Karolczyk, Ph.D., LL.M., Attorney at law at Domański Zakrzewski Palinka Law Firm LP in Warsaw (Poland)

T. Keresteš, Associate Professor at the Department of Basic Legal and Other Sciences, Faculty of Law, University of Maribor (Slovenia)

D.E. van Loggerenberg, Extraordinary Professor of Civil Procedure, Faculty of Law, University of Pretoria; Senior Counsel, Pretoria Society of Advocates (South Africa)

R. Mertens, Bachelor Student of Law, Faculty of Law, University of Maastricht (Netherlands)

P. Oberhammer, Professor of Civil Procedure, University of Vienna (Austria); Permanent Visiting Professor of Law, St. Gallen University (Switzerland); Rechtsanwalt, London (UK)

V. Poels, Bachelor Student of Law, Faculty of Law, University of Maastricht (Netherlands)

U.U. Rehman, Visiting Fellow, School of Law, City University of Hong Kong (Hong Kong, China); Barrister-at-Law (Hong Kong)

M. Repas, Associate Professor at the Department of Business Law, Faculty of Law, University of Maribor (Slovenia)

C.H. van Rhee, Professor of European Legal History and Comparative Civil Procedure, Faculty of Law, Maastricht University (Netherlands)

V. Rijavec, Professor at the Department of Civil, Comparative and International Private Law, Faculty of Law, University of Maribor (Slovenia)

D. Sehnálek, Assistant Professor at the Department of International and European Law, Masaryk University (Czech Republic)

E. Silvestri, Associate Professor of Civil Procedure and Comparative Civil Procedure; Scientific Director of the postgraduate program on Mediation and ADR, Department of Law, University of Pavia (Italy)

A. Uzelac, Professor of Civil Procedure, Faculty of Law, University of Zagreb (Croatia)

J. Valdhans, Assistant Professor at the Department of International and European Law, Masaryk University (Czech Republic)

T. Zoroska-Kamilovska, Associate Professor of Civil Procedure, Faculty of Law 'Iustinianus Primus', Ss. Cyril and Methodius University in Skopje (Macedonia)

ACKNOWLEDGEMENTS

The editors would like to thank Mrs. Marina Jodogne from the Maastricht European Institute for Transnational Legal Research (Maastrichts Europees Instituut voor Transnationaal Rechtswetenschappelijk Onderzoek or METRO) for her help and advice in editing the present volume. They are also grateful to Mr. Randolph Davidson (Pavia) for revising the English of the contributions of the non-native speakers; his language revision often went beyond what may be expected from a language revisor.

Most of the contributions collected in this book were initially presented and discussed at the postgraduate course and conference which took place between 27 and 31 May 2013 at the Inter-University Centre Dubrovnik, as a part of the Public and Private Justice (PPJ) series. The editors would like to thank the Inter-University Centre, led by Secretary General Ms. Nada Bruer, for their continuing kind assistance in providing an inspiring forum for high-quality professional and academic debates. The comprehensive PPJ discussions on fundamental issues and challenges of reforms of the European law of evidence would not have been possible without the help of the Maastricht and Zagreb Universities. In particular, helpful aid in all organisational matters on-site was provided by the team of the Law Clinic of the Faculty of Law in Zagreb, which also financially supported them. Some financial support for participation of individual participants was provided by two Croatian ministries (Ministry of Judiciary and Ministry of Science, Education and Sports), the HESP Programme of the Soros Foundation, and the Judicial Academy of the Republic of Croatia (the latter enabling the participation of judges from two superior Croatian courts, the High Commercial Court of the Republic of Croatia and the Commercial Court in Zagreb). The main source of support and financing, both of this book and the conference that prepared its birth, remains, however, the EU Project *Dimensions of Evidence in European Civil Procedure*. The results of the research presented in this book will, in the future, be used as the starting point of further research, in particular within the ambit of the scientific project *Transformation of Civil Justice under the Influence of Global and Regional Integration Processes. Unity and Diversity* (TCJust-UD, IP-11-2013) approved by the Croatian Science Foundation (HRZZ).

INTRODUCTION

C.H. van Rhee
A. Uzelac

EVIDENCE IN CIVIL PROCEDURE: THE FUNDAMENTALS IN LIGHT OF THE 21ST CENTURY

Introduction

If civil procedure lies at the heart of every legal system, the taking of evidence lies at the heart of every civil procedure. Yet, there are very few comparative works that attempt to present the topical issues of evidentiary proceedings in civil litigation.[1] The harmonization of procedural law in the European Union has not changed this situation, irrespective of the fact that mutual cooperation of European judicial systems as regards the taking of evidence in civil and commercial matters forms part of the European *acquis*.[2] Nevertheless, comparative research of the trends and developments in the national practices of evidence-taking in civil litigation has a lot to offer. Since the start of the new millennium, many contemporary jurisdictions are revisiting the fundamental principles of their civil procedures. The core areas of the civil process are not left untouched, including the way in which evidence is being introduced, collected and presented in court. One generator of the reforms in the field of evidence-taking in the past decades has been the challenge of slow and inefficient litigation. While the taking of evidence is not the only reason for the endemic deficiencies that have put into jeopardy the human right to a trial within reasonable time, in many national justice systems it has been contributing a fair share to it. Difficult access to information, inaccessibility of witnesses, and time-consuming processes of producing expert testimony have been the cause of frustration for many court-goers across the European continent and elsewhere. Both in Europe and globally, reaching a balance between the demands of factual accuracy and the need to adjudicate disputes in a swift, cost-effective and efficient way is still one of the key challenges. The rise in court backlogs, the difficulties of many national civil justice systems in securing a reasonable length of the central stages of their civil proceedings as well as an increased influx of new cases and reduced

1 See as one of the rare exceptions the work of Heinrich Nagel, revitalized and reconceptualized in collaboration with Ena-Marlis Bajons (Nagel 1967; Nagel & Bajons 2003).
2 Compare EU Regulation No 1206/2001 of 28 May 2001.

budgets of national judiciaries contribute to the reform trends aimed to streamline, simplify and accelerate fact-finding procedures.

The second reason why many countries are reforming their law of evidence is related to cultural and technological changes in modern societies. As the balance between, on the one side, traditional human rights such as the right to privacy and due process is shifting to, on the other side, the modern need for security, efficiency and quick access to justice, the perception of what is admissible or not in the context of evidence-taking is changing as well. In the same sense, the fast pace of modern life commands different practices of fact-finding, accompanied by new methods of selection of evidence that are appropriate for this purpose. Last but not least, the overwhelming penetration of new technologies into all spheres of public and private life has the capacity of dramatically changing the methods of the collection and presentation of evidence. The ubiquitous migration to paperless, online-based information systems is greatly changing the conventional landscape of civil courts, which were during many ages graphically presented as venues submerged in a sea of paper documents - and the biggest part thereof were the documents used as means of proof and those recording the results of evidence-taking. 'Digitalization' of civil procedure[3] challenges the conventional principles and routines, and may in the future bring much more than a mere conversion of dusty paper documents from court archives into electronic cyber-documents on court servers or cloud-based services.

Exploring these issues, the editors of this book invited the contributors to reflect on how these trends affect the situation in their countries and to present their views regarding further developments, both nationally and in comparison with the developments in other countries and regions. The impact of European and regional integration processes was also an element that could be discussed, in particular when exploring whether some common core elements may be identified in a cross-border or transnational context, and whether these common core elements have a chance to be further strengthened and developed. Our further goal was to inquire whether, in spite of national differences that are still dominant, the approaches to civil evidence converge, and whether reforms affecting fact-finding have a chance of leading to some forms of harmonization.

The contributions in this volume have been brought together under four different headings: 1) Fundamental and other Principles of Evidence in Civil Litigation; 2) Types of Evidence in Civil Litigation; 3) Evidence in Arbitration and National Civil Litigation; and 4) Evidence in Cross Border Litigation.

1. Fundamental and other Principles of Evidence in Civil Litigation

In this section, a series of fundamental and other important principles of evidence in civil litigation are discussed, amongst others: (1) proportionality in the taking of evidence, (2) access to information and evidence, (3) concentration in the administration of evidence, (4) the principle of loyalty and the taking of evidence,

3 On current debates in this context see Kengyel & Nemessányi 2012.

(5) the right to proof, (6) the admissibility of evidence, (7) equality of arms and language in the taking of evidence, and (8) immediacy and publicity as regards evidence.

The first contribution in this section by Alan Uzelac starts with the observation that some harmonization in the approach to the taking of evidence in civil matters is indispensable if the common European area of justice is taken seriously. The author advocates the role of the proportionality principle in this area. In order to show how matters should *not* be organized he discusses the way the ideas of the Austrian law reformer Franz Klein have been wrongly interpreted in Socialist legal systems to advocate the idea that it is the task of the judge to leave no stone unturned in the effort to establish the 'real truth' in the case, i.e. the so-called material truth. According to the author, after the demise of Communism the quest for the material truth is still pursued in former Socialist systems, leaving out of consideration whether the efforts invested in proof proceedings are justifiable in relation to the features of the specific case at hand. The modern trend is different if one takes into consideration various other civil procedural systems in Europe (the author specifically mentions the Woolf reforms in England & Wales) and recent EU legislation (e.g. the Small Claims Regulation). This trend suggests that the simplest and least burdensome method of taking evidence should be opted for in civil cases, and that the specific features of individual cases should give guidance in answering the question as to what evidentiary efforts should be made to establish the factual basis of the legal action.

In the second contribution to this section, Aleš Galič discusses access to information in the hands of the opponent party which could adversely affect the opponent party's case. In many Continental jurisdictions such access is problematic in civil litigation, amongst other things given the observance of the *nemo tenetur* principle and the fact that access to information is only available if the information can be identified adequately by the party in need of it and if the judge so orders. On the basis of a comparative overview of the approaches in different legal systems, the author claims that the traditional Continental approach to matters needs to be re-examined and that alternatives, for example the system of disclosure in England & Wales, should be considered. In the author's home country (Slovenia), the introduction of a new system of access to information in the hands of the opponent is especially urgent, since the existing system has abolished the far-reaching *ex officio* powers which the judge could exercise in Socialist times as regards evidence. The author states that the traditional *nemo tenetur* principle should be re-evaluated if it extends beyond the risk of exposure to criminal prosecution of the party holding the information, and that Slovenia should fully profit from the convergence in this area of civil procedure between England & Wales and some civil law systems such as Germany, Austria, Switzerland, the Netherlands and France, a convergence that can also be witnessed at the EU level (e.g. in the area of intellectual property rights legislation and competition law).

Next, Bartosz Karolczyk discusses the attempts of the Polish Legislature to concentrate allegations and evidence in civil procedure. He starts his contribution, however, with the remark that in modern Polish civil procedure the old Socialist maxim that the judge has the duty to search for the truth *ex officio* still applies. Nevertheless, modern Polish legislation seems to sacrifice the search for the truth to other important values. Attempts at concentration resulted in, for example, special procedural rules, introduced in 2000 and abolished in 2012, for commercial cases, providing for what the Polish Supreme Court called an *Eventualmaxime*. This meant that allegations, objections or defences as well as motions for evidence, when omitted from the statements of case, could not be introduced later unless the omission could be excused (for which only two bases existed). There was no judicial discretion in these cases and therefore no flexibility. The ordinary procedure, however, continued to follow the French 19th-century model, a model that did not advocate any concentration at all. In 2012, together with the abolition of the special procedure for commercial cases, the ordinary procedure was amended, aiming to introduce some concentration while avoiding the introduction of an *Eventualmaxime*. According to the Polish Legislature, the amendments allow for judicial discretion and the new rules are considered to be both flexible but at the same time rigorous. According to Bartosz Karolczyk, however, it is hard to see why the new system should be better than the former procedure in commercial cases. First, the new rules state that all the procedural acts by the parties should comply with the established standards of good behaviour. Second, they state that parties and participants in the proceedings are under a duty to submit allegations and evidence without delay, and third, that the court shall ignore untimely allegations and evidence unless the moving party can show that there is a good excuse for the late submission of allegations and evidence. The author provides various reasons why the new system is flawed and suggests that far-reaching reforms are needed in order to achieve the required balance between efficiency and fairness in Polish civil procedure.

The principle of loyalty in French civil evidence is the central topic of the contribution by Emmanuel Jeuland. The author states that evidence is not studied as a separate subject in France (neither is it in many other civil law countries), and as a result the topic is often neglected although it seems that currently the situation is subject to change. According to the author, written evidence is central in French private law. By way of an example, he remarks that a document is needed to prove a legal act if the value of the act exceeds the relatively small sum of 1,500 euros. Witnesses rarely appear in court to give oral evidence, but their statements are submitted to the court by way of witness depositions. The judge has extended case management powers in the French civil process, also as regards the administration of evidence, and the cooperation principle implies that the parties must assist the judge in arriving at a decision in the case in an efficient manner. A central element in the contribution by Emmanuel Jeuland is the so-called loyalty principle in relation to the right to proof. This loyalty principle, which is not generally recognized in France, is said to apply in the area of the administration of evidence in civil matters and means that the parties must exercise good faith when obtaining evidence. This principle is, however, in competition with a right that is firmly recognized under French law, i.e. the right to proof. This right facilitates the parties in proving their case in civil litigation and is opposed to limiting the use of evidence. The right to proof is widespread in France and according to the author it 'fits within the new procedural interactions, based on human rights interests and the principle of proportionality'.

The theme of the contribution by Vesna Rijavec and Thomas Keresteš is restrictions on the admissibility of evidence. The authors provide a comparative overview, focusing on differences in how illegal and illegally obtained evidence are treated within the various jurisdictions discussed by them. These differences are especially problematic where cross-border cases are involved, and where evidence is taken in a state that is different from the state where the evidence needs to be used in court proceedings. The authors distinguish three groups of jurisdictions in Europe. In the first group the use of the relevant evidence is forbidden without much further ado, and this is, according to the authors, most likely the case in Croatia (if the constitutional provision that contains a blanket prohibition of illegally obtained evidence is interpreted literally). The second group contains jurisdictions where a balancing test is used, i.e. where the interests of the litigant who wants to use the evidence is weighed against the interests of the litigant whose rights have been infringed by the use of or the methods used for obtaining the evidence. In a third group of countries, there are no restrictions on the use of the relevant evidence in a civil action, although the litigant producing this evidence may be subject to an action in tort.

Martina Repas discusses evidence in civil claims for damages in relation to competition cases and leniency programmes. Within the context of leniency programmes, companies provide information to the authorities about the cartel in which they have participated in return for immunity from fines. However, these companies will not be exempt from civil liability for the consequences of competition law infringement. The problem that arises in civil actions for damages before national courts is that the claimant may not have access to relevant evidence, especially to information provided by the defendant company to the authorities within the context of the leniency programme. The author discusses various possible venues for obtaining the relevant information and to what extent these venues offer any relief to the claimant. Of special interest here are the CJEU *Pfleiderer* and *Donau Chemie* cases, in which it was decided that the national authorities may not exclude the disclosure of the relevant documents (including the leniency documents themselves) completely and categorically, but have to take the merits of the individual case into consideration when deciding about the matter (i.e. there is a balancing test between public and private interests). The future implementation of Directive 2014/104/EU may, however, mean that the balancing test would be short-lived where it concerns the leniency documents themselves (the Directive only knows such a test for pre-existing documents).

The contribution by Elisabetta Silvestri is devoted to language and evidence. A fair trial may require the translation of documents (including documents used as evidence) and the availability of language interpretation (also for witnesses). The author was, however, only able to find one case at the European Court of Human Rights 'hinting at the problem of language in adjudication as a potential obstacle interfering with the principle of "equality of arms"' (an element of the right to a fair trial), and in this case the claim of an alleged violation of Article 6(1) ECHR was rejected. Nevertheless, the author holds that a dialogue on language and translation in civil litigation is necessary since these are closely related to the right to be heard. It is not justified that legal translation is underestimated in legal practice and that the profession of interpreter is not regulated in some jurisdictions such as Italy.

Finally, Viktória Harsági and Tjaša Ivanc address the questions whether the 'virtualization of court procedure' (litigation with the help of IT) is compatible with the traditional principles of procedural law, to what extent these principles prevent the use of IT, and whether the traditional principles are in need of reform given technological developments. In order to answer these questions, the authors discuss several examples of the use of IT in the court room, especially those in relation to the administration of evidence. One example is the hearing of witnesses by way of video link. In this case the principle of immediacy is at stake since communication by video link replaces the personal and direct contact between the court and the witnesses. A second example concerns public documents such as those produced by a Latin notary or other competent authority which have a special evidentiary status in various legal systems. Traditionally, these documents are paper-based and therefore the requirements these documents need to meet are related to this format. These requirements, which allow the courts to establish the integrity and authenticity of such documents, have to be re-evaluated and may be subject to change where such documents can be submitted in electronic format. The third example concerns the principle of the publicity of court hearings (where evidence is administered) and judgments (where evidence is evaluated). Obviously, this principle dates from a period in which the publicity of court hearings meant that access to the court room was granted to the public at large and making hearings available to a larger audience by television broadcasting or through the Internet was not possible since these modern communication technologies did not exist. The same holds true for the publication of court judgments. These were published in professional law journals or series which were mainly accessible to professional lawyers and getting access to these judgments for laypersons was nearly impossible. How different the situation is in the modern Internet age, where searching judgments, e.g. by 'googling' the names of the parties involved (e.g. the name of a neighbour) would certainly give rise to the necessary 'hits'. These and other examples demonstrate, according to the authors, that it is time to reconsider the traditional principles of civil procedure and to evaluate them in the light of developments in modern technology in order to provide for procedural principles that would stand the technological test of the 21st century.

2. Types of Evidence in Civil Litigation

The second section of this volume discusses two types of evidence: witness evidence in the Netherlands, and expert evidence in Hong Kong and the Former Yugoslav Republic of Macedonia.

In the first contribution in the section, Fokke Fernhout and his students report on an empirical study performed by them to assess the efficiency and the quality of witness examinations in Dutch commercial cases. As in most Continental legal systems, the hearing of witnesses is performed by the judge with only the limited participation of the parties. In their research, the authors have taken into consideration (1) the length of the examination of witnesses, (2) the way the available time is spent, (3) the way the witness is informed about his position by the judge (his or her rights and obligations), and (4) the extent to which the parties participate in witness examinations. From their research it appears that the average length of time used for hearing an individual witness in Dutch commercial cases is 36 minutes, of which 51 per cent is used for the actual interrogation of the witness. The remaining time is needed for making a written record of the witness statements, which in the Netherlands, just as in many other jurisdictions, is done by way of a summary dictated by the judge to the court clerk. On average 37 per cent of the time appears to be needed for drafting the summary, whereas an additional average of 12 per cent of the time is used for reading the summary to the witness, allowing him or her to make objections against the text where he or she considers this necessary. The authors come to the conclusion that the procedure followed in the Netherlands is of good quality, whereas they also consider that the time used for compiling an accessible and clear written record of the hearing (i.e. a summary, which in their opinion is far superior to an audio or video recording since it provides a clear report of the relevant issues in the witness statement which is authorized by the witness instead of an at times unclear, lengthy and not easily accessible audio or video recording of the proceedings in court) is well spent. Problems are noted as regards the quality of the information provided by the judge to the witnesses about their rights and obligations. Additionally, it seemed that at various courts staff had forgotten about the fact that civil court proceedings are public, since the researchers were sometimes initially denied access to the court room to observe the hearing of witnesses.

Peter Chan and Ubaid-Ur Rehman address expert evidence in Hong Kong within the context of recent changes that have been introduced in that jurisdiction. The aim of the changes was to curb the adversarial excesses in the administration of expert evidence. The Hong Kong changes have not gone as far as in England & Wales, where the judge has been given considerable powers to exclude expert evidence altogether. In Hong Kong, the general feeling is that there are already sufficient procedural tools for the court to manage the use of expert evidence. The Hong Kong reforms limit themselves to stating that the expert witness owes a duty to the court which overrides any obligation to those instructing or paying the expert, a set of declarations the expert needs to make in order to have his report received by the court, and the introduction of a code of conduct for experts. Chan and Rehman describe in detail how the system of expert evidence works in Hong Kong, including the use of the joint examination and joint report of experts that have been appointed on each side, respectively, and the Single Joint Expert. When discussing an area of litigation where the use of expert evidence is prevalent, i.e. personal injury litigation, they note that especially the use of the single joint expert, a measure that in England & Wales was thought to result in more efficiency, is not very frequent in Hong Kong. Although the authors explain that many personal injury cases are too complicated for a single joint expert to be used and therefore single joint experts are not frequently used, the limited use of such experts may also be proof of the fact that in Hong Kong the judge has not been given sufficient powers to manage the administration of expert evidence due to the successful opposition of the legal profession and 'the majority of stakeholders'.

Tatiana Zoroska discusses recent changes in the area of expert evidence in the Former Yugoslav Republic of Macedonia (FYROM). There, a shift has occurred from a Continental civil law approach to matters to a more adversarial, Anglo-American approach to expert evidence. Surprisingly, Macedonia has abolished court-appointed experts and adopted party-appointed experts even though in European common law jurisdictions the adversarial character of expert evidence has recently been reduced. Under the new rules, the Macedonian court may not order expert evidence at its own motion anymore. Another rule is that the parties must introduce expert evidence at the same time they submit their statements of claim and defence, respectively. The court cannot restrict expert evidence under the new rules. Only when the party-appointed experts provide vague, incomplete or contradictory reports, and re-examination of the experts does not eliminate the problems, may the court appoint an additional expert by way of random selection from the register of experts, and this is known as 'super-expertise'. Obviously, this system has many drawbacks, one of them being that the expert reports must be submitted prematurely, i.e. together with the statements of case. This may result in double work being done by the party-appointed experts, and in the event of problems super-expertise will be expensive. Also, under this system the defendant is disadvantaged, since the limited time period available to submit a statement of defence which must be accompanied by an expert report may mean that the defendant will not be able to find an expert who is willing to draft an expert report. The results are not favourable from the perspective of, amongst other things, complexity and costs.

3. Evidence in Arbitration and National Civil Litigation

The initial contribution to the section on Evidence in Arbitration and National Civil litigation is written by Paul Oberhammer. The author holds that in the area of evidence in civil matters (outside the area of small claims), one might learn from experiences in arbitration practice, especially where larger and more complex cases are concerned. The practice in arbitration is qualified by the author as user-friendly and efficient, and may serve as an example for court proceedings. The author states that the oral hearing in arbitration is very well prepared by way of written preliminary proceedings and this is done to such an extent that no new facts and evidence are admitted at the hearing stage. New facts and evidence are even precluded at the hearing stage. Experts are party-appointed, and court-appointed experts only appear in the case when this is really needed. Court-appointed experts may be avoided by way of a confrontation of party-appointed experts, as this confrontation usually leads to very reliable results. Witnesses are examined by the parties since they know their own case best, but the arbitration tribunal may ask additional questions. Another feature is that no distinction is made between party-witnesses and ordinary witnesses since there is no evidence that ordinary witnesses are more reliable then party-witnesses. The author also advocates witness conferencing and especially expert conferencing (i.e. bringing witnesses and experts together in order to discuss the evidence given by them), which is common in arbitration practice. In his final section, Paul Oberhammer advocates a method that is used in arbitration practice to deal with materials that are claimed to be privileged, i.e. the use of the so-called 'confidentiality advisor'. This advisor consults the materials that are claimed to be privileged and reports on the issue to the tribunal. In the event privileged materials are at stake, the advisor will not disclose the content of the materials to the tribunal or to the parties.

Remco van Rhee discusses the current system of civil evidence in the Netherlands. This system underwent major reforms in 1988, but has remained loyal (at least in part) to its 19th-century French origins. Since 1988 partial reforms have been introduced in the Dutch system of civil evidence, including some designed to deal with the latest developments in law and technology. Furthermore, the system has profited from a recasting of the civil procedural rules in 2002. Especially the introduction of the so-called 'post-defence hearing model' has led to concentration of the hearing and to the parties having an incentive to be as complete as possible as regards the facts of the case and the available means of evidence at an early stage. Concentration and efficiency are further advanced by the various discretionary powers of the judge in the conduct of the civil action, which are also the result of these reforms. Current reform plans may again bring some additional beneficial changes (although the planned abolition of the cause-list and the introduction of a digital 'My Case Environment' which is only accessible to a limited group of people may not be a good idea). The Dutch model may certainly be a source of inspiration for civil law jurisdictions which are aiming at a gradual reform of their civil procedural system and which are unwilling to embrace the extremes of more adversarial systems of civil procedure.

Slađana Aras addresses the scope of appeal in civil cases in Croatia, comparing it with other jurisdictions. One of her central questions concerns the possibility of re-examining evidence that has been introduced at first instance before the appellate courts. In Croatia, oral hearings for the re-examination of evidence are allowed on appeal, amongst other reasons to remove the need for remittals to the court below. In practice, however, Croatian appellate courts still prefer remittals of cases to the lower courts instead of re-examining the evidence themselves. This is problematic since the European Court of Human Rights has identified successive remittals as a systemic problem in Croatian civil procedure. Croatian appellate courts are, nevertheless, of the opinion that they are unable to organize oral hearings on appeal. The author concludes that recent law reforms may not be able to solve the present problematic situation.

Danie van Loggerenberg describes the powers of the judge and the parties in the taking of evidence in South Africa. On the basis of his contribution, it may be concluded that the South African legal system is conservative in its approach to limiting the adversarial system by increasing the case management powers of the judge in taking evidence. The author describes a traditional common law approach to matters, where the trial judge is rather passive. The judge may, for example, only ask witnesses questions if this is needed to clarify obscure points. In addition, the parties themselves do not have much duty to enhance the efficiency of the trial itself either where evidence is concerned. As a rule, they do not have to inform their opponent of the evidence they are going to present at trial. According to the author, in South Africa '[t]he result is that the surprise element plays a major role in the context of the presentation of oral evidence at the trial'. It seems that the present situation is not going to change quickly and the judge is unlikely to be given more case management powers in the taking of evidence in the near future. Van Loggerenberg concludes his contribution with the following, telling remark: In South Africa '[t]he parties remain in control of the taking of evidence, and distinctly so.'

4. Evidence in Cross Border Civil Litigation

The central theme of the contribution by Jiří Valdhans is the relationship between the 1970 Hague Evidence Convention and the 2001 EU Evidence Regulation. Where it concerns the Hague Convention, the author especially studies the relationships and roles of the European Union and its Member States as regards the Hague Convention's implementation. Furthermore, the author compares the mechanisms of evidence taking of both instruments. Valdhans states that it is clear that the Hague Convention addresses the same issues of evidence taking as the EU Regulation, and he comes to the conclusion that despite differences in wording, the substantive scope of both instruments is also the same. The Hague Convention remains relevant where it concerns the relations between EU Member States and non-member states, whereas among the Member States the EU Regulation has to be applied. This is an advantage within an EU context, since the Regulation offers measures for the taking of evidence that reach further than those of the Convention. These far-reaching measures are not a surprise given the fact that issues of national sovereignty are less emphasized in an EU context than in a wider international context. Especially the possibility of the taking of evidence abroad directly by the requesting court is a revolutionary aspect of the Regulation which is absent in the Convention. The Convention puts greater emphasis on measures protecting against interference in the national sovereignty of the requested state than the Regulation.

The editors of the present volume are convinced that the contributions provide valuable information on recent trends in the area of civil evidence in Europe and beyond. The various contributions form in their opinion important materials that may be used in identifying areas of the law of civil evidence that are problematic within legal systems that operate in a justice area where national frontiers have become less relevant and where modern technology exercises an ever greater influence on the manner in which the civil process unfolds. And hopefully, the suggestions of the various authors to solve problems that have been identified will provide useful information in the hands of law reformers, both at the national level and in an international context.

Maastricht/Zagreb, July 2015

Bibliography

Kengyel & Nemessányi 2012
Kengyel, M. & Nemessányi, Z. (eds.), *Electronic Technology and Civil Procedure. New Paths to Justice from Around the World*, Dordrecht: Springer, 2012.

Nagel 1967
Nagel, H., *Die Grundzüge des Beweisrechts im europäischen Zivilprozeß - Eine rechtsvergleichende Studie*, Baden-Baden: Nomos, 1967.

Nagel & Bajons 2003
Nagel, H. & Bajons, E-M., *Beweis - Preuve - Evidence*, Baden-Baden: Nomos, 2003.

FUNDAMENTAL AND OTHER PRINCIPLES OF EVIDENCE IN CIVIL LITIGATION

A. Uzelac

EVIDENCE AND THE PRINCIPLE OF PROPORTIONALITY. HOW TO GET RID OF EXPENSIVE AND TIME-CONSUMING EVIDENCE?

1. Introduction

European civil procedural law deals with the taking of evidence in civil matters only marginally. Admittedly, cooperation in the taking of evidence is among the areas that may be subject to measures adopted by the European legislators.[1] But in the context of evidence-taking, 'cooperation' and 'harmonization' are two rather different, and sometimes contradictory concepts. As initially stated in the now almost 15-year-old EU instrument regarding the taking of evidence in civil and commercial matters, the aim of the Regulation was to 'improve, simplify and accelerate cooperation', and to 'make [it] easier to take evidence in another Member State'.[2] Yet, the very core of the evidence-taking - *who* (and *when* and *how*) has to select, present and assess the evidence - was left untouched.

Moreover, in line with the principles of subsidiarity and proportionality entrenched in the EU Treaty, the European legislators cannot go beyond what is absolutely necessary to achieve the imminently set objective, i.e. to improve the cooperation between the national courts of different European jurisdictions. Whether these courts have diametrically opposite approaches and rules to evidence-taking, from the EU law perspective it does not matter. As, allegedly, the desired objective of facilitating judicial cooperation has largely been achieved,[3] no further actions that would go beyond the friendly cross-border judicial assistance between courts and promotion of mutual knowledge of different evidence-taking systems in the EU countries are either desired or permissible.

1 Treaty on the Functioning of the European Union, Art. 81 para. 2(d).

2 See Council Regulation no 1206/2001 of 28 May 2001 on cooperation between the courts of the Member States in the taking of evidence in civil or commercial matters, preamble.

3 See EC Report on the application of Council Regulation (EC) 1206/2001 of 28 May 2001 on cooperation between the courts of the Member States in the taking of evidence in civil or commercial matters, COM(2007) 769 final of 5 December 2007, p. 6-7.

Is this really the case? Can cooperation be successful within the 'common area of justice' if the practices of the taking of evidence in civil and commercial cases are exceedingly different and are rooted in different rationales and different core practices? In this text, I will argue that if a 'common area of justice' is to be taken seriously, some harmonization in the approach to the taking of evidence is indispensable.

The developments regarding the taking of evidence conform to the wider trends of convergence triggered by the change in the setting of the goals of civil litigation. In all recent reforms, the key is the principle of proportionality.[4] In the context of evidence-taking, the principle of proportionality, when properly understood and accepted, may prompt far-reaching changes - in particular where the principle of proportionality was largely unknown in the field of civil procedure.

To support this assessment, in this text I will briefly outline some specific features of the style of civil procedure in selected countries of the European South and East that differ greatly from the values of 'acceleration' and 'simplification' proclaimed at the EU level. I will submit that some elements of the European *acquis* on civil procedure do contain the seeds of a uniform approach to evidence, which may have a certain horizontal effect of making the judicial practices and reforms of national legislation that regulate court proceedings in civil and commercial matters similar.[5] A few provisions on evidence-taking from recent civil procedure reforms in Croatia will be used as an example of a new approach in evidence-taking.

2. Ideology of 'Material Truth' and its Impact on Evidence-taking

This text is written from the perspective of the post-socialist EU Member States, in particular those from the South-East. After two decades of 'transition', the transformation of civil justice systems there still seems to be incomplete. As I have extensively discussed elsewhere,[6] many elements of the former legal tradition managed to successfully survive. Among them, two were particularly influential in the context of the taking of evidence: the doctrine of the 'material truth' and the inquisitorial and paternalistic position of judges *vis-à-vis* the parties. Their specific amalgam led to the formation of a mainstream style in evidence-taking proceedings, which can be best described in a negative way, by three insurmountable challenges that lead to a triple deficiency: the lack of procedural concentration, the lack of proper time-management, and the hostility to preclusions of any kind in respect of the presentation of new (additional) evidence.

Every post-socialist country added a specific flavour to this amalgam. Also, some other countries of the European South that technically cannot be regarded as

4 Beware: in the context of civil procedure it has a different meaning in comparison with the same substantive principle in European law. It relates to the need of balancing the value of accuracy with the values of timeliness and appropriate costs.

5 On the potential horizontal effect in respect to remedies required to achieve a full effective judicial protection see Van Gerven 1995, p. 679-702.

6 See Uzelac 2010; see also Van Rhee & Uzelac 2012, p. 6-7.

post-socialist (e.g. Italy or Greece) share to a certain extent some similar features, so that we can distinguish a 'transition' and 'Mediterranean' subspecies of the same approach to evidence-taking.[7] Therefore, we should focus on the presentation of models, comparable with Max Weber's 'ideal types', without insisting on their perfect match with a precisely defined circle of jurisdictions or legal orders.

The adherence to the value of 'material (substantive) truth' and the active role of the judge in the process of evidence-taking is indeed not uniquely present only in the socialist and post-socialist civil procedures. The promotion of rules and practices that give priority to the accuracy of the factual findings is at the core of other approaches to the taking of evidence, most prominently in the context of one of the most successful procedural models ever, the model of Austrian civil procedure as developed at the end of 19th century by Franz Klein.[8] Prior to World War II, some countries of Central and Eastern Europe that were later a part of the socialist bloc, like Hungary, Czechoslovakia, Poland and Yugoslavia, experienced reforms inspired by Klein's ZPO.[9] The historical memory of the pre-socialist reforms remained prominent in the legal textbooks and doctrine during socialist times, which regularly supported the idea that the socialist codes of civil procedure essentially continue and further develop the model of civil procedure originally framed by Klein. While this can, to a certain extent, be true where the bare text of the procedural legislation is concerned, the ideas of Franz Klein were dramatically different from the practice of litigation in the times of 'real socialism'. On the other hand, the fact that the 'law in books' always interpreted existing codes of civil procedure as a continual development inspired by the Austrian (i.e. non-socialist) civil procedure prevented the legal positivists' circles from becoming aware that, also after the fall of socialism, the reality in court proceedings still remained in crass contradiction with the goals and ambitions of Klein's model.

Klein's model and the socialist model are best distinguished where the taking of evidence is concerned. Both models start with the idea of judicial activism, propagating that judges should actively participate in the taking of evidence. However, the underlying rationale and the practical implementation of the two models are radically different. Franz Klein wanted to moderate the adversarial structure of civil proceedings, which had become 'a war without a Red Cross'.[10] He did not, however, intend to dismantle this structure. The role of the judge in his model was the one of the moderator who actively participates in the lively discussion of the parties or their representatives, setting limits when necessary or stimulating actions if the course of the process slowed down. Klein's judge had the right to question witnesses and experts on equal footing with the parties. He could take evidence *ex officio*, but only in the interests of justice, subject to his best judgment and discretion. The powers of the judge would in his view include the

7 See on 'Mediterranean' subspecies more in Uzelac 2008, p. 71-99.
8 See Frodl 2012; Verkerk 2010, p. 33-45.
9 More in Jelinek 1991, p. 41-89.
10 Klein 1891, p. 40.

right to restrict the evidentiary proposals of the parties, and to set time limits for the collection and presentation of evidence. Imposing sanctions in the form of preclusions for belated evidence is a natural and necessary component of such an approach. Altogether, the key element in Klein's model was the perception of civil procedure as a joint responsibility of the parties and the court. They were supposed to work together in order to come to a fair and accurate result with minimum waste of effort, money and time. 'Material truth' in such a concept is not an imperative imposed from the outside; it is the likely outcome of the loyal procedural collaboration of all the actors that participate in civil procedure.

On the other hand, the socialist concept of 'material truth' had a different starting point. The parties and their lawyers were from the very beginning labelled as an unreliable and *par excellence* suspect factor in civil proceedings. The early understanding of the revolutionary period was that the law and lawyers are an instrument of the class society, which will have to die out over time in the new communist society.[11] Later, the trust in 'socialist legality' and 'socialist justice' as powerful instruments of the socialist regimes secured more space for civil procedure, but the strengthening of judicial structures relied on judicial hierarchies controlled and governed from above, not on trust in private parties who dealt with their personal and economic disputes (which were anyway only an aberration in the state-governed economies).[12] Therefore, civil procedure was always aimed to maintain a firm grip on the way parties handle a dispute. It dominated the proceedings in the spirit of 'socialist paternalistic inquisitorialism'. This approach also was reflected in the evidentiary process. The judges ('the court') had not only an option, but also a *de facto* duty to take evidence on their own initiative, while controlling the evidence introduced by the parties from the perspective of order and (socialist) morality.[13] However, with the shifting of duties and initiative, the parties' role in the procedure was increasingly marginalized. In the evidence-taking process, their obligation was only to indicate possible sources of information (and sometimes not even that), the rest was up to the court, which should procure documents, invite witnesses, appoint experts... Consequently, the failure in procuring evidence could be attributed more to the failure of the court. A passive and obedient attitude would pay off, or at least not be penalized by negative inferences. And, when the ball is in the other player's court, the way for various dilatory tactics was wide open, and even more so, because the failure of the official judicial structures as representatives of the state apparatus was hardly tolerable. Since the failure of official inquiries implied the failure of the regime, the doctrine of 'material truth' imposed the duty

11 The representative doctrine of that period is formulated in the works of Pashukanis, Stuchka & Reisner. See more in Pashukanis 1980.

12 For a representative understanding of the position of 'socialist justice' in the context of evidence see Vyshinski 1946.

13 As representatives of the public interest, judges had an obligation to act. Private interests had little weight. As stated by Lenin, '[W]e do not recognise anything "private", and regard everything in the economic sphere as falling under public and not private law' – see Lenin's statement in his letter to Kursky, in Lenin 1971, p. 560.

to continue to inquire, pursuing all possible sources of evidence, until the options were definitely exhausted. In the words of a foreign observer of judicial practices in Croatia (long after the start of the transition), the ruling principle in official evidence-taking was 'no stone should be left unturned'. Therefore, the system of preclusions in which strict time limits were imposed on the introduction and presentation of evidence was unthinkable,[14] as it would also suggest that the omnipotent investigatory machine of the state had not done everything in its power to establish the truth. And, the precedence of 'truth' over efficiency was backed by the general view that channels for the control of the Judiciary have to remain open. In the same sense, avenues for possible reopening of already closed cases had to exist. To that extent, new (or 'new') evidence could be introduced throughout the proceedings, including its appellate and further stages. Therefore, the 'material truth' construct in that model of evidence-taking was not an inherent and internal value of the process, but a value imposed from the outside. Essentially, the 'material truth' was the product of the ideological imperative of the inquisitorial and paternalistic attitude towards the private dispute resolution process.

After the 1990s, much of the ideological basis for this model of procedure disappeared, but the customary style of evidence-taking largely continued in the judicial practice of transition countries, even when some of them became Member States of the EU. The scars left were deep, and they continued to manifest in various typical features. One of them was the absence of trial *stricto sensu*. The lack of concentration led to a style of oral hearing that took place over a longer period of time in multiple short meetings where few substantive arguments occurred, and new documents could be introduced and exchanged. The tolerance for new evidence and the weaknesses in the system of summons and service made proper time-management and planning of the proceedings virtually impossible. Ultimately, as no deadlines could be introduced for factual allegations and submission of evidence, the 'activist' judges could not use preclusions to prevent parties from using dilatory and protracting strategies. The 'activist' Judiciary therefore collapsed where it was supposed to be the strongest – in controlling the course of the court action and the behaviour of the parties.

Indeed, the style of proceedings inherited from the past was not very sympathetic towards the idea of weighing the evidentiary efforts against the background of their expense and time-use. The catchy phraseology of 'material truth' was apparently ideologically neutral. At least in its pure form, the idea of material truth was independent from the subject matter of dispute and its value. Truth, as an absolute value, would have to be established even in the smallest of small claims. Concurring with this statement, the textbooks on civil procedure, long after the fall of socialism, kept repeating that it was not permissible to neglect small cases: the *de minimis non curat praetor* principle was generally rejected, even though

14 See Galič 2014, p. 241, disclosing the non-liberal and paternalistic nature of those who oppose the system of preclusions that emphasises the responsibility of the parties for the active conduct of the case.

the procedural codes here and there contained some - largely ignored - special rules that were supposed to accelerate proceedings in small claims cases.

Of course, the depicted model of procedure is a simplification. Many scholars and practitioners would find that in this or that aspect the practice of the post-socialist countries, in particular those that have entered into the EU, has moved forward. But a more careful analysis points to many areas in which the once-shared procedural tradition has survived.[15] The test for checking whether the 'old' procedure is finally gone or not can be found in the acceptance of the principle of proportionality in the context of the taking of evidence.

3. The Seeds of Proportionality and the New Wave of Thinking about Procedure and Evidence-taking

The European perspective on the principle of proportionality actually does not start on the European Continent, but in the British Isles. The principle of proportionality was in a prominent form introduced by the 1999 CPR reform in England, and locally and globally represented by its main proponent, Lord Woolf.[16] As stated in CPR Rule 1.1.1: '[T]hese Rules are a new procedural code with the *overriding objective* of enabling the court to deal with cases *justly and at proportionate cost*'. Though the word 'proportionate' in 1.1.1 relates only to costs, the equation is a bit more complex. The definition of dealing with a case justly includes again the proportionality - proportionality 'to the amount of money involved ... to the importance of the case ... to the complexity of the issues ... and to the financial position of each party'. Zuckerman called this a three-dimensional concept of justice, denoting thereby a concept in which '... efficiency and expedition are as important as the correctness of the outcome'.[17] Three dimensions that have to be balanced and put into the relationship of proportionality are the time needed to adjudicate, the costs incurred in the proceedings, and the just and accurate result of litigation.

How does this concept affect the process of evidence-taking? Obviously, the costs and efforts engaged to establish disputed facts should be put into correlation with the value and complexity of the case. In other words, the type of evidence used to prove disputed facts, the scope of evidentiary efforts and the method of assessment of proof should be adjusted to the value and complexity of the disputes. In the English CRP reform, this aim was pursued through the allocation of each case to one of three tracks (small claims track, fast track and multi-track) to which all cases are allocated, with a certain degree of flexibility. Another method was the pre-action protocols - routine steps that have to be pursued in particular types of

15 See Uzelac 2010; Manko 2013. The study of survival of the Socialist tradition in Central and Eastern Europe continues to be topical. E.g. it is the central topic of the Brno conference '25 Years after the Transformation: Law and Legal Culture in Central and Eastern Europe between Continuity and Discontinuity' in April 2015.

16 See Woolf Report 1996.

17 Zuckerman 2009, p. 49.

disputes. Among them an important place is attributed to the identification of the disputed issues and to the preparation and disclosure of evidence.[18]

The proportionality in the approach to the selection of evidence after the Woolf reforms in England may be illustrated by the example of experts. In small claims cases (currently: claims of a value of not more than 10,000 GBP), in principle no experts are permitted without special permission of the court.[19] In fast track cases (currently: claims of a value of not more than 25,000 GPB), if expert evidence is required, the parties are encouraged to agree on the use of a single joint expert. Failing their agreement, 'the court is to give directions on its own initiative and ... its general approach will be ... to give directions for a single joint expert unless there is good reason not to do so'.[20] In any case, fast track limits the use of experts to one expert per party in relation to any field of expertise, and to a maximum of two fields. In a multi-track procedure, there are no general limitations on the number of experts and the fields of expertise. However, having the overriding objective in mind, the court will give a direction granting permission to use expert evidence in each individual case, stating whether it grants permission to use oral evidence or reports or both and it will name the experts concerned.[21]

The level of detail with which English law of procedure attempts to regulate proportionality as the guiding approach to evidence is generally not possible to find in most other European national laws. However, the prominence and global attention that the Woolf reform raised did have an impact on subsequent national reforms of civil procedure. It also had a small, but not insignificant impact on the European law of civil procedure.

This impact is probably least visible in the EU instrument that in its title expressly concerns evidence - Regulation No. 1206/2001. However, even in that document (drafted only slightly later than the Woolf reforms in England) one can find some seeds of proportionality. The Regulation has as its main target the improvement of cooperation in the taking of evidence, and not the improvement of the taking of evidence in and of itself; but what applies to cooperation can be applicable, at least partly, also to evidence-taking. Therefore, when the Regulation speaks of 'improving', 'simplification' and 'acceleration' as regards cooperation between courts in the taking of evidence,[22] this may be taken as a signal that the taking of evidence as such should also move in the same direction. More so, because the Regulation also cites the need for the efficiency of judicial procedures in civil and commercial matters, and encourages that, at least when cross-border requests for the taking of evidence are executed, the transmission (and fulfilment?) of such requests is 'made directly and by the most rapid means possible.'[23] Thereby, the

18 See e.g. for fast track Practice Direction (supplement to CPR Part 28), p. 3.3.
19 See CPR 27.5.
20 See Practice Direction 28, 3.9. p. (4).
21 Practice Direction 29, 9.2. p. (4).
22 Regulation 1206/2001, preamble, p. (2).
23 *Ibid.*, p. (8).

need for speed warrants the use of 'all appropriate means'[24] and requires that requests for the performance of the taking of evidence be executed 'expeditiously', if possible within 90 days of receipt by the requesting court.[25] For the purpose of facilitation of the proceedings, the direct taking of evidence in another EU Member State is also permitted, which is again motivated by reasons of cutting time and, possibly, the costs of proceedings. The latter motivation is certainly at the core of the provisions that encourage the use of communication technologies, such as videoconferences and teleconferences. However, no rules from that early regulation have a bearing on the selection and assessment of evidence, as this is firmly in the hands of the national authorities that request assistance in evidence-taking.

A more direct approach to evidence-taking in EU law can be inferred from the two autonomous European procedures, the European Order for Payment procedure[26] and the European Small Claims procedure.[27] In the discussion of the proportionality principle in evidence-taking, we will focus on the latter one. Small claims are as such a wonderful litmus test for the principle of proportionality. The very fact that the first contentious procedure in Europe regulates small claims can be proof of proportionality considerations, as the motive was again to 'simplify the procedure', again in order to balance the input with the importance of the foreseeable output. In its policy documents, the European Commission mentioned 'costs and delays inherent in ordinary civil proceedings' and stated that the lack of streamlined procedures for small claims in some Member States often involve costs *disproportionate* to the amounts at stake.[28] While planning the Small Claims Regulation, the Commission apparently drew inspiration from the discussions in England, referring expressly to the 'three-headed hydra' of costs, delay and vexation.[29]

Proportionality in dealing with small claims in Regulation 861/2007 is encountered on several levels. At a more technical level, it is the keenness for the use of standard forms in all stages of the proceedings. By the use of standard forms, the proceedings are better prepared and concentrated. *Inter alia*, the standard claim

24 *Ibid.*, p. (9); see also Art. 6 that mentions 'swiftest possible means'.

25 *Ibid.*, p. (10).

26 See Regulation (EC) No 1896/2006 of the European Parliament and of the Council of 12 December 2006 creating a European order for payment procedure.

27 See Regulation (EC) No 861/2007 of the European Parliament and the Council of 11 July 2007 establishing a European Small Claims Procedure.

28 Green Paper on a European order for payment procedure and on measures to simplify and speed up small claims litigation, COM(2002) 746 final, part III, see note 122 (citing J. Jacob's book).

29 So the Green Paper, citing J. Jacobs, states that '[f]or many the judicial systems are too expensive, too slow and too difficult to deal with. The smaller the claim is, the more the weight of these obstacles increases, since costs, delay and vexation (the "three-headed hydra") do not necessarily decrease proportionally with the amount of the claim.' See Part III, nte 122.

form (Form A) has to include a description of the evidence supporting the claim, and be accompanied by relevant supporting documents.[30]

More important is the concept of the European Small Claims Procedure as an essentially written procedure. In the Green Paper on a European order for payment procedure and on measures to simplify and speed up small claims litigation, one of the options that was suggested was the introduction of the possibility of a purely written procedure.[31] It was stated that '[t]his possibility can in "easy" cases significantly cut costs, particularly in cross-border cases, and reduce the time necessary for the judgment to be rendered'. However, after a comparative study of the way various European jurisdictions deal with small cases, the rule that the small claims procedure shall be a written one was softened. In the initial Commission proposal, whether an oral hearing would take place or not depended solely on the discretion of the court.[32] The final text added that an oral hearing shall be held 'if a party so requests'. Thereby, the edge of the principle was considerably blunted, but it was not entirely abandoned, since the court can refuse by a reasoned decision to hold an oral hearing if it considers that it is 'obviously not necessary for the fair conduct of the proceedings'.[33]

But, the core of the efforts to make the proceedings more proportionate is, in the self-understanding of the European Commission, to be found in the evidence-taking rules. The Green Paper expressly states: 'A crucial issue in most existing Small Claims procedure[s] is the simplification of the rules concerning the taking of evidence which aim at shortening the procedure and cutting costs.' Exploring this 'crucial issue', the Green Paper first discussed whether, in order to achieve the set goal, the policy of restricting the means of evidence which are admitted should be pursued. As candidates for such restriction(s), means of evidence which are 'especially costly' are mentioned (such as expert witnesses).[34]

However, in conclusion, the Commission found that a total exclusion of 'costly evidence' could 'in certain cases make the establishment of facts almost impossible', and therefore proposed 'flexible rules' that would target 'simplification of the rules concerning the taking of evidence instead of limitations to the means of evidence'.[35] In the original proposal, the simplification of the rules was indicated by such options as the admission of written statements of parties and witnesses, the use of telephone and videoconferences, and 'submitting certain means of evidence to the admission by the judge'.[36]

This approach, although formulated as a compromise that puts the burden on judges who should make appropriate determinations in concrete cases, found its

30 See Art. 4, Small Claims Regulation.

31 Green Paper, at 6.5.

32 See Art. 4 of the Commission Proposal (SEC(2005) 351 & 352, COM(2005) 87 final, Brussels, 15 March 2005.

33 Art. 5 para. 1 of the Small Claims Regulation.

34 Green Paper, at 6.4.

35 *Ibid.*

36 *Ibid.*

way into the final text of the Small Claims Regulation,[37] which puts on display a good example of proportionality considerations regarding evidence-taking:

> 1. The court or tribunal shall determine the means of taking evidence and the extent of the evidence necessary for its judgment ... The court or tribunal may admit the taking of evidence through written statements of witnesses, experts or parties. It may also admit the taking of evidence through video conference or other communication technology if the technical means are available.
> 2. The court or tribunal may take expert evidence or oral testimony only if it is necessary for giving the judgment. In making its decision, the court or tribunal shall take costs into account.
> 3. The court or tribunal *shall use the simplest and least burdensome method* of taking evidence.

These provisions, together with some other rules, in particular those on representation and the costs of the proceedings,[38] are sufficient to legitimate the statement that the Small Claims Regulation can be assessed - as much as this is possible in the cumbersome process of European rule-making - as a procedural subsystem that is almost entirely built around the considerations of procedural proportionality.

The practical utilization of the Small Claims Regulation in the past several years may have been relatively limited, due to its limited scope and other reasons.[39] However, the approach set by the Regulation is probably more important than its direct legal and economic impact. The seeds of proportionality, once converted into national procedural law through direct application of European law, may encourage a new wave of thinking about procedure and evidence-taking.

In the final part of this contribution, I will present one - so far rather modest - example from recent civil procedure reforms in Croatia.

4. Reforming Rules on Proof in Croatia: Free Assessment of Evidence

In 2011, one in a series of amendments to the Croatian Code of Civil Procedure[40] introduced several new rules on evidence-taking and assessment of evidence. These changes have not been very prominent, as some other provisions in the

37 See Art. 9.

38 See Art. 10 and, in particular, Art. 16 (the costs of the proceedings are to be awarded only if they are not 'disproportionate to the claim').

39 The EC may have been right when it asserted in the initial proposal that '[i]t would not only be inappropriate but even counterproductive to constrain the scope of application of the European Small Claims Procedure to cross-border cases' (Commission Proposal (SEC(2005) 351 & 352, COM(2005) 87 final, Brussels, 15 March 2005, at 2.2.1.). The limitation to cross-border cases in the adopted text failed to stimulate the creation of generally available 'procedures which are proportional to the value of the litigation'. Duality of regimes is indeed not consistent with the objective of a single and coherent area of justice for all (*ibid.*, p. 6).

40 See Off. Gaz. 57/11.

amendments raised more attention among the general and professional public.[41] However, to put it briefly, these few almost unnoticed new rules managed to introduce the principle of proportionality into the evidence-taking process, and indicate some potentially far-reaching changes to the customary approach to evidence.

The changes introduced assert and further develop a rarely used exceptional rule on discretionary evaluation of evidence. Essentially, the rule authorizes the court to decide based on its own 'free assessment' when, in claims for damages and certain other claims 'the amount or quantity cannot be established, or can be established only subject to *disproportionate difficulties*'. While this provision raised some attention in terms of procedural theory, the case law on this provision started to accumulate only in the 2000s.[42] In 2011, this rule was supplemented by two new rules, Article 223(2) and Article 223a.

In the new § 2 of Article 223, the authority of the court to decide based on 'free assessment' was extended to 'claims that are [in their scope and value] insignificant compared to the total value of all claims', again under condition that decision-making on such claims is subject to difficulties *disproportionate to the importance of these claims.* Most important, however, is the new provision of Article 223a that applied the same approach to all claims below a certain value:

> For disputes before municipal courts, if thc amount in dispute is not higher than 5,000 kuna, and for disputes before commercial courts, if the amount in dispute is not higher than 10,000 kuna, the court may decide on disputed facts based on its free assessment, if it deems that the establishment of relevant facts would be connected with disproportionate difficulties and expenses. On the existence of disputed facts the court shall decide taking into consideration the documents submitted by the parties and their statements, if such statements were submitted as evidence ...

In 2011, the initial monetary thresholds of 5 thousand kuna in civil cases (about € 700) or 10 thousand kuna in commercial cases (about € 1,400) were set lower than the border for small claims. However, two years later, by another amendment,[43] these amounts were raised to 10 thousand (about € 1,400) and 50 thousand (about € 6,500) kuna. Thereby, they were brought into line with the statutory amounts for small claims procedures (and also brought closer, on average, to the monetary threshold of € 2,000 in the European Small Claims Regulation).

41 Other changes dealt *inter alia* with audio recording of the oral hearings, introduction of rules on collective redress, limitation in the number of remittals and the secondary (further) appeal (*revizija*) at the Supreme Court. When listing the 'important changes' in the introduction of the legislative proposal, no mention was made of this change. See CCP Amendments – Legislative Proposal of the Government, PZE 792, April 2011, p. 1-3.

42 See e.g. VSRH Rev x 324/2012-2, VSRH Rev x 611/2009-2, VSRH Rev 612/2009-2, VSRH Rev 574/2010-2, VSRH Revr 448/2011-3, VSRH Rev x 1018/2010-2, VSRH Rev x 846/2010-2, VSRH Rev 877/2010-2, VSRH Rev x 214/2009-2 etc. (data from <iusinfo.hr> database, consulted in March 2015).

43 See Off. Gaz. 25/13.

But, another novelty from the 2011 'free assessment' rules is a specific directive given to the court in relation to the taking of evidence. Prior to the introduction of the two new provisions, the notion of 'free assessment' was differently interpreted in the case law and doctrine. In some decisions, higher courts criticized the summary way of decision-making of the lower courts, remitted the case and ordered the taking of additional evidence.[44] The two new provisions both contain an identical clause that specifies the means of evidence which should, in particular, be considered: documentary evidence and statements of the parties (when the parties are heard as witnesses). It is important to note what is missing: namely, documents submitted by the parties, and their statements, are obviously the means of evidence that are easily available. Such evidence is, in doctrine, also called 'liquid evidence'.

On the contrary, the means of evidence that are not on the list of the 'considered means' include other oral evidence (witnesses), and expert statements and reports. Both types of evidence belong to the means that are, in practice, often the cause of delays and thereby can be included in the category of the evidence that is, in the words of the European Commission cited above, 'especially costly' and time-consuming. In short, the same rationale of proportionality that is motivating the Small Claims Regulation, though in another form, may be diagnosed in the newest wave of procedural reforms, i.e. the intention to use the 'simplest and least burdensome method of taking evidence'.[45]

5. Conclusion – A Change, but not too Fast

It is still early to assess whether these new provisions will cause any significant changes in the practice of civil procedure in Croatia. They are important at the symbolic level, as they indicate further departure from the deeply entrenched adherence to the 'material truth' principle. However, there may be a few problems that could potentially impede the effectiveness of the new provisions.

First, they are anything but obvious. Hidden in a bundle of other legislative changes and inserted without a comprehensive explanation, they are easily overlooked, in particular in the legal tradition in which the courts and judges often have more esteem for their accustomed practices than for ever-changing statutory norms. Also, their language is complex and conditional, full of 'ifs' and unspoken premises. The conclusions which stimulate proportionality in evidence-taking have to be drawn *per negationem,* interpreting closely the legislative text.

Interpretation of the new concept of 'free assessment' of Croatian and post-Yugoslav law can also be challenging from the perspective of legal doctrine. The notion of 'free assessment' (*slobodna ocjena*) is traditionally connected with the

44 E.g. in VSRH Rev 693/2004-2; VSRH Rev 563/2005-2; VSRH Revr 47/2009-2; VTS Pž-4356/08.

45 See above, Art. 9 para. 3 of the Small Claims Regulation. This intention is also mentioned in the legislative history, where the change was explained by the wish to simplify and accelerate the proceedings by cutting the 'often unnecessary evidence-taking'. CCP Amendments – Legislative Proposal of the Government, PZE 792, April 2011, p. 20-21.

evaluation of evidence that is free of any pre-set legal rules on proof[46] (German *freie Beweiswürdigung,* French *intime conviction*). The new wave of rules on decision-making based on 'free assessment' is by nature entirely different. It may be interpreted in various ways: as a practical instruction for case-management which suggests selection of the least burdensome method of evidence-taking (reducing the intensity of the pursuit for proof); as a command to give priority to certain means of evidence (filtering of certain categories of evidence); or, as permission to base the decision on a lower degree of probability than in the other cases (easing the standard of proof from certainty to probability).[47] The expression 'free assessment' is also closely connected with the idea of giving the judges a considerable discretion in decision-making, which is something that is generally considered to be abhorrent and inappropriate in the hyper-positivist tradition of the post-socialist legal systems.[48]

Therefore, some of the barriers against 'arbitrariness' have been integrated in the very structure of the new norms, such as the condition that full-fledged taking of evidence can be avoided only if it is 'disproportionately difficult'. The test of the proportionality of 'difficulties' is still not sovereignly in the hands of the first-instance judges, but is subject to the assessment of the higher courts - and in their present case law there is already a number of decisions that have held that the lower courts erred, instructing them to make further inquiries and take additional evidence.[49] Obviously, if the intervention of the higher tribunals, trained and educated in the old style of proceedings, sends a restraining message to the lower courts, it can again be: *plus ça change plus c'est la même chose.*

However, in spite of all the ambiguities inherent in the way European legislation is being drafted and adopted, the seeds of proportionality contained in European civil procedural law have been planted. In Southern and Eastern Europe, the fruits that have grown from these seeds are so far still small and weak. But, the proportionality between the procedure and its objective is increasingly becoming a global procedural principle. It is present in national laws of both common law and civil law countries,[50] so that it has been raised to one of the transnational principles

46 In carrying out his assessment of the facts of the case, the judge shall not be bound by any statutory rules regarding the quality and quantity of the means of proof that have to be collected, but must decide the factual issues in accordance with his personal conviction. See e.g. Croatian CCP, Art. 8; Austrian ZPO, § 272, or German ZPO, § 286.

47 In the older legal theory, the 'free assessment' provision of Art. 223 CCP was interpreted as 'certain reduction of certainty criteria in the establishment of relevant facts, but short of sheer arbitrariness', quoting also case law according to which 'one should come as close to the real facts as possible, if those facts cannot be exactly and precisely established'. Triva *et al.* 1986, § 28/13, p. 136.

48 On hyper-positivism see Manko 2013, p. 6. See also Uzelac 2010 (on fear to assume responsibility for decision-making).

49 See e.g. VSRH Revr 47/2009-2, or VTS Pž-6945/04-3 (explicitly instructing the first-instance court to use experts).

50 Compare Piché 2012 (for developments in Canada, but also elsewhere).

of civil procedure.[51] Indeed, the principle of proportionality 'must not impair greater justice objectives' and 'must instead work in favour of the true improvement of the system'.[52] But, without equal or at least comparable implementation of the principle of proportionality, the idea of a common area of justice will remain remote and illusory. Therefore, if Europe survives the current period of turbulence, we can expect a creeping harmonization of the national approaches to evidence, even in the areas of the South and East that have, due to their past traditions and legal cultures, so far successfully resisted the change. It may be a small step in the convergence of procedural laws and practices in Europe, but for the countries that have been dominated by the 'material truth' doctrines, it is a giant leap.

51 See Principle 11 of the ALI/UNIDROIT Principles of Transnational Procedure, which imposes an obligation both on the court and on the parties to promote fair, efficient and reasonably speedy resolution of court proceedings. See ALI/UNIDROIT 2006, p. 16-50.

52 Piché 2012, p. 164.

Bibliography

ALI/UNIDROIT 2006
American Law Institute/UNIDROIT, *Principles of Transnational Civil Procedure*, Cambridge: Cambridge University Press, 2006.

Frodl 2012
Frodl, S., 'The Heritage of the Franz Klein Reform of Austrian Civil Procedure in 1895-1896', *Civil Justice Quarterly*, 2012, Vol. 31(1), p. 43-68.

Galič 2014
Galič, A., '(In)compatibility of Procedural Preclusions with the Goals of Civil Justice: An Ongoing Debate in Slovenia', in: Uzelac, A. (ed.), *Goals of Civil Justice and Civil Procedure in Contemporary Judicial Systems*, Cham/Heidelberg/New York/ Dordrecht/London: Springer, 2014, p. 221-243.

Jelinek 1991
Jelinek, W., 'Einflüsse des österreichischen Zivilprozeßrechts auf andere Rechtsordnungen', in: Habscheid, W. (ed.), *Das deutsche Zivilprozeßrecht und seine Ausstrahlung auf andere Rechtsordnungen*, Bielefeld: Gieseking, 1991, p. 41-89.

Klein 1891
Klein, F., *Pro futuro. Betrachtungen über Probleme der Civilproceßreform in Oesterreich*, Leipzig, Wien: Deuticke, 1891.

Lenin 1971
Lenin, V.I., *Collected Works*, Moscow: Progress publishers, 1971.

Manko 2013
Manko, R., 'Survival of the Socialist Legal Tradition? A Polish Perspective', *Comparative Law Review* 4.2 (2013). Available at: SSRN: <http://ssrn.com/-abstract=2332219>.

Pashukanis 1980
Pashukanis, E., *Selected Writings on Marxism and Law* (eds. P. Beirne & R. Sharlet), London & New York: Academic Press, 1980.

Piché 2012
Piché, C., 'Figures, Spaces and Procedural Proportionality', *International Journal of Procedural Law*, 2012, Vol. 2(1), p. 145-166.

Triva *et al.* 1986
Triva, S., Belajec, V. & Dika, M., *Građansko parnično procesno pravo*, Zagreb: *Narodne novine*, 1986.

Uzelac 2008
Uzelac, A., 'Reforming Mediterranean Civil Procedure: Is There a Need for Shock Therapy?', in: C.H. van Rhee & A. Uzelac (eds.), *Civil Justice between Efficiency and Quality: From Ius Commune to the CEPEJ,* Antwerp/Oxford/Portland: Intersentia, 2008, p. 71-99.

Uzelac 2010
Uzelac, A., 'Survival of the Third Legal Tradition?' in: Walker, J. & Chase, O. (eds.), *Common Law, Civil Law and the Future of Categories,* Markham: LexisNexis, 2010, p. 377-396.

Van Gerven 1995
Van Gerven, W., 'Bridging the Gap Between Community and National Laws: Towards a Principle of Homogeneity in the Field of Legal Remedies?', *Common Market Law Review,* 1995, Vol. 32, p. 679-702.

Van Rhee & Uzelac 2012
Van Rhee, C.H & Uzelac, A., 'The Pursuit of Truth in Contemporary Civil Procedure: Revival of Accuracy or a New Balance in Favour of Effectiveness?, in: Van Rhee, C.H. & Uzelac, A. (eds.), *Truth and Efficiency in Civil Litigation,* Cambridge/Antwerp/Portland: Intersentia, 2012, p. 3-10.

Verkerk 2010
Verkerk, R.., *Fact-finding in Civil Litigation. A Comparative Perspective,* Antwerp: Intersentia, 2010.

Vyshinsky 1946
Vyshinsky, A.J., *Teoriya sudebnikh dokazatelstv v Sovetskom prave* [Theory of Court Evidence in Soviet Law], Moscow: Yurisdat, Ministry of Justice of the USSR, 1946.

Woolf Report 1996
The Right Honourable The Lord Woolf, Master of the Rolls, *Access to Justice – Final Report to the Lord Chancellor on the Civil Justice System in England and Wales,* London: Her Majesty's Stationery Office, July 1996. Available at: <http://www.dca.gov.-uk/civil/final/index.htm>.

Zuckerman 2009
Zuckerman A., 'The Challenge of Civil Justice Reform: Effective Court Management of Litigation', *City University Hong Kong Law Review,* 2009, Vol. 1(1), p. 49–71.

A. Galič

DISCLOSURE OF DOCUMENTS IN CIVIL PROCEDURE: THE PRIVILEGE AGAINST SELF-INCRIMINATION OR A QUEST FOR PROCEDURAL FAIRNESS AND SUBSTANTIVE JUSTICE

> *'Nobody is obliged to testify against himself and to offer evidence, unfavourable to him.'*
>
> Triva, Belajec and Dika, *Građansko parnično procesno pravo,* 1986, p. 425

> 'In this country litigation ... is conducted 'cards face up on the table'. Some people ... regard this as incomprehensible. 'Why', they ask, 'should I be expected to provide my opponent with the means of defeating me?' The answer, of course, is that litigation is not a war or even a game. It is designed to do real justice between opposing parties and, if the court does not have all the relevant information, it cannot achieve this object.'
>
> Sir John Donaldson MR *in Davies v. Eli Lilly & Co.* [1987] 1 WLR 428.

1. Introduction

In Slovenian (and in former Yugoslav) civil procedure, party access to relevant information and documents, which are in the possession of the opponent and which could adversely affect the opponent's case, is limited. Traditionally, based on a German and Austrian heritage of civil procedure, the principle that no one is obliged to help his adversary win the case (*nemo tenetur edere contra se*) applied.[1] Experience and recent developments abroad - not only in common law jurisdictions, which have for a long time embraced broad duties to disclose, but also in civil law systems which were traditionally restrictive in requiring the parties to contribute to the establishment of the true facts - show that this approach needs to be re-examined.

1 Triva, Belajec & Dika 1986, p. 425.

The alternative to the principle that the party to a civil case cannot be obliged to 'put weapons in the hand of its opponent'[2] is the common law concept of disclosure of documents. Thereby especially the English Civil Procedure Rules of 1998 (which have done away with some extremes of discovery)[3] seem to be an important source of inspiration for Legislatures in civil law jurisdictions nowadays.[4] The main idea of 'disclosure' is that the parties should as early as possible give advance notice of all relevant documents – not just those supporting their case but including those which adversely affect their case or which support the other party's case.[5] The so-called 'cards on the table' approach strives to fulfil the overriding objective of doing justice, to enable better preparation and unfolding of a case and to prevent ambush strategies (taking the opponent by surprise) during the hearing.[6] Enabling parties to realistically assess the strength or weakness of their positions at early stages of proceedings is also a powerful device for promoting settlements. It has been acknowledged in Slovenia as well, though in a different context, that if a party cannot know before the main hearing what arguments and evidence are 'in the hands' of his opponents, he cannot realistically assess his prospects of success. In such a case, settlement negotiations during the early stages of litigation can hardly be effective.[7]

In the modern era the importance of effective access to information in general and of disclosure of documents in particular is growing. The number of complex litigations, which cannot be effectively pursued without broad access to information, not already in possession of the aggrieved party, is increasing. The same goes for the number of cases where the economically stronger party (large companies, public entities) has in its possession relevant documents and information, whereas the weaker party (consumer, aggrieved individual) does not. Therefore, procedural tools aimed at access to information and disclosure of documents can contribute to a more genuine equality of arms.[8]

On the other hand, the importance of privacy and of protection of business secrets should not be underestimated and the attorney-client privilege along with confidentiality of without-prejudice documents related to settlement negotiations should be protected. In addition, proportionality should also be achieved in order to avoid excessive burdens and costs inevitably connected with the obligation to

2 Leipold 2005, § 142, No. 9.

3 Andrews 2003, p. 597.

4 See e.g. Van Rhee 2008, p. 206 *et seq.*; Groen 2007, p. 250 *et seq.*

5 Pursuant to CPR, advance notice is given, generally, in the early stages of litigation, shortly after the allocation stage, by serving a list of documents, which are material to the case and in a party's control, on the other side. Disclosure is the first stage of a two-stage process – the second one being an 'inspection', where the other party can request insight into the disclosed documents – either in the form of copies or by physically inspecting them at the disclosing party's offices. Sime 2004, p. 279. For the construction of concepts such as 'documents', 'control', 'duty to search' and 'privileges' see: *ibid.*, p. 282-285.

6 Andrews 2003, p. 597.

7 Brus 2007, p. 336; Trampuš 2002, p. 1549.

8 See e.g. Andrews 2003, p. 597.

disclose. The main dilemma therefore is how to strike a proper balance between competing values and underlying policies - not only from the viewpoint of the individual interests of litigants at hand but from the viewpoint of public purposes of litigation as well.

Another dilemma relates to the question as to what extent can rights of access to information existing under substantive law compensate for insufficiencies in the disclosure of the evidence system in procedural law. More recently another issue has been gaining in importance - the relationship between laws regulating personal data protection and the right of access to databases containing personal data, on the one hand, and rights to information before and during civil proceedings, on the other.

2. The Limited Scope of Disclosure of Evidence in Slovenian Civil Procedure

2.1. *Documents in the Possession of the Party Adducing Them*

It is understandable that the parties are required to produce documents in their possession to which they themselves have made reference. As this will normally concern documents that support the party's case, it is in principle in the party's own interest to produce them.[9] The major practical dilemma, however, is when should such documents be produced. It should be noted that there is no general pre-trial disclosure rule in Slovenian civil procedure. Pursuant to the Yugoslav Civil Procedure Act of 1976, the parties were free to submit new facts and evidence until the end of the last session of the main hearing. Such system did not allow for the proper organization of the preparatory stage of litigation, structuring of proceedings and early identification of disputed and relevant issues of the case. It was also not able to prevent the common - however, from the aspect of the efficiency of proceedings, outright fatal - practice that attorneys filed further preparatory briefs, adducing new facts and evidence, as late as during the main hearing. The lack of effective tools that would enable the timely gathering of procedural materials resulted in frequent adjournments of hearings, in a 'piecemeal' presentation of facts and evidence, and in culpably delaying a case's progress.

9 The party's consideration might be different if such a document contains business or trade secrets. However, the party must take into account that if he submits the document to the court, the opponent will inevitably get full access to it. The option that a protection of business and trade secrets in civil litigation could be achieved through some sort of a 'secret hearing' in such a way that it would also be kept secret from the opponent (and disclosed solely to the court or to a court-appointed expert entrusted with the task to inspect the document and provide a non-confidential edited summary) was rejected by Slovenian courts (Judgment of the Ljubljana Court of Appeals No. I Cpg 708/2013 dated 21 November 2013). The party who chooses to submit documents to the court must take into account that these documents will inevitably be accessible to his opponent ('lose the case or lose the secret approach').

Another feature of the style of litigation in the former system was the frequent use of 'ambush tactics' by attorneys. As there were no time limits for the adduction of fresh evidence and no obligation regarding advance disclosure, parties often filed documentary evidence only at the oral hearing. They counted on the other party being taken by surprise (admittedly, though, such late disclosure of relevant evidence was often not a result of any deliberate tactics, but a mere consequence of the negligent preparation of the case, or, more frequently, a tool that enabled the achievement of a desired adjournment of the hearing).[10] The idea that it is precisely in the interests of justice - not only procedural, but substantive as well - that evidence in the hands of one party should be disclosed to the other party in a timely fashion, such that both the opposing party as well as the court can properly consider it, found no response. And all this was done, supposedly, in the name of the 'quest for the material truth'.

Already the first Slovenian Civil Procedure Act (1999; hereinafter CPA[11]) introduced the rule that the parties may assert new facts and evidence at the first main hearing at the latest, whereas at the last stages the parties are allowed to present new facts and new evidence only with a proper excuse for the belated submission (Article 286 CPA). Further steps were made through an amendment in 2008.[12] In order to enable the other party's right to be heard and to organize his case, the first party is now obliged, whenever possible, to file new preparatory briefs in sufficient time for them to be served on the other party with adequate time before the main hearing. Furthermore, judges now have the discretionary power to require (and to impose binding time limits) that parties make further submissions and clarifications concerning facts, evidence and legal positions in the set time limit (Article 286a(1) CPA). The judge may exercise this discretion already in a written form before the main hearing. The system of procedural sanctions is flexible. The judge is empowered but not obliged to use the described tools and also has discretion to relieve the parties from the sanctions. It is also acknowledged that preclusions restrict the parties' right to be heard and thus they should be applied carefully and with a proper balance between competing policies.[13]

Sadly, the instruments that were introduced by the 2008 reform and designed to enable a comprehensive preparation for the hearing are still insufficiently used in practice. These tools require diligent preparation before the hearing, thus good knowledge of the file and a serious preliminary legal analysis by both the judge and the attorneys. However, such a preparation cannot be expected from a judge who cannot rid himself of the old habit of having 'the first serious look' at the file only at the first hearing and only then truly starting to work on the case. Inevitably, such a judge will neither be able to correctly apply the statutory provisions concerning

10 See also Uzelac 2010, p. 384.

11 *Zakon o pravdnem postopku*, Official gazette, No. 26/99.

12 *Zakon o spremembah in dopolnitvah Zakona o pravdnem postopku* (ZPP-D), Official Gazette, No. 45/2008.

13 Judgment of the Supreme Court of Slovenia No. II Ips 197/2009 of 7 April 2011.

binding time limits nor be able to exercise his duty to pose appropriate questions and promote clarification at the preparatory stage of proceedings.

2.2. *Documents in the Possession of the Other Party*

The Slovenian Civil Procedure Act provides only for a rather narrow scope of the duty to produce documents upon request of the opposing party (Article 227 CPA).[14] A party can request that the opponent produce documents, which the latter himself has referred to in his pleadings, without any restrictions; furthermore, where the latter, under substantive laws,[15] has a legal duty to produce certain documents (as is the case with shareholders vis-à-vis a corporation,[16] with agents vis-à-vis their principals or with keepers of accounting books) or when the document is, due to its content, regarded as mutual for both parties (for example, a contract between these parties).

In the circumstances referred to above, the obligation to produce documents is absolute. Different rules, however, apply for all other documents that are material to the case (e.g. the defendant company's accounts or financial documents or the defendant's file with findings on, for example, an internal investigation that the defendant has undertaken regarding the occurrence that gave rise to the dispute). If the requesting party is aware of the existence of such documents and can identify them to a sufficient degree (and can also explain how the documents requested are relevant to the case and material to its outcome), the other party who is in possession of such documents may be required to produce them. But here the duty to disclose is not absolute. The rules determining privileges of witnesses (cases, where witnesses are excused from the obligation to testify) apply *mutatis mutandis* (Article 227 and Articles 231-234 CPA). Hence, the production of a document may be denied if the document relates to what the party has confessed to the possessor of the document as their legal counsel (or their religious confessor) or facts of which he has learnt as a lawyer or a doctor or in pursuance of another profession, if he is bound to protect the secrecy of what he learns in the practice of such profession (Article 231 CPA). Nevertheless, the document may not be withheld on the grounds of protection of a professional secret (such as applies for e.g. attorneys-at-law, medical doctors, mediators, bankers, journalists ...) if the disclosure of certain facts

14 It is unclear whether data stored in an electronic form (including e.g. documents that are stored on servers or back-up systems, email and other electronic communications, word-processed documents, documents stored on memory sticks and mobile phones) are considered documents or tangible things subject to proof by observation (see e.g. Zobec 2006, p. 419; *cf.* also Stürner 2007, p. 174). However, the dilemma is not really practically important since the rules concerning the duty to disclose and the right to deny disclosure, applicable to documents, apply *mutatis mutandis* also in regard to inspection of tangible things in the possession of the opponent or third persons (Art. 222 CPA).

15 It remains unsettled both in the case law as well as in legal writing whether the reference to the statutory duty to submit a document should be construed broadly and hence includes also cases where such duty is established on a contractual basis.

16 See e.g. judgment of the Ljubljana Court of Appeals No. I Cpg 590/2006.

is to the benefit of the public or some other person, provided that such benefit outweighs the damage caused by disclosure of the secret (Article 232 CPA). The test of proportionality must be applied.

Moreover, a document may also be withheld if by producing it the party might expose himself, a spouse or close relative to serious disgrace, considerable financial loss or criminal proceedings (Article 233 CPA). In such case, the right to withhold the document is absolute, thus, irrespective of whether the benefit of disclosure for the requesting party would outweigh the damage caused by it to the possessor of the document.

The described system hence enables merely a limited scope of disclosure of documents. The first key difference between this system and the common law concept of disclosure is that in Slovenia a party has no duty to disclose unfavourable documents in his possession on his own motion. Although the law establishes the obligation of truth for the parties (Article 9 CPA), this is merely a programmatic proclamation without any sanctions and adverse consequences for cases of non-compliance. The second major difference is that in Slovenia the party seeking disclosure must sufficiently identify the document he is requesting. A request for production of a document can only be successful if the party is able to describe the content of the requested document in sufficient detail so as to clearly identify it. The regulation is hence merely proper to avoid the concealing of documents, the existence of which is already known, but not documents, for which the requesting party does not know to a quite concrete degree what their contents are or that the other party even possesses them. This system does not facilitate any kind of discovery of new information,[17] and purely exploratory evidence is not admissible.[18] The duty of the opponent to produce documents only applies if the requesting party has submitted his substantiated pleadings and explained his cases in detail beforehand. It should also be noted that in line with the Continental tradition (and in contrast to US-style notice pleading) the principle of fact pleading applies in Slovenian civil procedure. This means that the party must plead detailed facts and offer exactly specified means of evidence already in the statement of claim. According to the Continental procedural tradition of fact pleading, the judge will only order the taking of evidence on individual facts that have been asserted by the party.

Parties often try to avoid this limitation by requesting 'the entire correspondence' or 'all documents relating to a certain transaction' to be disclosed, but courts are usually quite restrictive in this regard.[19] In addition it should be noted that the party cannot demand of the opponent to disclose evidence; only the court is (upon the party's motion) authorized to do so. Consequently, documents are handed over to the court, not to the requesting party (who, however, will receive

17 Judgment of the Supreme Court No. II Ips 544/2002, dated 11 September 2003.

18 See e.g. judgment of the Supreme Court No. II Ips 560/2006.

19 See e.g. judgment of the Ljubljana Court of Appeals No. I Cpg 1205/2001: '... the law refers to specific, individualized documents, invoked by the party, and not to any documents relating to the case or even some undefined and undefinable "documentation"'.

copies or – in case of voluminous documentation – is entitled to inspect the documents in the court's file). More importantly, the court's order for disclosure of documents cannot be rendered already at the preparatory stage of civil litigation, but only after the commencement of the main hearing: the disclosure mechanisms are designed to be used after the commencement of the main hearing. Consequently, they can hardly contribute to a better preparation of a hearing and even less so to stimulate settlements at an early stage of proceedings. It has already been mentioned that since the CPA 2008 amendment, the judge has the power to order documents to be produced even before the main hearing. But this – at least according to the wording of the law – merely relates to the documents in the possession of the party who in his pleadings (the claim, the defence plea) adduced (but did not as yet produce) them. Unfortunately, there is no explicit provision authorizing the court in the preliminary stage of proceedings to order the party to produce documents in his possession which the other party has adduced as evidence.

On the other hand, the material scope of disclosure in the Slovenian Civil Procedure Act is relatively broad. It is important to note that the right to seek documents is not (as has traditionally been the case in civil law jurisdictions)[20] restricted to cases, where an independent substantive right to possession exists. The duty to disclose extends to documents, the production of which is sought solely on the basis of their relevance to the pending case. Thereby the approach of the Legislature that the duty to disclose is not unconditional and that a proper balance between the competing values is attempted is appropriate. It nevertheless seems that the attempt has not been entirely successful and that the legitimate interests of the possessor of documents have not been adequately protected. It is especially noteworthy that the protection of trade and business secrets is not explicitly mentioned as a legitimate ground for refusal of disclosure (as it is not a reason for excusing a witness from the duty to testify).[21] Protection of trade and business secrets is merely a ground for exclusion of the public from all or part of the main hearing (and access to the court file for the general public) (Article 230 CPA). This, however, does not solve the problem where the party wishes to safeguard business secrets *vis-à-vis* his opponent who might at the same time be his competitor in the market and to prevent serious damage that could result from improper communication of business secrets to such a party. Protection of professional secrets (which relate to professions where confidentiality of the professional-client relationship is essential) does enable withholding of documents; however, professional secrets are only rarely identical to trade and business secrets.[22] Certain authors have suggested that protection of business secrets could be covered by the provision that documents can be withheld if by producing them the party would expose himself (*inter alia*) to a *considerable financial loss* (Article 233 CPA). This seems

20 *Cf.* Trocker & Varano 2005, p. 255.

21 *Cf.* Testen 2011, p. 1506.

22 Bergant Rakočević 2011, p. 1483; Zobec 2006, p. 445.

like a plausible construction, although the problem is that – unlike with professional secrets and attorney-client privilege – the right to withhold documents for reason of threat of considerable financial loss is unrestricted. No test of proportionality applies here, and the court cannot rule that the benefit of producing the document outweighs the damage caused by disclosure of certain business secrets. This is, again, not a proper solution. The protection of trade and business secrets should be a legitimate ground for denial of disclosure of documents but not in absolute terms. It is necessary to strike a proper balance between the competing values (the right of effective access to court and the right to be heard on the one hand, and protection of confidentiality and business secrets on the other). Therefore the protection of trade and business secrets should not form an unconditional and absolute ground for withholding documents. The court should be authorized to weigh the respective interests in order to establish a proper balance between the adversarial principle and the right to observance of business secrets.[23] Thereby compromise solutions should also be possible (e.g. restricted access to the documents or the redaction of sensitive parts to the extent that it still provides the requesting party sufficient information, but only if there is a legitimate interest on the part of a party or third party).

Another dilemma concerns the extent of the attorney-client privilege. From the wording of Articles 227 and 231 CPA it would follow that only documents possessed by legal counsel are privileged[24] but not correspondence and work products received from an attorney and in the possession of the client. Some authors suggest that a broader construction of the norm is necessary so that all confidential communications between counsel and his client relating to the pending case are covered by the privilege, regardless of whether it is counsel or the client who possesses them.[25] Only in such manner, it is claimed, can the purpose of the attorney-client privilege be fulfilled: that is, to encourage clients to seek legal advice and to ensure that they communicate forthrightly with their attorneys. Still, there is no firm case law on this point yet. It should also be noted that a broader work-

23 For the specific area of anti-trust litigation (claims for damages for infringement of competition law) compare Directive 2014/104/EU of the European Parliament and of the Council of 26 November 2014 *on certain rules governing actions for damages under national law for infringements of the competition law provisions of the Member States and of the European Union*). Recital No. 18 of the Directive states that 'While relevant evidence containing business secrets or otherwise confidential information should, in principle, be available in actions for damages, such confidential information needs to be protected appropriately. National courts should therefore have at their disposal a range of measures to protect such confidential information from being disclosed during the proceedings. Those measures could include the possibility of redacting sensitive passages in documents, conducting hearings in camera, restricting the persons allowed to see the evidence, and instructing experts to produce summaries of the information in an aggregated or otherwise non-confidential form.'

24 Also pursuant to Art. 6 of the Attorney Acts, the lawyer is under the obligation of confidentiality in the interest of his client about matters entrusted to him and also facts revealed to him through his professional quality.

25 See Testen 2011, p. 1506.

product privilege in Slovenian law does not exist, one which would then exempt materials prepared in anticipation of litigation from the duty to disclose (except if they are already covered by the attorney-client privilege). That being said, the practical importance of these shortcomings is not particularly significant, since the party is only obliged to disclose documents which the other party has sufficiently specified (which presupposes that he is also aware of their existence). In most cases, however, the opponent will not be in a position even to be aware of the existence of such (specific) documents.

Furthermore, there is a question of consequences when the opponent fails to produce the required document.[26] Before the 2008 CPA reform the law provided that the court would assess, by discretion and taking into account all circumstances of the case, the significance of the fact that the party possessing a document failed to comply with a court order to produce it, or asserted, contrary to the court's belief, that they were not in possession of such document. In practice, this usually meant that the court drew adverse conclusions from any refusal to produce readily available documents when it came to the determining of the claim. This was a reasonable, adequate and at the same time flexible solution. Nevertheless, in 2008 the Legislature chose to change the system and introduced sanctions for non-compliance which are both harsher as well as more rigid. Now, if the party does not comply with the order to produce a document (which the court believes is in his possession), the court must regard the facts, alleged by the requesting party and supposedly supported by the document in question, as true. Presumably, the novelty was transplanted from § 427 of the German ZPO.[27] This 'transplantation', however, was not correct. Pursuant to the German law, based on the failure to comply with the order to produce the document, the allegations made by the party tendering evidence regarding the nature and content of the document may be assumed to be proven. The differences between this regulation and the Slovenian law are significant. Not only does the German judge still retain discretion not to draw adverse inferences ('may'), unlike in Slovenian law ('shall'), much more importantly, the rule that the asserted content of a certain document is considered proven (§ 427 of the German ZPO) is much less far-reaching than the rule that material facts, intended to be proven by the document in question, shall be considered proven (Article 227(5) of the Slovenian CPA). The German rule is much more adequate. After all, in the system of free evaluation of evidence where a judge has to weigh all evidence, even if the document was submitted and if its content was indeed such as the requesting party had contended, this would not automatically mean that the party would inevitably succeed in proving facts, which he intended to prove relying on this document.

26 First it should be noted that the order that the opposing party must produce the documents is not enforceable. The court has no power to force the opponent to produce such documents even in the case where the opposite party has a legal right to obtain them. There only remains the possibility for bringing a separate claim for handing over the document in question (*actio ad exhibendum*). Ude 2002, p. 267.

27 Zobec 2010, p. 177.

It is not clear why the Legislature opted for changing the previous rule concerning sanctions for non-compliance with the order to submit documents. But it might be just one further expression of a general animosity towards judicial discretion in Slovenia and a persistent preference for a rigid procedural regime.

2.3. *Documents in the Possession of Third Parties and Public Authorities*

Persons other than the parties may be ordered to submit documents only if such an obligation is imposed on them by substantive law or if the document to be submitted was created both for them and the party adducing it as evidence. Although (unlike the order directed to the other party) the order for the production of documents directed to a third person is directly enforceable (Article 228 CPA), the regulation is extremely unfavourable for the party relying on a document in the possession of a third person. There is no right to production if the request is based solely on the document's relevance for the pending case, no matter whether the person possessing it has any legitimate interest to withhold it. Here the Legislature entirely failed to strike a balance between legitimate interests of litigants (and their constitutional right of effective access to court) and legitimate interests of third parties who possess relevant documents.

In Slovenia, the present system has been criticized for being too restrictive and also for its logical inconsistency. It is not coherent that a third party may be obliged to testify about the content of a certain document in his possession, but is nevertheless not obliged to produce this document in court.[28]

If a document (relied upon by a party) is in the possession of a public body and if the public body refuses to produce it, the court may demand its production *ex officio* (Article 226(3) CPA). In addition, the court also has a general power to request that public authorities or public officials communicate records or provide official information (Article 10 CPA). On behalf of their clients, attorneys-at-law can also request public authorities to provide official information needed to support or bring individual legal proceedings (Article 10 of the Attorneys Act).[29]

2.4. *Lack of Access to Information in the Pre-action Stage*

It has already been mentioned that the production of documents in the possession of the opponent is part of the proof-taking stage of litigation and not of the preparatory stage. Consequently, there are even fewer possibilities of access to relevant information before the start of civil litigation (the pre-action stage). The Slovenian Legislature has so far failed to learn anything from one of the most interesting developments in recent years, which is that the law of civil procedure has been gradually extending to the phase when the prospective litigants only start

28 Testen 2011, p. 1507; Zobec 2006, p. 433.

29 *Zakon o odvetništvu*, Official Gazette No. 73/2007. See also Testen 2011, p. 1499 *et seq*.

preparing to bring the lawsuit.[30] Whereas the pre-action phase has traditionally not been the subject of extensive and detailed regulation, recent developments have changed this course, inspired foremost by the pre-action protocols introduced - for certain types of disputes - by the English CPR.[31]

Over time, numerous Legislatures in civil law jurisdictions came to realize that there is an inherent link between access to information and access to justice and recently started to study, consider and exploit the possibility that the prospective claimant could - at least in those types of disputes where the imbalance between parties as to the access to information is most pressing - ask for information from the presumed defendant.[32] There is a significant public interest in such developments. If access to relevant information is enabled even before the commencement of proceedings, it may prevent an escalation of the conflict and enable the parties to re-evaluate their positions and to engage in informed settlement negotiations.[33] This can often result in avoiding litigation altogether. In such a manner, the principle that litigation should be the last resort is most clearly promoted.[34] In Slovenia, however, this area has remained entirely underdeveloped. So far the issue has remained constrained to the question of access to information concerning debtors' assets,[35] which, however, predominantly benefits creditors, who have already obtained an enforceable judgment. Moreover, the recent introduction and rigid application of personal data protection legislation has resulted in ever more obstacles for access to information in the pre-action stage.[36]

3. A Short Comparative Overview - Disclosure of Documents in Civil Law Jurisdictions

Disclosure of evidence (or a more far-reaching, American-style discovery) has been an integral part of civil justice in the common law procedural model for a long time.[37] In civil law jurisdictions the idea has only recently been gradually gaining ground that if procedure aims at getting as close as possible to the truth concerning the litigated issues, it must rely on techniques through which each party can have access to items of evidence not in his possession.[38] Regarding disclosure of documents and access to information in general, as in many other areas of civil

30 Leipold 2008, p. 54.
31 See in detail: Andrews 2003, p. 614 *et seq.*; Andrews 2007, p. 224 *et seq.*
32 See Leipold 2008, p. 56 *et seq.*; Groen 2007, p. 252 *et seq.*; Trocker & Varano 2005, p. 257; Van Rhee 2008, p. 206-208.
33 Van Rhee 2008, p. 207.
34 Leipold 2008, p. 55.
35 See e.g. Testen 2011, p. 1500 *et seq.*
36 Brulc 2011, p. 1497.
37 See e.g. Andrews 2003, p. 595 *et seq.*
38 Trocker & Varano 2005, p. 255.

procedure a certain degree of convergence of the practices in common law and leading civil code countries has already been achieved.[39]

In *Germany*, party and court access to documents in the possession of the other party and of third persons was traditionally limited.[40] The doctrine of civil procedure has firmly adhered to the principle that no party is obliged to assist his opponent in winning the case.[41] Only substantive not procedural law could (but not should) constitute such a duty. Consequently, only when substantive law gave one party such a claim against the other party could this claim work procedurally as a duty to disclose (§ 422 ZPO).[42] It should be noted, however, that German substantive laws have quite extensively exploited the opportunity to establish rights of access to information.[43] In addition, although there is no general obligation to disclose information under substantive law, for certain types of contractual relationships such obligation may derive already from the general principle of good faith (*Treu und Glauben*).[44] Still, for cases where no such obligation existed under substantive laws, the Federal Supreme Court ruled that the party is not obliged to give the adverse party the material for winning the case, material which the adversary does not dispose of by himself.[45] In effect, such a standpoint allows the party to frustrate a potentially meritorious claim brought by his less informed opponent.[46] The position changed, however, with the ZPO reform in 2002. Since then, the court is empowered to seek production of documents - from the other party and from third persons as well - based solely on their relevance to the

39 On the level of academic thought, an important indication of convergence between civil and common law approaches can be found in the ALI/UNIDROIT Principles of Transnational Civil Procedure. The text of the Principles and the accompanying commentary were adopted by the American Law Institute (ALI) and by the International Institute for the Unification of Private Law (UNIDROIT) in 2004. Art. 16.2 provides for limited disclosure under the supervision of the court. It states that 'upon timely request of a party, the court should order disclosure of relevant, non-privileged, and reasonably identified evidence in the possession or control of another party or, if necessary and on just terms, of a non-party'. By stating that 'It is not a basis of objection to such disclosure that the evidence may be adverse to the party or person making the disclosure', the Principles explicitly do away with the old-fashioned Continental understanding of the privilege against self-incrimination in civil cases. On the other hand, the explanatory memorandum also makes clear that particular attention should be paid to preventing fishing expeditions; i.e. non-specific search of information in order to develop a case for which there is no support (typical for the American style of discovery). Non-parties are in principle also obliged to cooperate. See Stürner 2007, p. 174.

40 Murray & Stürner 2004, p. 241; Rosenberg, Schwab & Gottwald 2004, p. 740.

41 Leipold 2005, § 142, No. 9.

42 Prütting 2008, p. 257.

43 Rosenberg, Schwab & Gottwald 2004, p. 738; Leipold 2006, § 422, No. 8 *et seq*.

44 Staudinger 2009, § 242, No. 601.

45 'Eine allgemeine Auskunftspflicht kennt das materielle Recht jedoch nicht, und es ist nicht Aufgabe des Prozeßrechts, sie einzuführen. Es bleibt vielmehr bei dem Grundsatz keine Partei gehalten ist, dem Gegner für seinen Prozeßsieg das Material zu verschaffen, über das er nicht schon von sich aus verfügt.' BGH, 11.06.1990 - II ZR 159/89.

46 Wagner 2012, p. 105.

pending case.[47] Third parties are protected from having to submit evidence to the extent that such production would be unreasonable or the documents are protected by a statutory witness privilege.[48] How far-reaching this new rule is, is still a matter of debate, but the prevailing view is that it amounts to a paradigm shift and is a major step in the direction of a general duty to disclose and produce evidence.[49]

Concerning the duty to disclose and produce documents, *Austrian* law is quite similar to Slovenian law. The major difference is that - insofar as documents in the possession of the opposing party are concerned - it is explicitly stated that also business (and not just professional) secrets can form a legitimate ground for withholding a document. In addition, the regulation is flexible, since it acknowledges that also 'other important grounds' could justify departure from the duty to submit documents. Concerning documents in the possession of a third party, the Austrian law is as restrictive as the Slovenian: if there is no obligation of the third party to submit the document under substantive law (or if the document, concerning its content, is not considered to be common for both parties), the third party has no duty to submit it.[50] Regarding documents in the possession of third parties, important developments occurred in Croatia. The *Croatian* Legislature realized that the regulation, which Croatia (just like Slovenia) inherited from the Yugoslav era, was too restrictive. In 2003 the Croatian Civil Procedure Act was changed and under the newly adopted regime a third party is obliged to submit documents unless their contents is covered by witness privilege.[51]

In *France*, pursuant to Article 11 NCPC, when a party possesses relevant documents, the judge can, at the request of the other party, order the party to produce them, and, unless legitimate grounds for withholding the document exist, fine the party for delay (and draw adverse inferences in cases of non-compliance).[52] These rules are based on the general principle that everyone must cooperate in the administration of justice in view of pursuing the truth. The judge can, upon the request of a party, also request a third party to submit documents in his possession, unless legitimate grounds for withholding them prevail (e.g. protection of professional secrecy).[53] Also the new *Dutch* Civil Procedure Act of 2002 extended the possibilities through which a party to litigation can effectively seek production of documents in the possession of the opposing party (Article 22). A document can be requested if it is relevant to the pending dispute and it may be withheld only for 'compelling reasons'. This is in line with the (also newly introduced) and 'decidedly revolutionary'[54] principle that parties must 'fully and truthfully supply facts that are

47 See e.g. Walter 2005, p. 76.
48 Murray & Stürner 2004, p. 243.
49 Murray & Stürner 2004, p. 77; Prütting 2008, p. 257.
50 See Rechberger & Simotta 2003, p. 359.
51 See e.g. Triva & Dika 2004, p. 517.
52 Ferrand 2005, p. 27.
53 *Ibidem.*
54 Rutgers & Rutgers 2005, p. 140.

relevant for the judge's decision under the threat of drawing adverse inferences in case of non-compliance' (Article 21).

The new *Swiss* Federal Civil Procedure Act (in force since 2011) provides for far-reaching obligations of the parties and third parties to disclose and produce documents. Pursuant to Article 160, the parties and third parties have a duty to cooperate in the taking of evidence. *Inter alia* they have the duty to produce relevant documents (with the exception of documents forming correspondence between a party or a third party and a lawyer who is entitled to act as a professional representative) and to allow an examination of their person or property by an expert. In case of unjustified refusal, the court may infer that the alleged fact is proven. A party may refuse to cooperate if the taking of evidence would expose a spouse or close relative (thus, surprisingly, not the party) to criminal prosecution or civil liability or if the disclosure of a secret would amount to a criminal offence concerning breach of professional confidentiality or if the party is entrusted with legally protected secrets and if it is credibly demonstrated that the interest in keeping the secret outweighs the interest in finding the truth (Article 163). Swiss courts have traditionally been sympathetic especially towards protection of banking secrets. It is interesting that (with the exception of the specific criminal offence of breach of professional confidentiality) a party has no right to withhold documents which might have the effect of exposing himself to criminal prosecution. Such privilege applies only with regard to third parties. This rule has been criticized by some authors, but the majority view is - rather unconvincing, though - that it is not incompatible with the privilege against self-incrimination, since (in case of non-compliance with the order to produce documents which the party may choose to do if he fears criminal prosecution) adverse inferences supposedly affect the party merely in the civil case at hand.[55]

4. Some Lessons from EU Law

Recent developments in EU law, although still limited to certain specific types of disputes, are worth mentioning as well. Pursuant to Article 6(1) of Directive 2004/48/EC on the enforcement of intellectual property rights ('Enforcement Directive'), Member States must ensure that 'on application by a party which has presented reasonably available evidence sufficient to support its claims, and has, in substantiating those claims, specified evidence which lies in the control of the opposing party, the competent judicial authorities may order that such evidence be presented by the opposing party, subject to the protection of confidential information'. Furthermore the opposing party may be ordered to produce banking, financial or commercial documents relevant to the resolution of a dispute involving the infringement of intellectual property rights on a commercial scale (Article 6(2)). Such developments on the EU level, although restricted to specific types of legal

55 Schmid 2010, p. 657.

disputes, might trigger a move in the national legislation of Member States towards a more general recognition of the duty to disclose and produce documents.[56]

Another specific area where claimants experience many difficulties in obtaining the evidence they need to bring a successful claim concerns actions for damages for infringement of competition law. Especially documents or records held by competition authorities can be particularly valuable for victims of cartels. The CJEU has ruled that a blanket ban on access to documents on file with the competition authority and relating to leniency proceedings is not permitted.[57] It rejected the pleas for an almost absolute protection of voluntary self-incriminating statements on file with competition authorities and made by a leniency applicant from disclosure to third parties who claim damages for anti-trust infringements.[58] A balanced approach must be adopted, and any request for access to the documents in question must be assessed on a case-by-case basis. This balancing of interests does not apply only to conflicting private interests of the individual parties concerned. In the course of assessment, it is for the national courts to appraise public interests also: the public interest relating to the effectiveness of the leniency programme (it is essential that members of the cartel bona fide and fully cooperate with competition authorities and disclose incriminating documents), on the one hand, and the public interest of ensuring effective private enforcement of anti-trust and maintenance of effective competition through individual claims for damages, on the other.[59] Further clarification is brought by the *Directive on certain rules governing actions for damages under national law for infringements of the competition law provisions of the Member States and of the European Union*,[60] which contains elaborate rules on disclosure of evidence (Articles 5-8). On the one hand, it aims at ensuring that claimants are afforded the right to obtain the disclosure of evidence relevant to their claim, whereas, on the other hand, it also contains safeguards to ensure that the incentives for offending companies to voluntarily cooperate with competition authorities were not diminished.

5. Evaluation and Conclusion

The privilege against self-incrimination is a principle of criminal procedure and as with many other properties of the law of evidence (e.g. burden of proof, standard of proof, exclusion of illegally obtained evidence ...) one should be cautious when

56 Wagner 2012 p. 105.

57 CJEU judgment of 6 June 2013, C-536/11, *Bundeswettbewerbsbehörde v. Donau Chemie AG and Others*.

58 Such a view was advocated also by AG Jääskinen in his opinion of 7 February 2013 in case C-536/11 *Donau Chemie and Others*.

59 CJEU judgment of 6 June 2013, C-536/11, *Bundeswettbewerbsbehörde v. Donau Chemie AG and Others*.

60 Directive 2014/104/EU of the European Parliament and of the Council of 26 November 2014 on certain rules governing actions for damages under national law for infringements of the competition law provisions of the Member States and of the European Union.

'transplanting' such doctrines into civil cases. Undoubtedly, in the context of disclosure of documents in civil procedure, the privilege against self-incrimination is legitimately applicable insofar as it relates to the party exposing himself to the risk of being prosecuted for a criminal offence.[61] It is, however, an entirely different question whether this privilege should apply when the party would, by disclosing unfavourable evidence, merely risk losing the civil case at hand. The reason why many doctrines concerning safeguards developed in criminal procedure cannot be transplanted into the sphere of civil disputes is not because more is at stake for the affected person in the criminal case. Realistically, for the parties involved in the civil case legal, economic and personal interests involved are often much bigger than in certain criminal cases. What is decisive is that the structure of a civil case differs from a criminal one as it inevitably involves the need to strike a proper balance in the conflict of rights between two equal parties. When striving to protect the constitutional rights or legitimate expectations of one party in a civil case, the court should take into account equally important constitutional rights and legitimate interests of the other party in the dispute. Concerning disclosure of documentary evidence (just as in case of e.g. use of illegally obtained documents in a civil case), the goal to protect the rights of the party possessing such documents cannot be considered isolated from the rights of the other party involved - his right of effective access to court and effective right to be heard. In addition, since both parties are - in contrast to a criminal case - in an equal position, there is no reason to ensure a more favourable position for one party (e.g. concerning burden and standard of proof). For these reasons the traditional absolute application of the principle *nemo tenetur edere contra se* in civil litigation must be rejected insofar as it extends beyond the risk of exposing oneself to criminal prosecution. A proper balance between legitimate expectations and the constitutional rights of both parties should be struck. It should be borne in mind that especially in litigation which is either complex or characterized by an unequal position of the parties concerning possibilities to obtain evidence effective access to justice is inherently linked to access to information. The present situation in Slovenia, where - and even this to a rather limited extent - the court's order for disclosure of evidence can only be made at the hearing, is unsatisfactory. This is important not only because of the goal of a focused hearing and its proper preparation or because of the goal to foster settlements as early as possible, it is additionally important because of the substantive aspect of adjudication: achieving justice on merits.

In its traditional negative stance towards placing a burden on the party to disclose unfavourable documents in his possession, Slovenian law does not differ from other procedural systems of continental Europe. Hence, this is not some relict from the procedural system of the communist era. Nevertheless, there might be some reasons linked to the fate of civil justice during communist Yugoslavia that add to the general underdevelopment of this topic - not only in legislation and case law but also in legal writing. On the face of it, it might seem surprising that a

61 See Andrews 2003, p. 55.

procedural system which highly valued the so-called principle of material truth in fact contained so few instruments which would enable parties to search for the truth. However, it should be noted that the lack of such instruments in the hands of the parties was 'compensated' by the broad inquisitorial powers of the judge. Hence, it is not too surprising that the lack of the party's access to documents in the possession of either the opponent or a third party was not perceived as important. Since the judge was empowered to take evidence *ex officio* (alongside broad inquisitorial powers to require the production of any kind of documents irrespective of in whose possession they were in), it was simply expected that in the event the party himself did not gain access to relevant evidence, the judge would take it *ex officio* and invoke his broad inquisitorial powers. The rule that the judge has broad powers to seek documents from any person still remains in the law (Article 10 CPA). But it has lost much of its significance due to the fact that the judge is no longer empowered to take evidence *ex officio* - except in regard to procedural prerequisites, e.g. jurisdiction, or in exceptional circumstances and certain specific types of disputes, e.g. family cases. Consequently, the judge can use his powers to seek documents from persons possessing them only in exceptional circumstances. Another reason why the lack of a party's access to documents has until very recently not been perceived as really important is linked to the powers of court-appointed experts. These persons are perceived as assistants of the court and consequently the broad powers of the judge to seek documents applied to the court-appointed experts as well. Terms of reference for the experts stating that the expert shall 'review all documents in the defendant's company's file' or 'all documents relevant for the dispute' were - and to a certain extent still are - common. Such practice actually often enabled 'fishing expeditions'. However, recently the courts are increasingly becoming more careful in framing the terms of reference when appointing experts and a more specific description of documents that the expert is entitled to review is necessary.

While the principle of the 'quest for the material truth' was typical for the procedural system of the communist era, a certain animosity against the idea of effective protection of 'rich' creditors coupled with a high degree of protection of the 'poor' debtors was typical as well. Whereas this approach was foremost evident in the regulation of the enforcement of judgments, it affected litigation too. A closer look at certain principles and rules of civil procedure of communist Yugoslavia shows how unfavourable the creditor's position was. For example, the standard of proof in civil cases is very high and, according to the wording of the law, practically the same as in criminal cases ('the judge must be convinced ...').[62] At least until very

[62] The judge must be (practically) convinced (persuaded) about the existence of a certain fact, if not, the judge should find against the party whom the burden of proof for this fact rests, thus, even if the court finds it more probable - but still not with a degree beyond the doubt of a reasonable person - that this fact actually exists (Judgment of the Supreme Court, II Ips 492/2002 dated 8 July 2004: '... convinced of the existence of the material fact beyond doubt of any reasonable person'). In the doctrine as well as in case law, the harshness of the high standard of proof is sometimes relaxed and a solution applied that a standard of proof in a →

recently, a strict and unexceptional prohibition of so-called 'exploratory' or 'informative' evidence applied[63] (stricter than in e.g. Germany, where the doctrine and the case law have developed a balanced approach to the acceptability of *Ausforschungsbeweis*).[64] The prohibition is certainly justified when litigants know or could have known the facts they are supposed to assert. However, it is not justified in other not so rare cases, where the litigants must allege facts that lie outside their range of perception and hence do not have sufficient knowledge of the necessary facts.[65] In such cases, it is, on the one hand, necessary to alleviate the requirements of substantiated allegation of facts and, on the other hand, to allow informative evidence in order to ensure a fair trial.[66] This is especially important, bearing in mind that the rule of 'fact pleading' applies in Slovenian law, hence the creditor needs to make detailed statements of facts and offers of evidence already in the statement of claim. Furthermore, until the CPA reform of 2008 it was not necessary for the opponent to make a substantiated (reasoned) denial of facts. 'Escape clauses' that 'everything is denied except what is expressly admitted' were (and still are) common, although the facts fall entirely within the sphere and knowledge of the party denying them.[67] It should also be noted that in Slovenian civil procedure the claimant needs to – without exception – make a specific prayer for relief (the precise amount of money sought) already in the claim; he cannot wait for, for example, the results of expert evidence which enables the effective determination of the damage. At the same time, the strict principle of the 'loser pays' rule applies, and costs for pre-action party appointed experts are only exceptionally reimbursable. The 'loser pays' principle means that the claimant bears a substantial cost-risk in case of making an inflated claim (even in legitimate circumstances where at the start of the litigation he could not properly assess e.g. damage). On the other hand, if the claim is set at too low a level, the claimant risks that at the moment when he might want to readjust it, it would already fall under the statute of limitations. All of the aforementioned features – added to a lack of adequate possibilities of access to information – show that the claimant's position in Slovenian civil procedure is rather difficult, compared not only to the common law systems but to civil law systems as well. Many of these features were inherited from the procedural regime of the communist era even though that was the system which supposedly attached a

civil case should not, as Art. 216 CPA could imply, be practically identical as the one in criminal cases (beyond reasonable doubt); therefore a *clearly overwhelming degree of probability* should be sufficient in a civil case (see: ibid.). But in any case, a mere decision on the preponderance of probabilities is definitely not sufficient.

63 E.g. judgment of the Supreme Court No. II Ips 106/2001 dated 5 July 2002.

64 Dolenc 2011, p. 1467.

65 *Ibidem*.

66 II Ips 302/2011 dated 26 April 2012.

67 Now, the CPA explicitly provides that only facts that have been disputed need to be proved. In addition, a denial of facts must be substantiated; the party must in principle offer his version of disputed events. A statement of non-knowledge may resolve the party of the effect of presumed admission only if it concerns facts that are not in the sphere of this party (Art. 214/2, CPA).

very high importance to the finding of the 'material truth'. This programmatic and ideological background led many authors from former Yugoslavia to believe that the 'adversarial' common law style of civil procedure attached no importance to the quest for truth in civil litigation.[68] The quote of the learned English judge in the introduction to this article shows how erroneous such a perception was. What the aforementioned authors failed to understand is that different systems apply different concepts and methods that are regarded as producing most truthful results.[69] They also failed to realize that promoting the goal of searching for the truth out of an ideological reason to demonstrate the omnipotence of state power, inevitably linked to a disrespect for party autonomy and self-responsibility, has very little in common with pursuing the quest for the very same truth for the benefit of the individual rights of the parties.

68 Typically Šipec 1999, p. 1206.
69 Van Rhee & Uzelac 2012, p. XXIII.

Bibliography

Andrews 2003
Andrews, N., *English Civil Procedure*, Oxford: Oxford University Press, 2003.

Andrews 2007
Andrews, N., 'The Pre-action Phase: General Report - Common Law', in: Pelegrini Grinover, A., Calmon, P. (eds.), *XIII World Congress of Procedural Law*, Rio De Janeiro: Editora Forense, 2007, p. 201-241.

Bergant Rakočević 2011
Bergant Rakočević, V., 'Varstvo uradne, vojaške in poslovne tajnosti v civilnem sodnem postopku' (Protection of official, military and commercial confidentiality in civil proceedings), *Podjetje in delo*, 2011, No. 6-7, p. 1476-1486.

Brulc 2011
Brulc, U., 'Pridobivanje listinskih dokazov pred pravdo in med njo v razmerju do varstva osebnih podatkov' (Obtaining documentary evidence before and during litigation in relation to personal data protection), *Podjetje in delo*, 2011, No. 6-7, p. 1487-1498.

Brus 2007
Brus, M., 'Prvostopenjski civilni proces po nemškem ZPO' (Litigation in first instance courts pursuant to the German ZPO), *Podjetje in delo*, 2007, No. 2, p. 336-369.

Dolenc 2011
Dolenc, M., 'O vlogi informativnega dokaza v pravdnem postopku' (On the role of informative evidence in civil proceedings), *Podjetje in delo*, 2011, No. 6-7, p. 1467-1475.

Ferrand 2005
Ferrand, F., 'The Respective Role of the Judge and the Parties in the Preparation of the Case in France', in: Trocker, N. & Varano, V. (eds.), *The Reforms of Civil Procedure in Comparative Perspective*, Torino: Giappichelli Editore, 2005, p. 7-32.

Groen 2007
Groen, B., 'New Trends in Pre-action - General Report Civil Law', in: Pelegrini Grinover A. & Calmon P. (eds.), *XIII World Congress of Procedural Law*, Rio De Janeiro: Editora Forense, 2007, p. 242-256.

Leipold 2005
Leipold, D., in: Stein, F. & Jonas, M., *ZPO-Kommentar*, 22. Aufl., Band 3, Tübingen: Mohr Siebeck, 2005.

Leipold 2006
Leipold, D., in: Stein, F. & Jonas, M., *ZPO-Kommentar*, 22. Aufl., Band 5, Tübingen: Mohr Siebeck, 2006.

Leipold 2008
Leipold, D., 'Oral and Written Elements within the Introductory Phase of Civil Procedure', in: Ortells Ramos, M. & Carpi F. (eds.), *Oralidad y escritura en un proceso civil eficiente*, Valencia: Universitat de Valencia, 2008, p. 53-78.

Murray & Stürner 2004
Murray, P. & Stürner, R., *German Civil Justice*, Durham: Carolina Academic Press, 2004.

Prütting 2008
Prütting, H., 'International Sources of German Civil Procedure', in: Deguchi, M. & Storme, M. (eds.), *The Reception and Transmission of Civil Procedural Law in the Global Society*, Antwerp: Maklu, 2008, p. 249-260.

Rechberger & Simotta 2003
Rechberger, W. & Simotta, D.A., *Zivilprozessrecht*, 6th edn., Wien: Manz, 2003.

Rosenberg, Schwab & Gottwald 2004
Rosenberg, L., Schwab, K.H. & Gottwald, P., *Zivilprozessrecht*, 16th edn., München: Beck, 2004.

Rutgers & Rutgers 2005
Rutgers, G.R. & Rutgers, J.W., 'Reform of the Code of Civil Procedure in the Netherlands', in: Trocker, N. & Varano, V. (eds.), *The Reforms of Civil Procedure in Comparative Perspective,* Torino: Giappichelli Editore, 2005, p. 131-142.

Schmid 2010
Schmid, H., in: Oberhammer, P. (ed.), *Schweizerisches Zivilprozessordnung,* Basel: Helbing Lichtenhahn Verlag, 2010.

Sime 2004
Sime, S., *A Practical Approach to Civil Procedure,* 7th edn., Oxford: Oxford University Press, 2004.

Šipec 1999
Šipec, M., 'Med liberalnim in socialnim civilnim procesom' (Between a liberal and social civil procedure), *Podjetje in delo,* 1999, No. 6-7, p. 1200-1209.

Staudinger 2009
Staudinger von, J., *BGB Kommentar,* München: Beck, 2009.

Stürner 2007
Stürner, R., 'Duties of Disclosure and Burden of Proof in the Private Enforcement of European Competition Law', in: Basedow, J. (ed.), *Private Enforcement of EC Competition Law*, Alphen aan den Rijn: Kluwer, 2007, p. 163-194.

Testen 2011
Testen, M., 'Vloga odvetnika pri pridobivanju in (ne)razkritju dokazov za namen pravdnega postopka' (The role of the attorney in the obtaining of evidence and the (non)disclosure of evidence in civil proceedings), *Podjetje in delo*, 2011, No. 6-7, p. 1499-1509.

Trampuš 2002
Trampuš, Z., 'Materialno procesno vodstvo in sodna poravnava' (The judge's duty to seek clarification and settlement in court), *Podjetje in delo*, 2002, No. 6-7, p. 1545-1560.

Triva & Dika 2004
Triva, S. & Dika, M., *Građansko parnično procesno pravo*, Zagreb: Narodne novine, 2004.

Triva, Belajec & Dika 1986
Triva, S., Belajec, V. & Dika, M., *Građansko parnično procesno pravo*, Zagreb: Narodne novine, 1986.

Trocker & Varano 2005
Trocker, N. & Varano, V., 'Concluding remarks', in: Trocker, N. & Varano, V. (eds.), *The Reforms of Civil Procedure in Comparative Perspective*, Torino: Giappichelli Editore, 2005, p. 243-266.

Ude 2002
Ude, L., *Civilno procesno pravo* (Civil Procedure), Ljubljana: ČZ UL, 2002.

Uzelac 2010
Uzelac, A., 'Survival of the Third Legal Tradition?', *Supreme Court Law Review*, 2010, p. 377-396.

Van Rhee 2008
Van Rhee, C.H., 'Dutch Civil Procedural Law in an International Context', in: Deguchi, M. & Storme, M. (eds.), *The Reception and Transmission of Civil Procedural Law in the Global Society*, Antwerp: Maklu, 2008, p. 191-212.

Van Rhee & Uzelac 2012
Van Rhee, C.H. & Uzelac, A., (eds.) *Truth and Efficiency in Civil Litigation: Fundamental Aspects of Fact-finding and Evidence-taking in a Comparative Context*, Antwerp: Intersentia, 2012.

Wagner 2012
Wagner, G., 'Harmonisation of Civil Procedure: Policy Perspectives', in: Kramer, X., Van Rhee, C.H. (eds.), *Civil Litigation in a Globalising World,* Cham/Heidelberg/-Dordrecht/New York/London: Springer, 2012, p. 93-119.

Walter 2005
Walter G., 'The German Civil Procedure Reform Act 2002: Much Ado About Nothing', in: Trocker, N. & Varano, V. (eds.), *The Reforms of Civil Procedure in Comparative Perspective,* Torino: Giappichelli Editore, 2005, p. 67-89.

Zobec 2006
Zobec, J., in: Ude, L., *Pravdni postopek – zakon s komentarjem* (Civil Procedure: Act with Commentary), Vol. 2, Ljubljana: GV Založba in ČZ UL, 2006.

Zobec 2010
Zobec, J., in: Ude, L., *Pravdni postopek – zakon s komentarjem* (Civil Procedure: Act with Commentary), Vol. 4, Ljubljana: GV Založba in ČZ UL, 2010.

B. Karolczyk

PRECLUSION OF LATE ALLEGATIONS AND EVIDENCE AS A TOOL TO INCREASE THE EFFICIENCY OF CIVIL PROCEEDINGS IN POLAND: A SHORT STORY OF THE UGLY PAST AND THE WAY TO A BRIGHT FUTURE

1. Introduction

In this contribution I present selected issues regarding the preclusion of untimely allegations and evidence[1] in civil proceedings. In other words, this contribution deals with the doctrine of concentration of procedural material, as it is called in Poland. In the background there are inherent internal tensions between two key values of adjudication, namely, efficiency, on the one hand, and the reliability of the factual inquiry, on the other. I will carry out my presentation by mixing a healthy concoction of doctrine, law and practical observations. One caveat is in order, however. Given the limited space and the sheer size of the subject of inquiry, some readers may find this article a bit general. Although a side effect, this should be in fact beneficial for a foreign reader, as a meticulous discussion might have been too abstract and too detailed for comparative purposes.

I start with a brief characterization of the Polish system of procedure, including the still powerful dogma of truth-seeking. After a short historical comment on the principle of concentration, I move to the recent 'ugly past' and 'the bright future' ahead in light of recent amendments to the Polish Code of Civil Procedure (CCP).[2] I conclude with some thoughts on the new law.

2. The Polish Model of Procedure: A View from Above

I would like to start by making two points.

1 In this contribution the term 'allegation' means factual allegation or statement introduced, in principle, into the proceedings by the parties. The term 'evidence' is used to denote a motion to admit (take) evidence, unless otherwise indicated. Where the term 'procedural material' is used, it means both allegations and evidence.

2 In this contribution references to Articles are to the CCP, unless otherwise indicated.

2.1. *Theoretical Classification*

First, although it does not perfectly match Damaška's model, I would argue that the Polish system is a type of 'social' or 'policy-implementing' model of procedure.

Theoretically, this model has the following characteristics: (1) as a part of its function, the active state has adopted a certain idea of how a 'good society' should work; (2) a civil dispute is a social problem, because it disrupts the orderly workings of society; (3) so, the state needs to be actively involved in adjudication, should it be invoked; (4) accordingly, adjudication is about more than merely resolving civil disputes; it is also about that idea of social order; (5) thus, the lawmaker infuses procedural norms with substantive policies; (6) because otherwise these policies will remain on paper and the primary goal of civil proceedings is to make correct factual findings, which is a *conditio sine qua non* for giving a proper judgment. Given how important the ultimate outcome is, this model of procedure has a tendency to incorporate officialdom. Ultimately, the fate of the proceedings, in particular both identification and the taking of evidence, is left principally to the judge as an emanation of the state, so that neither the procedural nor the substantive goals of the process are compromised by private contest.[3] Procedural norms are mostly *ius cogens* in character, meaning neither the judge nor the joint accord of the disputants can alleviate their application.[4]

It is fair to say that this approach to adjudication was taken by the principal drafter of the Austrian Code of Civil Procedure of 1895,[5] Franz Klein. The Polish Code of Civil Procedure of 1930 was heavily based on the Austrian Code. The CCP was, in turn, heavily based on the Code of 1930.

However, due to political changes in post-war Poland and to Soviet influence, the social model was gradually turned into a socialist model. As a result, several key concepts were significantly modified. The prime examples relevant to this contribution are Articles 3(2), 7, 213 and 232 in their original wording (until 1996).[6]

3 See Damaška 1986, p. 80-88.

4 Regardless of Damaška's brilliant analytical framework, I should point out that Franz Klein is considered the father of this approach to civil litigation. Klein did not invent these elements, although he put them together in a unique manner. The literature on the topic is vast.

5 This code is commonly accepted as the most influential code of civil procedure in 20th-century Europe. See generally e.g. Van Rhee 2008a.

6 The court was under the duty to examine all material circumstances of the case in a comprehensive manner and discover the actual substance of factual and legal relations. The court, acting on its own, could take any steps, allowed given the stage of the proceedings, deemed necessary to supplement the (factual) material and evidence submitted by the parties (Art. 3(2)). Art. 7 (still) authorizes public prosecutors to initiate civil proceedings in any case in which they believe the protection of the rule of law, the rights of citizens or public interest so require. Pursuant to Art. 213(1), the court could order appropriate inquiry in order to supplement or clarify the parties' allegations. Moreover, in principle, the court was not bound by the defendant's acceptance of the complaint. The parties were obliged to submit evidence; the court could take evidence not submitted by the parties; the court could also order an appropriate inquiry, so that necessary evidence could be established (Art. 232).

Generally speaking, the sole responsibility for the efficiency[7] of proceedings has been placed with the courts (the judges).

Things have, of course, changed since 1989. Nonetheless, a significant consequence of these historical events is that many concepts of 'social' origin are frequently viewed as 'socialist'. There are many psychological and social reasons for this phenomenon, but they cannot be explored here.[8]

2.2. *A System in Flux*

Second, regardless of such categorization the Polish system is in a state of constant flux. As of June 2014, since its entry into force in 1964 the CCP has been amended over 173 times.[9] In spite of that, the structure of the first instance procedure remains generally unchanged.

Looking back at the last 20 years through the comparative lens reveals some disturbing results.

The first major reform took place in 1996. Much socialist tissue was removed from the patient, who at the same time was administered a healthy dose of measures oriented towards the production of an adversarial environment. Still, judicial discretion, a concept hardly recognized in the legalistic, bureaucratic and hierarchical system of justice,[10] was difficult to find.[11] What is more, there was no

7 Procedurally, in Europe this concept has two elements. First, cases should be decided within reasonable time and as economically as possible. Second, cases should be decided fairly on the merits, that is, in accordance with substantive law. See Taruffo 2008, p. 187; Pogonowski 2005, p. 61 and Łazarska 2012, p. 379 *et seq*. See also generally Ereciński & Weitz 2006. *Cf.* the overriding objective of the English Civil Procedure Rule 1.1 (available at: <http://www.justice.gov.uk/courts/procedure-rules/civil/rules/part01> (last consulted on 11 June 2014)).

8 Suffice it to say that this phenomenon may be observed because the differences between 'social' and 'socialist', despite changes in the law, may indeed be subtle at times and are not directly clear to many common observers. *Cf.* generally Uzelac 2010 (arguing that the socialist legal tradition has survived in post-socialist countries in the context of procedural law) and Uzelac 2012 (discussing the concept of opinion written by the court in support of the judgment). *Cf.* also conclusions and citations in Karolczyk 2013b (discussing reluctance towards judicial involvement in case management in Poland and its potential sources).

9 According to notes in the commercial digital database Lex Prestige (Wolters Kluwer). The current code is criticized by many as incoherent, vague, detailed and complicated. These claims are neither surprising nor false given the act was created in times of 'deep' socialism and has 'survived' the political, economic and social changes.

10 See Damaška 1986, p. 19, 21-22, 51-52. Thus the 'classic' attachment to rules and lack of standards. Moreover, as a result the taking of evidence is divided into many hearings spread over months and, in many cases, years ('piecemeal trial').

11 One casual way to explain this is to say that the legislator does not trust the judge. Still, two significant propositions can be made. One, in the Civil Law tradition the scholar is exceptionally close to the legislator. Two, the Polish scholar (who was raised in the civil law school, but then went to a socialist university for almost 50 years) had primarily two teachers, one French and one German. The French scholar distrusted judges because of the pre-Revolution association of judges with the aristocracy and the abuse of discretion. The →

preparatory stage, no judicial case management and the practice of commencing hearings for unprepared cases was both notorious and frequent.[12]

Meanwhile in England, in March of 1994 Lord Woolf was appointed to review the rules of civil procedure. The goal was to improve access to justice, reduce the cost of litigation and remove unnecessary complexity. I assume that every reader of this contribution is well familiar with the famous Woolf Reports. If not, it suffices to quote this sentence by Lord Woolf: 'Ultimate responsibility for the control of litigation must move from the litigants and their legal advisers to the court.'[13] In 1999, Adrian Zuckerman wrote about 'the universal assertion of judicial control' as a European trend in the search for efficiency in civil litigation.[14]

Yet, in 2000 the Polish lawmaker introduced preclusion to the special procedure for commercial matters,[15] arguing this would speed up the proceedings and increase the adversarial environment by forcing the parties to be more active. That year marked the beginning of a decade during which the doctrine, the lawmaker and the courts regularly fell victim to two fallacies. One, that entrepreneurs involved in civil litigation should be held to a higher standard because they do business. Two, that formalism promotes efficiency. Subsequent changes to this procedure prohibited amendments to the claim and the subject matter of the complaint, as well as limited the admissibility of the set-off defence.[16] Effectively, those and many other changes, by eliminating any traces of reason and flexibility, took this procedure back to the early 19th century. For a vibrant, developing economy based on small and medium, but legally unsophisticated, businesses it was the wrong decision. Probably it was mostly the courts that

German scholar remembered well Frederick the Great and the idea that the judge is merely an automaton to apply the law ('Subsumtionsautomat'). For a comparative account of these trends see generally Merryman 1985. Thus the following hypothesis can be formulated. Polish legal thought was formed by both German and French currents. These ideas were further galvanized by socialism, where judges were not supposed to have any real power. Therefore, the procedure was deprived of legal norms involving discretion. Still, although the law may have changed, these original currents are still certainly present today in Polish legal doctrine.

12 Unfortunately, this is still frequently the case. See Sect. II in Karolczyk 2013b.

13 See Woolf 1996, p. 5.

14 Zuckerman 1999, p. 47.

15 Generally, every matter between two entrepreneurs was a commercial matter. Any legal entity or natural person carrying out a business or professional activity on its own behalf was considered an entrepreneur. See Art. 43^1 of the Polish Civil Code of 1964. Thus this included, for example, sole proprietors and partners of civil law partnerships.

16 At the same time, the general (ordinary) procedure for civil disputes remained basically untouched. The only change to that procedure in 2000 was the introduction of Art. 207(3). This provision authorized the presiding judge to order a party to raise or submit procedural material (literally, 'allegations, defences and evidence') in writing by a certain date, provided that the party was represented by an attorney. Should the party fail to comply, it would be barred from raising allegations or defences or moving for evidence at a later stage, provided that these could have been made in response to the judge's order. The nature of that provision was disputed, while it remained in force until 3 May 2013. See Sec. 3.3 below for more details about the changes to the special procedure.

benefitted from the decision - because of preclusion they could easily get rid of a case on a technicality.

During the same period, in Austria and Germany (2002 and 2003, respectively) the courts were granted *the right* to disregard untimely submissions of procedural material.[17] And in Norway (in 2005) a new code of civil procedure was passed that abandoned its German heritage, leaning more towards common law standards.[18] By 2008 judicial case management was on the lips of everyone.[19]

2.3. *Constitutional Foundation*

The Polish Constitution of 1997 contains several key declarations about adjudication. Fundamentally, Article 45 stipulates that 'every person has the right to a fair and public resolution of the matter without undue delay'. Following the model of Article 6 of the European Convention for the Protection of Human Rights and Fundamental Freedoms of 1950, Article 45 of the Polish Constitution is a manifestation of a basic, substantive right to court. This right includes, *inter alia,* the right: (1) of access to courts; (2) to an effective judicial remedy; and (3) to have a matter resolved within reasonable time.[20] I would argue that all three elements, that is, 'fair, public and reasonably fast', have been given the same weight.

Unfortunately, until very recently the only provision in the CCP pertaining to the efficiency of judicial proceedings was Article 6(1). It reads: 'The court should counteract delay in the proceedings and strive to resolve the matter at the first hearing, if it is possible without compromising the inquiry into the dispute.' There was not a single hint in the Code that the speed with which the matter is decided also depends on the parties.

2.4. *The Dogma of Truth-seeking*

The second part of Article 6(1) brings me to the dogma of truth-seeking.

In the field of procedural theory, Polish doctrine has closely followed German thought. As such, much of it is based on the concept of fundamental principles of civil procedure.[21] One such principle is the principle of truth.

17 See §§ 179, 180(2) and 275 of the Austrian ZPO. See also Oberhammer 2004, p. 227; Oberhammer & Domej 2005, p. 116, 123; Verkerk 2010, p. 40. Not to mention that judicial case management has been in operation for decades.

18 See generally Act of 17 June 2005 No. 90 relating to mediation and procedure in civil disputes (The Dispute Act) (*om mekling og rettergang i sivile tvister* (*tvisteloven*)) and the contributions in Lipp & Fredriksen 2011. The English translation of the Dispute Act is available in that volume, as well as online. See <http://www.ub.uio.no/ujur/ulovdata/lov-20050617-090-eng.pdf> (last consulted on 11 June 2014).

19 See generally contributions in Van Rhee 2008b. See also sources cited in Karolczyk 2013b.

20 See Pogonowski 2005, p. 7, 16.

21 These are 'general assumptions', 'leading ideas' of the procedural system, which affect all other elements of that system and the relations between them. *Cf.* Andrews 2012, p. 12-38 (an →

Currently, this principle should be understood as a postulate to decide the matter on the merits after a diligent but reasonable factual inquiry. Arguably, given the existing model this is self-explanatory. However, many commentators believe that despite the change of the model (from socialist to social), the court is still under the duty to pursue 'the truth, while this command is clear and does not require any dogmatic justification'.[22] Moreover, even stronger claims are commonly made in the doctrine, namely, that determination of the truth is the goal of adjudication. Notably, also the Supreme Court seems to approve this line of thought in the context of judicial power to introduce evidence.[23]

Indeed, from my perspective the best example and a living testament to the socialist model is the court's authority to introduce evidence on its own accord (*ex officio*). Literally, this is discretionary.[24] Despite the clear wording of the provision, however, under certain circumstances this right turns into a duty.[25] Specifically, the Supreme Court has ruled that 'the court should introduce evidence on its own accord in special circumstances'. These include, among others, a risk that an unrepresented party's interest, deserving special protection, may be infringed due to the lack of activity on the party's part, despite proper instructions by the court.[26] In addition, it was ruled that 'sometimes due to the existence of public interest [which, by the way, always exists in social security cases] the discretionary right to introduce evidence *ex officio* becomes the court's duty'.[27]

Most importantly, this right (or obligation) is not subject to any time limitations. Accordingly, the court may (or must) admit evidence that would be

interesting attempt to synthesize a doctrinal approach to fundamental rules under English law).

22 Ereciński 2012, p. 120.

23 See the Supreme Court's resolution of 17 February 2004, III CZP 115/03, OSNC 2005, No. 5, Item 77 (Art. 232 2nd sentence is the manifestation of the limited, albeit still existing, principle of the material truth); the Supreme Court's judgment of 22 February 2006, III CK 345/05, OSNC 2006, No. 10, items 174 (since Art. 232 2nd sentence has remained unchanged, it is a good indication to conclude that the legislator still gives priority to the principle of the material truth).

24 See Art. 232 2nd sentence ('The court may admit evidence not indicated by the party'). It is interesting to contrast this with the Code of 1930 and its Art. 244, which read: 'The court may admit evidence which neither party has moved to admit, provided that the court took notice thereof from the file of the case or the parties' statements, and provided that this code does not stipulate otherwise.' A subtle, yet significant difference indeed.

25 Apart from historical and theoretical considerations, this may come as a surprise given the civil character of the Polish legal order and the relevant provisions of the Constitution. Specifically, according to its Art. 178, while performing their duties judges are only subject to the Constitution and statutes.

26 See e.g. the Supreme Court's judgment of 8 December 2009, I UK 195/09, OSNP 2011, Nos. 13-14, Item 190.

27 See e.g. the Supreme Court's judgment of 4 January 2007, V CSK 377/06, OSP 2008, No. 1, Item 8. *Cf.* the Supreme Court's judgment of 15 January 2010, I CSK 199/09, LEX No. 570114 (holding that if the only way to avoid an incorrect decision on the merits is to take expert witness evidence, then the court's lack of initiative in that regard violates Art. 232 2nd sentence, regardless of the parties' initiative).

otherwise barred as untimely. This was also the rule in commercial cases. Although it was considered controversial then, it very likely remains good law today.[28]

Nonetheless, the Code contains many provisions that sacrifice the search for truth for other equally important values.[29] Furthermore, two of these values are the (individual) right to have one's matter decided without undue delay and the efficiency of the court system (common interest). In civil litigation it is simply unreasonable to expect that the truth will be determined in each and every case.[30] What is essential, though, is that 'the legislator should provide the courts and the parties with tools, which used with reason and regular diligence', allow for proper inquiry into the facts of the case.[31] Accordingly, regardless of the soundness of the said postulate, it should not be understood as an absolute command. However unpleasant and costly that is, we need to accept that a judicial decision may sometimes not be based on the facts.

In light of recent amendments it is indeed conceivable that such situations could be caused by the parties themselves, specifically when a party intentionally or recklessly obstructs the proceedings, treats the court instrumentally, or exercises his or her procedural rights in such a manner or with such a (malicious) purpose.[32] I believe such acts or omissions should, after proper notice: (1) constitute a deemed waiver of the right to have the case decided pursuant to the facts; and (2) in consequence, relieve the court of the duty to decide the case pursuant to the facts.[33] This line of thought, however, has a long wait ahead before being seriously considered, if at all.

28 See Ereciński 2012, p. 135-136, 1042. The authors (K. Weitz and P. Grzegorczyk) limit the rule by writing that the court's initiative should be limited exclusively to allegations properly introduced by the parties.

29 *Cf.* Karolczyk 2014 (on the clash of values in the context of admitting in civil litigation evidence allegedly obtained contrary to the law).

30 This has been said many times before. *Cf. Pearse v. Pearse* (1846) 1 De G & Sm 12, per *Knight-Bruce* V-C: 'The discovery and vindication and establishment of truth are main purposes certainly of the existence of Courts of Justice; still, for the obtaining of these objectives, which, however valuable and important, cannot be usefully pursued without moderation, ... Truth, like all other good things, may be loved unwisely - may be pursued too keenly - may cost too much ...'; cited in *A (FC) and others (FC) v. Secretary of State for the Home Department* [2005] UKHL 71.

31 Gudowski 2005, p. 1027. *Cf.* Jakubecki 2006, p. 366 (citing A. Wach). See also the legislative opinion supporting the bill, p. 52 (available at: <http://orka.sejm.gov.pl/-Druki6ka.nsf/0/46931DF8C9071DE8C12578B1003FF809/$file/4332.pdf> (last consulted on 11 June 2014)).

32 This could be put under the umbrella of abuse of procedural rights. Although some authors argue prohibition against abuse of right is a general principle of the CCP, it does not contain any general provision that addresses procedural abuse by the parties or their attorneys (similar to, for example, Rule 11 of the Federal Rules of Civil Procedure). See generally Plebanek 2012.

33 Similarly Łazarska 2012, p. 670 ('Procedural rights end where their abuse begins').

3. The Concentration of Procedural Material

3.1. *Preliminary Remarks*

That proceedings should be swift is also expressed in Article 6(1) CCP, which is treated as a normative foundation of the concentration principle. This is understood as all provisions that facilitate the efficient collection of procedural material and - in turn - the conclusion of disputes at the first hearing.[34] Moreover, there is a formal aspect to it as well, since it is said to set time limits on certain actions, including raising certain procedural defences and initiating interlocutory proceedings.[35] I think it is fair to say that this theoretical approach is universally accepted both in Poland and in a number of other European countries.[36]

According to Polish legal writings, the concentration principle can be implemented in two ways.[37] First, through a system of preclusion that incorporates the rule of contingent accumulation (*Eventualmaxime*).[38] This system originated in the formalized, written Romano-canonical procedure and was further developed in the Germanic *gemeines Recht*.[39] Generally, it is based on express statutory deadlines for identification and submission of procedural material. The lapse of a deadline renders any omitted material belated. If a party submits such material nonetheless, the rule of preclusion will activate. Exclusion of such untimely allegations or evidence from the file thus (in theory) occurs automatically by mere operation of

34 This is both theory and fiction, indeed a harmful one since the disharmony between the reality and the letter of the law is striking even to a layperson. The ultimate outcome is lack of respect for the law.

35 One can build a rather extensive catalogue of procedural defences that need to be raised prior to appearance under pain of preclusion. Since this is a rather common rule I will not talk about it. What I would like to note is that in Poland there are nine defences that affect the admissibility of the complaint, which the court has to consider on its own motion. Accordingly, these are not subject to preclusion and can thus affect the outcome of the case even at the Supreme Court.

36 See Weitz 2009, p. 74 and sources cited there; Taruffo 2008, p. 198-199.

37 Historical research into that statement has been painfully limited. This claim was made consistently throughout the 20th century, mostly by reference to two important Polish books, namely Waśkowski 1932 and Wengerek 1958. These two scholars looked mostly into German sources. However, there are some interesting inconsistencies between their work and Engelmann 1927. Suffice it to say, the picture of the sequence of process and the legal doctrine one gets from the latter is definitely less coherent than the one presented by the former. The most comprehensive modern Polish research into these matters can be found in Weitz 2009.

38 Engelmann also referred to it as *Konzentration der Rechtsbehelfe*, whereas Millar wrote about *the principle of mass-attack or mass-defense*. See Millar 1923, p. 25.

39 Weitz 2009, p. 76.

law.[40] As Engelmann notes, very little room for manoeuvre, if any, is left to the judge.[41]

Many Polish authors argue that the rule of contingent accumulation is an inherent element of the system of preclusion.[42] The said rule makes it mandatory for the parties to submit *all* allegations and evidence, at a certain stage in the proceedings, including potential procedural material (*in omnum eventum*), namely, allegations and evidence that *could become* relevant.[43] In other words, you are expected to plead 'just in case', apparently regardless of how plausible such pleas may be or the (little) information you actually have. Thus, inconsistencies between such 'primary' and 'secondary' material do not matter. What matters, though, is that if you fail to allege or make a motion for evidence such material will be, at a later stage, automatically deemed untimely and thus inadmissible on procedural grounds.[44]

40 This is seen as rather artificial (and goes even beyond the concept of the judge as *Subsumtionsautomat*) as the nature of any exclusionary rule is that it is not self-executing. On the contrary, it needs application by the judge to have any effect.

41 *Cf.* Engelmann 1927, p. 32.

42 Wengerek 1958, p. 38; Weitz 2009, p. 75-76.

43 See Millar 1923, p. 26 (citing German sources) and Engelmann 1927, p. 28.

44 Even though I have researched this area rather extensively, I have not come across a comprehensive analysis of the actual purpose or function of this rule. K. Weitz concludes, with regard to both systems, that it is their preventive function that was essential. In other words, the rules were there to make sure parties would submit procedural material in a complete and concentrated manner, and thus their repressive function was secondary in that it enhanced the preventive function. See Weitz 2009, p. 78. This conclusion warrants the following observations. First, different historical roots of these systems speak against drawing a common conclusion. Specifically, preclusion was a product of a secret, inquisitive, written and formalized Romano-canonical procedure, whereas judicial discretion (during trial) was an essential element of unitary oral trial by jury under the common law. We should also remember the rigid common law pleading rules (which effectively worked the same way as preclusion), which were oriented towards simplifying the issue for the trier of fact (the jury). Second, given the origin of Germanic rules, the explanation seems unpersuasive. For any rule of law to operate as a preventive measure, its addressees need to take actual notice. How were the parties under German law supposed to know these highly technical rules? Were they obliged to use professional legal help? Did the court advise them about the preclusion? These themes have not been explored and the conclusion, therefore, is susceptible to challenge. I think the key question is: who benefited the most from this rule, and why? In light of what we know about the Germanic procedure at the time, my hypothesis would be: the judge. Given the inquisitive nature of this procedure resulting in a duty for the judge to pursue the truth, that answer seems to be plausible. The nature of the process could have been generally known to potential disputants, but that is a speculative claim. In any case, elimination of the information asymmetry between the parties was certainly not a concern. We should also remember that the principle of *nemo tenetur edere contra se* reigned on the Continent until the early 20th century. I would argue, therefore, that it was the repressive function that was essential. Simply put, it was there to punish the parties for not helping the judge do his or her job properly. *Cf.* paragraphs from the General Judicial Ordinance for the Prussian States, in Engelmann 1927, p. 591.

The second system of concentration, which originated in England, is based on judicial discretion.[45] Theoretically, this system does not incorporate strict statutory deadlines for submissions. On the contrary, it is the judge who decides whether to accept or reject new (potentially untimely) allegations or evidence late in the proceedings. In order to do so, the judge weighs different factors and evaluates how such material affects both the other party and the course of the hearings.[46] In other words, preclusion of evidence is in theory a result of judicial decision, not an automatic outcome of statutory rules.[47]

Regardless of its origin, neither the Austrian nor the German ZPO has incorporated the *Eventualmaxime*. In fact, both of these codes copied the liberal French rule.[48]

3.2. *The Ugly Past (Special Procedure for Commercial Matters until May 2012)*

As mentioned before, in 2000 the CCP was amended to 'adjust' the resolution of commercial disputes to 'the high standards of professional business' by introducing preclusion, especially at the pleading stage.[49] Effectively, it made the pleadings the sole means for identification and submission of evidence. As a consequence, a party would lose the right to make allegations and submit evidence at a later stage in the proceedings simply by failing to include these in his or her pleading. Prior to 2000 no such rules ever existed in 20th-century Polish civil procedure.

Three years after the amendment came into force the Supreme Court said that the new system was in fact based on the *Eventualmaxime*.[50]

45 On the Continent, it was the French who in 1806 introduced the rule that allegations and evidence can be submitted until the judgment is given.

46 *Cf.* Weitz 2009, p. 77; Wengerek 1958, p. 39.

47 See Weitz 2009, p. 77.

48 Neither did the Dutch Code of 1838 have it. See Verkerk 2010, p. 63. This changed over time, however. See Art. 111(3) and Art. 128(5) of the Dutch Code of Civil Procedure. See also Van Hooijdonk & Eijsvoogel 2009, p. 34. As I understand, professional representation before Dutch courts is, in principle, mandatory.

49 Art. 479[12](1) (after the year 2000): 'In the complaint, the plaintiff must provide all allegations and evidence [to support them] or he shall lose the right to submit them in the course of the proceedings, unless he can show that their submission in the complaint was not possible or that the need to submit them arose later.' Art. 479[14](2) (after the year 2000): 'In the answer, the defendant must provide all allegations, defenses and evidence [to support them] or he shall lose the right to submit them in the course of the proceedings, unless he can show that their submission in the complaint was not possible or that the need to submit them arose later.'

50 From today's perspective this is truly remarkable. Neither in the law nor in the legislative materials was there a single hint that this was the case. An alternative, more rational reading of the provisions was not even considered in the decision. See the Supreme Court's resolution of 17 February 2004, III CZP 115/03, reported in 'Prokuratura i Prawo' 2004(9), p. 33. This resolution announced the rule that under the system of preclusion both parties were required to submit all facts, evidence and defences known to them in the pleadings, including those which would become relevant only if the first line of allegations proved ineffective or got →

Allegations, objections or defences as well as motions for evidence, if omitted from pleadings, were by default deemed untimely.[51] Thus the court had no choice but to bar a party from acting or disregard such submissions altogether, if already made, regardless of their relevance or how they would affect the judgment.

That was the case unless the omission was excused. One had only two options, namely, to show either that earlier submission of material was impossible or that the need to allege or to move for evidence arose after the initial pleading had been filed with the court. Initially this was very difficult.

Fast forward to 2010 and the ultimate result is the snowball effect in case law on these two exceptions. The Supreme Court decided these points as questions of law, while they were actually fact-driven decisions based on judicial discretion. Thus, most of the time the Supreme Court would second-guess the decisions of the lower courts. No wonder then that quite quickly the case law became voluminous, detailed and not necessarily coherent.[52] Limited empirical data showed that preclusion was one of the most important aspects of every commercial court case.[53] To put it differently, the focus of adjudication shifted from the merits to technicalities.

Thus the Polish legislator, with the 'help' of the Supreme Court, 'succeeded' in creating a 19th-century style procedure in the 21st century. What Poland ultimately had were technical, blurry rules that fundamentally affected how a case was decided. Commercial, often complex suits began to hinge on the art of pleading, à la 19th-century common law style.[54] The plaintiffs' attorneys were literally expected to guess how the opponent would respond in his or her pleading, and the defendants' counsel - under the axe of the statutory, unchangeable deadline of two weeks to respond - would in turn come up with every allegation, claim, defence or objection

dismissed by the court. Should they fail to do so, they lost the right to submit that particular piece of procedural material that could have been included in the pleading in the first place, regardless of its weight or relevance, unless the delay could be excused. The Court has given zero thought to policy or functional considerations behind this formal, dogmatic reading, merely pointing out the need for efficiency in civil litigation.

51 An intention to modify a motion was often treated as a new motion. Importantly, preclusion did not apply to the court, which by exercising its right/duty could admit otherwise procedurally inadmissible evidence. This rule supports the repressive function of the system. See point 2.4 above. What is also important to note is that the answer had to be filed within two weeks following service of the complaint. This was a strict statutory deadline for every commercial case.

52 See generally Sadomski 2010, p. 83 *et seq.*

53 See Sadomski 2010, p. 123. The literature on the topic is extensive.

54 *Cf.* e.g. *Clark v. Pennsylvania R. Co.*, 328 F.2d 591, at 594 (2nd Cir. 1964): 'In the heyday of Common Law Pleading, when each of the numerous technicalities involved provided the members of the bench and bar with a source of continual intellectual amusement and pleasure, the sporting theory of justice prevailed. To win a lawsuit by guile and surprise or by the skilful manipulation of mysterious rules, understood only by the elite, was quite the thing to do.' This description, although taken from a different legal culture and from a different time, is an incredibly accurate description of the Polish reality in 2000-2013, except apparently nobody was amused or pleased.

imaginable in the answer.[55] Additionally, both parties were in fact invited to guess what the judge would make of it all. Since there was no opportunity to talk to the judge, this proved to be quite a game – to identify the law and to allege facts that fit the law right at the outset of the case!

As a result, just as under the *gemeines Recht*, this form of preclusion 'led to monstrous formalism and basic eccentricity, so that finally a party was compelled to allege wholly contradictory things, the one in the first line, the other for the case that the first was unavailing: the presentation of the case was a most unnatural one, and what is more, the use of such contradictory allegations prejudiced the cause of candor and honourable dealing'.[56]

It took the Supreme Court 10 years to recognize two crucial things. First, that preclusion is not *really* automatic and it *has* an important element of judicial discretion in it. Second, that the *Eventualmaxime* is not *really* there, or – at least – it is not as broad as initially announced.[57] These developments were important as they have introduced an urgently needed element of reason into the system. Also around the same time the special procedure came under heavy and widespread criticism that eventually led to its demise.

Calls for review of the ordinary procedure have also been growing louder. K. Weitz, professor at Warsaw University and Member of the Civil Law Codification Commission, has concluded that: (1) the CCP lacks general provisions that would stipulate the parties' responsibility for proper implementation of the concentration principle and burden them with the duty to support (diligent conduct of) the proceedings;[58] (2) the CCP lacks provisions based on judicial discretion that would provide for a general tool to achieve proper concentration of procedural material;[59] and (3) general rules addressing the parties' activity in the course of the proceedings are needed; on the other hand the court needs to be authorized, but not bound, to bar or disregard untimely submission of procedural material, unless the delay is excused.[60]

To summarize, the ordinary procedure for civil matters lacked a mechanism that would ensure and mandate the effective flow of information. Following the old French rule, the parties were allowed to amend their pleadings, allege new facts and introduce new motions for evidence until the judgment is given.

55 There was a rule in the CCP that was directed, perhaps intentionally, at mitigating these difficulties. Specifically, it was Art. $479^{12}(2)$. This article required the plaintiff to attach to the statement of claim a copy of either a notice of dissatisfaction (Polish, *reklamacja*) or a demand for voluntary satisfaction of the claim, sent to the defendant prior to commencing the case in court, as well as information or a copy of documents pertaining to pre-litigation settlement negotiations. A statement of claim lacking any of these would be formally deemed defective.

56 See Engelmann 1927, p. 591.

57 See Karolczyk 2012a, No. 1, p. 54-55 (noting the change in case law with regard to the *Eventualmaxime*).

58 Weitz 2009, p. 93.

59 *Ibidem*, p. 94.

60 *Ibidem*, p. 96-97.

3.3. *The Flexible Future under the New Law?*

On 3 May 2012 the separate procedure for commercial cases was abolished, whereas the ordinary procedure was heavily amended. According to the written opinion accompanying the bill, its overriding objective was to increase the efficiency of adjudication.[61] New provisions pertaining to the concentration principle are based on judicial discretion and are both flexible and rigorous enough 'to ensure that proceedings, also between entrepreneurs, will run efficiently'.[62]

Apart from general conclusions, however, the opinion seems to lack actual reasoning as to why the existing system of concentration should be changed from preclusion to judicial discretion. Arguably, one may search in vain for an explanation of exactly how the new system is better than the one employed to resolve commercial cases,[63] especially in light of recent case law that has rationalized preclusion. Moreover, the change may come as a surprise because statistical data from the Ministry of Justice clearly shows that commercial disputes took less time to decide than 'regular' civil disputes.[64]

Let us now take a closer look at what is new.

First of all, Article 3 was changed.[65] The new part is that all procedural acts by the parties should comply with the established standards of good behaviour.[66]

Second, a new Article 6(2) was introduced. It reads: 'Parties and participants in the proceedings are under the duty to submit allegations and evidence without delay, so that the proceedings can be concluded efficiently and swiftly.' All in all, this provision introduced a new procedural burden, namely, the duty to support (diligent conduct of) the proceedings.[67]

61 Legislative opinion 2011, p. 6-7.

62 *Ibidem*, p. 7.

63 Karolczyk 2012a, p. 52.

64 See sources cited in Karolczyk 2012a, p. 52. Still, in comparison to legislative materials concerning previous fundamental amendments to the CCP, the opinion at hand stands out as coherent and elaborate.

65 By stipulating that the parties should explain truthfully (as to the facts) and not withhold anything, as well as produce evidence, this provision is basically a translation of § 178(1) of the Austrian ZPO.

66 This is a rather awkward expression to use in procedural provisions. Ironically, I think the English translation captures that awkwardness nicely. Its use was criticized during the legislative process, but the wording did not change. As it stands today, it is hard to say whether this expression includes a fairly straightforward concept of 'good faith'. It remains to be seen how the courts will handle it. Although, it may be purely academic inquiry, since violation of the duty to act in compliance with established standards of good behaviour does not give rise to any meaningful sanctions under the CCP. Interestingly enough, for example, I am not aware of any published court decision which would refer to this article in the context of the duty to reveal unfavourable evidence (which was clearly the intention of the Austrian legislator). Therefore, it is likely that this provision will remain what it has always been - an ideological manifestation.

67 *Cf.* § 178(2) of the Austrian ZPO. *Cf.* also §§ 282, 283 of the German ZPO.

Third, pursuant to the new Article 207(6) the court ignores untimely allegations and evidence, unless the moving party can show with high probability (*semiplena probatio*)[68] that their omission from the complaint, answer or other preparatory submission has not been negligent, that their admission shall not delay the disposition of the case, or that other extraordinary circumstances exist.[69]

Another new provision is Article 217(2), which applies to hearings. It is similar to Article 206(6), yet the wording is subtly different. Specifically, the court ignores untimely allegations and evidence, unless the moving party can show with high probability that the lack of their submission *in due time* has not been negligent, that their admission shall not delay the disposition of the case, or that other extraordinary circumstances exist.

These provisions are there to sanction the new procedural duty. In essence, the statute requires the court to ignore untimely allegations and evidentiary motions, regardless of the opposing party's position in that regard.[70]

These amendments were heavily criticized at the bill stage. After entry into force, many reviews have been rather mixed[71] or outright negative.[72] Initially, both the Judiciary and the legal profession seemed utterly unhappy about them, or at least that part of the two groups that felt this way was very vocal about their objections.

4. Conclusions

The universal goal of civil proceedings in the Western world is to swiftly produce a fair judgment. The structure, including the sequence of the proceedings, must represent a certain compromise and balance between the swift part and the fair part. It seems that in Poland that has not been the case. Until very recently, a review of the law and literature suggested that the scales were clearly tipped in favour of the latter, to the disadvantage of the former. In fact, it is a fresh development that the imbalance has been acknowledged at all. Some members of the new generation of judges have lately spoken out about it – the problem of the depreciation of the swift approach to adjudication among the Judiciary.[73] The point can be made that the

68 As opposed to 'prove', where the expected standard is absolute certainty. *Cf.* generally Uzelac 2012.

69 Analogous provisions have been introduced in special proceedings (order for payment, simplified) as well as in relation to appeal against default judgments.

70 It remains to be seen whether the lack of objection by the other party will be treated as an extraordinary circumstance, and thus allow for admission of belated material.

71 See e.g. Arkuszewska & Kościołek 2012, p. 11.

72 See e.g. Piebiak 2012a, p. 618; Piebiak 2012b, p. 676. Judge Piebiak believes these amendments will be reversed sooner rather than later because they will in fact increase delay in the courts. Additionally, he has verbalized a very common reservation against the new law, i.e. that it was written by theorists or judges who lack actual court experience and thus '[their] assumptions are detached from practice and the needs of the [first instance] courts'.

73 Łazarska 2012, p. 670. She concludes that this is the legacy of the former (socialist) system, where the 'absolute dominance of the principle of objective truth' has 'degraded the right to →

May 2012 amendments to the CCP were intended to remedy this imbalance, at least partially. It remains to be seen whether desirable results will occur.

The discussed provisions are new and no case law exists yet. While, doctrinally, there is an ongoing debate over the interpretation of certain elements, this might not be necessarily engaging from the comparative perspective. In my evaluation of the new system of concentration I will, therefore, focus on some broader interrelated themes revolving around the lack of transparency and the lack of a preparatory stage.

Granted, there is a wide margin of discretion to admit untimely submissions under the new system, nevertheless Article 207(6) may still be viewed as a systemically flawed solution or a half-remedy. There are seven reasons that may be put forward in support of this conclusion.

First of all, this provision seems to manifest a view that the pleadings (i.e. complaint and answer) can be used as effective tools to crystallize both factual and legal issues. While this approach may work in courts dealing with law only or for simple cases, and with no doubt should be applied to the answer, its application to courts of fact (mostly first instance courts) and the complaint may be perceived as misguided. The lesson has been perhaps already taught by the 19th-century English common law where the pleading stage became a game of skill, just as in 21st-century Polish proceedings for commercial matters. From the practical point of view, in many, especially complex cases the pleadings provide for (and rightly so in my opinion) but an outline of the facts and some basic evidence to support them. The procedural material unravels as the dispute develops.

Second, what about the balance between the parties? Under Polish law the plaintiff is not required to hire an attorney to file a complaint.[74] If unrepresented, it is highly unlikely that the plaintiff will know about Article 207(6) and the sanction for the improper discharge of the duty to support the proceedings. Additionally, the court puts the defendant on notice about Article 207(6) upon service of the complaint. Thus, an important safeguard for the plaintiffs (at least in some cases) is gone and a procedural imbalance is created. I have already suggested elsewhere that this makes Article 207(6) susceptible to constitutional challenge.

Third, transparency. The problem is that the CCP does not really provide for a modern preparatory stage.[75] The structure that does exist is out of date and the mechanisms are inadequate. As a result, there is no effective exchange of information prior to hearings (formal taking of evidence). Here I will name just a few problems. Questioning of the parties for informative purposes and potential

have the case decided within reasonable time'. An inquiry into the reasons or incentives for this (still often prevailing) attitude warrants separate research.

74 Here it is significant to note that the 2011 bill prepared by the Codification Commission provided for mandatory professional legal representation in (upper) first instance courts (Polish, *sąd okręgowy*), which handle more complex cases (valued approximately € 18,500 and more). However, this did not become law.

75 See generally Karolczyk 2013b.

discussion may only take place once the hearing has begun.[76] The court may not rule on evidence outside of the actual hearing, except for motions for expert witnesses. Although the parties are under the duty to specify evidence in their pleadings, their access to each other's information is otherwise basically non-existent.[77] These are problems that attorneys face every day in practice, and some of them are insurmountable. As for the answer, it is still, in principle, a facultative pleading. It lacks comprehensive statutory regulation pertaining to admissions, denials, defences, etc., so as to actually improve efficiency.[78]

Fourth, neither a schedule for proceedings nor a trial plan is prepared in Polish courts. Most of the time all managerial decisions are made 'secretly' by the judge, in his or her own head, and without the parties' participation.[79] What is a party's or the court's point of reference to decide *ex ante* what should have been submitted at an earlier stage? The 2011 bill prepared by the Codification Commission attempted to slightly modify that territory by requiring the court to discuss with the parties the substantive law they believe should apply to the case. Unfortunately, this important change did not become law.

Fifth, as a result, every piece of evidence admitted at trial has the potential to open new avenues of inquiry and naturally affect the dynamic of a trial. As a consequence, in all those legitimate circumstance the courts must apply Article 217(2). Having put the party to the standard of high probability, the court will hopefully conclude that a new allegation or motion for evidence is in fact not untimely and, therefore, admissible. It may be the case that this will occur at every hearing.

Sixth, regardless of political manifestation by stipulating different procedural burdens (truthfulness, acting in conformity with established standards of good behaviour, etc.), existing provisions do not facilitate the exchange (disclosure) of information. There is simply no effective sanction.[80]

Seventh, the arguably 'open catalogue of evidence' is somewhat lacking. For example, Polish civil procedure does not recognize: written inquiry

76 See Art. 212(1).

77 With regard to the complaint and the answer, motions for admission of evidence have to be included in those pleadings. For example, how do you establish the address of Mr Smith, which you need to put in the pleading? Well, the fact of the matter is, you do not. You just ask the court to do that for you in the course of the proceedings. Moreover, it is still a common ethical belief that an attorney should not contact a potential witness. Curiously, there is not a single provision either in the law or in the codes of professional conduct that addresses the question.

78 See my observations and citations in Karolczyk 2012b, p. 509.

79 For a comprehensive discussion of the problem of lack of transparency and an analysis of the proposed Art. 212^1 that ultimately did not become law see Karolczyk 2013a, p. 348 *et seq*.

80 See Arts. 233(2) and 251. Refusal to produce evidence on the court's order is sanctioned by a fee of up to app. € 1,300. See also the Supreme Court's judgments of 14 February 1996 r., II CRN 197/95, Lex No. 24748, and 20 January 2010 r., III CSK 119/09, Lex No. 852564. But *cf.* Piasecki 2010, p. 1303 and 1309 (making the point that refusal to produce evidence should result in an application of a presumption favourable to the moving party).

(interrogatories), the taking of testimony out-of-court prior to trial, written statements (affidavits) made under oath or in the presence of a public officer, demand for written admission, and the examination of a location or an object by the party. With the existence of a civil law notary, the possibilities seem truly vast.

All in all, first instance proceedings in Poland suffer from a serious lack of transparency, which is an essential component of the modern process oriented towards fair results. Therefore, preclusion of belated allegations and evidence should be applied with great care (as the potential to violate the basic principles of justice is considerable).

Fortunately, that seems to be exactly the case in practice. Under the old law, one could be sure that the opponent would at some point argue that exclusion of (untimely submitted) procedural material was warranted. This standard litigation practice has basically disappeared under the new law. This phenomenon can be explained in two ways. First, despite the fact that the legal norms under the two systems are structurally the same ('exclude belated material, unless ...'), judges have duly noted the systemic change that is reflected by the nomenclature and has already been explained in major commentaries. Two, the parties are more diligent and lawyers who were exposed to the harshness of the old law practise as if it were still in force (because they see the structural similarity of legal norms). Alternatively, it is the judges who have noted the said similarity. As a result, in applying the new law they fall back on the reasonable interpretation of the old law, which started to prevail just before it was repealed.[81] Or perhaps it is a mixture of all these hypotheses.

In any event, the practice does not seem to suggest a cause for concern. Therefore, regardless of any objections that can be made, in this regard the amendment may prove to be a beneficial step in slowly changing the procedural landscape, while Poland waits for the new codification that it so urgently needs.

81 Elsewhere I have suggested that, due to the similarity of the legal norms, this 'last-stage' case law is still generally good law and should not be disregarded simply because the system of concentration has changed.

Bibliography

Andrews 2012
Andrews, N., 'Fundamental Principles of Civil Procedure: Order Out of Chaos', in Kramer, X.E. & Van Rhee, C.H. (eds.), *Civil Litigation in a Globalising World*, The Hague: T.M.C. Asser Press, 2012, p. 19-38.

Arkuszewska & Kościołek 2012
Arkuszewska, A.M. & Kościołek, A., *'Nowelizacja Kodeksu postępowania cywilnego – wybrane zagadnienia (I)', Przegląd Sądowy,* 2012, Vol. 5, p. 5-21. Available at: <https://www.ksiegarnia.lexisnexis.pl/gfx/lexisnexis/userfiles/-files/arkuszewska_kosciolek_nowelizacja_kodeksu_postepowania_cywilnego__wybrane_zagadnienia._czesc_i.pdf>.

Damaška 1986
Damaška, M., *Faces of Justice and State Authority. A Comparative Approach to Legal Process*, New Haven: Yale University Press, 1986.

Engelmann 1927
Engelmann, A. (ed. & translation by R.W. Millar), *History of Continental Civil Procedure*, Boston: Little, Brown & Company, 1927.

Ereciński 2012
Ereciński, T. (ed.), *Kodeksu postępowania cywilnego. Komentarz*, Vol. I, Warszawa: LexisNexis, 2012.

Ereciński & Weitz 2006
Ereciński, T. & Weitz, K., 'Effektivität des Rechtsschutzes vor staatlichen Gerichten in Polen', in Gottwald, P. (ed.), *Effektivität des Rechtsschutzes vor staatlichen und privaten Gerichten*, Bielefeld: Gieseking, 2006, p. 1-40.

Gudowski 2005
Gudowski, J., 'O kilku naczelnych zasadach procesu cywilnego - wczoraj, dziś, jutro', in Nowicka, A. (ed.), *Prawo prywatne czasu przemian, Księga pamiątkowa dedykowana Prof. Stanisławowi Sołtysińskiemu,* Poznań: Wydawnictwo Naukowe UAM, 2005, p. 1015-1033.

Jakubecki 2006
Jakubecki, A., 'Naczelne zasady postępowania cywilnego w świetle nowelizacji kodeksu postępowania cywilnego', in *Czterdziestolecie kodeksu postępowania cywilnego. Zjazd katedr postępowania cywilnego w Zakopanem (7–9 października 2005 r.),* Kraków: Zakamycze, 2006, p. 349-379.

Karolczyk 2012a
Karolczyk, B., 'Nowelizacja postępowania cywilnego a prekluzja procesowa przed sądem pierwszej instancji', *Przegląd Prawa Handlowego,* 2012, Vol. 1, p. 51-58.

Karolczyk 2012b
Karolczyk, B., ‚Odpowiedź na pozew w postępowaniu zwyczajnym: wybrane zagadnienia w świetle nowelizacji k.p.c.', *Monitor Prawniczy,* 2012, Vol. 12, p. 509-516.

Karolczyk 2013a
Karolczyk, B., ‚Formułowanie twierdzeń pozwu oraz zasada da mihi factum dabo tibi ius w postępowaniu zwyczajnym w świetle nowelizacji KPC', *Monitor Prawniczy,* 2013, Vol. 7, p. 343-352.

Karolczyk 2013b
Karolczyk, B., 'Pretrial as a part of judicial case management in Poland in comparative perspective', *Comparative Law Review,* 2013, Vol. 15, p. 151-188, Toruń: UMK. Available at: <http://wydawnictwoumk.pl/czasopisma/index.php/CLR/-article/view/CLR.2013.009>.

Karolczyk 2014
Karolczyk, B., 'Admissibility of "Illegal Evidence" in Civil Procedure: A Comparative Look through Polish and American Lenses', *Zeitschrift für Zivilprozess International* ZZP Int. Jahrbuch des Internationalen Zivilprozessrechts 18/2013, Wolters Kluwer Deutschland 2014 (forthcoming).

Łazarska 2012
Łazarska, A., *Rzetelny proces cywilny,* Warszawa: Wolters Kluwer, 2012.

Lipp & Fredriksen 2011
Lipp, V. & Fredriksen, H. (eds.), *Reforms of Civil Procedure in Germany and Norway,* Tübingen: Mohr Siebeck, 2011.

Merryman 1985
Merryman, J.H., *The Civil Law Tradition,* Stanford, CA: Stanford University Press, 1985.

Millar 1923
Millar, R.W., *The Formative Principles of Civil Procedure,* Evanston Illinois: Northwestern University Press, 1923.

Oberhammer 2004
Oberhammer, P., 'Speeding up Civil Litigation in Austria: Past and Present Instruments', in Van Rhee, C.H. (ed.), *The Law's Delay: Essays on Undue Delay in Civil Litigation,* Antwerp: Intersentia, 2004, p. 217-232.

Oberhammer & Domej 2005
Oberhammer, P. & Domej, T., 'Germany, Switzerland and Austria (ca. 1800-2005)', in Van Rhee, C.H. (ed.), *European Traditions in Civil Procedure,* Antwerp: Intersentia, 2005, p. 103-122.

Piasecki 2010
Piasecki, K., 'Kodeks postępowania cywilnego', in Piasecki, K. (ed.), *Komentarz,* Vol. 1, Warszawa: CH Beck, 2010.

Piebiak 2012a
Piebiak, Ł., 'Nowelizacja Kodeksu postępowania cywilnego - uwagi praktyczne (I)', *Monitor Prawniczy,* 2012, Vol. 12, p. 619-628.

Piebiak 2012b
Piebiak, Ł., 'Nowelizacja Kodeksu postępowania cywilnego - uwagi praktyczne (II)', *Monitor Prawniczy,* 2012, Vol. 13, p. 677-690.

Plebanek 2012
Plebanek, M., *Nadużycie praw procesowych w postępowaniu cywilnym,* Warszawa: Wolters Kluwer, 2012.

Pogonowski 2005
Pogonowski, P., *Realizacja prawa do sądu w postępowaniu cywilnym,* Warszawa: CH Beck, 2005.

Sadomski 2010
Sadomski, J., 'Prekluzja procesowa w praktyce sądów gospodarczych', *Prawo w działaniu,* 2010, Vol. 7, p. 81-132.

Taruffo 2008
Taruffo, M., 'Orality and Writing as Factors of Efficiency in Civil Litigation', in Carpi, F. & Cartells, M. (eds.), *Oral and Written Proceedings: Efficiency in Civil Procedure,* Vol. 1, Valencia: Univesitat de València, 2008, p. 185-204.

Uzelac 2010
Uzelac, A., 'Survival of the Third Legal Tradition', *Supreme Court Law Review,* 2010, Vol. 49, p. 377-396. Available at: <http://alanuzelac.from.hr/pubs/pubs.htm>.

Uzelac 2012
Uzelac, A., 'The Need to Provide Reasons in Court Judgments: Some Developments in East and West', in Gudowski, J. & Weitz, K. (eds.), *Aurea Praxis, Aurea Theoria,* Warszawa: LexisNexis Polska, 2012, p. 1547-1566. Available at: <http://alanuzelac.-from.hr/pubs/pubs.htm>.

Van Hooijdonk & Eijsvoogel 2009
Van Hooijdonk, M. & Eijsvoogel, P.V., *Litigation in the Netherlands: Civil Procedure, Arbitration and Administrative Litigation,* The Hague: Kluwer Law International, 2009.

Van Rhee 2008a
Van Rhee, C.H., 'The Development of Civil Procedural Law in Twentieth Century Europe: From Party Autonomy to Judicial Case Management and Efficiency', in Van Rhee, C.H. (ed.), *Judicial Case Management and Efficiency in Civil Litigation*, Antwerp: Intersentia, 2008, p. 11-25.

Van Rhee 2008b
Van Rhee, C.H. (ed.), *Judicial Case Management and Efficiency in Civil Litigation*, Antwerp: Intersentia, 2008.

Verkerk 2010
Verkerk, R., *Fact-finding in Civil Litigation: A Comparative Perspective*, Antwerp: Intersentia, 2010.

Waśkowski 1932
Waśkowski, E., *System procesu cywilnego*, Wilno: Drukarnia 'Zorza', 1932.

Weitz 2009
Weitz, K., 'Między systemem dyskrecjonalnej władzy sędziego a systemem prekluzji - ewolucja regulacji prawa polskiego', in Dołecki, H. & Flaga-Gieruszyńska, K. (eds.), *Materiały konferencyjna Ogólnopolskiego Zjazdu Katedr Postępowania Cywilnego Szczecin-Niechorze 28-30.9.2007*, Warszawa: CH Beck, 2009, p. 73-97.

Wengerek 1958
Wengerek, E., *Koncentracja materiału procesowego w postępowaniu cywilnym*, Warszawa, 1958.

Woolf 1996
Woolf, L., *Access to Justice: Final Report*, London: The Stationary Office, 1996.

Zuckerman 1999
Zuckerman, A., 'Justice in Crisis: Comparative Dimensions of Civil Procedure', in Zuckerman, A. (ed.), *Civil Justice in Crisis: Comparative Perspectives of Civil Procedure*, Oxford: Oxford University Press, 1999, p. 3-52.

E. Jeuland

THE 'RIGHT TO PROOF' AND THE 'LOYALTY PRINCIPLE': A FRENCH PERSPECTIVE

The subject of evidence is in fashion in France and probably elsewhere. I counted two important and international colloquia in France on the topic of evidence in 2013. It is a new topic in France. Traditionally, there were no textbooks, no papers and obviously no lectures on the topic. Evidence is basically taught during the first year of law school in a broad, introductory course on law. Depending on the course professor, the topic of evidence may or may not be covered; if it is, there are only three to nine hours dedicated to the topic.

Since the end of the nineteenth century there has been only one casebook written on evidence.[1] Obviously, evidence is studied in the context of procedural law - whether criminal, administrative or civil - but again this is in a wider context only, and covers the procedural aspects of evidence.

The renewal of evidence as a topic of interest may be explained by several factors: the 'proceduralization' of law, the influence of the common law and the difficulty of proving discrimination and harassment claims. This trend is accompanied by the development of the loyalty principle and its counterpart, the right to proof. This contribution will first present the general picture of evidence law in France, then the emergence of the loyalty principle and lastly the limitations of this principle imposed by the right to proof.

1. General Picture of Evidence Law in France

The rules of evidence in French law are very different from the rules in common law countries even though some parallels can be drawn. In English, the two words 'evidence' and 'proof' are equivalent to the French term 'preuve', which comes from 'épreuve', or ordeal. Thus, in French law proof is not what we can see and hear (through testimony, for example) as the etymology of evidence would imply; rather,

1 Bonnier & Larnaude 1888.

it is what the plaintiff and the defendant experience. This explains why proof by confession is still the basis – often repressed – of French criminal law.

Expertise (by this I mean the use of specialized knowledge provided by experts in particular fields) is now the most important means of proof in civil law, as it is in criminal law. Thus, physical or DNA evidence in tort law or family law, for instance, has been presented by certain scholars as an 'ordeal' in the sense of a response of the human body. It must be noted that the word for proof in German is 'Beweiss', which relates to the idea of showing reality. In German culture, proof is not a matter of what we see (evidence, in English law) or of what we experience ('ordeal', in French law); it is a matter of explanation and demonstration.[2] These hypotheses (certainly difficult to prove) are interesting even for a practitioner, because cultural aspects[3] must be part of legal strategy and may help in understanding the method of proceedings in a given country. Cultural notions may shed light on the reasons why French lawyers or judges are sometimes reluctant to admit certain pieces of evidence emanating from foreign authorities. Judicial truth, which is not the absolute truth (unattainable), is a cultural matter.

It should be added that written evidence is central in French law. This may be explained by the old, Roman idea of 'written reason' or by the Roman origins of French law and probably by the bureaucratic, Paris-centred and paper-centred French government. New technologies have not eliminated this aspect of French law, but have transformed it considerably. Today the electronic document has become a central piece of evidence in French law.

Evidence as a separate legal subject is not very important in French legal theory. There is no book on evidence and there are few research programmes in this field.[4] Rules on the manner in which evidence can be presented (expertise, inquiry, etc.) were spread across the Civil Code (means of evidence) and the Code of Civil Procedure (CPC) after the French Revolution in order to avoid making evidence a judicial matter. The principal means of evidence do not need to be judged: for example, a written contract is evidence of an agreement between the parties.

According to the Civil Code, a legal act has to be proved by way of a written document if the value of the act is more than € 1,500 (Article 1341). As such, the civil law is based on the system of legal evidence. Under € 1,500, a written document is not compulsory, and freedom of proof applies to prove points of fact. In criminal law, freedom of proof applies except with respect to certain facts for which only one means of proof is accepted. For example, breath and blood tests are the only acceptable means of proving drunkenness.

In the absence of a written document relating to an agreement where more than € 1,500 is at stake, the contract may be proven by way of confession or oath, though this is very rare. A written document that is unsigned, signed by one of the parties (e.g. a letter) or not signed in the presence of a notary may be considered

2 The author would like to thank Professor P. Oberhammer for his comments on this issue.
3 Girard 2013.
4 Except: Lagarde 1994. Also Bergeaud 2010, on the right to proof.

partial proof. In this situation, the legal act may be evidenced by way of testimony or presumption (but partial proof is necessary). There are some other rare exceptions for which it is impossible to require written proof. For example, in certain trades, such as the diamond trade, written contracts are not customarily used.

Traditionally, the civil judge from the Frankish period was neutral and passive (still according to the 1806 Code): he could not participate in the taking of evidence. Then in the twentieth century certain reforms made in France in 1937 and 1965 authorized French judges to be more 'interventionist', but these reforms were limited. Case management ('la mise en état') did not work very well because the judges did not have enough power. The new Code of Civil Procedure of 1976 broadened the powers of the judges in this respect. This reform was influenced by Alsatian procedural law, which was of German origin,[5] and by German procedure, directly through the figure of Henri Motulsky.[6]

Since this reform, the judge and the parties must cooperate to find a solution for their dispute. The scope of cooperation is different depending on whether facts or the law are concerned. The Latin adage *Da mihi factum, dabo tibi jus* ('Give me the facts, I will give you the law') is more or less applicable in France, but it is much more subtle than it seems.

Normally, a party must present the facts to the judge. If certain facts are contested by the opposing party, these facts must be proven. The burden of proof lies on the party who introduces the facts to justify the claim (Article 6 CPC and Article 1315 Civil Code). In the event of a counterclaim, the burden shifts to the defendant, who must establish his claim. Each party must try to prove his case; if he fails, the judge may order a particular type of proof taking (the hearing of witnesses, experts, etc. - see below). The judge may give these orders at the request of a party or *ex officio*. In the latter case, the proceedings are inquisitorial rather than adversarial. But the judge cannot base his decision on facts which are not on the record, whether these facts are presented by a party or the result of his orders for proof taking (Article 7 CPC). For example, the judge cannot use personal knowledge of the case. The judge may use any fact that is on the record even though no party relied on the fact as a basis for an argument. As an example, in one case a French judge used a minor provision in an insurance contract that no party had relied on or seen as the basis for his decision. Since the contract was part of the record, the judge was entitled to do so.

The adversarial principle is encompassed in the principle of equality of arms in the European Court of Human Rights (ECtHR) case *Montavanelli v. France*.[7] The

5 It should be noted that the Alsace region was part of Germany from 1870 until World War I, and its civil procedure was of German origin. When the region became part of France after World War I, it maintained its civil procedural rules until the reform of 1976 which unified French civil procedure and was, in part, influenced by Alsatian case management.

6 The great scholar who influenced the new Code of Civil Procedure of 1976 was educated in Germany where he practised law.

7 18 March 1997, 21497/93.

principle is rarely referred to alone, but rather in conjunction with the adversarial principle in French case law.

There are three tendencies in French civil procedure: 'managerialization', 'technologization' and 'fundamentalization'. The first tendency may be seen as much in the development of fast and efficient proceedings as in the development of efficiency, celerity and quality principles. The second tendency is based on new technology, software, new means of communication, electronic documents and scientific expertise. The third tendency is based on procedural principles, which are usually human rights-based, and the case law of the French constitutional council and the ECtHR. These tendencies are universal, but the tendency of 'fundamentalization' is still rather European.

My hypothesis is that recent developments, approaches and interests related to evidence in France are connected with these three strong tendencies and that the manner in which these tendencies are developing is specific to France. The idea of 'fundamentalization' refers to the development of human rights and human rights reasoning in the field of evidence; it is not a mere deduction, but rather a balance of interests according to the principle of proportionality. More precisely, there is a right to proof. This right is not totally clear. It concerns not only to the party's right to have proof taking ordered on request, but also to something more complex: the right to use a piece of evidence which may not have been obtained in good faith or the idea of obtaining from the Legislature and the judge a right to have less evidence admitted in order to create an asymmetric situation and shift the burden of proof. The nature of the right to proof is not clearly presented as a subjective right, but there is no debtor, so it is probably a human right and the reasoning applied is a human rights reasoning although there is no treaty provision on point. The right to proof appears as of 2012 in the case law of the French Court of Cassation. In Sec. 3 below I will describe its emergence in French law during the preliminary phase of the proceedings and recent developments relating to the right to proof. I will argue that the right to proof mirrors the loyalty principle, which I shall first turn to now, in the taking of evidence.

2. The Loyalty Principle

The plaintiff may prove his case using written documents although electronic documents are increasingly being used for this purpose. The authenticity of these documents is very difficult to dispute. Proceedings to contest the authenticity or accuracy of a document last long, so parties are usually discouraged from bringing a special action to contest a document (forgery proceedings), which is possible but rare, especially as far as 'public' documents are concerned (e.g. documents drafted by notaries). When proof can be obtained free of charge or the case relates to a contract valued at under € 1,500, or where proof is being presented on factual matters, the documents may be very diverse: even witness testimony can take the form of a written declaration. It is rare in civil proceedings that the witness appears in court. For example, in divorce proceedings the parties will generally present the written testimony of parents and friends.

The party who refers to a document in his complaint has to provide the document to the other party. If he does not provide this piece of evidence to the other party, a judge may impose an injunction and a fine that increases each day until the document is provided ('astreinte' is the functional equivalent in civil law of 'contempt of court' since it is used to obtain performance of an injunction). If the document is in the hands of a third party, the party wishing to use the document in court may ask the judge to order the third party to produce the document. The penalty of a fine that increases with each day may also be ordered. This procedure to obtain a document is the functional equivalent of common law discovery. The principal difference is that the document has to be identified or at least objectively identifiable (i.e. easy to locate among other documents; for example, the sales contract between X and Y of 2012: there is no date or number, but the holder of the document may locate it easily). The production of the document may be refused by the holder for legitimate reasons, such as professional privilege (if the holder is a lawyer), but trade secrecy does not justify a refusal.

The electronic document is admitted under certain conditions and the judgment itself can be provided digitally. The judge assesses the evidence and must check that it is relevant and conclusive.

The parties must exercise good faith when obtaining evidence. The principle of loyalty prohibits the use of tricks, telephone recordings without the speaker's knowledge,[8] surveillance by video or other means,[9] e.g. by observing a spouse in order to obtain a divorce or of an employee in order to obtain dismissal for cause.[10]

The principle of loyalty does not apply in criminal matters since the goal of criminal procedure is, above all, to discover the truth. The French Competition Agency had considered the principle as not applicable to competition law proceedings, but the French Court of Cassation eventually decided that the principle should apply since competition law proceedings resemble civil proceedings more than criminal proceedings.[11]

The principle of loyalty is specific to evidence and does not apply to procedure in general, except in arbitration. The principle of loyalty may be too general and difficult to distinguish from the legality principle or the good faith principle. The principle of loyalty may even be misplaced as far as evidence is concerned since nowadays everybody knows that a telephone call may be recorded. Interestingly

8 Cass. 2nd civ., 7 Oct. 2004: *JCP* 2005, II, 10025 LÉGER; *D.* 2005, 122, BONFILS referring to Art. 6 ECHR - Cass. com., 3 juin 2008: *Bull. civ.* 2008, IV, n° 112; *D.* 2008, 2476, BOURSIER-MAUDERLY, chron. C. cass. 2753, obs. SALOMON, et pan. 2823, obs. DELEBECQUE; *Gaz. Pal.* 10-11 sept. 2008, 7, note RODA, Cass. ass. plén., 7 janv. 2011, n° 09-14.316 and n° 09-14.667: *JCP* 2011, 43, MALAURIE-VIGNAL.

9 Cass. soc., 26 Nov. 2002: *JCP* 2003, I, 156, n° 5, CESARO; *D.* 2003, 1858, note BRUGUIÈRE; then Cass. 1st civ., 31 Oct. 2012, n° 11-17.476: *JCP* 2012, 1229, ABRAVANEL-JOLLY; *D.* 2013, 227, DUPONT; *RTD civ.* 2012, 117, n° 9, FAGES.

10 Cass. soc., 18 March 2008: *D.* 2008, 993; *Rev. huissiers* 2008, 218, FRICERO; *Procédures* 2008, n° 137, then: Cass. soc. 4 July 2012, n° 11-30.266: *Procédures* 2012, n° 286, BUGADA.

11 Cass. ass. plén., 7 Jan. 2011, n° 09-14.316 and n° 09-14.667: *JCP* 2011, 43, MALAURIE-VIGNAL et 666, n° 13, SERINET; *D.* 2011, 157, obs. CHEVRIER.

enough, the Second Chamber of the French Court of Cassation, which is specialized in civil proceedings, has never acknowledged the principle of loyalty. Moreover, this principle is in competition with the right to proof.

3. The Right to Proof as a Limitation to Loyalty

The principle of loyalty has exceptions. For example, an employee may produce a piece of evidence obtained without authorization on his firm's computers. There is now a so-called right to proof.[12] In a case decided on 5 April 2012, the French Court of Appeal rejected the evidence by way of a private letter since it was obtained in violation of the privacy principle, against the will of its author. The Court of Cassation reversed the decision of the Court of Appeal to set aside the letter 'without checking whether the letter was necessary for the exercise of the right to proof and proportionate to the ... conflicting interests'. In other words, the Court of Cassation reversed the judgment because the Court of Appeal should have checked whether this piece of evidence was necessary for the claimant to exercise his right to proof and was proportionate to the rights of the different parties. The right to proof is not a right to obtain a measure from the judge; it is the right to use a piece of evidence, such as a document.

Moreover, the principle of loyalty does not prohibit evidence by email, Short Message Service (SMS)[13] or USB key. In one case, a USB key was presented in evidence by an employer. There was no privacy issue, so the USB key could be used as a document in court. The same rule was found to apply to an SMS when the person who wrote the SMS knew that it could be read and preserved for litigation. An employer can even use a personal file found on an employee's work computer against the employee since the computer is used in a professional context. Conversely, an employee can use secret files of his employer in a case against the employer if this means of evidence is necessary to prove the claim.[14] Lastly, in October 2012 evidence obtained by a detective hired to follow someone was found admissible and not contrary to the principles of loyalty or privacy since the detective took pictures in a public area.

In 2007, an SMS was used to prove harassment by an employer. Harassment and discrimination claims raise important issues in relation to the right to proof in a wider sense. The European Directive of 27 November 2000 establishing a general

12 Cass. 1st civ., 5 Apr. 2012, n° 11-14177: *D.* 2012, 1596, LARDEUX; *D.* 2013, pan. 274. FRICERO; *RTD civ.* 2012, 506, HAUSER, free translation of '*sans rechercher si la production litigieuse n'était pas indispensable à l'exercice de son droit à la preuve, et proportionnée aux intérêts antinomiques en présence*'.

13 See about emails Cass. 1st civ., 18 May 2005: *Gaz. Pal.* 16-18 oct. 2005, 19, MASSIP and Cass. 1re civ., 17 June 2009, n° 07-21.796: *D.* 2009, 1758, obs. EGEA in divorce matters if there is no fraud or violence, then Cass. soc., 12 Feb. 2013, n° 11-28.649, *Procédures* 2013, n° 152 obs. BUGADA (USB key).

14 If strictly necessary to the employee: Cass. soc., 30 juin 2004: *Bull. civ.* 2004, V, n° 187; *JCP* 2005, I, 122, n° 16, PÉTEL-TEYSSIÉ.

framework for equal treatment in employment and occupation has been implemented in France. Under this Directive evidence is used to protect a fundamental right. The burden of proof is alleviated for the employee because of the asymmetry of access to information as compared to the employer. The employer may only establish that his decision was objective. To respect the right to proof, the Directive considers that the employee only has to present facts which establish a presumption of discrimination or harassment. In 2002, the French Constitutional Council oversaw the implementation of the Directive in France. The implementing statute stated that the victim had to present the facts establishing discrimination and that it was up to the defendant to prove there was no discrimination. The Constitutional Council considered that the victims had to establish the facts establishing a presumption of discrimination or harassment in order to avoid creating an imbalance in the relationship between employers and employees. The statute had to be modified: instead of 'facts which supposedly establish discrimination', the statute provides that the employee has to present facts which establish a presumption of discrimination. This solution complies with the right to defence.

Later the French Court of Cassation (Soc. 24 September 2008) decided that it would review the qualification of harassment and discrimination to verify how judges decided on the merits after hearing evidence of an employer's behaviour. Whether it was a matter of qualification or a matter of evidence was unclear. In 2011, the Court of Cassation specified that judges should decide on the merits of a case after an appreciation of all of the elements taken together rather than after an assessment of separate elements. Then in 2013 (Soc. 29 January 2013) the Court of Cassation specified that a medical certificate was not enough to establish a presumption of discrimination or harassment. The right to proof allows the admission of a large amount of information even obtained without loyalty but, in a way, the right to proof is recognized for the employee who cannot establish the discrimination or harassment. The employee may request an order from the judge or legislator in order to alleviate his burden of proof.

By way of conclusion, the principle of loyalty is different from the legality principle of evidence, but is more or less a moral principle. It may be without limitations and may, therefore, be dangerous. It is limited by the right to proof and even regarding specific means of evidence such as expert evidence. The right to proof is widespread and fits within the new procedural interactions, based on human rights interests and the principle of proportionality.

Bibliography

Bergeaud 2010
Bergeaud, A., *Le droit à la preuve*, Paris: LGDJ, 2010.

Bonnier & Larnaude 1888
Bonnier, E. & Larnaude, F., *Traité des preuves en droit civil et criminel*, 5nd edn., Paris: Plon et Marescq, 1888.

Girard 2013
Girard, F., *Essai sur la preuve dans son environnement culturel*, Aix: Presses universitaires d'Aix-Marseille, 2013.

Lagarde 1994
Lagarde, X., *Réflexion critique sur le droit de la preuve*, Paris: LGDJ, 1994.

V. Rijavec
T. Kresteš

RESTRICTIONS ON THE ADMISSIBILITY OF EVIDENCE

1. Introduction

Restrictions on the admissibility of evidence are closely connected with the establishment of the truth in civil procedure. It is obvious that restrictions and especially the exclusion of evidence would hinder the quest for the truth in certain cases. Restrictions are also closely related to the principle of procedural justice. Procedural justice presupposes that just results should be obtained through a just procedure - fairness of procedure. To be able to talk about fairness, procedure should be oriented towards correctness. However, is it possible to have correctness in the procedure with evidence obtained illegally or in violation of human rights?

The equality principle generally favours the admissibility of all evidence relevant to the trial. By excluding a piece of relevant evidence categorised as inadmissible, evidence law places the risk of error associated with this evidence on its proponent, whose opponent consequently acquires an immunity from that risk. This one-sided outcome is generally inferior to a system of free proof. Arguably, a free-proof system apportions the risk of error more equitably by allowing fact-finders to consider all relevant evidence and determine its probative value on a case-by-case basis. This system avoids any systematic skewing of the risk of error. Fact-finding errors are thus entirely accidental in their occurrence. Free proof, however, only guarantees rudimentary equality in risk allocation and is still far from guaranteeing equality in the final apportionment of the risk of error. Application of this system in civil litigation only installs primary equality and requires corrective equality mechanisms. These mechanisms render inadmissible any evidence (or impose other restrictions on evidence) that creates inequality between the litigating parties by imposing a non-reciprocal - and, therefore, inequitable - risk of error on the opponent.[1]

These corrective mechanisms can include evidentiary privileges, restricting the means of evidence, restricting methods of taking evidence, prohibiting specific

1 Stein 2005, p. 225.

evidence or a general exclusion of evidence. The problem has cross-border dimensions - the question of whether a court of another country will accept evidence taken in the first country, for example in a manner that is considered to be problematic. Another problem is the feasibility of taking evidence in another country in case of evidence that is considered illegal according to the *lex fori*. These problems are also problematic in the enforcement stage, e.g. as regards enforceability of the judgment in another country.

The issue of restrictions on evidence has been briefly touched upon by the European Court of Human Rights in *Schenk v. Switzerland*, a criminal case, questioning the police methods of investigation.[2] In the case, the Court examined the fairness of the proceedings as a whole and found no violation of Article 6(1) of the European Convention on Human Rights (ECHR), even though the obtaining of a tape recording by the police was unlawful not only according to the ECHR, but also under domestic law.[3] However, the Court did not address issues about the admissibility of evidence in the abstract nor did it deal with them as issues of principle. The conclusion could be that Article 6 ECHR simply guarantees the right to a fair trial and that the admissibility of evidence (even in criminal cases) is primarily a matter for regulation under national law. And this conclusion is valid for both criminal and civil cases.

There is a similar situation at the level of EU rules on civil procedure. Council Regulation (EC) No. 1206/2001 of 28 May 2001 on cooperation between the courts of the Member States in the taking of evidence in civil or commercial matters does not directly cover the issue of restrictions on evidence or even its admissibility and exclusion. The only relevant provisions are those covering feasibility (e.g. Article 10 regarding the feasibility of complying with a request for evidence).4 It is thus clear that this issue is left open to different solutions in national law.

In the comparative perspective we can notice various approaches in national laws - from express regulation in law across the utilisation of evidence after the balancing of interests, or a combination of both, all the way to the lack of mention in the national law. It is not uncommon, however, to find particular restrictions on evidence in legislation. A good example is the prohibition against applying the materials gained in mediation or conciliation as evidence in civil proceedings. All countries following the UNCITRAL Model Law on International Commercial Conciliation (2002) have also introduced the restrictions on the admissibility of evidence as regulated under Article 10.[5] On the other hand, none of the countries

2 *Schenk v. Switzerland* (App. No. 10862/84), 12 July 1988, Series A, No. 140 (1991) 13 EHRR 242.

3 White & Ovey 2010, p. 280.

4 'The requested court shall comply with such a requirement unless this is incompatible with the law of the Member State of the requested court or by reason of major practical difficulties. ...'

5 'Article 10. Admissibility of evidence in other proceedings
1. A party to the conciliation proceedings, the conciliator and any third person, including those involved in the administration of the conciliation proceedings, shall not in arbitral,
→

follows the example of restrictions on evidence as were developed in criminal law (rules of exclusion, fruit of the poisonous tree doctrine, the infected judge, etc.).

2. General Principle of Inadmissibility

Express rules restricting the admissibility of evidence as a general principle are rare. One possible, but not necessarily good, example does appear in the Republic of Croatia. The amendments to the Constitution of 2000 created a general principle of procedural law according to which illegal evidence is inadmissible in judicial proceedings. Although this principle is generally related to criminal cases, the text of the Constitution does not differentiate between criminal and civil cases.[6] The fact that such differentiation is omitted in the constitutional text leads to the conclusion that the principle is also applicable to civil cases. However, it seems that the real value of this principle in civil procedure is still open to debate.[7] It is not entirely clear what 'illegally obtained evidence' means. In literature it is stated that it only covers the methods of collecting evidence, but not the taking of evidence in court.[8] The final interpretation of these provisions is up to the Constitutional Court, and it is not yet entirely clear how much the balancing of interests will be regarded by the Court.

To some extent there is a similar situation in Greece. There, a constitutional prohibition against illegal evidence exists, but this principle is supplemented by the application of the balancing of interests in cases where some higher values are involved. Article 19 III of the Greek Constitution provides for the inadmissibility of evidence obtained in violation of Articles 19, 9 and 9A of the Greek Constitution concerning the protection of the confidentiality of correspondence, the protection of every person's home ('asylum'), the inviolability of private and family life and the inviolability of personal data, respectively. This is qualified as 'illegally obtained evidence'. The specific constitutional provision is also applicable as regards the

judicial or similar proceedings rely on, introduce as evidence or give testimony or evidence regarding any of the following:
(a) An invitation by a party to engage in conciliation proceedings or the fact that a party was willing to participate in conciliation proceedings;
(b) Views expressed or suggestions made by a party to the conciliation in respect of a possible settlement of the dispute;
(c) Statements or admissions made by a party in the course of the conciliation proceedings;
(d) Proposals made by the conciliator;
(e) The fact that a party to the conciliation had indicated its willingness to accept a proposal for settlement made by the conciliator;
(f) A document prepared solely for purposes of the conciliation proceedings.'

6 Art. 29 of the Constitution of the Republic of Croatia: '(1) Everyone shall be entitled to have his or her rights and obligations, or suspicion or accusation of a criminal offence decided upon fairly before a legally established, independent and impartial court within a reasonable period. ... (4) Evidence obtained illegally may not be admitted in court proceedings.'

7 Uzelac 2003, p. 348.

8 Triva & Dika 2004, p. 483.

relations between private citizens (Article 25 I c of the Greek Constitution). According to decision No. 1/2001 of the Areios Pagos (the Supreme Civil and Criminal Court of Greece) (in plenary), the above-mentioned illegally obtained evidence is inadmissible on the basis of a violation of Article 8 ECHR as well. More specifically, the inadmissibility of tape recordings, as a means of evidence, consists in its being obtained without the consent of the persons involved, which entails their entrapment and therefore constitutes a commitment and a restriction on the free exercise of communication. The consent should be given before the recording of the conversation. The use of the illegally obtained evidence is prohibited not only regarding the conversation partner that was not informed but regarding any other third person as well. However, an exception is valid exclusively in favour of a constitutionally higher-in-rank legal value (e.g. human life). Any other exception, even if introduced by a formal law, should be considered as invalid. The prevailing opinion within the context of Greek doctrine accepts the inadmissibility of the illegally obtained evidence on the basis of the violation of human dignity or of rights relating to personality. The full extent of this principle is, however, still not entirely clear.[9]

3. Balancing of Interests and Restrictions on Evidence

3.1. *Slovenia*

In Slovenian civil procedure there is no express provision on restrictions on evidence (with the exception of rules regarding mediation). However, the Constitutional Court of Slovenia has developed a doctrine of restrictions on evidence on the basis of a balancing of interests. In decision Up-472/02 (7 October 2004) it ruled that the encroachment upon the right to privacy is admissible under certain conditions; however, well-grounded circumstances have to exist in legal procedure where evidence obtained in violation of privacy is admitted. The taking of such evidence should have a special purpose for the exercise of certain constitutionally protected rights. In such a case the court should apply the principle of proportionality and carefully determine to which right it shall give precedence. In other words, there is no general principle of inadmissibility (rule of exclusion) in Slovenian law, but the balancing of interests is applicable. Notwithstanding this, there is an interesting decision from the Higher Court of Ljubljana (I Cp 376/2009) stating that the results of polygraph tests are inadmissible in civil proceedings as they also are in criminal proceedings. The reason for the inadmissibility is that the polygraph test has elements of coercion. Since the civil courts have the power of free evaluation of evidence there is no need for additional polygraph testing. This

9 Katiforis 2014, p. 26-72.

decision does seem to introduce a general prohibition on the use of polygraph tests as evidence in civil proceedings in Slovenia.[10]

3.2. *Austria*

Austrian civil procedural law distinguishes between three types of exclusion of evidence: (1) the inadmissibility of evidence in regard to certain facts (*Beweisthemenverbote*); (2) the exclusion of certain means of evidence (*Beweismittelverbot*); and (3) the inadmissibility of using a certain method of taking evidence (*Beweismethodenverbot*).[11] These types of inadmissibility constrain in different ways the judge's obligation to establish the truth. In Austrian law there is a distinction between illegally obtained evidence and illegal evidence; however, this distinction is not explicitly laid down in the ZPO (Code of Civil Procedure). There is no explicit legal provision on how to treat illegally obtained evidence. However, the literature has developed some particular rules in this regard: the obtaining of evidence is generally illegal if (1) the means of obtaining evidence violate constitutionally granted fundamental rights, such as the prohibition of torture (Article 3 ECHR) or the right to liberty and security of a person (Article 5 ECHR) (this could be the case if evidence was gained by way of force or torture) or (2) the means of obtaining evidence contravene the applicable rules of procedural law. If evidence was obtained illegally, this generally represents a ground for appeal. There are several problems concerning illegal evidence. Some of them are explicitly regulated in the Austrian ZPO, others are treated in legal literature and case law. According to § 320(1) ZPO, witnesses that are unable to perceive impressions or reproduce their perceptions must not be heard in court; this is a restriction of regarding a means of evidence in general. Besides that, there are several restrictions due to the information that may be gained from the evidence: for example, priests must not be heard on facts covered by the secrecy of confession (§ 320(2) ZPO); state servants must not be heard on facts that can be classified as official state secrets unless they are freed from keeping the information secret by their superiors (§ 320(3) ZPO) and mediators must not be heard on facts they were entrusted with by their clients (§ 320(4) ZPO). Also, under certain circumstances witnesses and parties can refuse to testify (§ 321 and § 380 ZPO) or to produce evidence (§ 305). Another problematic area is illegal evidence produced by one of the parties. The literature draws a distinction here: if there was only a contravention of civil law, the evidence has to be considered by the court; the party whose interests have been violated can only demand compensation. If a criminal offence was committed, however, and the producing party's behaviour violates the core of another person's fundamental rights, the evidence must not be accepted by the court. If the court nonetheless

10 Clearly under the influence of German case law – *cf.* BVerfG NJW 1982, 375 and BGH NJW 2003, 2527.

11 *Cf.* Mayr 2004, p. 42-43.

accepts the evidence, this constitutes a ground for appeal. Constitutional limitations (such as the protection of privacy) are also to be regarded in civil proceedings.[12]

3.3. *Germany*

In German law there is a clear position that certain means of evidence (*Beweismittel*) are inadmissible. In certain proceedings all the means of evidence but documents are inadmissible, and polygraph testing results are in principle inadmissible even when a person consented to the testing. However, it is disputable whether German law contains a general principle prohibiting the use of illegally obtained evidence (*Verwertung rechtswidrig erlangter Beweismittel*). The position of German law seems to be somewhere between the precedence of the material truth principle and the rule of exclusion. Not every materially illegal piece of evidence is, however, necessarily inadmissible.[13] Just the bare illegality of evidence does not make it inadmissible. For instance, evidence is not admitted if the evidence is obtained by way of violating the other party's possessory rights. But if obtaining the evidence itself resulted in a violation of the other party's basic rights, then there is a ground for exclusion which is, however, subject to the balancing of interests. Typical cases are those which regard audio recordings, where the court takes into account whether the words were directed to a certain individual only, a limited circle of persons or to the general public. Home audio recordings are in general inadmissible.[14]

3.4. *Denmark*

The general opinion is that since no rule within Danish civil procedure forbids illegally obtained evidence, such evidence may under some circumstances be produced. In an announcement written by the permanent Danish advisory board on civil procedure (*Retsplejerådet*) from 1972, it was stated that

> in civil and criminal cases it may occur, that the use of evidence may be justified even if there is doubt about the validity of the evidence and even if evidence has been taken by means that are dubious or illegal, for instance because it is obtained from a witness who has listened by the door or by a window or because the evidence produced has in fact been stolen.

Case law within this area is fairly limited, though in a provisional judgment from 2001 the Eastern High Court ruled that an employer was allowed to present a video recording of an employee in spite of the employee's protests. The Court stated that due to the fact that the evidence was, among other factors, not illegally obtained, the evidence should not be rejected. Thus the Court implied that in some cases it may be possible to use the above-mentioned discretion under Article 341 and reject

12 Nunner-Krautgasser & Anzenberger 2014, p. 81-84. *Cf.* Nagel & Bajons, p. 449-450.
13 *Cf.* Rosenberg, Schwab & Gottwald 2010, p. 617.
14 Balzer 2005, p. 45. *Cf.* Nagel 2003, p. 105-106.

evidence if it has been illegally obtained. Nevertheless, depending on the circumstances, the court might allow the evidence even if it has been obtained illegally. The discretion permitted under Article 341 to accept unlawful evidence is, on the other hand, subject to the rights guaranteed in the ECHR, including the rights of third parties. No case law exists as to the use of polygraphs in Danish courts. However, in light of procedural law in other Scandinavian countries, it has been claimed that such evidence would be rejected.[15]

3.5. *Estonia*

Estonian law does not provide for any restrictions as to the use of unlawful (illegal) evidence. The only norm that regulates unlawfully obtained evidence is Sec. 238(3) of the Code of Civil Procedure. It provides that the court may refuse to accept evidence if the evidence has been obtained by a criminal offence or unlawful violation of a fundamental right. However, the court has no obligation to refuse such evidence and may accept it despite the violations. Sec. 238(3) of the Code does not specify any specific fundamental rights that it is designed to protect nor does it specify any particular criminal offence that would give grounds to refuse the evidence. Thus it can be concluded that committing any criminal offence or unlawfully violating any fundamental right while obtaining the evidence may give grounds to refuse the evidence. However, there is no court practice in this matter nor can any further information be obtained from the preparatory materials of the Code.[16]

3.6. *Switzerland*

The solution in Swiss law is interesting, as it does contain an express provision regarding illegal evidence. However, at the same time the provision refers to the balancing of interests. Article 152(2) of the Swiss Federal Code of Civil Procedure states that 'illegally procured evidence is only to be considered if the interest of truth finding prevails'. The opposing interests are the interests in the protection of human rights and the interests of other affected persons.[17] Even though a clear provision of Swiss law deals with the admissibility of evidence in civil cases, the exclusion of evidence depends on the prevailing interests.

3.7. *Finland*

As a starting point, Finnish procedural law does not make a distinction between illegally obtained evidence and illegal evidence. According to the principle of free assessment of evidence, the main rule is that all evidence is accepted and issues

15 Waage & Herborn 2014, p. 32.
16 Poola 2014, p. 46.
17 Kofmel Ehrenzeller 2003, p. 575.

related to obtaining the evidence have effect on its evidentiary value.[18] However, a distinction is made between limitations due to witness professional confidentiality (*todistamiskiellot*) and limitations on obtaining evidence (*hyödyntämiskielto*). The doctrines on professional confidentiality and limitations on obtaining evidence have been developed in national case law and based on ECHR Article 6 and on the case law of the European Court of Human Rights. For example, if there has been a breach of the fair trial principle in the police investigation, the accused's narrative may not be used as evidence against him or her.[19] However, the limitation of using such evidence - as in Supreme Court decision 2012:45 - applies only to evidence against the accused; whereas evidence supporting the accused's innocence cannot be limited. Also, such limitations cannot be applied in civil cases. Neither does Finnish evidence law provide a normative solution to establish the illegality of the means of obtaining evidence.[20]

3.8. *Poland*

There is no legal concept or definition of 'illegal evidence' in Poland. It is also unclear whether there is a general principle of inadmissibility of illegally obtained evidence.[21] Only evidence obtained according to the rules of the taking of evidence can be taken into consideration while establishing the facts, and appraising evidence and the other materials relevant for the case.[22] The establishment of facts according to evidence that is not formally permitted and not taken during a court action violates general rules of procedure such as immediacy, publicity, equality of the parties and the adversarial principle,[23] and also of the principle of the free evaluation of evidence (Supreme Court judgment of 9 March 2005, III CK 271/04).[24]

18 See Supreme Court decision 2011:91. In this case, nursing staff filed a police report based on a patient's narrative on the crimes he had committed which he had given while committed to a psychiatric ward. Although the staff did not have a right to file the report due to their official confidential role, the medical certificates could be used as evidence in the criminal proceedings. Koulu 2014, p. 31-32.

19 See Supreme Court decision 2012:45. In the case, the defendant was found guilty of an aggravated drug offence partly based on the narrative he had given during the police investigation. As it was uncertain whether the accused had waived his right to have an attorney present or understood the meaning of such waiver, the Court held that the accused's right not to assist in incriminating himself had been violated and thus the police reports could not be used as evidence. Similar reasoning is found in Supreme Court decision 2013:25. Koulu 2014, p. 31-32.

20 Koulu 2014, p. 31-32. *Cf.* Möller 2003, p. 156.

21 *Cf.* Mokry & Sobkowski 2003, p. 486.

22 Court of Appeals in Katowice, judgment of 22 January 2009, V ACa 551/08.

23 Verdicts of the Supreme Court: 13 November 2003, IV CK 212/02; 20 August 2001, I PKN 571/00; 23 June 1999, II UKN 9/99; 3 February 1997, I CKN 60/96; 20 August 2001, I PKN 571/00, OSNP 2003/14/330.

24 Bagan-Kurluta & Fiedorczyk 2014, p. 66-67.

3.9. *Sweden*

In Swedish civil and commercial litigation there is, as a starting point, no distinction between illegally obtained evidence and illegal evidence. The circumstances under which evidence may be rejected by the court follow from Chapter 35, Sec. 7 of the Code of Civil Procedure. All means of evidence are allowed if they may serve as proof, and this according to the far-reaching principles of the free production of evidence and the free evaluation of evidence. The limitations are stated in Article 6 ECHR and the Instrument of Government regarding the right to a fair trial, which is an integral part of the Swedish legal system. The right to a fair trial is also clearly expressed in Chapter 2, Sec. 11, second para, of the Instrument of Government, which was added as directly inspired by Article 6 ECHR through the latest reform of the Constitution in 2010. The Swedish system does not provide for rules establishing the illegality of the manner in which evidence is obtained.[25]

3.10. *Romania*

Romanian legal doctrine does not consistently structure the concept of unlawful evidence. Disparate observations and legal texts allow, nevertheless, some considerations to be made. The notion of 'illegal evidence' may refer to the proposition of such means of evidence which are not explicitly listed by the law, to evidence that does not meet the general conditions of admissibility, to evidence taken without observing other procedural requirements, or to false evidence (such as the production of forged documents, false testimony, etc.). A general principle of the inadmissibility of illegally obtained evidence is not explicitly stated by the Code of Civil Procedure. However, the Romanian Constitution states that the public authorities respect and protect private and family life; that the home, the confidentiality of correspondence, phone and other means of communication are inviolable (Articles 26, 27 and 28). Moreover, Romania has ratified the European Convention on Human Rights. The principle of legality, as prescribed by Article 7 of the new Code of Civil Procedure, also states that the civil process takes place according to the provisions of the law and that the judge has the duty to ensure the observation of the provisions of the law regarding the attainment of the rights and the fulfilment of the duties of the parties. The new Code also contains a particular rule which states that photographs, photocopies, video recordings, disks, magnetic tapes and other similar means of evidence are considered physical evidence, as long as they were not obtained by violating the law or morality (Article 341). The civil procedure literature mentions that the use of letters as evidence by their addressee or by a third person is not always without restrictions; such use may depend upon their content and the manner in which the letter was obtained. These may be reasons for a court to proceed cautiously when confronted with evidence that contravenes the aforementioned principles and rules. Civil courts can annul illegal

25 Bylander 2014, p. 22-23. *Cf.* Lindell 2003, p. 528-530.

evidence; the exclusion of certain evidence is also practised (in the sense that the evidence is not considered by the court) if there are justifiable grounds. The fact that evidence was illegally obtained may represent such grounds.[26]

3.11. *Latvia*

Latvian civil procedural rules do not expressly define the concepts of 'illegal evidence' or 'illegally obtained evidence' and do not directly regulate issues related to these concepts. However, special meaning shall be devoted to Sec. 95 of the Code of Civil Procedure referring to the admissibility of evidence. This section states: (1) the court shall admit only such kinds of evidence as provided for by law; (2) facts that, in accordance with the law, may be proved only by a particular kind of evidence, may not be proved by any other kind of evidence. Legal doctrine points out that this section highlights only the procedural form of the information contained in the norm; however, attention should also be drawn to the method of obtaining such information. This opinion is closely connected with the provision under para 1 of Sec. 8 of the Code that establishes the facts of the case by examining evidence gathered in accordance with a procedure provided for by law. Thus the Code in general determines that the evidence to be examined by the court to establish factual circumstances shall be legal and shall be gathered in accordance with a procedure provided for by law and not contrary to it. Latvian civil procedural rules do not directly define illegal evidence and evidence that is obtained illegally, but these issues should be taken into consideration when considering the admissibility of evidence. Analysis of the admissibility of evidence encompasses not only the evidence itself, but also the manner in which it has been obtained.[27]

3.12. *Hungary*

The Hungarian Code of Civil Procedure, which is founded on the principle of the free evaluation of evidence, contains a rather small number of provisions the violation of which would result in the unlawfulness of evidence. With regard to the *use of unlawfully obtained evidence*, the Code does not formulate generally applicable clauses of the type contained in the Act on Criminal Procedure. Prohibitions are concentrated around the witness statement and expert opinion, but in other areas the lack of general and special prohibitions results in uncertainty concerning such illegalities as, for example, the stealing of documents or obtaining an electronic letter through unauthorised access to the email system. In the literature the evidence obtained unlawfully - through the actual violation of personal rights - is regarded to be admissible (e.g. a stolen letter), but it is considered to be sharply distinguishable from unlawful conduct violating the authenticity or genuineness of

26 Spinei 2014, p. 27-28.
27 Rozenfelds 2014, p. 48-50.

documents. However, there are also general objections to the admissibility of evidence obtained through the violation of personal rights, and it is regarded as part of the ethos of the free evidentiary system that unlawfully obtained evidence cannot not be used in court.[28]

3.13. *Ireland*

Unlawfully obtained evidence may be divided into two types: firstly, evidence obtained in breach of the Constitution, and ordinarily in Irish law such evidence is inadmissible; and, secondly, evidence obtained in breach of statute or the common law, known as illegally obtained evidence which is admissible at the discretion of the trial judge. In *People (Attorney General) v. O'Brien* [1965] IR 142, Walsh J. stated his view of how the admissibility of evidence obtained in violation of constitutional rights should be determined:

> The courts in exercising the judicial powers of government of the State must recognise the paramount position of constitutional rights and must uphold the objection of an accused person to the admissibility at his trial of evidence obtained or procured by the State or its servants or agents as a result of the deliberate and conscious violation of the constitutional rights of an accused person where no extraordinary excusing circumstances exist, such as the imminent destruction of vital evidence or the need to rescue a victim in peril.

In *DPP v. Kenny* [1990] 2 IR 110, Finlay C. J. stated the rule in the following terms:

> I am satisfied that the correct principle is that evidence obtained by invasion of the constitutional personal rights of the citizen must be excluded unless a court is satisfied that either the act constituting the breach of constitutional rights was committed unintentionally or accidentally or is satisfied that there are extraordinary excusing circumstances which justify the admission of the evidence in its discretion.

While the rule was originally formulated in the context of criminal cases, it later became apparent that it also applied in the context of civil law. Thus unconstitutionally obtained evidence is also excluded in civil cases. In *Universal City Studios v. Mulligan,* Unreported, High Court (Laffoy J.) 25 March 1998, Laffoy J. recognised *obiter* the entitlement of a party in civil proceedings to the exclusion at trial of evidence obtained in breach of that party's constitutional rights. The action involved a breach of copyright, and a videocassette seized from the defendant's vehicle was important evidence for the plaintiff. The search warrant pursuant to which the evidence was obtained had been lost. In the circumstances, the High Court found that the unlawfulness did not amount to a breach of the accused's constitutional rights. However, the Court said that had there been such a breach the same rule would apply as applied in criminal proceedings, and the evidence would have been automatically excluded (similar in *Universal Studios v. Mulligan*). In *PMcG*

28 Harsági 2014, p. 48. *Cf.* Németh & Papp 2003, p. 670.

v. AG, Unreported, High Court (Budd J.) 28 January 2000, the Court excluded evidence in family law proceedings obtained after an unlawful search by one spouse of the other spouse's dwelling in violation of Article 40.5 of the Constitution: the medical inspector was not entitled to base his findings on a diary seized by one party to the proceedings in violation of the other party's right to privacy. In the literature the evidence is considered to have been obtained illegally if the investigator acted without or beyond his lawful authority under statute or the common law or if the evidence was obtained by the commission of a crime, tort or breach of contract. Where evidence is obtained illegally as opposed to unconstitutionally, the trial judge has discretion whether to admit or exclude the evidence. These rules apply to all types of evidence.[29]

3.14. *France*

The issue of unlawful evidence is related in French law to the principle called *loyauté de la preuve*: loyalty – or fairness – of evidence. According to this, evidence is not admissible in court if it was obtained and/or provided unfairly. This principle has emerged in recent years in civil procedure and is currently spreading in various branches of law. Of course, this is not to say that, in the past, evidence taking was absolutely 'disloyal' or unfair. The 'contradictory principle' itself can be regarded as an application of a general principle of fairness. The principle of loyalty also underlies more precise evidentiary rules, e.g. Article 259-1 *Code civil* according to which, in divorce proceedings, a spouse cannot produce evidence obtained 'by violence or fraud'. Apart from such rules, courts have always tended to reject 'fraudulent' or 'illicit' evidence.[30] But only recently the judges have started to refer expressly to the principle of loyalty, which they derive not only from Article 9 of the Code of Civil Procedure but also from Article 6 ECHR (right to a fair trial). There is no precise definition of what unfair evidence is. One can only find various illustrations in case law. For instance, the Cour de cassation has decided that the recording of a phone call, made and retained secretly and without the agreement of the other party, is 'an unfair practice that makes the evidence obtained this way inadmissible before a court'.[31]

4. Countries with no or Limited Restrictions on Evidence

In the EU there are some countries where restrictions on evidence have not been developed. In these countries the finding of truth has an absolute precedence. In

29 Moriarty 2014, p. 105-106. *Cf.* Fennell 2003, p. 264.

30 See for instance Cass. soc., 22 mai 1995: Bull. civ. 1995, V, n° 164: shadowing of an employee by a private investigator on request of the employer.

31 Cass. 2e civ., 7 oct. 2004: Bull. civ. 2004, II, n° 447; D. 2005, p. 122, note Ph. Bonfils; JCP G 2005, II, 10025, note N. Léger; RTD Civ. 2005 p. 135, obs. J. Mestre et B. Fages. Oudin 2014, p. 43.

Bulgaria there is no concept of illegally obtained evidence or illegal evidence.[32] There is also no concept of illegally obtained evidence or illegal evidence in Malta.[33]

In the Netherlands, the concept of restrictions on evidence is not unknown, but it is of very limited relevance in civil litigation. In 1988, the Legislature decided not to regulate this issue in the Code of Civil Procedure but to leave the development of it to case law. As a general rule, the judge may use any means of evidence in civil litigation in the Netherlands. Examples are where a conversation had been secretly recorded and then submitted as evidence, or where video recordings had been made secretly and then subsequently submitted to the court. The judge freely evaluates whether or not the case has been proven by way of this evidence (although it has been argued that this could be different if the violation of a right such as the right to privacy outweighs the public interest in establishing the truth in civil cases). Parties against whom this evidence is used may, however, consider whether an action in tort can be brought against the opponent party who makes use of the illegal or illegally obtained evidence.[34] The position is rather similar in the Slovak Republic, where there is no distinction between illegally obtained evidence and illegal evidence. There is no normative solution either. Evidence is taken by the court, and there is a presumption that the court will not act *contra legem* (for example, the court would not take evidence that is recorded illegally).[35]

In English law it had previously been the case that in a civil action the court had no power to exclude evidence even on the ground that it had been obtained illegally. Nevertheless, the Civil Procedure Rules have recently been amended (Rule 32.2(3)) to provide as follows: *(1) The court may control the evidence by giving directions as to (a) identifying or limiting the issues to which factual evidence may be directed; (b) Identifying the witnesses who may be called or whose evidence may be read; or (c) Limiting the length or format of witness statements.* This rule is remarkable in the context of the centuries-long tradition of the non-interventionist judge in the common law. But in exercising this power the court is not to lose sight of the 'overriding objective' to ensure that the case is dealt with justly. This rule was included following a major review of the cost of civil litigation by Lord Justice Jackson. Similar powers are given to the judges hearing cases listed in the small claims track. There are statutory provisions for excluding certain classes of evidence on the grounds of 'public policy' (Regulation of Investigatory Powers Act 2000).[36]

5. Conclusions

This survey clearly demonstrates that a certain concept of restrictions on evidence is evidently present in a great part of the national legislations of European states. Even

32 Bonchovski 2014, p. 40-41.
33 Sammut 2014, p. 63-64.
34 Van Rhee 2014, p. 44. *Cf.* Granow & Bervoets 2003, p. 398.
35 Vnukova 2014, p. 57-58.
36 Turner 2014, p. 13.

the traditionally non-interventionist English law has recently seen a certain shift towards restrictions regarding illegal evidence. The practical implementation of restrictions, however, differs significantly from one country to another. In some countries (e.g. Croatia and Greece) the restrictions have been raised to the constitutional level. In other countries the main development of the area is by court practice. It is nevertheless common that at least certain restrictions are regulated in the legislation as particular exceptions in evidence law. As a predominant rule, in Europe we can identify that violation of fundamental rights could lead to the inadmissibility of such evidence. However, such inadmissibility is rarely automatic (e.g. as it is in Greece) and normally subject to some balancing of interests. This is somehow expected because fundamental rights serve as the highest principles in a legal order and have as such a dimension of weight. This enables them to be taken into account in cases where collisions between different constitutional principles occur. Here a proportionality test is applied. A clearly separate but still similar case is French law, where the issue of unlawful evidence is related to the principle of loyalty/fairness of evidence. This means that evidence is not admissible in court if it was obtained unfairly. Even though the concept of restrictions on evidence is underdeveloped in certain countries (e.g. Hungary), it still exists at least in legal literature. In the Netherlands, the concept is familiar but of very limited relevance in civil procedure. There are only rare examples of countries where no restrictions on evidence are reported to exist (e.g. Bulgaria and Malta). However, the described diversity in approaches does pose difficulties in the cross-border taking of evidence and a more harmonised approach within Europe would be desirable.

Bibliography

Bagan-Kurluta & Fiedorczyk 2014
Bagan-Kurluta, K. & Fiedorczyk, P., *Dimensions of Evidence in European Civil Procedure - Draft National Report for Poland*, unpublished, 2014.

Balzer 2005
Balzer, C., *Beweisaufnahme und Bewieswürdigung im Zivilprozess: eine systematische Darstellung und Anleitung für die gerichtliche und anwaltliche Praxis*, 2nd edn., Berlin: Erich Schmidt Verlag, 2005.

Bonchovski 2014
Bonchovski, P., *Dimensions of Evidence in European Civil Procedure - Draft National Report for Bulgaria*, unpublished, 2014.

Bylander 2014
Bylander, E., *Dimensions of Evidence in European Civil Procedure - Draft National Report for Sweden*, unpublished, 2014.

Fennell 2003
Fennell, C., 'Irland', in Nagel, H. & Bajons, E.-M. (eds.), *Beweis - Preuve - Evidence: Grundzüge des zivilprozessualen Beweisrechts in Europa*, Baden-Baden: Nomos, 2003, p. 235-266.

Granow & Bervoets 2003
Granow, H.M. & Bervoets, C.M., 'Niederlande', in Nagel, H. & Bajons, E.-M. (eds.), *Beweis - Preuve - Evidence: Grundzüge des zivilprozessualen Beweisrechts in Europa*, Baden-Baden: Nomos, 2003, p. 387-417.

Harsági 2014
Harsági, V., *Dimensions of Evidence in European Civil Procedure - Draft National Report for Hungary*, unpublished, 2014.

Katiforis 2014
Katiforis, N., *Dimensions of Evidence in European Civil Procedure - Draft National Report for Greece*, unpublished, 2014.

Kofmel Ehrenzeller 2003
Kofmel Ehrenzeller, S., 'Schweiz', in Nagel, H. & Bajons, E.-M. (eds.), *Beweis - Preuve - Evidence: Grundzüge des zivilprozessualen Beweisrechts in Europa*, Baden-Baden: Nomos, 2003, p. 557-590.

Koulu 2014
Koulu, R., *Dimensions of Evidence in European Civil Procedure - Draft National Report for Finland*, unpublished, 2014.

Lindell 2003
Lindell, B., 'Schweden', in Nagel, H. & Bajons, E.-M. (eds.), *Beweis - Preuve - Evidence: Grundzüge des zivilprozessualen Beweisrechts in Europa*, Baden-Baden: Nomos, 2003, p. 519-555.

Mayr 2004
Mayr, P.G., 'Das Beweisrecht in Österreich', in Lebre de Freitas, J.M. (ed.), *The Law of Evidence in the European Union*, The Hague: Kluwer Law International, 2004, p. 33-67.

Mokry & Sobkowski 2003
Mokry, J. & Sobkowski, J., 'Polen', in Nagel, H. & Bajons, E.-M. (eds.), *Beweis - Preuve - Evidence: Grundzüge des zivilprozessualen Beweisrechts in Europa*, Baden-Baden: Nomos, 2003, p. 477-503.

Möller 2003
Möller, G., 'Finnland', in Nagel, H. & Bajons, E.-M. (eds.), *Beweis - Preuve - Evidence: Grundzüge des zivilprozessualen Beweisrechts in Europa*, Baden-Baden: Nomos, 2003, p. 139-165.

Moriarty 2014
Moriarty, B., *Dimensions of Evidence in European Civil Procedure - Draft National Report for Ireland*, unpublished, 2014.

Nagel 2003
Nagel, H., 'Deutschland', in Nagel, H. & Bajons, E.-M. (eds.), *Beweis - Preuve - Evidence: Grundzüge des zivilprozessualen Beweisrechts in Europa*, Baden-Baden: Nomos, 2003, p. 95-137.

Nagel & Bajons 2003
Nagel, H. & Bajons, E.-M. (eds.), *Beweis - Preuve - Evidence: Grundzüge des zivilprozessualen Beweisrechts in Europa*, Baden-Baden: Nomos, 2003.

Németh & Papp 2003
Németh, J. & Papp, Zs., 'Ungarn', in Nagel, H. & Bajons, E.-M. (eds.), *Beweis - Preuve - Evidence: Grundzüge des zivilprozessualen Beweisrechts in Europa*, Baden-Baden: Nomos, 2003, p. 661-688.

Nunner-Krautgasser & Anzenberger 2014
Nunner-Krautgasser, B. & Anzenberger, Ph., *Dimensions of Evidence in European Civil Procedure - Draft National Report for Austria*, unpublished, 2014.

Oudin 2014
Oudin, M., *Dimensions of Evidence in European Civil Procedure - Draft National Report for France*, unpublished, 2014.

Poola 2014
Poola, M., *Dimensions of Evidence in European Civil Procedure - Draft National Report for Estonia*, unpublished, 2014.

Rosenberg, Schwab & Gottwald 2010
Rosenberg, L., Schwab, K.H. & Gottwald, P., *Zivilprozessrecht*, 17th edn., München: Verlag C.H. Beck, 2010.

Rozenfelds 2014
Rozenfelds, J., *Dimensions of Evidence in European Civil Procedure - Draft National Report for Latvia*, unpublished, 2014.

Sammut 2014
Sammut, I., *Dimensions of Evidence in European Civil Procedure - Draft National Report for Malta*, unpublished, 2014.

Spinei 2014
Spinei, S., *Dimensions of Evidence in European Civil Procedure - Draft National Report for Romania*, unpublished, 2014.

Stein 2005
Stein, A., *Foundations of Evidence Law*, Oxford: Oxford University Press, 2005.

Triva & Dika 2004
Triva, S. & Dika, M., *Građansko procesno pravo*, Zagreb: Narodne novine, 2004.

Turner 2014
Turner, R., *Dimensions of Evidence in European Civil Procedure - Draft National Report for England*, unpublished, 2014.

Uzelac 2003
Uzelac, A., 'Kroatien', in Nagel, H. & Bajons, E.-M. (eds.), *Beweis - Preuve - Evidence: Grundzüge des zivilprozessualen Beweisrechts in Europa*, Baden-Baden: Nomos, 2003, p. 335-357.

Van Rhee 2014
Van Rhee, C.H., *Dimensions of Evidence in European Civil Procedure - Draft National Report for the Netherlands*, unpublished, 2014.

Vnukova 2014
Vnukova, J., *Dimensions of Evidence in European Civil Procedure - Draft National Report for the Slovakia*, unpublished, 2014.

Waage & Herborn 2014
Waage, F. & Herborn M., *Dimensions of Evidence in European Civil Procedure - Draft National Report for Denmark*, unpublished, 2014.

White & Ovey 2010
White, R.C.A. & Ovey, C., *The European Convention on Human Rights*, Oxford: Oxford University Press, 2010.

M. Repas

TAKING LENIENCY DOCUMENTS AS EVIDENCE IN DAMAGES ACTIONS IN CASES OF COMPETITION LAW INFRINGEMENT

1. Introduction

Taking evidence in competition cases is particularly delicate since companies are careful to hide any evidence that may prove wrongdoing on their part. This is due to the severe penalties that are prescribed for infringement of competition rules. This problem is especially acute in cartel cases,[1] and consequently competition authorities use different methods to detect and prove cartel activities. One of the most effective methods that is currently used to fight cartels is the leniency programme, whereby companies that provide information about the cartel in which they participate may receive full or partial immunity from fines.[2] In addition to fines that can amount to up to 10 per cent of the total turnover of the company in the preceding business year,[3] companies are liable for the civil consequences of the competition law infringement (e.g. damages) as well. Claims for compensation for

1 A cartel is an agreement and/or concerted practice between two or more competitors with the intention of coordinating their competitive behaviour on the market, and/or influencing the relevant parameters of competition through practices such as, but not limited to, the fixing or coordination of purchase or selling price, or other trading conditions, including in relation to intellectual property rights, the allocation of production and sales quotas, the sharing of markets and customers, including bid-rigging, restrictions of imports or exports and/or anti-competitive actions against other companies. See Art. 2(14) of Directive 2014/104/EU of the European Parliament and of the Council of 26 November 2014 on certain rules governing actions for damages under national law for infringements of the competition law provisions of the Member States and of the European Union (*OJ* L349, 5 December 2014, p. 1-19; Directive 2014/104/EU).

2 Commission Notice on immunity from fines and reduction of fines in cartel cases (*OJ* C298, 8 December 2006, p. 17) and Art. 76 of the Slovenian Prevention of Restriction of Competition Act (*OJ* RS Nos. 36/2008, 40/2009, 26/2011, 87/2011, 57/2012, 39/2013, 63/2013 and 33/2104; SCA).

3 See Art. 23(2) of Regulation 1/2003 and Art. 73 of the Slovenian Competition Act.

damages caused are made before national courts in private law actions[4] from which there is no immunity under the leniency programme. Private law actions in competition cases have been acknowledged as highly important in recent years, and the EU Commission stimulates such private enforcement, which is still low in the EU as compared with the USA. This 'improvement' of private enforcement, however, requires adequate access to information, essential for preparing lawsuits by the private damages claimants, that is in the possession of the defendants and competition authorities.[5]

Since competition authorities, including the EU Commission, are bound by the rule of confidentiality of sensitive documents, which is part of the leniency programme as well, the question is how to adequately protect the individual interests of victims, on the one hand, and not jeopardise the effectiveness of the leniency programme, on the other hand. The Court of Justice of the European Union (CJEU) and the General Court tackled this issue in several cases that will be analysed in this article. As a result of the decisions made in these cases, case law does not favour leniency applicants entirely, while Directive 2014/104/EU takes the opposite view. Finally, this article explores how this issue is handled in Slovenia, and its compatibility with EU law. So far, there is no recorded case that refers to the disclosure of leniency documents in the Republic of Slovenia.

2. Public and Private Enforcement of Competition Law Rules

Two different categories of competition rule enforcement can be distinguished: public enforcement and private enforcement. Public enforcement is executed in the public interest realised through public authorities (the EU Commission and national competition authorities), while private enforcement is realised through private actions before national courts, filed by private claimants (competitors, suppliers and consumers) who are claiming, in particular, compensation for damage caused by the competition law infringement. While the primary goal of public enforcement is to deter anti-competitive conduct, the goal of private enforcement is to compensate the victims of anti-competitive conduct for losses suffered,[6] although private enforcement has a deterrent effect as well given that compensation may be high. Private and public enforcement are closely connected. This is the result of *inter alia* the fact that public enforcement facilitates private enforcement; that national courts must not make a decision that runs counter to the decision of the competition authorities; that public enforcement may provide evidence helpful in establishing causation and harm in civil proceedings; and that private enforcement can reinforce public enforcement by increasing deterrence.[7]

4 See more in Bratina 2012 and Ahtik & Vlahek 2011.
5 Kellerbauer 2014, p. 56.
6 Faull & Nikpay 2007, p. 1121. See also Komninos 2006, p. 10.
7 See Jones & Sufrin 2014, p. 1089 and Wils 2009, p. 15-16.

The enforcement of competition rules in the EU is based on a system of public enforcement, while private enforcement plays only a minor role.[8] According to the EU Commission,[9] in only 25 per cent of the competition infringement decisions the Commission has made in the past seven years did the victims seek compensation before national courts. The reasons behind such low rates of private enforcement vary and are mainly connected to the diverging legislation across the EU.[10] Most of these reasons will disappear due to the new directive which aims to facilitate actions for damages in competition cases.[11]

The EU institutions, including the EU courts, thus seek to improve private enforcement of competition rules. The CJEU has widely acknowledged private enforcement and ruled in the *Courage v. Crehan* case[12] that each individual has the right to claim compensation for damage suffered as a result of competition infringement before the national courts. This position was reaffirmed several times by the CJEU in subsequent cases.[13] For a successful claim, private claimants need adequate access to information (documents) which are in the possession of third parties, mainly the competition authorities. There are several routes for private claimants to take in order to obtain the required information from the EU Commission and national competition authorities.

First, private claimants may seek to obtain the documents under Article 30 of Council Regulation (EC) No. 1/2003 of 16 December 2002 on the implementation laid out in Articles 81 and 82 of the Treaty[14] (Regulation 1/2003) or relevant national law (e.g. Article 22(6) of the Slovenian Competition Act[15] (SCA)) according to which the EU Commission is obliged to publish only the main content of the decision, although it is entitled to publish the full, non-confidential version of the decision, which has usually been done up to now.[16] The non-confidential version does not include information such as business secrets, specific references to leniency submissions and the other information covered by the principle of the presumption

8 As for the reasons for such underdeveloped private enforcement, see Scharaw 2014, p. 357.

9 European Commission Press Release, Antitrust: Commission proposes legislation to facilitate damage claims by victims of antitrust violations, Brussels, 11 June 2013.

10 See Green Paper - damages actions for breach of the EC antitrust rules (COM(2005) 672, 19 December 2005).

11 See Scharaw 2014, p. 352-360 and Howard 2014, p. 51-55.

12 Case C-453/99, *Courage Ltd v. Bernard Crehan and Bernard Crehan v. Courage Ltd and Others* [2001] ECR I-06297.

13 Cases C-295/04, *Manfredi v. Lloyd Adriatico Assicurazioni SpA* [2006] ECR I-6619; C-360/09, *Pfleiderer AG v. Bundeskartellamt* [2011] **ECR** I-5161; C-199/11, *Europese Gemeenschap v. Otis NV and Others* [2012]; C-557/12, *Kone AG, Otis GmbH, Schindler Aufzüge and Fahrtreppen GmbH, Schindler Liegenschaftsverwaltung GmbH, ThyssenKrupp Aufzüge GmbH v. ÖBB-Infrastruktur AG* [2014].

14 *OJ* L1, 4 January 2003, p. 1.

15 According to this Article, the Slovenian competition authority shall publish on its website its final decisions in an administrative procedure and minor offences procedure, as well as final orders by which the procedure is concluded, without confidential data.

16 Kellerbauer 2014, p. 56.

of innocence.[17] Often it is precisely this information, unattainable through this route, that is the most important for private claimants preparing a lawsuit. Second, information can be obtained under Regulation (EC) No. 1049/2001 of the European Parliament and the Council of 30 May 2001 regarding public access to European Parliament, Council and Commission documents[18] (Regulation 1049/2001), according to which the public has a right to access to EU Commission's documents. Appropriately, this right is also enjoyed by private claimants under the national law of the Member States (e.g. the Slovenian Public Information Access Act; PIAA).[19] Third, private claimants might obtain information from direct intervention in appeals against the Commission's decision in cartel cases, although this route was barred by the CJEU in the *Schenker* case.[20] The fourth and final route is to obtain the relevant information by means of a request made by national courts requiring competition authorities to disclose documents.[21]

The disclosure of documents is highly problematic in the case of a leniency programme, as the documents often contain highly sensitive information in the form of detailed accounts of the cartel arrangements, and the participation of the leniency applicant in those arrangements.[22] Allowing the disclosure of documents that were submitted in order to avoid fines prescribed by competition law could jeopardise the whole operation of the leniency programme, since cartel participants would then be unwilling to reveal cartel arrangements and open themselves up to high compensation costs for damages. It must be stressed that already the incentive for private enforcement could jeopardise the effectiveness of the leniency programme,[23] but revealing certain documents from that programme to private claimants is even more troublesome.

Since the publication of the decision by competition authorities does not contain confidential information, and since direct intervention in appeals against the EU Commission's decisions was barred by the CJEU, only the public access route and the national route are considered as options for obtaining leniency documents.

3. The Purpose and Aims of the Leniency Programme

Since it is very difficult to prove the existence of cartel behaviour due to the ever complex nature of cartels and the increasingly assiduous effort of companies involved in them to prevent detection,[24] competition authorities introduced a special method for effective detection, the so-called leniency programme. Under this

17 De Stefano 2012, p. 97.
18 *OJ* L145, 31 May 2001, p. 43-48.
19 Kellerbauer 2014, p. 56.
20 Case C-602/11 P(I), *Schenker v. European Commission* [2012].
21 See also De Stefano 2012, p. 96.
22 Sanders *et al.* 2013, p. 175.
23 See also Faull & Nikpay 2007, p. 1123.
24 *Ibidem*, p. 960.

programme, cartel participants who reveal information and offer proof of the cartel's existence may receive full, or partial immunity from fines. The aim of the leniency programme is to increase the probability of detecting cartels, to effectively punish cartel participants who are not part of this programme, and to prevent cartel behaviours in the first place. In addition, leniency is also a cost-effective enforcement tool since competition authorities do not have to use other costly and time-consuming methods of investigation.[25] It must be stressed that, as stated, the programme gives leniency applicants immunity from, or reduction of, fines only and not immunity from having to provide compensation for damages caused.[26] Thus, leniency applicants can still be found liable for the damages caused by their participation in the cartel. The leniency programme is not used only by the EU Commission, similar programmes have also been introduced and utilised in a number of EU Member States.[27] Just as the Commission faces problems with leniency disclosure, so too do the national competition authorities.

4. Protection of Business and Other Professional Secrets

4.1. *The Position of the EU Commission*

Under Article 399 of the Treaty on the Functioning of the European Union[28] (TFEU), members of the institutions of the EU, members of the committees, and the officials and other servants of the EU are required not to disclose information of the kind covered by the obligation of professional secrecy, in particular, information about companies, business relations or cost components. This provision is repeated in Article 28(2) of Regulation 1/2003 and in Article 16(1) of the Commission's Regulation (EC) No. 773/2004 of 7 April 2004 relating to the conduct of proceedings by the Commission pursuant to Articles 81 and 82 of the EC Treaty[29] (Regulation 773/2004).

Professional secrecy probably extends to all information that comes into the hands of the EU Commission or national competition authorities in the exercise of their functions except those already in the public domain. Of all the information covered by professional secrecy, business secrets and other confidential information are the most disputed.[30] The General Court held in the *Postbank* case[31] that business secrets constitute information of which not only disclosure to the public, but also mere transmission to a person other than the person who provided the information,

25 *Ibidem*, p. 700 and 800. See more about the leniency programme in Sandhu 2007; Podobnik 2009; Breathnach 2013, and others.

26 Para 31 of the Leniency Notice. About the reasonableness of such exclusion from leniency, see Ferčič 2011. p. 110-113.

27 See e.g. Art. 76 of SCA and Repas 2010, p. 446-458.

28 *OJ* C326, 26 October 2012, p. 47.

29 *OJ* L123, 27 April 2004, p. 18.

30 Faull & Nikpay 2007, p. 151.

31 Case T-353/94, *Postbank* [1996], ECR II-921, para 87.

could seriously harm the latter's interests. These business secrets are, for example, methods of assessing costs, production secrets and processes, supply sources, quantities produced and sold, etc.[32] As for other confidential information, Recital 13 of Regulation 773/2004 states that such information also includes information other than business secrets that may be considered confidential insofar as its disclosure would significantly harm a company or person.

With respect to this professional secrecy, it must be stressed that the EU Commission and the national competition authorities (members of the European Competition Network; ECN) apply EU competition rules in close cooperation and are thus able to exchange information between them, including confidential information (Articles 11, 12(1) and 28(2) of Regulation 1/2003). However, as for the leniency documents, under points 40 and 41 of the Commission Notice on cooperation within the Network of Competition Authorities[33] (ECN Notice), ECN members will only transmit information voluntarily submitted by a leniency applicant to another ECN member when the leniency applicant consents to such an exchange, with the exception of instances provided for by point 41 of the ECN Notice. The same applies to the information gathered as a result of the leniency application. This rule is quite logical given that a potential leniency applicant will no longer apply for leniency if the information can be used against the applicant by another ECN member.[34]

In addition, Article 15 of Regulation 1/2003 establishes cooperation between national courts and competition authorities, which is further explained in the Notice on the co-operation between the Commission and the courts of the EU Member States in the application of Articles 81 and 82 EC[35] (Co-operation Notice). Such cooperation is established in different ways, *inter alia*, a national court may request that the EU Commission transmit information in its possession or provide it with an opinion concerning the procedural or substantive application of the EU competition rules: transmission of information does not cover confidential information and business secrets unless the national court can guarantee their protection.[36] Of importance for the leniency application, the Commission will not transmit to national courts any information voluntarily provided by the leniency applicant without the applicant's consent, because such transmission could jeopardise the accomplishment of the task entrusted to it.[37] As a result, the Commission strictly upholds the view that the protection of leniency documents is a high priority.

32 Faull & Nikpay 2007, p. 152.
33 *OJ* C101, 27 April 2004, p. 43.
34 See also Faull & Nikpay 2007, p. 142.
35 *OJ* C101, 27 April 2004, p. 54.
36 Co-operation Notice, paras 23-25.
37 Co-operation Notice, para 26.

4.2. *The Position of National Competition Authorities – The Case of Slovenia*

National competition authorities are bound to a similar obligation of professional secrecy under national rules as the institutions of the EU. For example, the Slovenian competition authority is bound by Article 13a of the SCA to protect confidential information, that being trade secrets (data that is known to a limited number of persons, the disclosure of which would cause considerable damage[38]), business correspondence concerning the economic activity of a company, personal data and any other information that, under the SCA or other regulations, is subject to a special arrangement for protection and to special conditions for assessment.[39] However, it may disclose information in its possession to administrative bodies; other state authorities and holders of public authorisation on the basis of a substantiated written request clearly indicating that the purpose of the request is to be able to carry out their statutory responsibilities; to the EU Commission according to Regulation 1/2003; to authorised authorities of foreign countries under international treaties; and to authorities for the purpose of execution under the SCA (Articles 13b(1), (2) and (3) SCA).

In addition, the SCA clarifies the relationship between the protection of professional secrecy contained in the SCA and the PIAA. It states in Article 13b(4) that, notwithstanding the provisions of the law regulating access to public information, the competition authority shall refuse a person requesting access to public information access to information relating to the secrecy of the source and to information constituting business secrecy of a company. Thus, the SCA is *lex specialis* in relation to PIAA, meaning that the purpose of the legislator is to avoid applying the balancing test under Article 6(2) of the PIAA, under which confidential information shall be disclosed if the public interest in disclosure prevails. With such a regulation, Slovenia has avoided problems, analysed below, that face the EU Commission in cases where personal claimants require public access to documents contained in its files.

Special provisions regarding the secrecy of leniency documents are contained in Article 6 of the Decree on the Procedure for Immunity from Fines and Reduction of Fines in Cartel Cases[40] (Decree). The Slovenian Government issued the Decree under Article 76(5) of the SCA. According to this Article, the Government is required to lay down rules on the procedure for immunity from, or the reduction of, fines. Under Article 6(1) of the Decree, a competition authority may disclose information and evidences from a leniency application only to a company under an infringement procedure after a statement of the objections has been issued in an administrative procedure and in accordance with para 7 of Article 18 of the Act, i.e. if disclosure might objectively prevail over the interest of protecting such

38 See Art. 3, point 17 SCA.
39 Art. 3, point 16 SCA.
40 *OJ* RS, Nos. 112/2009 and 2/2014.

information as a trade secret. In addition, according to Article 6(2) of the Decree, a leniency application shall be transmitted to the members of the ECN provided that:

- an offender consents to the transmission of information; or
- an offender has also submitted an application for immunity from, or reduction of, a fine for the same infringement to the competition authority of the Member State that has requested the information, or provided that the competition authority of the Member State that requested the information has made a written statement, a copy of which shall be transmitted to the offender by the Slovenian competition authority, stating that the information obtained shall not be used for the imposition of sanctions on the offender, persons subject to the application, employees, or former employees of the offender or persons subject to the application; and
- the level of protection against disclosure afforded by the receiving Member State is equal to that conferred by the Republic of Slovenia.

It follows that Slovenian regulation, as far as leniency documents are concerned, does not leave any room for competition authorities to transmit leniency documents to national courts, or any other person, natural or legal, except for the persons and authorities mentioned above.

5. Disclosure of Leniency Documents in Damages Actions

5.1. *General*

As already stated, leniency documents often contain very sensitive information about the cartel members and their involvement in the cartel, which may be very helpful to private claimants seeking damages suffered as a result of the cartel behaviour. In particular, they help to prove the existence of damage, and the causality between the damage and the infringement.[41] It has to be emphasised that leniency documents fall into two categories: (i) corporate statements and (ii) other leniency documents, i.e. other pre-existing documents submitted by the leniency applicant that are not subject to the leniency procedure because they exist, unlike corporate statements, independently, and could be discovered elsewhere.[42] The distinction between those two categories of leniency documents has not played a role in case law thus far.[43]

In this section, the case law of the European Union relating to the disclosure of leniency documents is analysed. First, disclosure through right of access under Regulation 1049/2001 will be analysed, followed by an analysis of disclosure upon

41 de Zárate Catón 2013.

42 See De Stefano 2012, p. 102, note 97.

43 However, this position will obviously change according to the Proposal, as explained below.

the request of national courts. Finally, the use of these two routes for obtaining leniency documents is explored and analysed according to Slovenian law.

5.2. *Right to Access under Regulation 1049/2001*

In cases *CDC*,[44] *EnBW*[45] and *Netherlands v. Commission*,[46] private claimants used Regulation 1049/2001 to access documents in the EU Commission's files. It must be noted that these cases did not deal with the leniency documents directly, however, decisions made by the EU courts carry significant importance for those documents as well.

Under Regulation 1049/2001, all documents in the possession of EU institutions must be open to public access, except where overriding interests of non-disclosure exist. Article 4(2) of Regulation 1049/2001 provides that institutions shall refuse access to a document where disclosure would undermine, *inter alia*, the protection of the commercial interests of a natural or legal person, including intellectual property, and the purpose of inspections, investigations or audits, unless there is an overriding public interest in disclosure. In the past, the EU Commission has relied on these exceptions in cartel cases.[47]

The EU Commission is generally bound to carry out an assessment of the documents on an individual basis before refusing access to the documents under Regulation 1049/2001. However, there are exceptional circumstances where such individual assessment is not needed, and the refusal of access is based on a general presumption.[48] General presumptions apply to certain categories of documents where similar general considerations are likely to apply to requests for disclosure given that the documents are of the same nature.[49] In particular, the CJEU has recognised such general presumption in state aid[50] and merger proceedings.[51] In the *CDC* case, the General Court held that the EU Commission was not entitled to refuse access based on the general nature of the documents. Instead, it must assess each document separately to determine whether the exception in Article 4(2) of Regulation 1049/2001 applies. It also held that the interest of a cartelist to avoid action for damages is not a commercial interest, and does not constitute an interest deserving protection.[52] In *EnBW*, the General Court came to the same conclusion. It annulled the Commission's decision because concrete, individual examination of

44 Case T-437/08, *CDC Hydrogene Peroxide Cartel Damage Claims v. European Commission* [2011] 8251.
45 Case T-344/08, *Energie Baden-Wuerttemberg AG* [2012].
46 Case T-380/08, *Netherlands v. Commission* [2013].
47 Sanders *et al.* 2013, p. 177.
48 De Stefano 2012, p. 97.
49 See cases C-532/07 P, *Sweden and Turco v. Council*, [2010] ECR I-8533, para 50; C-139/07 P *Commission v. Technische Glaswerke Ilmenau* [2010] ECR I-5885; C-404/10 P *Commission v. Éditions Odile Jacob* [2013] ECR, etc.
50 Case C-139/07 P *Commission v. Technische Glaswerke Ilmenau* [2010] ECR I-5885.
51 Case C-477/10 P, *European Commission v. Agrofert Holding a.s.* [2012].
52 Para 49 of the T-437/08 [2011].

the content of the requested documents had not been carried out. A different conclusion was reached in the *Netherlands v. Commission* case, where it was held by the General Court that the EU Commission may use a general presumption if the disclosure of documents during the procedure undermines the protection of commercial interests and the objectives of investigation activities.[53] The General Court acknowledged that the same conclusion applies regardless of whether the application for access concerns a proceeding that has already been closed, or a proceeding that is pending. The reason for this acknowledgment was that the publication of sensitive information is likely to harm the commercial interests of companies regardless of whether the proceeding is pending.[54]

During an appeal brought by the European Commission in the *EnBW case,*[55] the CJEU had an opportunity to clear up this issue. It upheld the Commission's pleas alleging misinterpretation of Article 4 of Regulation 1049/2001, and set aside the General Court's judgment. In particular, the CJEU noted that, according to Regulation 1/2003 and Regulation 773/2004, only the parties to cartel proceedings, and to a certain extent the complainants, have the right to access documents that are in the hands of the EU Commission.[56] Consequently, if third parties were able to access such documents, the access system under Regulations 1/2003 and 773/2004 would be undermined.[57] Accordingly, the CJEU held that the Commission is entitled to rely on a general presumption under which exceptions to the right of access under Article 4(2) of Regulation 1049/2001 apply. Thus, there is no need to conduct individual review of each and every document in the Commission's file, since it is presumed that disclosure of such documents will, in principle, undermine the protection of the commercial interests of the parties involved, as well as the purpose of the investigation.[58] However, that general presumption does not rule out the possibility of demonstrating that the disclosure of a specific document that has been requested is not covered by that presumption, or that there is an overriding public interest in the disclosure of the document. Nevertheless, the CJEU specifically held that the interest in obtaining damages for loss suffered as a result of a breach of Article 101 TFEU cannot, in and of itself, constitute an overriding public interest.[59] According to the CJEUs reasoning, it is difficult to predict a case of successful rebuttal of such a general presumption for the purpose of damages actions.

The CJEU noted that it is irrelevant for the general presumption to apply that documents were provided to the EU Commission voluntarily by the parties involved in the leniency programme. Namely, Regulation 1/2003 and Regulation 773/2004 strictly govern documents regardless of the way in which they were

53 Para 42 of the C-380/08 [2013].
54 Para 43 of the C-380/08 [2013].
55 Case C-365/12 P, *European Commission v. EnBW Energie Baden-Württemberg AG* [2014].
56 Para 87 of the C-365/12 P [2014].
57 Para 88 of the C-365/12 P [2014].
58 Para 93 of the C-365/12 P [2014].
59 Para 108 of the C-365/12 P [2014].

obtained from the parties (voluntarily or under compulsion).[60] The impact of the decisions of the General Court in *Netherlands v. Commission* and of the CJEU in *EnBW* is quite unfavourable for private claimants seeking access to cartel documents under Regulation 1049/2001. As a result, private claimants are left with the option of accessing relevant documents under the national rules following the rulings in *Pfleiderer*[61] and *Donau Chemie*,[62] which are analysed below.

5.2.1. Right of Access under the Slovenian PIAA

As mentioned, access to public information in Slovenia is generally provided by the PIAA, according to which any person may acquire information of a public nature from the state authorities. According to Article 6(2) of the PIAA, there are exceptions to the disclosure of such information, but only after the balancing test has been applied, meaning that confidential information can be disclosed if the public interest in disclosure prevails over the public interest or the interest of other persons not to disclose. However, this Article is not applicable in competition cases since the SCA applies in this regard as *lex specialis*. According to Article 13b(4) of the SCA, the competition authority shall refuse a person's request for access to public information when that information relates to the disclosure of a secret source, or when that information is covered under business secrecy of companies. It is obvious that with such a regulation the purpose of the legislator was to avoid applying the balancing test under the PIAA. As a result, Slovenia has avoided problems facing the EU Commission in cases where personal claimants require public access to documents contained in its files.

5.2.2. Right of Access on the Request of National Courts

In addition to access under Regulation 1049/2001, private claimants may acquire leniency documents through national courts. The CJEU first tackled this issue in the *Pfleiderer* case[63] wherein the private claimant, Pfleiderer, requested access to all material in the file including the leniency documents which had been voluntarily submitted by the leniency applicant, in addition to the evidence seized. The German competition office restricted access to the file to the version from which confidential business information, internal documents and leniency documents had been removed, and refused access to the evidence seized. Pfleiderer then brought an action before the German local court which referred the question in this regard to the CJEU for a preliminary ruling. The CJEU held that, under EU law, private claimants are not prevented from gaining access to leniency documents, and that it is for the courts and tribunals of the Member States, on the basis of their national

60 Para 97 of the C-365/12 P [2014].
61 Case C-360/09, *Pfleiderer AG v. Bundeskartellamt* [2011] I-5161.
62 Case C-536/11, *Bundeswettbewerbsbehörde v. Donau Chemie AG* [2013].
63 Case C-360/09, *Pfleiderer AG v. Bundeskartellamt* [2011] I-5161.

law, to determine the conditions under which such access must be permitted, or refused, by weighing the interests that are protected by EU law. The CJEU rejected the distinction between leniency statements and pre-existing leniency documents as proposed by Advocate General *Mazák*,[64] and thus endorsed the same balancing test for all leniency documents.

It is clear from the CJEU's decision in *Pfleiderer* that it refused to strike a balance of conflicting interests at the EU level. Further still, the CJEU did not provide any guidance as to how this balance should be struck, and instead left this delicate issue to the courts of the Member States. Thus, no basis for a standardised approach has been provided by the CJEU.[65] Consequently, following *Pfleiderer*, leniency documents fall under a different category of protection in the EU. According to the case law of the Member States, Germany considered the private interest to be outweighed by the public interest in an effective leniency programme, and thus refused access to leniency documents.[66] A different position was taken by the United Kingdom's courts where a limited disclosure of leniency document was ordered.[67]

In the *Donau Chemie* case,[68] the CJEU was given another opportunity to clarify this issue. The company, Donau Chemie, was fined for competition infringement on the market in the wholesale distribution of printing chemicals. Verband Druck & Mediatechnik (VDMT) applied to the Austrian court for access to the file relating to the judicial proceedings between the Austrian Federal Competition Authority and Donau Chemie and Others. The purpose of that application was to gather evidence enabling an assessment of the nature and amount of the potential loss suffered by the VDMT's members due to the infringement committed by Donau Chemie and Others, and to determine whether it was appropriate to bring an action for damages against those companies. According to Austrian legislation (§ 39(2) of the *Kartelgesetz*), disclosure of documents is not to be granted unless all parties agree to the disclosure. For the preliminary ruling, the Austrian court referred the question of whether the requirement of such consent from the parties conforms to EU law to the CJEU, as the court was not in a position to conduct the *Pfleiderer* balancing test.

The CJEU ruled that such a national provision under which access to leniency documents is granted solely upon the consent of all parties to the proceedings jeopardises the effectiveness of the right to private enforcement of competition rules,[69] and thus contradicts EU law since it leaves no possibility for the national courts to weigh the interests involved. The CJEU insisted on a case-by-case

64 See more in De Stefano 2012, p. 102.

65 Sanders *et al.* 2013, p. 175, see also Slot 2013 and Singh 2014 about the impact of the *Pfleiderer* judgment on the effectiveness of the leniency programme.

66 See cases S 51 Gs 53/09, *Pfleiderer v. Bundeskartellamt*, GRUR-RR 2012, 178, and V-4 Kart 5+6/M (OWi), *Roasted Coffee*, BB 2012, 2459. For further explanation, see Sanders *et al.* 2013, p. 175-176.

67 See Sanders *et al.* 2013, p. 176.

68 Case C-536/11, *Bundeswettbewerbsbehörde v. Donau Chemie AG* [2013].

69 Para 39 of the C-536/11 [2013].

assessment that takes into account all the relevant factors of the case,[70] especially (i) the interest of the requesting party in obtaining access to documents in order to prepare an action for damages, in particular in the light of other possibilities it may have, and (ii) actual harmful consequences which may result from such access regarding the public interest, or the legitimate interests of other parties.[71] With respect to the public interest, the CJEU pointed out that unless it is clearly demonstrated that disclosing leniency documents will actually undermine the leniency programme, the potential threat that it will do so is in itself not enough to justify a refusal of access to said documents.[72] Unfortunately, the CJEU did not provide an example of when such is the case.

The CJEU's judgment in *Donau Chemie* thus extends the principle already established in the *Pfleiderer* judgement that access to leniency documents should be assessed by national courts on an individual basis. It must be stressed that both judgments refer to access to the leniency documents of national competition authorities. However, there seems to be no reason that the judgments in the two cases mentioned above would not also affect access to leniency documents in the possession of the EU Commission when so required under Article 15 of Regulation 1/2003.[73] This position was affirmed by the EU Commission itself in the *National Grid* case[74] where it emphasised that Article 15 of Regulation 1/2003 does not prevent national courts from ordering the disclosure of leniency documents according to the *Pfleiderer* ruling.[75]

5.2.3. Court's Intervention under Slovenian Law

In the Republic of Slovenia, there are legal grounds under which private claimants can acquire leniency documents through the intervention of the national court as well. However, it must be stressed that access to the competition authority's file or the administrative court's file in judicial protection procedure is not provided for third parties under the provisions of the SCA.[76] Third parties can thus acquire access to a file only in accordance with the PIAA, where Article 13b(4) of the SCA applies as *lex specialis*.

The first route through which leniency documents can be obtained with the court's intervention is through an administrative dispute against the decision in accordance with the PIAA. In such a case, the national administrative court will have to decide whether the refusal to grant access to public information was

70 Para 43 of the C-536/11 [2013].

71 Paras 44 and 45 of the C-536/11 [2013].

72 Paras 46 and 48 of the C-536/11 [2013].

73 See more about the effectiveness of this route in de Zárate Catón 2013 and Kellerbauer 2014, p. 60-62.

74 Judgment of the English High Court of Justice, Chancery Division, *National Grid Electricity Transmission Plc v. ABB & others*, 4 April 2012, case No. HC08C03243.

75 See more in de Zárate Catón 2013.

76 See Arts. 18 and 60 SCA.

legitimate. The second route is to get the court to intervene in civil proceedings before civil courts. According to the Slovenian Civil Procedure Act[77] (CPA), the court shall order, *ex officio,* a governmental body (competition authority) to deliver a document that is inaccessible to the party. Under this provision, the national court can thus require that the Slovenian competition authority deliver leniency documents. Since there is the possibility that the competition authority will refuse to deliver such a document, the question is what the consequences for this omission are, especially in cases where such a document is the only documentary evidence. According to Article 215 of the CPA, the court's decision as to what consequences for withholding the documents shall be drawn pursuant to ruling on the burden of proof. Due to the fact that the private claimant should prove not only the existence of damage caused, but also the causal link between infringements of competition rules and the damage caused, the non-delivery of such documents would be to his detriment.

Another route through which to obtain leniency documents is Article 227 of the CPA in cases where one party to the proceedings (private claimant) requires a document in the possession of an opposing party to the proceedings (leniency applicant against whom an action for damages is filed) directly. If such documents are in the possession of the leniency applicant, then the national court can order the leniency applicant to deliver it. The leniency applicant can refuse the delivery of the document if excusable reasons provided by Articles 231 to 234 of the CPA exist, i.e. reasons under which witnesses can refuse testimony. Among them, Article 233 especially enables the leniency applicant to refuse to deliver the documents if doing so will result in considerable pecuniary damage. Since compensation for damage in competition cases can be extremely high, it seems that Article 233 offers reasonable grounds upon which a leniency applicant can refuse to deliver a leniency document. If there is an excusable reason on the part of the leniency applicant, then the court will not take the request to deliver the document into consideration. If there are no excusable reasons not to deliver the document, and the leniency applicant does not produce it, then whatever fact the private claimant is attempting to prove with the document is assumed to be proven (Article 227(5) CPA).

Considering the system of the CPA, the above-mentioned routes through which leniency documents can be obtained are applicable only in the course of litigation. The question is whether the CPA enables private claimants to obtain required documents even before the litigation. Article 264, in relation to Article 265, of the CPA refers to the securing of evidence prior to the commencement of civil proceedings if there is a legitimate concern that evidence could not be produced later or that producing said evidence would be more difficult. In this respect, two situations need to be explored. First, where the securing of leniency documents is required from the competition authority, and second, where required from the leniency applicant. In the first situation, there seem to be no grounds for the private

[77] *OJ* RS Nos. 73/2007 (UPB), 45/2008, 11/2008, 57/2009, 12/2010, 50/2010, 107/2010, 75/2012, 30/2013, 92/2013 and 10/2014.

claimant to obtain documents under these provisions, since it would be very difficult for him to prove that it would not be possible to produce the leniency document at a later stage, or that doing so would be more difficult considering that the leniency documents are in the hands of the competition authority. As for the second situation, there could be a legitimate concern that the leniency document would be destroyed by the leniency applicant. However, it must be stressed that this is a specific situation since the leniency document is in the hands of the competition authority as well, but because there is a possibility that such document would not be delivered by the competition authority, it seems that the conditions prescribed by Article 264 of the CPA are met. However, meeting the conditions in Article 264 of the CPA does not necessarily mean that the private claimant would actually obtain the document from the leniency applicant. It has to be emphasised that before litigation the leniency applicant would not be an opposing party in the proceedings, which means that the rules regarding the delivery of evidence as prescribed for other persons are applicable, and not those prescribed for the opposing party.[78] Accordingly, Article 228 of the CPA, under which other persons are obliged to deliver documents only in the following two cases applies: (i) other persons are obliged to deliver documents if there exists such an obligation to deliver them under the law; and (ii) if the content of the required document is related to the leniency applicant and private claimant. Since no such grounds exist on the part of the leniency applicant, it seems that there are also no legal grounds upon which private claimants would be successful in requiring that a leniency document be turned over according to the provision of Article 264 in relation to Article 265 of the CPA.

Although there are ways for the national court to require the disclosure of leniency documents, such disclosure is, under current regulation, barred by the SCA and the Leniency Decree. Therefore, there is no room to apply the balancing test. Consequently, it seems that the present Slovenian law is incompatible with European Union law in light of the CJEU's rulings in *Pfleiderer* and *Donau Chemie*. However, after these two rulings, the Slovenian competition authority and national courts will have to use the balancing test in order to assess the potential disclosure of leniency documents.

6. Directive 2014/104/EU and Disclosure of Leniency Documents

Directive 2014/104/EU was adopted on 26 November 2014 and needs to be transposed into national laws of the Member States by 27 December 2016. Its purpose is mainly to ensure that victims obtain full compensation for the damage suffered due to competition law infringement.[79]

Since it is well acknowledged that private claimants need sufficient evidence and information to prepare a solid claim, Directive 2014/104/EU contains special

[78] Rijavec 2006, p. 534.

[79] See more at Weidt 2014, p. 438-444.

provisions on this issue in Articles 5 to 8, the most important for leniency applicants being Article 6, which regulates sensitive issues on disclosure of leniency documents. Article 6(6) provides that Member States shall ensure that, for the purpose of actions for damages, national courts cannot at any time order a party or a third party to disclose leniency statements. Leniency statements are thus contained in the black list of evidence,[80] meaning that access to them is barred. Directive 2014/104/EU also regulates the destiny of leniency statements in cases where they are obtained by a natural or legal person solely through access to the file of a competition authority. According to Article 7(1) of Directive 2014/104/EU, Member States shall ensure that such evidence is either deemed inadmissible in actions for damages or otherwise protected under the applicable national law in order to ensure the full effect of the limits on the use of such evidence.

It is important to note that access is refused only to leniency statements and not to pre-existing leniency documents as well. According to Article 2(16) of Directive 2014/104/EU, a leniency statement is an oral or written statement voluntarily provided by, or on behalf of, a company or a natural person. The statement, or a record thereof, is presented to a competition authority and describes the company or natural person's knowledge of a cartel and its role therein as drawn up specifically for submission to the authorities with the intention of obtaining immunity or a reduction of fines under the leniency programme concerning the application of EU competition law or national competition law. It is specifically mentioned that a corporate statement does not include pre-existing information. According to Article 2(17) of Directive 2014/104/EU, pre-existing information is evidence that exists irrespective of the proceedings of a competition authority, whether or not such information is in the file of a competition authority.

As for the pre-existing documents contained in the leniency file, the disclosure of evidence shall be limited to that which is proportionate. In determining the proportionality, national courts shall consider in particular three factors: the extent to which the claim or defence is supported by the available facts and evidence; the scope and cost of disclosure; and the nature of the evidence with respect to confidential information (Article 5(3) of Directive 2014/104/EU). In addition, information prepared for or by the competition authority may be disclosed only after the proceeding has been concluded by adopting a decision (Article 6(5) of Directive 2014/104/EU).

Moreover, it provides that the national court shall access leniency statements upon the justified request of the claimant, but for the sole purpose of ensuring that the content is actually a leniency statement. In obtaining such documents, the national court must not provide access to the documents to the other parties or third parties (Article 6(7) of Directive 2014/104/EU).

Considering the case law of the CJEU in the *Pfleiderer* and *Donau Chemie* cases, it could be argued that Directive 2014/104/EU contradicts the balancing test introduced by the CJEU. The balancing test refers to leniency documents in their

80 *Ibidem*, p. 438.

entirety, including statements and pre-existing documents, while Directive 2014/104/EU provides for such balancing for pre-existing documents only. This means that the effect of the CJEU's rulings in *Pfleiderer* and *Donau Chemie* would be short-lived, although for that time important with respect to leniency applicants and private claimants.

7. Conclusion

Public and private enforcement are both important to ensure that competition rules are followed, and assessing which has priority over the other is a difficult task. Competition authorities and courts are faced with two conflicting interests: the right to compensation for the damage caused to the victims of competition law infringement, on the one hand, and the protection of effective public enforcement through the leniency programme, on the other. According to the CJEU's rulings in *Pfleiderer* and *Donau Chemie,* this difficult task has now been shifted to the national courts and tribunals.

Private claimants claiming damages suffered as a result of the infringement of competition rules have very limited ability to obtain leniency documents under Regulation 1049/2001, or none according to the Slovenian access to public information legislation. Therefore, they need to explore other alternatives, those being Article 15 of Regulation 1/2003 when the information is in the possession of the EU Commission, or alternative national routes to obtain information when it is in the hands of national competition authorities. Until Directive 2014/104/EU is implemented, national courts and tribunals shall follow the precedent of the *Pfleiderer* and *Donau Chemie* cases, and thus use the balancing test to determine whether leniency statements and pre-existing leniency documents shall be disclosed.

Bibliography

Ahtik & Vlahek 2011
Ahtik, M. & Vlahek, A., 'Določanje odškodnin v primeru kršitev antitrusta', *Podjetje in delo*, 2011, Vol. 37, p. 1344-1359.

Bratina 2012
Bratina, T., 'Ekonomski vidiki določanja odškodnin v primeru kršitev pravil konkurenčnga prava', *LeXonomica - Journal of Law and Economics*, 2012, Vol. IV, p. 73-90.

Breathnach 2013
Breathnach, S., 'Sweetening the Carrot: The Role of Leniency Programmes in the Fight against Cartels', *European Competition Law Review*, 2013, Vol. 34, p. 12-16.

de Stefano 2012
de Stefano, G., 'Access of Damage Claimants to Evidence Arising out of EU Cartel Investigations: A Fast-evolving Scenario', *Global Competition Law Review*, 2012, Issue 3, p. 95-110.

de Zárate Catón 2013
de Zárate Catón P. G., 'Disclosure of Leniency Materials: A Bridge between Public and Private Enforcement of Antitrust Law', College of Europe, Department of Legal Studies, No. 8, 2013.

Faull & Nikpay 2007
Faull, J. & Nikpay, A., *The EC Law of Competition*, Oxford: Oxford University Press, 2007.

Ferčič 2011
Ferčič, A., 'Das Kronzeugenprogramm im slowenischen Kartellrecht: Grundsätzlich EU-konform, aber in der Praxis fast wirkungslos?', *Wirtschaft und Recht in Osteuropa*, 2011, Vol. 20, p. 110-113.

Howard 2014
Howard A., 'The Draft Directive on Competition Law Damages - What Does it Mean for Infringers and Victims?', *European Competition Law Review*, 2014, Vol. 35, p. 51-55.

Jones & Sufrin 2014
Jones, A. & Sufrin, B., *EU Competition Law (Text, Cases, and Materials)*, Oxford: Oxford University Press, 2014.

Kellerbauer 2014
Kellerbauer M., 'The Recent Case Law on the Disclosure of Information Regarding EU Competition Law Infringements to Private Damages Claimants', *European Competition Law Review*, 2014, Vol. 35, p. 56-62.

Komninos 2006
Komninos, A., 'Public and Private Antitrust Enforcement in Europe: Complement? Overlap?', *Competition Law Review*, 2006, Vol. 3, p. 5-26.

Podobnik 2009
Podobnik, K., 'Komentar k členu 76', in Grilc, P. *et al.* (eds.), *Zakon o preprečevanju omejevanja konkurence s komentarjem*, Ljubljana: GV Založba, 2009, p. 579-599.

Repas 2010
Repas, M., *Konkurenčno pravo v teoriji in praksi: omejevalna ravnanja in nadzor koncentracij*, Ljubljana: Uradni list, 2010.

Rijavec 2006
Rijavec, V., 'Komentar k členu 266', in Ude, L. & Galič, A. (eds.), *Pravdni postopek – zakon s komentarjem*, Part II, Ljubljana: GV Založba, 2006, p. 533-535.

Sanders *et al.* 2013
Sanders, M., Jordan, E., Dimoulis, C., Schwedt, K., DiLuigi, B., Wissen van, M., 'Disclosure of Leniency Materials in Follow-on Damages Actions: Striking "the Right Balance" between the Interests of Leniency Applicants and Private Claimants?', *European Competition Law Review*, 2013, Vol. 34, p 174-182.

Sandhu 2007
Sandhu, S.J., 'The European Commission's Leniency Policy: A Success?', *European Competition Law Review*, 2007, Vol. 28, p. 148-157.

Scharaw 2014
Scharaw, B., 'Commission Proposal for a Directive on Antitrust Damages and Recommendation on Principles for Collective Redress - The Road towards "Private Antitrust Enforcement" in the European Union?', *European Competition Law Review*, 2014, Vol. 35, p. 352–360.

Singh 2014
Singh A., 'Pfleiderer: Assessing its Impact on the Effectiveness of the European Leniency Programme', *European Competition Law Review*, 2014, Vol. 35, p. 110–123.

Slot 2013
Slot, P.J., 'Does the Pfleiderer Judgment Make the Fight against International Cartels more Difficult?', *European Competition Law Review*, 2013, Vol. 34, p. 197-206.

Weidt 2014
Weidt, C.F., 'The Directive on Actions for Antitrust Damages after Passing the European Parliament', *European Competition Law Review*, 2014, Vol. 35, p. 438-444.

Wils 2009
Wils, W.P.J., 'The Relationship between Public Antitrust Enforcement and Private Actions for Damages', *World Competition*, 2009, Vol. 32, p. 3-26.

E. Silvestri

LOST IN TRANSLATION? LANGUAGE DIFFERENCES AND THEIR IMPACT ON EVIDENCE-TAKING IN LITIGATION

1. Introduction

The idea of addressing the topic of the impact of language differences on litigation was prompted by the reading of the essays collected in a special issue of *Erasmus Law Review* under the heading 'Law and Language: Implication for Harmonization and Cross-Border Litigation'. These essays helped me frame some thoughts on the problems that may arise when the *dramatis personae* of a judicial proceeding do not share the same native language.

Language differences can affect litigation in many ways, and most of all in transnational cases or, to use the preferred expression in the EU context, in cross-border cases.[1] Cross-border litigation implies that at least one party to a case will have to litigate in a foreign language, since the rule is that the court language is the official language of the forum state. Whenever international rules on jurisdiction allow the plaintiff to do some forum shopping, they also allow him to engage in language shopping. Therefore, often the defendant is the one who is faced with language obstacles. It is clear that these obstacles must not harm his right to a fair trial, nor must they contribute to delaying the proceedings.

Language differences may arise at the very beginning of a case (just think of the problems brought about by service of process), but in this contribution I would like to make some remarks on the impact of language differences at the evidence-taking level, that is, with reference to the documents that are produced as evidence, and to oral evidence, namely, witness testimony or the interrogation of the party himself, as regards the legal systems - such as the Italian system - in which the parties cannot be heard as witnesses, but are subject to a particular form of examination that in Italy is qualified as 'formal interrogatory'.[2]

1 See in particular Kramer 2012, p. 133-134; Ontanu and Pannebakker 2012, p. 169-186.

2 Arts. 230-232 of the Italian Code of Civil Procedure.

2. The Protection of Language Rights

The problem of language differences and their impact on litigation and on the rights of the parties can be dealt with from different angles. One is to see the problem within the framework of so-called language rights. Scholars have emphasized that 'the concept of language rights is in an embryonic stage only',[3] and, as a matter of fact, it is difficult to offer a clear definition of what is meant exactly by 'language rights', if one steps back from the perspective in which they are often analysed, namely, the protection of minority languages. Social scientists, and scholars in sociolinguistics in particular, have developed different categories of language rights, so as to distinguish between linguistic human rights (LHR) and minority language rights (MLR), both stemming from a common background, the so-called Language Ecology (LE) movement.[4] Sophisticated analyses of these categories do not seem suitable for the purpose of this contribution that revolves around a simple (or maybe simplistic) notion of 'language rights', meaning the right of individuals to express themselves in their native languages, not only in their private lives, but also in their contacts with public authorities.

Language rights are protected in various ways at the national and international level, even though – as mentioned earlier – the protection concerns essentially minority languages. In this regard, at the European Union level it is worthwhile to mention the European Charter for Regional or Minority Languages, which was adopted by the Council of Europe in 1992 and entered into force in 1998.[5] Actually, the Charter is not directly relevant for transnational litigation; rather, it concerns domestic cases handled by the courts of a state in which minority languages other than the official language of the state exist. In any event, it should be of interest to mention Article 9 of the Charter, which lays down some important principles applicable to 'Judicial authorities'. According to this article, the signatory states commit themselves to guarantee that in civil proceedings (a) whenever a litigant has to appear in person before the court, he or she may use his or her minority language, without having to bear additional expenses; and (b) documents and evidence can be produced in the minority language. In both situations, court interpreters or translations must be made available, 'if necessary' says the rule, without any further specifications. Article 9 goes on to provide that the signatory states undertake both to accept the validity of legal documents drafted in the minority language and to allow the documents to be invoked against interested third parties that are not users of the minority language, provided that the content of the documents is made understandable for the third parties themselves.

The reader may find it interesting to hear that Italy signed the Charter only in 2000, even though the protection of minority languages is a constitutional mandate

3 Malksoo 2000, p. 432.

4 See extensively May 2005, p. 319-347.

5 The text of the Charter is available at: <http://www.coe.int/t/dg4/-education/minlang/textcharter/default_en.asp> (last consulted on 12 September 2014). For a commentary, see Dunbar 2001, p. 90-120.

that state authorities are expected to discharge.[6] In 2012, the government then in power announced that a bill for the ratification of the Charter had been presented: unfortunately, the bill got lost in the labyrinth of Italian politics, since – at least to this author's knowledge – it was never adopted as a statute.[7]

More relevant for the problem of cross-border litigation and language differences is what the European Convention on Human Rights says – or, as we shall see, does not say – about the relevance of language in judicial proceedings. Actually, the Convention protects the right to one's language only with reference to criminal proceedings. The relevant principles are laid down by Articles 5 (Right to liberty and security) and 6 (Right to a fair trial). According to Article 5(2), 'Everyone who is arrested shall be informed promptly, in a language which he understands, of the reasons for his arrest and of any charge against him.' Among the 'minimum rights' granted to the individuals charged with criminal offences by Article 6(3) are both the right 'to be informed promptly, in a language which he understands and in detail, of the nature and cause of the accusation against him' and the right 'to have the free assistance of an interpreter if he cannot understand or speak the language used in court'.[8]

Along the lines of the Convention, in October 2010 Directive 2010/64/EU of the European Parliament and of the Council on the right to interpretation and translation in criminal proceedings was adopted.[9] From a general point of view, the Directive lays down several important principles. First of all it bestows an unconditional right to be assisted by an interpreter upon individuals suspected or accused of a crime when they do not speak or understand the language of the forum State. Member States are instructed to recognize and implement this right not only during the development of a criminal proceeding, but also at the stage of police investigations and questioning and in the communications between the suspect (or the accused) and his legal counsel.[10] Similarly, the Directive guarantees the right to a

6 See Art. 6 of the Italian Constitution, according to which 'The Republic shall protect linguistic minorities by means of specific measures' (official translation, available at: <http://en.camera.it/application/xmanager/projects/camera_eng/file/costituzione-aggiornata_EN_10_10_12.pdf> (last consulted on 12 September 2014)).

7 On the ambivalent attitude of the Italian government and Constitutional Court toward the problem of the minority languages spoken in a few areas of the national territory, see Podetta 2012, p. 1-20.

8 The literature addressing the right to a fair trial in criminal proceedings under the Convention is extensive: for a general overview, see, for instance, Rainey, Wicks & Ovey 2014, p. 247-278. With specific reference to the principles mentioned in the text (above), see Danisor 2013, p. 26-31; Rafaraci 2013, p. 331-343; Van Puyenbroeck & Vermeulen 2011, p. 1017-1038; Brems 2005, p. 294-326; Mahoney 2004, p. 107-129; Henrard 2001, p. 15-29.

9 Directive 2010/64/EU of the European Parliament and of the Council of 20 October 2010 on the right to interpretation and translation in criminal proceedings, *OJ* L280 of 26 October 2010, p. 1-7, available at: <http://eur-lex.europa.eu/legal-content/ EN/TXT/PDF/-?uri=OJ:L:2010:280: FUL_L&from=EN> (last consulted on 13 September 2014). On the Directive, see Cras & De Matteis 2010, p. 153-162. Italy implemented the Directive only in 2014, well beyond the deadline set for its transposition: see Gialuz 2012, p. 1193-1206.

10 See Art. 2 of Directive 2010/64/EU, note 9 *supra*.

written translation of all the documents that are 'essential to ensure that [suspected or accused persons] are able to exercise their right of defense and to safeguard the fairness of the proceedings'.[11] Special attention is paid to the quality of interpretation and translation, a quality that Member States are expected to guarantee by 'concrete measures', including the institution of a register of independent translators and interpreters who are deemed to be 'appropriately qualified' and shall be bound by a duty of confidentiality as regards the information gained while providing their services.[12]

No legal basis exists to advocate the applicability of the rights granted by the Directive to individuals who are parties to civil proceedings. As far as the European Convention on Human Rights is concerned, as mentioned above the Convention per se does not guarantee the right to use the language of one's choice in communications with authorities at large; in particular, the Convention does not say anything about language in civil proceedings, even though the principle of 'equality of arms' enshrined in the right to a fair trial as regards the party to a case pending before a court whose language is not the party's own language could come into play. It is true that in civil cases the parties are virtually always represented by their attorneys (I am thinking, for instance, of the Italian legal system, in which litigants in person are almost unheard of), but still there are procedural rules requiring the direct examination of the parties, for instance in family proceedings or in a number of special proceedings, such as some non-contentious proceedings for the protection of the interests of minors and incompetent persons, as well as in a variety of proceedings (before both civil and administrative courts) arising out of immigration law.

Under these circumstances it seems possible to argue that if a party to a litigation is not able to understand some aspects of the proceedings due to his lack of knowledge of the court language (or his limited knowledge of it), the party would suffer a serious disadvantage, in clear disregard of the principle of 'equality of arms', since this principle, in criminal and in civil proceedings as well, implies that 'each party must be afforded a reasonable opportunity to present his case – including his evidence – under conditions that do not place him at a substantial disadvantage *vis-à-vis* his opponent'.[13] Therefore, it does not appear unreasonable to advance the thesis according to which, in certain circumstances, the right to a fair hearing in civil matters should include also the right to an interpreter, as well as the right to have the documents of the proceedings translated, most of all the documents produced as evidence against the party unfamiliar with the court language. To subscribe to this thesis, though, raises at least one delicate issue.

This issue is condensed into a simple question: Who is supposed to bear the risk of the translation? Perhaps here I should clarify my choice of words: when I

11 See Art. 3 of Directive 2010/64/EU, note 9 *supra*.

12 See Art. 5 of Directive 2010/64/EU, note 9 *supra*.

13 See, e.g., *Dombo Beheer B.V. v. The Netherlands* (1993) (Application No. 14448/88, 27 October 1993), at para 33. For a discussion on the case law of the European Court of Human Rights on the ramifications of the right to a fair trial in civil proceedings, see Rozakis 2004, p. 96-106.

speak of the 'risk' of the translation, I make reference to the problem of the quality and reliability of the translation, since we are all well aware that the translation of legal language is extremely difficult and requires special skills. I shall come back to this question shortly; for now, I just wanted to mention that one can debate whether there is a specific right to an interpreter and to the translation of documents in civil proceedings under the 'umbrella' of the right to a fair trial according to the European Convention on Human Rights. It may be worth mentioning that browsing through the case law of the European Court of Human Rights I was able to find only one case hinting at the problem of language in adjudication as a potential obstacle interfering with the principle of 'equality of arms'.[14] In this case, though, the Court rejected the claim of an alleged violation of Article 6(1) of the Convention due to the incompetence of the interpreter assisting the applicant, a German citizen married to a French national, who had been fighting a legal battle over the custody of the children before French courts. According to the Court, no breach of Article 6(1) of the Convention could be found, since the applicant was represented by a lawyer who was equally proficient in French and in German. The lack of the European Court's case law on interpretation and translation as aspects of the right to a fair hearing in civil cases is in sharp contrast with the number of judgments that the Court has rendered on the same issues as regards criminal proceedings: as mentioned above, it is true that the European Convention only mentions the right to the assistance of an interpreter as regards individuals who are charged with a criminal offence, if they cannot understand the court language, but, at the same time, it seems curious that the Court's creativity in interpreting the right to a fair trial has not produced, at least so far, an equivalent right for those who are parties to civil cases and are equally impaired by a lack of knowledge of the language spoken in the proceedings.

3. Interpreting and Translating in Italian Civil Courts: Some Evidence-Related Issues

I shall now turn my attention to the Italian rules that have a bearing on the topic of this contribution. Article 122 of the Italian Code of Civil Procedure provides for a general rule that – I suppose – has been adopted by most legal systems: Italian is the court language, that is, the language in which, the rule says, the entire proceedings must be conducted. Well-established case law clarifies that this rule applies only to the so-called 'procedural acts in the proper sense': they are the judgments and orders issued by the court; the records kept by the clerks, bailiffs, and other auxiliary personnel of the court; the pleadings and motions drafted by the parties; and the minutes of the hearings.[15] Therefore, documents written in languages other

14 *Tiemann v. France and Germany* (2000) (Application No. 47457/99, 47458/99, 27 April 2000), at para B. 3.

15 Among the most recent judgments issued by the Italian Supreme Court (the *Corte di cassazione*) on the meaning of Art. 122 of the Code of Civil Procedure, see Cass. (s.u.) →

than Italian are admissible evidence, and can be produced by the parties freely: specifically, the parties do not have any duty to provide the court with a translation into Italian of the documents drafted in a foreign language. According to Article 123, when documents of this kind are produced as evidence the court may appoint a translator. I draw your attention to the word 'may', which signals the liberty of the judge in charge of the proceedings to choose an alternative way to get acquainted with the content of the document: the judge may rely either on his personal knowledge of the foreign language or on a translation that the interested party (i.e., the party offering the document for evidentiary purposes) supplies. Is this arrangement a sound one? The case law on the rules of the Code of Civil Procedure that I have just mentioned is quite limited, and Italian legal scholars do not pay much attention to them,[16] oblivious of the fact that cross-border litigation, even though it does not crowd the dockets of the courts yet, is a growing trend at least in some parts of the country, which should make one think that the use of documentary evidence written in languages other than Italian is likely to become quite common.

Be that as it may, every possible solution contemplated by the Code (i.e., the appointment of a translator, the reliance on the personal knowledge of the judge, or the acceptance of a 'private' translation supplied by the interested party) brings about a number of problems. The discretionary power of the judge to rely on his own knowledge of the foreign language might seem unusual, if one takes into account the general rule according to which the judge is forbidden to rely on his private knowledge, but he is allowed to take judicial notice of *fatti notori* (well-known facts), as well as of 'factual notions based on common experience'.[17] One must not forget, though, that this rule applies to the facts of the case, facts that the judge can know only through the evidence offered by the parties; on the contrary, the rule does not apply to the mental process that is necessary in order to know the facts of the case through the medium of the evidence aimed at proving these same facts. In other words, in examining a document, whether written in Italian or in another language, the activity performed by the judge is the interpretation of the document itself, and interpretation is, by its very nature, subjective. Therefore, it appears to me that it is not of paramount importance to decide whether the choice by the judge to rely on his personal knowledge of a foreign language is wise and legitimate, while, on the contrary, it is important to emphasize that the judge must grant the parties an opportunity to express their opinions on his translation of the document, most of all if they disagree with the meaning assigned to certain expressions.

02/13/2013, No. 26937; Cass. 12/03/2013, No. 6093; Cass. 16/06/2001, No. 13249, all available (in Italian) at <http://pluris-cedam.utetgiuridica.it> (last consulted on 22 September 2014).

16 The only outstanding exception is Cavallone 1968, p. 271-290: the 'age' of this essay does not detract from the clarity of the analysis that the author devotes to the problems of interpretation and translation in Italian civil procedure.

17 See Art. 115(2) of the Code of Civil Procedure.

Similarly, if a court translator is appointed or the court is satisfied with a 'private' translation offered by the interested party, there should be room for a dialogue both between the parties and between the parties and the judge as to the meaning of the document. I realize that the emphasis I place on such a peculiar application of both the 'right to be heard' (as far as the parties are concerned) and the principle of collaboration between the parties and the court may sound time-consuming and not in line with the tenets of an expedited procedure, but I believe that the special nature of the translation of documents requires a collaborative approach and eventually an agreement reached on the meaning of the document.

I shall return now to the question I mentioned earlier, the question concerning what I called the 'risk of the translation'. Upon reflection, it seems to me that this risk must be accepted as it is: there is no recipe for a perfect translation, since no translator is infallible or, better yet, of a single document several translations equally 'exact' and reliable can be produced. This holds true, in my opinion, especially for legal documents: I am not an expert in linguistics, nor am I able to elaborate on the subtleties of legal discourse, but – based upon my personal experience – I think that whatever translation, even one made by a skilled official translator accredited by the court or by another public authority, can only come close to the authentic meaning of the original document: therefore, if the document is offered as evidence, it is necessary that, one way or another, there is a high degree of consent as to its 'true' meaning.

The same remarks can be made with reference to the interpreter the judge may appoint when a person (either a witness or one party) who does not speak Italian must be heard. The role of the interpreter is even more difficult than the one played by the translator of a document, who has the benefit of a written text as the basis of his task. The interpreter participates in the dynamics of the dialogue at the core of the taking of oral evidence. That is the reason why I think that even if the judge is able to understand the foreign language, he can avoid the appointment of an interpreter only insofar as all the individuals who are present at the hearing (the parties and their lawyers) have the same level of knowledge of the foreign language, so that the dialogical aspect of the process by which oral evidence is taken is preserved.

In the final part of this contribution, I would like to make some remarks that arise from what I discovered about legal translators and court interpreters. When I began my research, a whole world opened up for me. Again, based on my limited experience, I had perceived the difficulties both professionals may face, but certainly I had underestimated the complexities of their tasks, and the different levels of expertise required to carry out functions that are becoming more and more important for the proper administration of justice, not only in criminal cases, but also in civil proceedings. I think that the extent to which a faithful, reliable rendition in the court language of both documentary and oral evidence drafted or expressed in foreign languages can affect the rights of the parties and, in the end, the outcome of adjudication is seriously underestimated, at least in some legal systems. In Italy, for instance, legal translators and court interpreters are not considered experts in the proper sense, but are included in the hazy group of 'assistants' the court may appoint on a case-by-case basis whenever the need arises: according to the Code, they can be individuals 'proficient in certain arts or crafts and, in general, able to carry out activities that [*the court*] cannot perform by itself'.[18] In practice, the law in force does not impose any specific requirements or qualifications for legal translators and court interpreters. While experts in other fields must be appointed from among the professionals listed in special records kept by the courts, often translators and interpreters are appointed randomly, frequently starting from the mistaken assumption that native speakers of foreign languages are by default excellent translators and interpreters. This situation is brought about by several factors, an important one being that in Italy interpreters and translators do not belong to a regulated profession, and therefore there is no regulatory authority in charge of licensing them after an official and serious check of their necessary qualifications. Those who are interested in working as court interpreters or legal translators must apply to the court of the district in which they reside, supporting their applications by qualifications such as diplomas, degrees and the like. Applications are scrutinized by a special board, but the criteria that are supposed to be followed in deciding whether or not applicants can be granted the possibility to be called upon to act as interpreters or translators in civil cases vary from court to court. It must be emphasized, though, that even if the professional status of court interpreters and translators were recognized in an official way, it would be difficult to make these positions attractive: the remuneration is very low,[19] and those who have high qualifications can certainly find more profitable employment.

4. Conclusions

According to UNESCO, 'Language is not only a tool for communication and knowledge but also a fundamental attribute of cultural identity and empowerment, both for the individual and the group. Respect for the languages of persons belonging to different linguistic communities therefore is essential to peaceful cohabitation.'[20] If this statement is deemed worth subscribing to, legal systems should be ready to face the challenges that a multilingual society brings about. One of these challenges is to provide linguistic assistance to individuals who are parties to civil cases but who do not have mastery of the majority language of the forum state: in this regard, Italy still has a long way to go. Unfortunately, while the problem of the quality and reliability of court interpretation and translation has raised some interest, not only in legal circles, but also in public opinion as regards

18 See Art. 68 of the Code of Civil Procedure.

19 According to a tariff that dates back to 2002, the maximum remuneration for court interpreters and translators is € 39 (gross) *per diem*. On the disparaging state of Italian court interpreting and translating services, see Garwood 2012, p. 173-189.

20 See *Education in a Multilingual World*, UNESCO Education Position Paper 2003, <http://unesdoc.unesco.org/images/0012/001297/129728e.pdf>, at p. 15 (last consulted on 25 September 2014).

high-profile criminal cases that have created a stir even in the foreign press,[21] nobody seems aware of the extent that this very problem has in the proceedings pending before civil courts. Therefore, I want to end my essay with a plea that more attention be paid to this issue by legal professionals and legal scholars, but most of all by legislators.

21 Reference is made, for instance, to the trial of the American Amanda Knox, accused of the murder of a British, fellow student Meredith Kercher: the inadequacy of the court's interpreting services was so clear that eventually Ms. Knox decided to give up the interpreter and express herself in her poor Italian. For further details and other examples, see Garwood 2012, p. 180-185.

Bibliography

Brems 2005
Brems, E., 'Conflicting Human Rights: An Exploration in the Context of the Right to a Fair Trial in the European Convention for the Protection of Human Rights and Fundamental Freedoms', *Human Rights Quarterly*, 2005, Vol. 27, p. 294-326.

Cavallone 1968
Cavallone, B., 'Discrezionalità del giudice civile nella nomina del traduttore e dell'interprete', *Rivista di diritto processuale*, 1968, Vol. XXIII, p. 271-290.

Cras & De Matteis 2010
Cras, S. & De Matteis, L., 'The Directive on the Right to Interpretation and Translation in Criminal Proceedings. Genesis and Description', *Eucrim-The European Criminal Law Associations' Forum*, 2010, Vol. 4, p. 153-162.

Danisor 2013
Danisor, D.D., 'Right to a Fair Trial: The Role of the Translator-Interpreter in the Criminal Trial', *AGORA International Journal of Juridical Sciences*, 2013, Vol. 4, p. 26-31.

Dunbar 2001
Dunbar, R., 'Minority language Rights in International Law', *International and Comparative Law Quarterly*, 2001, Vol. 50, p. 90-120.

Garwood 2012
Garwood, C.J., 'Court Interpreting in Italy. The Daily Violation of a Fundamental Human Right', *The Interpreters' Newsletter*, 2012, Vol. 17, p. 173-189.

Gialuz 2012
Gialuz, M., 'Il diritto all'assistenza linguistica nel processo penale. Direttive europee e ritardi italiani', *Rivista di diritto processuale*, 2012, Vol. LXVII, p. 1193-1206.

Henrard 2001
Henrard, K., 'Language and the Administration of Justice: The International Framework', in Deprez, K. *et al.* (eds.), *Multilingualism, the Judiciary and Security Services*, Pretoria: Van Schaik Publisher, 2001, p. 15-29.

Kramer 2012
Kramer, X., 'Introduction: Law and Language; Implications for Harmonisation and Cross-Border Litigation', *Erasmus Law Review*, 2012, Vol. 5, p. 133-134.

Mahoney 2004
Mahoney, P., 'Right To A Fair Trial In Criminal Matters Under Article 6 E.C.H.R.', *Judicial Studies Institute Journal*, 2004, Vol. 4, p. 107-129.

Malksoo 2000
Malksoo, L., 'Language Rights in International Law: Why the Phoenix is Still in the Ashes', *Florida Journal of International Law*, 2000, Vol. 12, p. 431-465.

May 2005
May, S., 'Language Rights: Moving the Debate Forward', *Journal of Sociolinguistics*, 2005, Vol. 9, p. 319-347.

Ontanu & Pannebakker 2012
Ontanu, E.A. & Pannebakker, E., 'Tackling Language Obstacles in Cross-Border Litigation: The European Order for Payment and the European Small Claims Procedure Approach', *Erasmus Law Review*, 2012, Vol. 5, p. 169-186.

Podetta 2012
Podetta, M., 'Il lungo, maldestro surplace del legislatore statale a proposito della tutela delle lingue minoritarie e le recenti aperture regionalistiche del giudice costituzionale' (12 luglio 2012). Available at: <http://www.forumcostituzionale.it/-site/images/stories/pdf/documenti_forum/paper/0335_podetta.pdf>.

Rafaraci 2013
Rafaraci, T., 'The Right of Defense in EU Judicial Cooperation in Criminal Matters', in Ruggeri, S. (ed.), *Transnational Inquiries and the Protection of Fundamental Rights in Criminal Proceedings*, Berlin-Heidelberg: Springer Verlag, 2013, p. 331-343.

Rainey, Wicks & Ovey 2014
Rainey, B., Wicks, E. & Ovey, C., *Jacobs, White and Ovey: The European Convention on Human Rights*, 6th edn., Oxford: Oxford University Press, 2014, p. 247-278.

Rozakis 2004
Rozakis, C., 'The Right to a Fair Trial in Civil Cases', *Judicial Studies Institute Journal*, 2004, Vol. 4, p. 96-106.

Van Puyenbroeck & Vermeulen 2011
Van Puyenbroeck, L. & Vermeulen, G., 'Towards Minimum Procedural Guarantees for the Defence in Criminal Proceedings in the EU', *International and Comparative Law Quarterly*, 2011, Vol. 60, p. 1017-1038.

V. Harsági

EVIDENCE, INFORMATION TECHNOLOGY AND PRINCIPLES OF CIVIL PROCEDURE – THE HUNGARIAN PERSPECTIVE*

1. Role of Principles in Civil Proceedings

Undoubtedly, the development of IT has an impact on every aspect of civil proceedings.[1] This was clearly formulated at the 2007 World Congress of the International Association of Procedural Law: '[The] new technologies have the capacity to change the core values of civil litigation by making litigation more efficient and effective, by making the civil justice system more accessible, and by changing the way we determine the facts and decide the case.'[2] And so at the outset of this contribution it should be noted that the technology of today can provide more than we could ever need with respect to the 'electronification' of judicial proceedings and what could lay the foundations for more effective and up-to-date litigious and non-litigious proceedings while still ensuring the required guarantees. The task of the experts of civil procedural law is to find the limits of the applicability of the technology instead of integrating all technical possibilities into the proceedings without criticism.

When establishing these limits attention should be paid to numerous theoretical and practical aspects, and one should find the 'core' of the procedural rules according to the aim of the proceedings, the basic values the continuity of which must be ensured. In W. Rechberger's words, 'the cultural core of our procedure should not be "sacrificed on the altar of modern technology"'.[3] This does not necessarily mean that the traditional interpretation should prevail and that the basic principles should not be touched; however, it is obvious that it is within this circle of rules that the above-mentioned stable core is to be looked for. For this very

* The conribution was written within the framework of OTKA (Hungarian Scientific Research Fund) research project (registration number K-105559).

1 Sherwin, Feigenson & Spiesel 2006, p. 227.

2 Walker & Watson 2007, p. 122, 142.

3 Rechberger 2008, p. 18.

reason, when analysing this problem it is necessary to carry out a thorough review of basic principles,[4] to be open to modern solutions, but to apply criticism and to search for equilibrium at the same time.

Specific attempts have been made to identify the principles the unchanged nature of which must be guaranteed. In Leipold's view, instrumental principles may be overridden or reinterpreted, e.g. the principles of orality and immediacy.[5] However, the question is far from being that simple; it must be dealt with in a more refined way, for it is difficult to distinguish between basic principles on this ground. For it goes without saying that the principles of orality and immediacy are interrelated with the principle of fair hearing and the basic values of civil procedural law. Only those principles that are of a purely instrumental nature can be replaced (substituted) without affecting the quality of proceedings.[6]

In consideration of the foregoing, it may not be an exaggeration to claim that the development of IT constitutes one of the greatest challenges for procedural cultures deeply rooted in traditions.[7] Citing Lord Woolf's remark on the subject, several authors draw attention to the fact that IT not only contributes to the improvement of the present-day system, but may also serve as a catalyst for radical change.[8]

The question arises as to whether the virtualization of court proceedings is compatible with the traditional principles of procedural law.[9] On reviewing legislative actions concerning electronic proceedings, it is apparent that the legislator has not delved deeply into the question of basic principles. This contribution endeavours to find an answer to the question, In which area do the principles of procedural law related to evidence, the majority of which originate in the 19th century, obstruct the application of IT? and whether it may be justified to review or even redefine these principles in the 21st century.[10] When looking for an answer, the following two basic possibilities must be examined: either one may adjust the limits of electronification to the standard of basic principles or, going beyond this, one may reflect on whether the traditional principles still stand the test of modern times[11] and fulfil the original function they were meant to fulfil in litigation in the era when they were created and incorporated into the systems of procedural law.

During the analysis attention should be paid to the fact that the complex structure of litigious proceedings impedes, to some extent, the application of new information technologies – if only for technical reasons. Court proceedings – as opposed to electronic commerce and even some areas of electronic public

4 Walker & Watson 2007, p. 119.
5 See Iqbal 2002, p. 497.
6 Rechberger 2008, p. 13-14.
7 Walker & Watson 2007, p. 119, 122.
8 Lord Woolf 1996; Gilles 2003, p. 276; *cf.* Marcus 2008, p. 1828-1829.
9 *Cf.* Fischer 2007, p. 186.
10 *Cf.* Gilles 2007, p. 31-32.
11 Fischer 2004, p. 59.

administration – cannot be considered an everyday routine process, but rather an exceptional phenomenon. The extraordinary function of civil litigation constitutes the most important counter-argument against the implementation of all technically possible changes (complete virtualization) in judicial proceedings. G. Kodek thinks that in addition to the technical features there are other aspects that must also be taken into consideration, such as the 'loss of humanity' and the reduction of all the symbolic functions of proceedings that would contribute to the acceptance of judgments.[12]

2. Development of the Field

The first period of the application of IT was still characterized by a traditional approach, which, to some extent, could be traced back to technical limits but, to a greater extent, more so to the traditional approach of experts of civil procedural law. At the beginning, IT was mainly applied in the electronic administration of court affairs. Creating a legal environment for the electronic signature[13] soon rendered the use of the electronic form of documents possible.

The possibilities of electronic data processing in the administration of justice have gradually widened. Today the main possibilities are the following: the possibility of processing texts; the setting up and use of databases (e.g. an electronic database of judgments, summonses by publication on the court's electronic bulletin board on the internet); the use of auxiliary programmes (e.g. for the calculation of maintenance allowances, costs or deadlines) and organizational programmes for connecting offices to the network; the possibility of audio- or videoconferences; the creation of e-files (records), etc.[14]

3. Communication during the Lawsuit: The Principles of Orality and Immediacy

As a starting point, it must be noted that communication during the lawsuit has a two-way impact. In some cases the introduction of IT may restrict the realization of the mentioned basic principles, as automated proceedings presuppose the written form of communication.[15] In other cases the technical possibilities may give new impetus to the realization of orality[16] and they may also contribute to the realization of immediacy. Orality may also be implemented without the need for physical presence via videoconferencing. Or let us consider the situation where the request concerning the taking of evidence is not complied with traditionally but with the help of a videoconference.

12 Kodek 2002, p. 488-489.
13 *Cf.* Stadler 2002, p. 414.
14 *Cf.* Hendel 2002; Selbmann 2005, p. 283.
15 *Cf.* Taruffo 2008, p. 202.
16 Amrani-Mekki 2008, p. 96.

The weight of both orality and immediacy could be enhanced if the visual recording (video recording) of hearings and local inspections could become widespread, and the recording stored digitally as a part of the electronic file could be consulted by the judge before the decision-making several months (or perhaps years) later.[17] The advantages of such a system are obvious: this way the transformation of oral evidence into written evidence could be avoided,[18] as through the judicial intranet the recording would be available to the appeal court, the court could have access and replay it easily. However, the retention of video recordings and access to them may pose a problem from the aspect of data protection.

Orality plays an important role mainly at the hearing, where it also ensures the implementation of the principle of immediacy. In the traditional model of litigation, public control is also mainly guaranteed by the hearing. The hearing (oral proceedings) and the evidentiary proceedings have always been considered the central element, the core of civil litigation.[19] Consequently, they may also be regarded the 'most sensitive' points of proceedings. Any effect on them may concern questions of basic principle directly or indirectly.

Stadler considers that, as a result of technological progress, the culture of court presentations and hearings also undergoes changes.[20] With regard to the evidentiary proceedings, electronic communications widen the pool of the means of evidence. In addition to electronic documents the legal background of which today has become stable, other documents with various file formats[21] (e.g. video and music files) may be presented to the court and easily attached to the electronic file. Moreover, a Power Point presentation (simulation) may render the reconstruction of facts less complicated. However, besides constituting evidence the presentation may also be used as a means of reasoning and persuasion by the lawyer as he or she goes about laying out the case.[22]

The question of orality and immediacy arises primarily concerning the taking of evidence, where during the process of establishing the facts a decisive role is played by the personal conviction of the judge, directly and personally perceived impressions concerning people or objects, which serve as the guarantee for the legitimacy of the decision. Nevertheless, Kodek does not think that most technologies would cause changes in basic principles. The situation is different concerning the use of videoconferences. Kodek's conclusion about the need for a more refined examination of this question is justified: videoconferences only serve as substitutes for personal and direct contact.[23] While in most countries the use of videoconferences in criminal proceedings has been regulated primarily with regard

17 *Cf.* Landoni Sosa 2007, p. 191; Peyrano 2008, p. 168-169.
18 Taruffo 2008, p. 202.
19 *Cf.* Nagel 1967, p. 20; Coester-Waltjen 1983, p. 1.
20 Stadler 2002, p. 443.
21 Benneth 2009, p. 528; *cf.* Sherwin, Feigenson & Spiesel 2006, p. 233-235.
22 Landoni Sosa 2007, p. 189.
23 Kodek 2002, p. 485-486.

to the protection of witnesses, in civil proceedings reasons of cost efficiency play the dominant role. From the aspect of the implementation of immediacy, videoconferences may be described as being somewhere 'halfway'. The hearing and the taking of evidence via a videoconference ensures the realization of immediacy to a greater extent than the records prepared and submitted at the request of the court, yet the possibilities are limited compared to direct perception. The use of videoconferences will increase the 'distance' between the participants in the court action without a doubt, but it may also enhance the role of orality at the expense of the written form.[24] The interposing of a technical device restricts direct perception (technical limit), but it does not mean the interposing of another means of evidence or person or the substitution of another means of evidence for the witness. The witness whose testimony is broadcasted in the courtroom via picture and sound will remain the same witness; similarly, the judge hearing the witness is not being substituted by an intermediary.[25]

In accordance with the principle of immediacy, evidentiary proceedings are usually conducted by the first-instance court during the hearing. The indirect taking of evidence is possible via exceptional means: through a requested court (which may also be a foreign court) or through a dispatched judge if the conduct of the evidentiary proceedings by the first-instance court should cause significant difficulty or disproportionately high extra costs. In such cases, in Hungary the first-instance court addresses the district court in the area in which the persons to be examined reside or where evidence may be most expediently taken (§ 201(1) Hungarian Code of Civil Procedure - HCCP/the Act). The district court operating at the seat of the first-instance court cannot be requested to take evidence.

The possibility of performance of requests on the part of foreign courts outside the European Union to take evidence in Hungary must be adjudged based on the provisions of the Code on Private International Law. Since Hungary's accession to the European Union, Regulations are directly applicable in Hungary. Such a Regulation exists in the area of evidence as well, namely Regulation (EC) 1206/2001 of 28 May 2001 on cooperation between the courts of the Member States in the taking of evidence in civil or commercial matters, which, on entering into force, replaced the Hague Convention of 1970 signed in the same field.

4. The Principle of Free Evaluation of Evidence

Evidentiary proceedings in Hungarian civil litigation are based on the principle of the free evaluation of evidence; they are not regulated by strict methodological rules. In the free evidentiary system it is left to the court to decide which means of proof it will use in order to establish the facts of the case and the application of which method of proof it will find suitable for this purpose; in the free evidentiary system the evaluation of the probative force of the particular evidence is committed

24 *Cf.* Stadler 2002, p. 443.

25 *Cf.* Bachmann 2005, p. 139-140.

to the court's discretion. 'Free evaluation of evidence is necessitated by the general impossibility to establish the probative force of factual proof in advance, therefore, it is more reasonable to entrust it to the court to draw inferences from them about the facts to be proved.'[26]

> *However,* free evaluation of evidence *does not allow unlimited scope of action* either for the parties (the intervening party) or the court. The former are bound by the requirement of the bona fide conduct of the lawsuit and the court is bound by the rules referred to by the Hungarian Code of Civil Procedure as exceptions. The Act restricts the procedure of the court by binding or guiding (programme-like) norms relating to the formal requirements concerning evidence as well as the specific methods of proof and the specific means of proof (or "means of proof"), although to differing degrees. Evidentiary rules are, as a matter of fact, always rules containing formal requirements in the sense that the announcement of the means of proof, the order about the taking of evidence, the dismissal of the application for the taking of evidence, the taking of evidence and the recording of its result and process in the records of the court must be carried out in a predefined order laid down by procedural law.[27]

In the HCCP this is formulated as follows: unless the Act provides otherwise, in civil actions the courts in Hungary are not bound by formal rules of evidence, particular methods of evidence or the use of particular means of proof. They may freely use the pleadings of the parties and all evidence suitable for establishing the facts of the case. These provisions shall not affect statutory presumptions, including the legal rules according to which some circumstance must be regarded true until the opposite is proved (§ 3(5) HCCP). These statements do not fully prevail in Hungarian procedural law, as limitation is caused by certain restrictive elements in this respect, thus, for example, the legally regulated probative force of public documents and private documents having full probative force, the statutory presumptions and the rules relating to the burden of proof, court judgments passed in criminal cases within a circle defined by Sec. 4(2) of the HCCP and prohibitions relating to evidence.

The court establishes the facts of the case based on the comparison of the parties' pleadings and the evidence presented to the court during the evidentiary proceedings; the court assesses all the evidence in its entirety and adjudges it based upon its conviction. The court also has discretion in evaluating, based on a comparison with the data of the case, what importance must be attributed to the fact if a person summoned to appear personally in court did not appear, or the party or the party's representative did not comply with some instruction, did not reply to the question addressed to him or her, or declared that he or she had no knowledge of a fact or did not remember it (§ 206(1)-(2) HCCP).

The adjudication of legal disputes turning into civil action rests on two pillars: the facts of the case and the legal rule (legal rules).[28] The court carries out the

26 Magyary & Nizsalovszky 1924, p. 403.
27 Gáspárdy & Harsági 2009, p. A/23-24.
28 Novák 1997, p. 416.

evaluation of evidence and establishes its probative value (substantive probative force) in order to establish the facts of the case. This is a procedural act performed by the court exclusively. However, the free evaluation of evidence does not result in a judge's arbitrary decision. A guarantee for controlling judicial discretion is constituted by the judge's obligation to provide justification for his or her decision. Consequently, in the judgment the judge must present the established facts of the case with the indication of the related evidence; reference has to be made to the legal regulations on which the court's judgment is founded. Brief mention should be made of the circumstances given priority by the court during the evaluation of evidence, and finally the reasons must be indicated as to why the court did not find some fact proven or why it disregarded the offered evidence (§ 221(1) HCCP).

Free evaluation of evidence is laid down by the HCCP as a general rule, but there are cases when the probative force of some means of proof may be determined in advance, in the abstract. In such cases, based on the Act, during the taking of evidence restrictive elements are applicable, which may only be found as exceptions in modern codes of civil procedure. Free and not so free systems of evidence may also be distinguished based on the key notions of persuasion and conviction. Following this line of thought, we may speak of free evaluation of evidence if the judge accepts as true a fact, regarding the reality of which he or she has become convinced. If the court is obliged to accept a fact as the basis for its judgment, one may speak of restrictions.[29] A decision based on free conviction means that the judge is only bound by generally applicable logical, natural and empirical rules, but otherwise the judge has discretion and he or she is not bound by law when balancing the knowledge acquired by him or her during the proceedings.[30] The process of the development of the judge's conviction must be traceable rationally so that it could stand the test of a hearing at second instance if necessary. In the free evidentiary system, a statement may be deemed proven in the particular case if the court has ascertained its reality. However, the court must not be expected to meet impossible requirements. As absolute certainty is rarely achievable and the possibility of its opposite cannot, as a rule, be completely excluded,[31] the required degree of certainty must be determined in accordance with the practical realities. For a person capable of clearly understanding life relations, this means such a high level of probability that it pushes his or her doubts into the background (but without fully excluding them).[32]

The free evidentiary system is not usually implemented in a thoroughly clear form in practice. The restrictive elements that are necessary concomitants of the free evidentiary system may be divided into two groups depending on whether they are related to the use of the means of proof (of evidence) or the evaluation of evidence. In the first case, the court's activity is determined in relation to *the means of proof to*

29 Sárffy 1946, p. 248-249.
30 Zöller 2002, p. 822.
31 Farkas & Kengyel 2005, p. 65-68.
32 *Cf.* Rosenberg, Schwab & Gottwald 2004, p. 768.

be applied or not to be applied; in the second case, the legislator restricts judicial discretion by pre-defining *the probative force of a specific means of proof.*

Public documents. A paper-based or electronic document issued by the court, a notary public or other authority or administrative organ within their competence and in due form as a public document fully proves the measure or decision laid down by it, the reality of the data and facts certified by it, the making of the statement contained in the document and also the date and the way this is done. The document deemed a public document based on another legal instrument has the same probative force (§ 195(1) HCCP). If any of the above requirements are not met, the document cannot be considered a public document, which, however, does not exclude the possibility of evaluating it as a private document.

Although the probative force of the public document is partly founded on the authority of the person issuing it, another important ground for it is the procedure preceding the issuance of the document.[33] Thus, apart from the person issuing the document it is also of crucial importance - when establishing whether a document may be evaluated as a public document - whether the person or authority entitled to issue the public document has issued the document concerning a matter falling within the scope of that person's authority. Formal requirements relating to public documents vary depending on the type of document.

The public document must be considered authentic until the opposite is proved; nevertheless, the court may - if it finds this necessary - address the issuer of the document *ex officio* to make a statement concerning the authenticity of the document (§ 195(7) HCCP). In accordance with the presumption of authenticity there is no need to prove the authenticity of the public document in case of an apparently flawless document. The document is dubious if it contains, for example, deletions, insertions, gaps, changes executed in violation of the relevant legal rules, and if it has other external deficiencies (e.g. tears, spots, faded writing, etc.). The presumption of authenticity reverses the burden of proof in the event of a party's use of a public document as evidence, in which case the opposing party must prove that the original unadulterated public document is counterfeit or has been falsified. A document is considered counterfeit if it was not issued by the issuer, as opposed to a falsified document, which is authentic as a matter of fact - that is, it was issued by the issuer - but subsequent unlawful changes have been made to it. All documents, including public documents, may be subject to counterproof, but only if this is not excluded or limited by statute (§ 195(5) HCCP). At present, Hungarian law does not contain any rule that would exclude or limit counterproof. Documentary evidence may be rebutted by showing that the document is not suitable for proving the particular fact. Rebuttal may be founded on formal deficiency, external irregularity or it may be directed against the substantive probative force of the document. In the first case just mentioned, the aim to be achieved is to prove that the document is counterfeit or falsified or it was not properly executed, while in the second case, it must be proved that the apparently

33 Hámori 1970, p. 605.

unobjectionable document does not correspond to the intentions of the person making the declaration.[34] Rebuttal may extend to the following: the decision contained in the public document was not passed, the measure contained in the document was not taken, the statement was not made, or these events did take place but at a time, place or in a form different from the one indicated in the document, etc.[35] For rebuttal, any means of proof may be used; however, the rebuttal of public documents is rarely successful in practice.

The above provisions are applicable to foreign public documents as well, provided the foreign document has been endorsed by the Hungarian foreign representation authority having jurisdiction according to the place of issue. In case of an international agreement signed by the Hungarian state to the contrary or based on European Community legal regulation, there is no endorsement requirement.

The issues giving rise to debate concerning text processing by modern office technology or the *appearance of electronic documents*, concern the integrity of their content and the authenticity of such documents. Moreover, one must find answers to further specific questions, e.g. concerning the presentation and safe storage of electronic documents. The problems emerging in this field are different from the ones arising in connection with 'classic' documentary evidence that evolved over centuries in the soil of litigation cultures with divergent historical development and is still grounded in them, although there has been some approximation in recent years. In the field of electronic documents the problems encountered are different. In this case, novelty rendered it possible for European Community regulation to precede national legislation in most Member States. Therefore, it may be concluded that the frameworks of legal regulation of electronic trade and the electronic signature have evolved on uniform grounds, but civil procedural systems holding divergent views have incorporated virtual documents into their evidentiary systems in different ways, sometimes not even evaluating them as documents. Hence, individual systems of civil procedural law provide different responses to the new phenomenon. This difference in reaction also results from the divergence in approaches among the litigation cultures. Consequently, the best way of finding an explanation for such divergence would be to examine the ideas held by the models under analysis about traditional documents.[36]

5. Publicity – Inspection of Documents – Data Protection

In the era of modern IT, electronic publicity has a different meaning than in earlier times. The use of the internet – as a result of its nature – may lead to wider publicity in any case; *it may ensure access to the data of the lawsuit and the litigation materials for a*

34 Balogh 1935, p. 15.
35 Gátos 1999, p. 775-776.
36 For more detail: Harsági 2011, p. 108-117; Harsági 2012, p. 205-213.

substantially wider group of people than publicity taken in its traditional sense would imply.

The question arises as to whether the requirement of public hearings refers only to the courtroom. Is it possible or required to go beyond the traditional interpretation according to which the principle of publicity would mean that apart from the participants to the lawsuit, third parties or outsiders can also be (physically) present at the hearing? Could it be the aim of litigation that, by broadcasting the hearing via the internet, anybody could keep track of it? Could the principle of publicity really mean this in our era? In all circumstances, the answer is no, as the over-extension of the principle of publicity in this direction could cause conflict with other constitutional rights (e.g. data protection, protection of business secrets, personal rights). For this very reason it is also true that technology may offer more possibilities than one should necessarily incorporate into the 'texture' of the rules of civil procedure. It is not easy to strike the right balance in this field though.

Substantially more theoretical and practical problems are generated by the question of possible public access to files and data protection. Providing access to electronic court files may be easily implemented technically and it may have numerous practical advantages. Making the whole of the material of files accessible for anybody is obviously undesirable (from the perspective of data protection). Electronic files may contain content (such as judgments) which may be of 'public importance'. Within this circle the primary question presenting itself could be the need for anonymizing, which, in the majority of cases, may lead to the over-restriction of publicity. On the other hand – despite the main rule of public hearings – in legal literature, for example, one may encounter objections to the electronic publication of case records.[37] This seems closely connected with the question of whether the webcasting of cases should be allowed; therefore the counter-arguments are also similar.

However, a solution must be found to ensure the security of the system from the perspective of data protection and to prevent unauthorized access to electronic court files. During the inspection of documents, access should be recorded and a solution must be found to preserve the integrity of the content of e-files. Another important data protection problem is constituted by files sent by electronic delivery to incorrect (e-mail) addresses, which may occur more easily than in the case of delivery by postal service.

There are several technical possibilities for 'inspecting' electronic court files, e.g. a court office may ensure public access to these documents by printing them; or by forwarding them as electronic documents; or by the installation of a court terminal for the inspection of documents; or perhaps by providing online access to the files so that they could be viewed on the screen of a distant computer. Online access to court files would have numerous advantages both for the court and for those entitled to inspection. For example, it would be possible for multiple persons

[37] Kodek 2002, p. 486.

to have simultaneous access to the same online file for the purpose of reading it and the inspection of files would be possible 24 hours a day; it would not depend on the court timetable. Consequently, the protraction of proceedings partly caused by the transportation of files could be reduced to some extent. As a result of the lists of contents and the search functions provided by the software and applicable to the entire text, some files would become more transparent and easier to handle. Access to information about ongoing proceedings and their different stages would be improved substantially both for the court and for the parties.[38]

6. Principle of Party Control v. Evidence *Ex Officio*

Who takes the initiative and plays an active role during the taking of evidence in the civil lawsuit has a decisive effect on the structure of the lawsuit.[39] In this respect, the Amendment of 1995 to the HCCP provided a new basis[40] for evidence in civil litigation by setting as an objective to ensure the implementation of the principle of party control, and it confined the operation of the law within narrow, precisely defined limits.

During the taking of evidence based on the *principle of party control* it is the parties' responsibility to find the means of proof and present the facts and evidence that are relevant for the resolution of the case to the court. This may also be formulated in the following way: during litigation based on the principle of party control, the legislator imposes the obligation to produce material relating to the lawsuit on the parties. As opposed to this, procedural solutions where this task is partially or fully taken over by the court are based on the *inquisitorial principle*. The Amendment of 1995 abolished the earlier general authorization to take evidence *ex officio*: thus, since this amendment the court has been entitled to order the taking of evidence *ex officio* only based on special authorization.

Among the general principles the HCCP lays down is that the obligation to produce the evidence necessary for the adjudication of the legal dispute - unless it is provided otherwise by statute - forms part of the duties of the parties (§ 3(3) HCCP). Thus, effective statutory regulation basically expects active parties in finding and supplying evidence. Only in exceptional cases is it possible for the court to assume the initiative during the evidentiary proceedings in a civil lawsuit: the court may order the taking of evidence *ex officio* only if it is permitted by the Act (§ 164(2) HCCP). In the absence of the party's express request for the taking of evidence, the court shall not take evidence *ex officio*. This may occur only if it is expressly permitted by legal regulation.[41]

The court shall initiate proceedings in connection with civil disputes when so requested. Such a request (unless otherwise provided for by law) may only be

38 Hähnchen 2005, p. 2258.
39 Magyary 1942, p. 388.
40 Kengyel 2007, p. 99-101; Németh & Papp 2003, p. 665.
41 See *Bírósági Határozatok*, 1999, No. 565.

submitted by a party to the dispute. The requests and legal statements made by the parties shall be binding upon the court. The court shall take into consideration the requests and statements made by the parties according to their content, rather than their formal arrangement. A request for the performance of the taking of evidence or the court's decision ordering the taking of evidence shall not be binding upon the court. The court shall not order the taking of evidence if deemed unnecessary for rendering a decision in the dispute. The court must forego the ordering of the taking of evidence if the party has submitted the request for evidence taking in delay for reasons within the party's control, or if the request is presented contrary to good faith (§ 3(1)-(2), (4) HCCP).

When analysing the content of the principle of party control two elements must be emphasized. Beyond doubt, its most important manifestation is the initiation of the legal action itself, in which party control prevails. According to the modern conception of civil procedure, this means that 'the court should provide legal protection only if so requested by the party, but in that case, the court is by all means obliged to provide this protection'.[42] The right to initiate legal action is granted to the holder of a substantive right. However, some exceptions may be found to this rule, namely, when the actual claimant and the formal claimant are different persons.[43] Based on statutory authorization, the prosecutor, for example (see: § 9 HCCP), or a particular organization (e.g. the guardianship authority) may also be entitled to initiate legal action. Besides the principle that legal proceedings may be commenced only at the request of the parties pursuant to the above, mention should also be made of the principle of the court's being bound by the parties' request, which is, in fact, a result of a negative approach to the principle of party control, since, according to the principle of party control, the parties' autonomy extends not only to their right to initiate legal action, but also to the fact that the court is obliged to carry out certain procedural acts based on a request of the party concerned - even in ongoing proceedings.

A basic principle the content of which contrasts with that of the principle of party control is the principle of officiality (*ex officio* proceedings), which is rarely afforded a role in modern codes of civil procedure. The principle of *ex officio* proceedings prevails, for example, in the following situations. Pursuant to § 78(2) of the HCCP, the court shall decide *ex officio* as to court costs, unless the successful party asked the court not to adopt a decision concerning the court costs. Pursuant to § 153(3) of the HCCP, in an action for child maintenance, if deemed necessary, the court may adopt a decision of its own motion for awarding temporary support payments. If the identity of the person signing the electronic document issued with, at least, an advanced signature or the authenticity of the document is doubtful, the court shall, in the first place, address the authentication service provider issuing the certificate for the electronic signature. In case of doubt concerning the time stamp

42 Magyary & Nizsalovszky 1924, p. 229.
43 For more detail, see: Kengyel & Harsági 2013, p. 326.

attached to the electronic document, the court shall, in the first place, address the service provider carrying out the time stamping (§ 197(4) HCCP).

7. Specialities - Order for Payment Procedure

Act No. 50 of 2009 provided the order for payment procedure with completely new foundations in Hungary. Similar to most European countries in Hungary it has been possible to have recourse to the order for payment procedure exclusively in order to enforce pecuniary claims since the entry into force of these provisions.[44] The order for payment procedure has as such been transformed into a non-litigious procedure where the issue of the order for payment may take place *without the examination of the legal basis or proof of the claim*.[45] After the order for payment procedure acquired legal force, it also fell within the competence of the notary public to order its enforcement. An innovation which has an essential influence on the character of the procedure is constituted by electronic, automated processing. The explanation to the Act refers to a computer system to be set up as a 'nationally uniform computer system', which contains and automatically processes declarations and documents relating to order for payment procedures. All notaries public are granted direct access to the computer system. They carry out their procedural acts through this system, electronically. The automated system creates the decisions during the proceedings always on behalf of the 'proceedings' notary public, and the decisions bear the name and the stamp of the given notary public. According to the explanation, the notary public is liable for the decision so issued in his or her name. The parties and their representatives are also granted access to the system so that they can directly register their submissions in the internet-based system (on a Web surface). The processing of applications is automated, in other words the computer system can carry out the procedural acts without requiring human participation if the statutory conditions for this are met. The acts performed in this way are to be regarded as measures taken by the proceedings notary public.

8. Summary

To summarize, we could say that the use of IT does not have the same impact on all basic procedural principles; problems may arise to a greater extent with respect to some principles and to a lesser extent with respect to others. At the same time, in recent years as a result of modern technology several procedures have become available that could – in the event of the incorporation of the appropriate legal guarantees – serve the better realization of some principles. This may lead us to the

44 In accordance with the Hungarian law, for a long time it was possible to enforce two types of claims by the order for payment procedure: firstly, pecuniary claims and, secondly, claims directed at the surrender of personal property. This was not a common solution in international comparison.

45 Szécsényi-Nagy 2010, p. 853.

relative reconstruction of some traditional principles. Problems present themselves more intensively concerning litigious proceedings and to a lesser degree in the case of non-litigious or, at least, some types of non-litigious proceedings. However, both the experts of procedural law encouraging change and those holding more conservative views are likely to agree that IT may generate positive changes concerning both the procedural input and the output (the forwarding of petitions, service of documents, issuance of official copies, administration). Stronger differences in opinion concern the hearing itself accompanied by questions of procedural law relating to it, that is, the problem of the virtualization of the hearing.

Bibliography

Amrani-Mekki 2008
Amrani-Mekki, S., 'El impacto de las nuevas technologías sobre la forma del proceso civil', in Carpi, F. & Ortells Ramos, M. (eds.), *Oralidad y escritura en un proceso civil eficiente,* València: Universitat de València, 2008, p. 93-133.

Bachmann 2005
Bachmann, G., '"Allgemeines Prozessrecht" – Eine kritische Untersuchung am Beispiel von Videovernehmung und Unmittelbarkeitsgrundsatz', *Zeitschrift für Zivilprozeß,* 2005, p. 133-159.

Balogh 1935
Balogh, B., *Az okirati bizonyítás egynémely kérdése a bírói gyakorlat megvilágításában,* Debrecen: Városi ny., 1935.

Benneth 2009
Benneth, S.C., 'Records Management: The Next Frontier in E-Discovery?', *Texas Tech Law Review,* 2009, p. 519-528.

Coester-Waltjen 1983
Coester-Waltjen, D., *Internationales Beweisrecht,* Ebelsbach am Main: Verlag Rolf Gremer, 1983.

Farkas & Kengyel 2005
Farkas, J. & Kengyel, M., *Bizonyítás a polgári perben,* Budapest: Közgazdasági és Jogi Könyvkiadó, 2005.

Fischer 2004
Fischer, N., *Justiz-Kommunikation,* Berlin: Verlag für Wissenschaft und Forschung, 2004.

Fischer 2007
Fischer, N., 'E-Justice in Germany. Critical Comments about "Electronification" of Civil Litigation and Civil Justice', in Storme, M. *et al.* (eds.), *The Recent Tendencies of Development in Civil Procedure Law – Between East and West,* Vilnius: Justitia UAB, 2007, p. 177-186.

Gáspárdy & Harsági 2009
Gáspárdy, L. & Harsági, V., 'Alapvető elvek', in Petrik, F. (ed.), *Polgári eljárásjog. Kommentár a gyakorlat számára,* Budapest: HVG-Orac, 2009, p. D/85-102/12.

Gátos 1999
Gátos, G., 'A bizonyítás', in Németh, J. (ed.), *A Polgári perrendtartás magyarázata,* Budapest: Közgazdasági és Jogi Könyvkiadó, 1999, p. 645-821.

Gilles 2003
Gilles, P., 'Zur beginnenden Elektronifizierung von Zivilgerichtsverfahren und ihrer Verrechtlichung in der deutschen Zivilprozessordnung durch Sondernormen eines neuen "E–Prozeβrechts"', in Kiss, D. & Varga, I. (eds.), *Magister artis boni et aequi. Studia in honorem Németh János,* Budapest: ELTE Eötvös Kiadó, 2003, p. 271-285.

Gilles 2007
Gilles, P., 'Civil Justice Systems in East and West 2007 Plus – Fundamental Current Reform Movements and Some Speculations about Civil Conflict Resolution Systems of the Future', in Storme, M. *et al.* (eds.), *The Recent Tendencies of Development in Civil Procedure Law – Between East and West,* Vilnius: Justitia UAB, 2007, p. 26-42.

Hámori 1970
Hámori, V., 'Okirati bizonyítás a polgári perben', *Jogtudományi Közlöny,* 1970, p. 599-606.

Hänchen 2005
Hähnchen, S., 'Elektronische Akten bei Gericht – Chancen und Hindernisse', *Neue Juristische Wochenschrift,* 2005, p. 2257-2259.

Harsági 2011
Harsági, V., 'Trends of Development of Documentary Evidence in Civil Litigation – Comparative Analysis', in Zhang, B. (ed.), *Proceedings of the 3rd International Conference on Evidence Law and Forensic Science. Part 2,* Beijing, China: Institute of Evidence Law and Forensic Science - CUPL, 2011, p. 108-117.

Harsági 2012
Harsági, V., 'Documentary Evidence in Comparative Perspective', in Geimer, R., Schütze, R.A. & Garber, Th. (eds.), *Europäische und internationale Dimension des Rechts. Festschrift für Daphne-Ariane Simotta,* Wien: LexisNexis, 2012, p. 205-213.

Hendel 2002
Hendel, D., 'Der moderne Zivilprozess zwischen Mensch und Maschine – elektronische Akte, summarisches Verfahren und langfristige Reform des Zivilprozesses', JurPC Web-Dok. 68/2002, Abs. 10. Available at: <http://www.jurpc.de/aufsatz/20020068.htm>.

Iqbal 2002
Iqbal, Y., 'Bericht über die Diskussion zum Thema "Der Zivilprozess und neue Formen der Informationstechnik"', *Zeitschrift für Zivilprozeß,* 2002, p. 491-499.

Kengyel 2007
Kengyel, M., 'Recent Developments in Hungarian Civil Procedure', in Storme, M. *et al.* (eds.), *The Recent Tendencies of Development in Civil Procedure Law – Between East and West,* Vilnius: Justitia UAB, 2007, p. 94-103.

Kengyel & Harsági 2013
Kengyel, M. & Harsági, V., 'Hungary - Civil Law', in Eliantionio, M. *et al.* (eds.), *Standing up for Your Right(s) in Europe. A Comparative Study on Legal Standing (Locus Standi) before the EU and Member State Courts,* Cambridge/Antwerp/Portland: Intersentia, 2013, p. 322-344.

Kodek 2002
Kodek, G.E., 'Der Zivilprozeβ und neue Formen der Informationstechnik', *Zeitschrift für Zivilprozeß,* 115 Band, Heft 4, 2002, p. 445-490.

Landoni Sosa 2007
Landoni Sosa, Á., 'New Information Technologies in Civil Procedure. Synthesis Report', in Pellegrini Grinover, A. & Calmon, P. (eds.), *Direito Processual Comparado,* Rio de Janeiro: Editora Forense, 2007, p. 186-197.

Lord Woolf 1996
Lord Woolf, *Access to Justice. Final Report,* 1996.

Magyary 1942
Magyary, G., 'Magyar perjogi reformmozgalmak', in Magyary, G., *Összegyűjtött dolgozatai,* Budapest: Magyar Tudományos Akadémia, 1942, p. 3-19.

Magyary & Nizsalovszky 1924
Magyary, G. & Nizsalovszky, E., *A magyar polgári perjog,* Budapest: Franklin, 1924.

Marcus 2008
Marcus, R.L., 'The Impact of Computers on the Legal Profession: Evolution or Revolution?', *Northwestern University Law Review,* 2008, p. 1827-1867.

Nagel 1967
Nagel, H., *Die Grundzüge des Beweisrechts im europäischen Zivilprozeβ,* Baden-Baden: Nomos, 1967.

Németh & Papp 2003
Németh, J. & Papp, Z., 'Ungarn', in Nagel, H.. & Bajons, E.-M. (eds.), *Beweis – Preuve – Evidence. Grundzüge des zivilprozessualen Beweisrechts in Europa,* Baden-Baden: Nomos, 2003, p. 661-688.

Novák 1997
Novák, I., *Tényállás a polgári perben,* Magyar Jog, 1997.

Peyrano 2008
Peyrano, J.W., 'La prueba entre la oralidad y la escritura', in Carpi, F. & Ortells Ramos, M. (eds.), *Oralidad y escritura en un proceso civil eficiente,* València: Universitat de València, 2008, p. 149-173.

Rechberger 2008
Rechberger, W.H., 'Die Auswirkung des Einsatzes der Informationstechnologie im Zivilprozess auf die Prozesskultur', in Kengyel, M. (ed.), *Das elektronische Zivilverfahren in der österreichischen und ungarischen Justiz,* Pécs: Dialóg Campus, 2008, p. 9-18.

Rosenberg, Schwab & Gottwald 2004
Rosenberg, L., Schwab, K.H. & Gottwald, P., *Zivilprozeßrecht*, München: Beck, 2004.

Sárffy 1946
Sárffy, A., *Magyar polgári perjog,* Budapest: Grill, 1946.

Selbmann 2005
Selbmann, R.H., *Das Mahnverfahren – Außergerichtlicher und gerichtlicher Forderungseinzug und konventionelles und automatisiertes Mahnverfahren*, 3rd edn., Freiburg: Heufe, 2005.

Sherwin, Feigenson & Spiesel 2006
Sherwin, R.K., Feigenson, N. & Spiesel, C., 'Law in the Digital Age: How Visual Communication Technologies Are Transforming the Practice, Theory and Teaching of Law', *Boston University Journal of Science and Technology Law,* 2006, p. 227-270.

Stadler 2002
Stadler, A., 'Der Zivilprozeβ und neue Formen der Informationstechnik', *Zeitschrift für Zivilprozeß*, 115 Band, Heft 4, 2002, p. 413-444.

Szécsényi-Nagy 2010
Szécsényi-Nagy, K., 'A fizetési meghagyásos eljárás', in Varga, I. (ed.), *A polgári nemperes eljárások joga,* Budapest: ELTE Eötvös Kiadó, 2010, p. 844-945.

Taruffo 2008
Taruffo, M., 'Orality and Writing as Factors of Efficiency in Civil Litigation', in Carpi, F. & Ortells Ramos, M. (eds.), *Oralidad y escritura en un proceso civil eficiente,* València: Universitat de València, 2008, p. 185-204.

Walker & Watson 2007
Walker, J. & Watson, G.D., 'New Technologies and the Civil Litigation Process. Common Law – General Report', in Pellegrini Grinover, A. & Calmon, P. (eds.), *Direito Processual Comparado,* Rio de Janeiro: Editora Forense, 2007, p. 119-151.

Zöller 2002
Zöller, R., *Zivilprozessordnung,* 23rd edn., Köln: Verlag Otto Schmidt, 2002.

T. Ivanc

THE POTENTIAL IMPACT OF ELECTRONIC PROCEEDINGS ON TRADITIONAL PRINCIPLES OF CIVIL PROCEDURE - THE SLOVENIAN EXPERIENCE

1. Introduction

Until recently, new means of information and communication technology (ICT) had a limited effect on traditional civil procedure. Currently, new methods for storing, gathering and disseminating data are being considered by the courts, and using digital technology in courtrooms has become a reality. However, the incorporation and use of new technologies does not merely signify a technical challenge; it has an impact on traditional procedural values and, moreover, procedural and especially evidentiary rules. While the use of electronic technology in civil proceedings may promote efficiency and raise the quality of civil proceedings, the focus on efficiency should not overshadow the perceived legitimacy of the proceedings.

Civil procedure is selective as regards the information that can be considered in court actions. It provides for rules, which the court has to follow when reaching its decision.[1] Civil proceedings consist of a series of acts by the parties and the court. These acts are performed simultaneously or consecutively, and the civil procedural rules determine the ensuing procedural consequences.[2] The principle of legality is the basic criterion for the admissibility or inadmissibility of procedural acts.

The use of modern technology may improve the functioning of some traditional procedural principles if appropriate legal guarantees are provided. One of the main concerns is whether ICT, as a generator of swift proceedings and simplified solutions, will influence the right of access to justice and comprehensively contribute to the judicial protection of rights and the efficiency of litigation.

Due to recent developments in the use of ICT in different fields of everyday life as well as in the field of justice, the concept of e-justice used in the frameworks

1 Juhart 1961, p. 2.
2 Dika 2008, p. 1.

of both European procedures and national justice systems should be further defined. E-justice could be broadly defined as covering the use of ICT in all fields of justice. In the European context,[3] an e-justice system should provide the following functions: 1. Access to information in the field of justice;[4] 2. 'Dematerialization' of cross-border judicial and extrajudicial proceedings;[5] and 3. Communication between judicial authorities.[6] At the national level, EU Member States have yet to make significant changes, according to the Report by the Council Working Party on Legal Data Processing (E-justice) (hereinafter The Report), written in 2007.[7] The Report shows that only half of the Member States have implemented technical standards for electronic communication and maintaining electronic documents as well as for enabling electronic access to case files. Moreover, while the use of videoconferencing (VCF) in civil proceedings is possible in more than half of the Member States, the rate of use of this technology is consistently lower than 10 per cent.[8]

The impact of the use of ICT can be examined for the different stages of civil proceedings:

- gathering evidence and preparing the statement of claim;
- filing the claim with the court;
- the exchange of briefs and documents;
- the preparatory hearing;
- the main hearing; and
- delivering the judgment.

In the Slovenian Civil Procedure Act (*Zakon o pravdnem postopku* (CPA)),[9] there is no need for the plaintiff to meet specific requirements before filing the claim,[10] but

3 Notices from European Union Institutions and bodies, Multi-Annual European E-justice Action Plan 2009-2013 (2009/C 75/01), *OJ* L C 75/1, 31.3.2009, available at: <http://eur-lex.europa.eu/LexUriServ/LexUriServ.do?uri=OJ:C:2009:075:0001:0012:EN:PDF> (last consulted in May 2015).

4 Access to information is an important theme in European legislation and case law as well as that of the Member States. See n. 3.

5 'Dematerialization' involves electronic communication between a court and the parties to the proceedings, in particular in order to implement European instruments adopted by the Council. See n. 3.

6 Communication between judicial authorities should be simplified by introducing e.g. videoconferencing. See n. 3.

7 Council of the European Union, Report by Council Working Party on Legal Data Processing (E-justice), Brussels, 5 June 2007, available at: <http://register.consilium.europa.eu/-doc/srv?l=EN&f=ST%2010393%202007%20INIT> (last consulted in May 2015).

8 See further n. 3.

9 Official Gazette RS, No. 73/07 - official consolidated text, 45/08 - ZArbit, 45/08, 111/08 - odl. US, 57/09 - odl. US, 12/10 - odl. US, 50/10 - odl. US, 107/10 - odl. US, 75/12 - odl. US, 40/13 - odl. US, 92/13 - odl. US in 10/14 - odl. US.

10 In the Anglo-American system, more precisely in the United States, discovery dominates the process of fact-finding. The centre of gravity in the fact-finding process has shifted from trial →

there is a question as to whether the parties may submit electronic evidence at this stage in order to comply with their duty to produce evidence.

Although the evidentiary rules of the Slovenian CPA apply to all evidence and the evidence-taking procedure, the introduction of ICT in the proceedings raises special problems.

The questions with respect to the presentation of digital evidence regard the impact of ICT on the definition of a document and whether the carrier of the relevant information is of significance. Are audio and video recordings or digital images to be regarded as documents, or are they within the scope of an inspection as a means of evidence? In addition, how does the principle of the free evaluation of evidence relate to the evaluation of the credibility and authenticity of electronic documents and information produced and stored by electronic means?

Digital evidence must, as any other form of evidence, meet certain requirements in terms of the integrity of the electronic document and the identification of its author. A variety of issues may be considered within this context, such as the legal standards ensuring the trustworthiness of the documents (a legal requirement), the authenticity of electronic evidence, or digital archiving. However, these issues are not the subject of this contribution.

A significant question that needs to be discussed here is how digital information is or should be evaluated by the court and whether there is a need for the creation of new procedural rules of evidence-taking in this respect (examples of digital evidentiary materials include e-mails, computer data, electronic records, audio or video recordings of party or witness statements and personal information on social networks). This evaluation is closely linked to court culture, the ways of communication between the parties and the court (electronic filing and service), and the use of videoconferencing for the holding of court hearings.

The evidentiary stage is the core of civil litigation and it is directly linked to the question of special principles of evidence-taking. The main result of the introduction of electronic proceedings is certainly a shift from strictly fixed proceedings, recorded on paper, to dematerialized, more flexible proceedings.[11]

The use of 'e-justice' not only requires modifications in court organization, but also serves as a ground for the traditional principles of civil procedure to be re-examined.

Problems with the applicability of ICT especially arise in cross-border cases, as the different procedural structures in national jurisdictions and the tendency to use VCF is encouraged by EU civil judicial cooperation instruments. Specifically, obtaining evidence is more complicated when it has to be obtained from another country; barriers can be created by the physical distance between the court and the person to be examined.

to discovery and thereby from the courtroom to the lawyer's office. The process of fact-gathering in civil litigation has been privatized with the minimum of court intervention. Verkerk 2010, p. 136.

11 De Resende Chaves Junior 2012, p. 116.

2. Relationship between the Law and New Technologies

The general theory on the relationship between the law and new technologies in civil procedure[12] emphasizes that it could be characterized as potentially conflicting.[13] This conflict arises from the objectives of both subject areas. While the objective of civil procedure is to normatively ensure basic, regular and general methods for the protection of the substantive rights of the parties, technology serves as a functional tool and is 'outcome oriented'.[14] While the law is used for the regulation of technology, it also employs ICT to pursue its own goals. Technology may thus operate as an auxiliary tool for better achieving a legal aim.[15]

The placement of ICT in regulated court environments requires sets of formal rules, and a range of activities must be given legal or valid effect. Formal regulation is needed in terms of filing claims via online systems, and hearings held via VCF, as well as electronic service of court documents; which means that the validity of such procedural acts is judged from a legal perspective and not merely from a technological perspective, which enables the functionality and efficiency of individual e-justice services.[16] Therefore, ICT may change the contents of constitutionally protected human rights (for example, the right to privacy),[17] but the law must provide adequate rules to protect specific legal interests. In some cases, the use of ICT implies the need to re-frame traditional[18] concepts or to draw on new[19] concepts of court proceedings.

12 Lupo & Bailey 2014, p. 356, available at: <http://www.mdpi.com/2075-471X/3/2/353> (last consulted on 14 July 2014). Velicogna stresses that interaction between technology and highly regulated courts may lead to negative results. Velicogna 2008, available at: <http://www.coe.int/t/dghl/cooperation/cepej/series/Etudes7TIC_en.pdf> (last consulted on 14 July 2014).

13 There is an extensive body of literature discussing the relationship between the law and technology: Hildebrandt 2009; Cockfield 2004, p. 383-415; Cockfield & Pridmore 2007, p. 475-513; Tranter 2011, p. 754-762.

14 Mohr & Contini 2011, p. 998.

15 Palmerini 2013, available at: <http://www.robolaw.eu/RoboLaw_files/documents/-Palmerini_Intro.pdf> (last consulted on 14 July 2014).

16 The entanglement of formal rules and technology is analysed in three case studies illustrating different approaches using ICT: Money Claim Online, handling small claims in England and Wales; Civil Trial Online, a project developed in Italy to digitize all civil proceedings; and speed cameras used in Australia. See Mohr & Contini 2011, p. 994-1019.

17 Recent developments in information technology threaten privacy and have consequently reduced control over personal data. Easy access to personal data may result in a range of negative consequences.

18 Harsági argues that the use of modern technologies may lead to the 'relative reconstruction of some traditional principles' and that the impact is more intense in litigious proceedings than in non-litigious proceedings. Harsági 2012, p. 125-133.

19 In the paper 'Proceedings on the Web' the author claims that it is not adequate to import classic principles of paper proceedings into electronic proceedings and, in addition, suggests seven new principles adapted to electronic proceedings: namely the principles of 'immateriality', 'connection', 'intermediality', 'interaction', 'hyper-reality', 'instantaneousness' and 'de-territorialization'. De Resende Chaves Junior 2012, p. 110 *et seq*.

Scholars[20] argue that new principles and legal rules should be defined and drawn from the experience (or at least the anticipation) of using specific technologies.[21] The important question is which basic principles correspond to the new dimensions offered by ICT. The sections that follow will give a critical review of the use of ICT and its influence on civil procedure.

2.1. *The Use of Videoconferencing and the Question of the Oral Character of Procedural Acts*

VCF, the telephone, and audio recordings could be considered oral elements of civil proceedings. It could be argued that with new ICT the principle of orality has gained new content. If the new technologies enable renewed orality, they promote orality as well, but an orality that is 'depersonalized'. With the use of VCF, depersonalization can occur due to the lack of personal contact between the subjects (court and parties) acting in the proceedings.

VCF represents a combination of both written and oral elements in the court's procedural activities. The recordings of the main hearing may be considered written elements. Such recordings offer numerous advantages, since they can be heard again for the assessment of the evidence if there are doubts as to what was said, or even if there are doubts as to the manner in which it was said. Orality is also guaranteed. Since VCF can be used at geographically distant places, the main characteristic is that physical contact with the parties, witnesses or experts is absent. Proceedings held by VCF respect orality and publicity, but not the actual presence of the parties, the witnesses or the experts.

According to Slovenian law, witnesses give statements and are examined orally (Article 238 CPA). Parties may submit written statements of the witnesses if the court orders them to do so or at the request of the parties (Article 236(a) CPA). Furthermore, experts may give their opinions orally or in written form, depending on the court's decision (Article 253 CPA). The interesting question in practice regards the admissibility of witness or expert statements recorded on video and submitted by a party as written statements. Could such recordings be regarded as documents or should other rules apply, e.g. the rules on inspection of evidence by the court?

If the rules on inspection are applied, the video recording would need to be authenticated, which means that a witness familiar with the video content (e.g. the person who captured the video images) would probably have to be examined. Another approach would be to verify by using the opinion of an expert whether the images have been altered in any improper way. In contrast, the reliability of written witness statements could be examined by inviting the relevant witnesses to give oral testimony about the content of their written depositions.

20 Székely, Szabó & Vissy 2011, p. 180-194.

21 *Ibidem*, p. 182-183.

The Slovenian CPA regulates the use of VCF in civil proceedings (Article 114(a)) and the possibility of direct service (including electronic service) between counsel of the parties in civil proceedings (Article 139(a)). The law contains only one provision regarding the use of VCF for main hearings, and this provision also relates to the examination of parties, witnesses and experts.

With the consent of the parties, the court has the right to allow the parties and their counsel to be at another place at the time of the hearing and to perform procedural acts there, provided that audio and video transmissions have been provided for between the site of the hearing and the place, or places, where the party (parties) and their counsel are located, and vice-versa. In the event that the court decides that a hearing will be made via a VCF system, it issues a decision against which there is no appeal. This is an option and not an obligation for the courts. VCF eliminates the cost of travelling long distances, and consequently reduces the time needed for justice to be effectively administered. VCF is certainly a new form of orality by which a hearing is held at a distance. This method is also explicitly authorized under Regulation (EC) No. 1206/2001 on cooperation between the courts of the Member States in the taking of evidence in civil or commercial matters (hereinafter 'The Regulation').[22]

The Regulation provides that the requesting court may ask the requested court to use communication technology for the taking of evidence, in particular, VCF and teleconferencing (sound transmission). If the court in Slovenia directly hears a witness situated in another Member State by means of a video-link, the use of VCF is allowed only if the conditions stated in Article 17 of the Regulation are met. This means that the procedure for the direct taking of evidence of the requesting court would apply.[23] If the hearing of a witness is executed by the requested court, then the taking of evidence could be realized through the representatives of the requesting court and the parties via VCF (Article 12). The requesting court may also request the participation of court representatives according to the conditions set by the requested court (Article 12(3) and (4)). Since the Slovenian CPA allows the taking of evidence via VCF, the only impediment to the implementation of such a request may be the lack of technical equipment at the courts.

In Slovenia, there are at present no rules on how to use VCF in civil litigation. This lack of regulation is important because there are some significant differences between face-to-face civil litigation in the courtrooms and the main hearing held via VCF. One good example of a better practice is the English Videoconferencing Guidance in Annex 3 of Practice Direction 32,[24] [25] which covers the use of VCF equipment both (a) in a courtroom, whether via equipment which is permanently placed there or via a mobile unit, and (b) in a separate studio or conference room.

22 *OJ* L174 of 27 June 2001, p. 1-24.

23 Galič 2010, p. 93-94.

24 Videoconferencing Guidance in Annex 3 of Practice Direction 32. Available at: <https://-www.justice.gov.uk/courts/procedure-rules/civil/rules/part32/pd_part32#annex3> (last consulted on 23 April 2014).

25 Kawano 2012, p. 23.

The guidance applies to cases in which VCF is used for the taking of evidence and to its use for other parts of any legal proceedings (e.g. interim applications, case management conferences, pre-trial reviews). The guidance also contains some important remarks for courts using VCF. It states that although the use of VCF may be an ideal means of saving time and money, it is, however, 'inevitably not as ideal as having the witness physically present in court'. There is also guidance for the judge when deciding about the use of VCF in a particular case. The judge needs to consider whether the use of VCF will enable an overall cost saving, i.e. 'whether its use will be likely to be beneficial to the efficient, fair and economic disposal of the litigation'. There are considerably greater limitations in the degree of control that the court may exercise when having a witness physically present than when having a witness giving a statement at a remote site.[26]

When we recall the traditional principle of orality, we can see that the use of new technologies may influence the basic elements of this principle. It seems that the traditional need for the physical attendance of the parties, witnesses and experts is eclipsed. Even a court inspection via VCF could become a reality. The principle of the traditional written form has already been influenced by ICT, at least to a limited extent in some procedures in the Slovenian judicial system. The e-Justice portal allows electronic enforcement, electronic land register entries, and electronic insolvency proceedings; in some cases the use of electronically prepared forms is obligatory. Furthermore, the CPA introduced the (promising) possibility of audio and video recordings of hearings (e-hearings). Thus, Article 125(a) of the Slovenian CPA determines that the presiding judge may order the audio or video recording of the hearing, in which case the judge will inform the parties and the other participants at the hearing.

Currently, the common practice of Slovenian courts is to make an audio recording of the hearing of witnesses, the parties or, in particular, court experts, while the entire main hearing is not recorded. In accordance with the rules mentioned above, clerks transcribe the audio recordings and transcriptions are then served to the parties.

Certainly, it may also be stated that audio recordings disburden the judge in terms of removing the need of dictating the party, witness and expert statements for the record at the main hearing. Furthermore, the parties, their representatives, witnesses and experts are not interrupted when stating their thoughts for the court record.

2.2. *Adversarial System or Equality of Arms*

An important question is whether new technologies also favour respect for the adversarial procedure.

Generally speaking, procedural rules should make a swift resolution of the dispute possible. This is *inter alia* connected with the cost efficiency of the

26 Videoconferencing Guidance in Annex 3 of Practice Direction 32.

proceedings. A decision, taken by one party, regarding the type of evidence needed in order to prove certain facts will affect the costs of the civil action.[27] The question of costs is also affected by the willingness of the parties to invest in the process of fact-finding,[28] in which, for example, travel costs of a witness or costs for photocopies of documents for the court and opposing parties may be incurred.[29] In complex cases, it would be cost efficient if evidence were delivered to the court electronically.

Under Slovenian law, electronic documents are admissible as evidence. From a theoretical perspective, a document represents any object on which a human thought is expressed in writing.[30] According to the CPA, the rules that apply to the evidential value of electronic documents are the same as those that apply to that of ordinary, written and public documents used as evidence (Article 224(1)).[31] For the evidential value of electronic documents, the Electronic Commerce and Electronic Signature Act (ZEPEP)[32] prohibits any discrimination against the electronic form and specifies that electronic data must not be denied validity or evidential value simply because they are in electronic form (Article 4 ZEPEP). The condition for equal treatment is that electronic data are accessible and suitable for future use.

An example of what could be an adversarial procedure reinforced by the use of new technologies can be found in the Civil Procedure Rules and Practice Directions of England and Wales, under which the e-filing of documents is a reality.[33] The Rules allow for three methods of electronically filing documents: by e-mail,[34] via Online Forms Service and via Electronic Working Scheme.[35]

If a system further enabled access to electronic documents by the parties and the court, the adversarial principle would be guaranteed. Since digitization makes retrieval so straightforward, parties can have full access to statements and recorded interviews or opinions of experts. All examinations of witnesses and documents can be filed with the court in digitized form.

27 More details on the (in)efficiency of the adversarial principle can be found in Verkerk 2010, p. 329-355.

28 *Ibidem*, p. 345.

29 Galič & Wedam Lukić 2005, p. 65.

30 Ude 2002, p. 265; Juhart 1961, p. 369; Rosenberg, Schwab & Gottwald 2004, p. 814.

31 In contrast, Rüßmann argues that electronic documents with declarations in an electronic form lack the necessary embodiment of the written expression and, as such, electronic documents used as a form of evidence are not subject to the rules on documentary evidence, but to the rules governing inspection. Rüßmann 2012, p. 329.

32 Official Gazette RS, No. 98/04, 46/14.

33 Gascón Inchausti 2012, p. 151-154.

34 However, a party must not use e-mail to take any steps in a claim for which a fee is payable.

35 Where a party files a document electronically, the party must not send a hard copy of that document to the court. A document is not filed until the transmission is received by the court, regardless of the time shown as to when the document was sent. For more: The practice directions to the Civil Procedure Rules – Practice directions 5B – Electronic communication and filing of documents, available at: <https://www.justice.gov.uk/courts/procedure-rules/civil/rules/part05/pd_part05b> (last consulted on 12 February 2015).

The adversarial system in electronic proceedings will certainly be more intense and authentic if the electronic filing of claims, defences and evidence (witness and party statements, expert opinions) could be made available and accessed through an e-system.[36] Such paperless proceedings would lead to a higher quality of legal protection.[37]

2.3. *Electronic Service of Documents*

Closely linked to the adversarial principle is the service of documents. Therefore, how this principle is affected by electronic service should be examined. A necessary condition for the exercise of the right to be heard is that the party becomes aware of an act in respect of which he has a right to be heard. Thus, an important procedural institution, which ensures a right to be heard, is the service of process.

In Slovenia, electronic service of process is legally equivalent to traditional service if a secure electronic channel via a computer system is used by the organization that operates the electronic service. E-service can be used for court documents (e.g. judgments) that originate in physical form, but the electronic document must have been made on the basis of a physical original. Additionally, an electronic document has to be equipped with a secure electronic signature of the court, certified by a qualified certificate.

The address of a secure e-mail post box will be considered to be equal to the address of the party's residence or registered office (Article 132 CPA). If a party submits a document by secure electronic means, that party will be considered to accept documents served by secure electronic means until the party informs the court of the contrary. If the court has found the service of process to a secure e-mail post box to be impossible, the document will be served in physical form, and the reasons for such service will be given. Service of process by electronic means to a secure e-mail post box is mandatory if state authorities, lawyers, notaries, enforcement officers, court experts, court assessors, court interpreters, official receivers and other official persons and bodies are concerned.

Since service by electronic means, unlike the conventional methods of service, is not disruptive and does not interfere with the parties' privacy, the time of the day at which electronic service is allowed is not limited.

Assuming that the court would use only e-service for the service of documents, there are no reservations with regard to a judge issuing the judgment only in an electronic form. Article 323 CPA states that the judgment issued in electronic form will be signed by the presiding judge by means of his or her secure electronic signature and a secure electronic signature of the court certified by a qualified certificate. If the secure electronic signature of the presiding judge is

36 'In the United States, final statements sent by electronic methods contain links to evidential documents.' Amrani-Mekki 2008, available at: <http://www.uv.es/coloquio/-coloquio/ponencias/6tecmek2.pdf.> (last consulted on 17 July 2014).

37 Gottwald 2012.

certified by a qualified certificate of the court, a secure electronic signature of the court will not be required.

Any judgment issued in physical or electronic form may be delivered to the parties by way of a certified or electronic (scanned) transcript, or in electronic form. However, this option applies only to current procedures that are included in the Slovenian e-Justice portal. Litigation and special procedures under the Civil Procedure Act (for example, the procedure for issuing an order for payment) are not included in this system.

2.4. *Free Evaluation of Evidence*

'Free evaluation of evidence' implies that all evidence is admissible, and there are no formal rules for the assessment of evidence. There is no limitation on the means of evidence, with the result that parties may propose any evidence, not only that which is foreseen in the CPA.

Witness testimony is the most commonly used means of evidence in Slovenian civil proceedings. However, it is also considered to be the most unreliable means of evidence.[38] Thus, the factors affecting the reliability of witnesses are evaluated, and the most trusted way for examining the reliability of a witness is thought to be an oral examination, which also allows for the observation and consideration of the witness's body language. Consequently, and according to the main rules, witnesses are always to be examined orally in court, because the hearing of a witness at a distance via videoconferencing might pose problems for the evaluation of the witness's statements by the judge in the sense of gaining an overall impression of the witness. Therefore, judges in civil proceedings are usually very conservative when it comes to the use of VCF.

2.5. *Electronic Form versus Paper or Physical Form*

The question arises as to whether digital (electronic) documents should be judged differently than traditional (written) documents. When comparing electronic and paper documents, courts certainly need to recognize the changing nature of documentation. Electronic evidence appears in many forms, including electronic documents, audio and video recordings, digital images, e-mails, web content and more. Each form of electronic documentation has its distinctive technical characteristics, which may give rise to particular procedural issues also connected to the question of reliability and authenticity.[39] With e-mail, electronic signatures can be used to prove authorship, and other technical data may provide proof of the source of certain files. With audio and video recordings, possible witnesses with knowledge of the circumstances under which the evidence was produced, including

38 Zobec 2006, p. 435.
39 O'Neill, Sentilles & Brinks 2012.

the author of the recording, may give evidence. Furthermore, experts may also be needed to give opinions about the authenticity of the recording in question.

Generally speaking, procedural rules offer little guidance on how electronic evidence needs to be assessed when its authenticity is in question. Slovenian courts apply standard evidentiary rules and procedures to electronic evidence and make determinations about its probative value on a case by case basis.

As mentioned earlier, in theory,[40] a document can be defined as any object on which a human thought is expressed in writing. Consequently, what the material substrate of the document is and what it is composed of are irrelevant. The significant characteristic is the expression of a thought.[41]

All the same, electronically stored information differs from traditional documents. It includes metadata,[42] system data,[43] deleted data and legacy data.[44] [45] Electronic documents reflect dynamic forms of communication and the exchange of information between individuals through e-mails, text messages and chatroom communications; digital images; website content, including social media postings; computer-generated data; and computer-stored records. In comparison to paper documents, electronic documents last longer and are more easily changed, and they contain additional information about the document itself.

Digital evidence may be defined[46] as 'any information of probative value that is either stored or transmitted in a digital form'. It includes files stored on a computer hard drive, digital video, digital audio, network packets transmitted over local area networks, etc.[47] In Slovenia, the submission of evidence via microfilm, or an electronic copy of a document, or by reproduction of such a copy, will be regarded as equal to the submission of evidence via a document in physical form, or an electronic copy or reproduction thereof, which has been issued by a competent state authority, self-managing local community or a body exercising public powers. Consequently, photographs, photocopies, video recordings, electronic disks, magnetic tapes and other similar data carriers are considered physical evidence as long as they were not obtained illegally or unethically. As with a physical document, microfilm or electronic copies or reproductions of these copies can be proven to differ from the original document.

When starting from the definition that a 'document' represents any object on which human thought is expressed, then an electronic document would seem to fall into the category of documentary evidence. Some opinions hold that in cases in

40 Ude 2002, p. 265; Juhart 1961, p. 369; Rosenberg, Schwab & Gottwald 2004, p. 814.

41 Zobec 2006, p. 419.

42 Metadata provide information about electronic resources and are indispensable for their localization. Kavčič-Čolić 2010, p. 99-119.

43 System data relate to the performance of a computer task, such as which website a user has visited, which password has been used, which documents have been printed, etc. Curreri 2005, p. 15544.

44 Legacy data represent stored information which is no longer in use. *Ibidem*.

45 *Ibidem*, p. 15543-15544.

46 Morgan Whitcomb 2002, available at: <www.ijde.org> (last consulted on 14 January 2015).

47 Zhang & Chen 2012, p. 305.

which specialist knowledge is required to establish the authenticity of electronic documents, the rules of expert evidence apply.[48] In the study 'The admissibility of electronic evidence in court'[49] carried out in 16 countries,[50] four terms were analysed: evidence, electronic evidence, admissibility of evidence and admissibility of electronic evidence. In all of the countries concerned, the results of the analysis of the legislation show that electronic evidence is considered equivalent to traditional evidence. The majority of countries[51] permit electronic evidence and give it the same value as ordinary documentary evidence. None of the participating countries define exactly what electronic evidence is.

In cases in which it is debatable whether a document is authentic, the court often consults experts. Challenges to the reliability of an electronic document mean that more complex or unusual forms of data require more elaborate knowledge and impose more obstacles for the court in establishing the authenticity and integrity of a proposed piece of evidence. A party may also have difficulty in proving that information found on the Internet (e.g. via Facebook, Twitter, etc.) represents the truth. It has been emphasized that parties seeking to introduce information from the Internet would do well to provide evidence establishing the credibility of the website from which the information is drawn, particularly if the source is a government site that carries an official imprimatur.[52] [53]

3. Conclusion

New technologies are modern methods of expression in court proceedings. They appear to bring speed and quality to the procedure. They speed up communications and efficiency in the exchanges between the parties and the court. The new technologies could also contribute to a fair and equitable procedure with respect for the adversarial principle. The adversarial system in electronic proceedings will certainly be more intense and authentic if the electronic filing of claims, defences and evidence (witness and party statements, expert opinions) could be executed and accessed through an e-system.

48 Rüßmann states that electronic declarations of intent lack the necessary embodiment of a written expression of thoughts. Rüßmann 2012, p. 250.

49 The main objective of the project was to answer the following questions: What is electronic evidence? Is electronic evidence regulated in Europe? European Commission, Cybex: The admissibility of electronic evidence in court, available at: <https://www.itu.int/-osg/csd/cybersecurity/WSIS/3rd_meeting_docs/contributions/libro_aeec_en.pdf> (last consulted on 14 January 2015).

50 Germany, Austria, Belgium, Denmark, Spain, Finland, France, Greece, the Netherlands, Ireland, Italy, Luxembourg, Portugal, the United Kingdom, Romania and Sweden.

51 Germany, Belgium, Spain, Finland, France, Ireland, Italy, Luxembourg, Portugal and Romania.

52 Chorvat 2007.

53 Thus, the important question is also: To what extent can the Internet be used as a source of information and consequently to what extent can it be used as evidence in civil proceedings? In connection with that question the main problem is: Can all the information found on the Internet be regarded as public knowledge?

However, it remains necessary to determine the place of ICT next to the oral and written elements of procedural acts. It could be argued that with new ICT the principle of orality has gained new momentum. Above all, the civil procedural rules when using new technologies have to overcome the obstacle of breaking direct contact between the parties and the court. This depersonalization will influence the principle of immediacy and the contact between the judge and the source of evidence. A proceedings held by videoconference respects orality and publicity, but not the presence of the parties in court, thus the new technologies reveal the risk of losing a physical link that is essential for efficiency in litigation. As far as the use of videoconferences is concerned, these would be useful in cases where the distance is such that the cost of travel is disproportionate to the benefits of immediacy.

An important issue is to what extent the existing principles and evidentiary rules should apply not only to traditional paper-based documents, but also to electronic documentary evidence. One can argue that an ICT-neutral approach should be adopted, so that the term 'documentary evidence' should apply to traditional paper-based documents and to electronic documents. This would mean that there would be no fundamental differences in the application of the law of evidence to traditional paper-based documentary evidence and electronic evidence. For documentary evidence, there is a need for a clear definition of a document. The law of evidence of course must continue to accommodate the traditional notion of a document, since such documents will continue to be relevant to court proceedings. However, the concept of document must also be updated to accommodate electronically generated information or information stored in electronic form. Generally, countries do not include in their legal codes a specific definition of what electronic evidence is and consequently electronic evidence is considered to be equivalent to traditional evidence.

For the suggested changes, we would like to speak in favour of the adaptation of national regulations toward changes that add specific rules for a distinct definition of electronic evidence. There should also be rules on minimum standards at the international level. There is certainly a need to develop European rules that would guarantee at least a minimum unified approach in the treatment of electronic evidence in civil procedure.

Bibliography

Amrani-Mekki 2008
Amrani-Mekki, S., 'The Impact of the New Technologies on the Shape of Civil Procedure'. Available at: <http://www.uv.es/coloquio/coloquio/ponencias/-6tecmek2.pdf>.

Chorvat 2007
Chorvat, T.J., 'E-Discovery and Electronic Evidence in the Courtroom, A Primer for Business Lawyers', *Business Law Today*, 2007, Vol. 17(1), p. 13.

Cockfield 2004
Cockfield, A.J., 'Towards a Law and Technology Theory', *Manitoba Law Journal*, 2004, Vol. 30, p. 383-415.

Cockfield & Pridmore 2007
Cockfield, A. & Pridmore, J., 'A Synthetic Theory of Law and Technology', *Minnesota Journal of Law, Science and Technology*, 2007, Vol. 8(2), p. 475-513.

Curreri 2005
Curreri, S.M., 'Defining Document in the Digital Landscape of Electronic Discovery', *Loyola of Los Angeles Law Review*, 2005, Vol. 38, p. 1541-1590.

de Resende Chaves Junior 2012
de Resende Chaves Junior, J.E., 'Proceedings on the Web', in Kengyel M. & Nemessanyi, Z. (eds.), *Electronic Technology and Civil Procedure*, Dordrecht-Heidelberg-New York-London: Springer, 2012, p. 101-124.

Dika 2008
Dika, M., *Građansko parnično pravo, Parnične radnje*, Zagreb: Narodne novine, 2008.

Galič 2010
Galič, A., 'Komentar 114.a člena ZPP', in Ude, L. & Galič, A. (eds.), *Pravdni postopek: Zakon s komentarjem*, Book 4, Ljubljana: Uradni list Republike Slovenije, GV založba, 2010, p. 91-94.

Galič & Wedam Lukić 2005
Galič, A. & Wedam Lukić, D., 'Komentar 7. člena ZPP', in Ude, L. & Galič, A. (eds.), *Pravdni postopek: zakon s komentarjem*, Ljubljana: Uradni list Republike Slovenije, GV založba, 2005, p. 65-83.

Gascón Inchausti 2012
Gascón Inchausti, F., 'Electronic Service of Documents National and International Aspects', in Kengyel, M. & Nemessanyi, Z. (eds.), *Electronic Technology and Civil Procedure*, Dordrecht-Heidelberg-New York-London: Springer, 2012, p. 137-180.

Gottwald 2012
Gottwald, P., 'Introduction', in Kengyel, M. & Nemessanyi, Z. (eds.), *Electronic Technology and Civil Procedure*, Dordrecht-Heidelberg-New York-London: Springer, 2012, p. ix-xiv.

Harsági 2012
Harsági, V., 'Digital Technology and the Character of Civil Procedure', in Kengyel, M. & Nemessanyi, Z. (eds.), *Electronic Technology and Civil Procedure*, Dordrecht-Heidelberg-New York-London: Springer, 2012, p. 125-133.

Hildebrandt 2009
Hildebrandt, M., 'Technology and the End of Law', in Claes, E., Devroe, W. & Keirsbilck, B. (eds.), *Facing the Limits of Law*, Dordrecht: Springer-Verlag, 2009, p. 443-464.

Juhart 1961
Juhart, J., *Civilno procesno pravo Jugoslavije*, Ljubljana: Univerzitetna založba Ljubljana, 1961.

Kavčič-Čolić 2010
Kavčič-Čolić, A., 'Metapodatki za trajno ohranjanje elektronskih virov', *Knjižnica*, 2010, Vol. 54(1-2), p. 99-119.

Kawano 2012
Kawano, M., 'Electronic Technology and Civil Procedure - Applicability of Electronic Technology', in Kengyel, M. & Nemessanyi, Z. (eds.), *Electronic Technology and Civil Procedure*, Dordrecht-Heidelberg-New York-London: Springer, 2012, p. 3-27.

Lupo & Bailey 2014
Lupo, G. & Bailey, J., 'Designing and Implementing e-Justice Systems: Some Lessons Learned from EU and Canadian Examples', Laws 2014, 3. Available at: <http://www.mdpi.com/2075-471X/3/2/353>.

Mohr & Contini 2011
Mohr, R. & Contini, F., 'Reassembling the Legal: The Wonders of Modern Science in Court-related Proceedings', *Griffith Law Review*, 2011, Vol. 20(4), p. 994-1019.

Morgan Whitcomb 2002
Morgan Whitcomb, C., 'Historical Perspective of Digital Evidence: A Forensic Scientist's View', *International Journal of Digital Evidence*, 2002, Vol. 1(1), p. 1-9, available at: <www.ijde.org>.

O'Neill, Sentilles & Brinks 2012
O'Neill, K., Sentilles, D. & Brinks, D., 'New Wine in Old Wineskins? New Problems in the Use of Electronic Evidence in Human Rights Investigations and Prosecutions' - Report prepared under the auspices of the Bernard and Audre Rapoport Center for Human Rights and Justice, 2012. Available at: <http://www.crl.edu/sites/-default/files/d6/attachments/pages/Rapoport-E-evidence-report.pdf>.

Palmerini 2013
Palmerini, E., 'The Interplay between Law and Technology, or the RoboLaw Project in Context', in Palmerini, E. & Stradella, E. (eds.), *Law and Technology: The Challenge of Regulating Technological Development*, Pisa: Pisa University Press, 2013. Available at: <http://www.robolaw.eu/RoboLaw_files/documents/Palmerini_Intro.pdf>.

Rosenberg, Schwab & Gottwald 2004
Rosenberg, L., Schwab, K.H., & Gottwald, P., *Zivilprozessrecht*, 16th edn., München: C.H. Beck, 2004.

Rüßmann 2012
Rüßmann, H., 'Electronic Documents. Security and Authenticity', in Kengyel, M. & Nemessányi, Z. (eds.), *Electronic Technology and Civil Procedure: New Paths to Justice from Around the World. Ius Gentium: Comparative Perspectives on Law and Justice*, Vol. 15, Dordrecht-Heidelberg-New York-London: Springer, 2012, p. 233-260.

Székely, Szabó & Vissy 2011
Székely, I., Szabó, M.D. & Vissy, B., 'Regulating the Future? Law, Ethics, and Emerging Technologies', *Journal of Information, Communication & Ethics in Society*, 2011, Vol. 9(3), p. 180-194.

Tranter 2011
Tranter, K., 'The Laws of Technology and the Technology of Law', *Griffith Law Review*, 2011, Vol. 20(4), p. 754-762.

Ude 2002
Ude, L., *Civilno procesno pravo*, Ljubljana: Uradni list, 2002.

Velicogna 2008
Velicogna, M., 'Use of Information and Communication technologies (ICT) in European Judicial Systems', European Commission for the Efficiency of the Justice, 2008. Available at: <http://www.coe.int/t/dghl/cooperation/cepej/series/-Etudes7TIC_en.pdf>.

Verkerk 2010
Verkerk, R.R., *Fact-Finding in Civil Litigation. A Comparative Perspective*, Antwerp-Oxford-Portland: Intersentia, 2010.

Zhang & Chen 2012
Zhang, B. & Chen, H., 'Applications and Trends of Digital/Electronic Evidence in Chinese Litigation', in Kengyelm M. & Nemessanyi, Z. (eds.), *Electronic Technology and Civil Procedure*, Dordrecht-Heidelberg-New York-London: Springer, 2012, p. 305-323.

Zobec 2006
Zobec, J., 'Dokazi in izvajanje dokazov', in Ude, L. & Galič (eds.), A., *Pravdni postopek: zakon s komentarjem*, 2nd book, Ljubljana: Uradni list Republike Slovenije, GV založba, 2006, p. 327-528.

TYPES OF EVIDENCE IN CIVIL LITIGATION

F. Hoogers
F. Fernhout
H. Jans
R. Mertens
V. Poels

WITNESS TESTIMONY IN DUTCH CIVIL PROCEDURE: FACTS, FIGURES AND STATISTICAL RELATIONS

1. Introduction

When it comes to assessing the administration of justice it is likely that there is a consensus about one thing: the justice system needs to be efficient. A higher investment of time and money than strictly necessary is disadvantageous for citizens, the government and economic interests. Thus the complaints that adjudication takes too long.[1]

Efficiency is largely dependent on the way the administration of justice is organized; it depends primarily on the procedural model. Researchers often look at the time proceedings take, for a short procedure is beyond doubt an efficient one.[2] However, this is not enough: a judge deciding a case by rolling the dice will hardly need any time for his decision, but the result is a judgment of meagre quality. The best way to assess in an objective manner whether (an aspect of) a justice system is efficient is therefore to look for factors that influence the efficiency of proceedings and assess their working. In that way, the question whether quality is suffering under the desire to have an efficient procedure can be taken into account.

This empirical study is about witness examinations in Dutch civil procedure in commercial cases.[3] Examining witnesses is part of giving evidence or – seen from a more inquisitorial point of view – finding the truth. It is therefore a crucial part of civil procedure. Dutch civil procedure is only partly adversarial and is strongly modelled towards efficiency by giving the court extensive powers to determine the course of the proceedings. A procedural model such as this, aiming at a quick judgment, harbours the risk of inaccuracy. This is a real risk in Dutch procedure

1 Frissen 2012, p. 2. See also Van Rhee 1997, p. 57-67.
2 Wemmers 1995.
3 These are the cases for which no specific procedure has been prescribed (Art. 78 CCP, Code of Civil Procedure; hereafter CCP), including all monetary claims not based on family law. In court practice, the term 'commercial cases' is common, but not very precise.

since, especially compared with common law countries, there is not that much room left for the parties during witness examination.[4] Observing witness examinations in Dutch courts can be useful in determining whether overzealousness plays too big a role.

This contribution will start with a description of civil procedure in commercial cases. Next, the four indicators that were used to assess witness examinations in Dutch courts will be introduced. What follows is a brief description of the research design, the research method and the actual research, with mention of some of the difficulties that had to be overcome in order to gain access to public hearings.

In the last part, the results of this research will be summarized. On the basis of the four different indicators introduced, some detailed information on witness examination can be given. Graphs and charts will illustrate the conclusions that follow from the data. Based on these data, some concluding statements will be made about the efficiency of witness examinations in Dutch civil procedure, followed by a few recommendations.

2. Dutch Civil Procedure

2.1. *Two Basic Principles of Dutch Civil Procedure*

Dutch civil procedure strikes a balance between two conflicting principles, that of autonomy for the parties and case management by the court. Unfettered adversariality would lead to procedures going on forever, but an over-inquisitorial court would violate the freedom of the parties to determine their mutual relations under civil law.

Therefore, party autonomy is restricted to the extent of the dispute the court has to decide. It is up to the parties to decide on the contents of the claims, the nature and scope of the defences and the facts that support them. The court itself has a passive role in this respect; it may only base its judgment on facts that have been put forward by the parties. Uncontested facts have to be accepted as true.[5] The court is not allowed to investigate facts that have not been stated.[6] However, the court has to supplement the parties' legal arguments if these can be upheld by relying on other legal provisions.

The procedure itself is the domain of the court. The judge is the 'master of the procedural universe'. The judge sets time limits for each step in the proceedings and decides whether or not further evidence is needed. Obviously, the judge operates within the limits of procedural law, which means that within a certain context the judge may have an obligation to order evidence. The judge also fully decides on what will have to be proved by which party.

4 Rueb 2011, p. 169-170.
5 Art. 149 CCP.
6 HR (Supreme Court) 9 September 2011, *LJN* BR1653: the court is not allowed to 'google'.

2.2. *Post-defence Hearing Model*

The procedural model is simple and elegant. It is labelled as the 'post-defence hearing model'.

The procedure is commenced by a writ of summons drafted by the plaintiff and served by a bailiff on the other party.[7] There is no prescribed form, but the writ of summons should describe all facts and all available evidence in sufficient detail. The plaintiff is even bound to mention and refute the arguments put forward by the defendant in the pre-procedural phase, which is labelled as 'the duty of substantiation'.[8] Next, the defendant has the opportunity to present his side of the debate in the statement of defence.[9]

In practice, in 75 per cent of the cases these two documents are enough to order a post-defence hearing.[10] The hearing is ordered in an interlocutory judgment, which if necessary announces the issues that will be on the agenda of the hearing and orders the parties to submit supplementary documentary evidence. The parties are usually ordered to appear in person.[11]

At the hearing there is an open discussion between the court, usually a single judge, and the parties aimed at establishing the facts and exploring the possibilities of reaching a settlement. Surveys on the success rate of reaching a settlement show a success rate varying from 32 per cent to 50 per cent.[12] If the case is not settled, a date is set for judgment. This judgment could be a final judgment, but frequently an order is given to supply further evidence by witness testimony. An interlocutory judgment like this is also used to appoint one or more experts or to announce a court visit to a specific place.[13]

2.3. *Sieve Model*

The court functions as a sieve with regard to the facts. When it comes to establishing the facts, we could therefore speak of a 'sieve model'.

To support their position, both parties state a number of facts. Some of these facts will be undisputed or admitted by the other party, but obviously some facts will be asserted by one party and disputed by the other. In the interlocutory judgment, the court will select the applicable legal rules and apply those to the case.

7 Arts. 111-124 CCP. Procedures can also be initiated by a petition (Art. 261(2) CCP) or a referral (e.g. Art. 486 CCP). These procedures will not be dealt with here, since they apply to another type of cases.

8 Art. 111(3) CCP; for the term see Snijders 2011, p. 47.

9 Art. 128 CCP.

10 Verschoof 2004, p. 339. To fully understand Dutch civil procedure in first instance commercial cases, it should be borne in mind that the concept of a 'trial' does not apply. There may be several hearings, but there is no 'trial' as the central event of civil proceedings.

11 Snijders 2011, p. 50.

12 Van der Linden 2008, p. 48.

13 Rueb 2011, p. 129.

Here is the sieve at work, because many facts, undisputed or not, will turn out to be irrelevant in the light of the applicable law.[14]

If the relevant facts that remain are all undisputed or admitted, the judgment will be a final judgment. If some relevant facts are asserted by one party and disputed by the other, their truth will have to be established and an interlocutory judgment is then inevitable, provided that the parties offered to prove their statements by testimonial or expert evidence.

The party that invoked legal consequences for the support of his claim or defence is the party that will bear the burden of proof, unless the law specifically provides otherwise or unless it would be inconsistent with the principles of reasonableness and fairness.[15] The other party will have the opportunity of providing counter evidence, which is - in general - easier than providing full evidence. If the order to give evidence is directed at the parties and does not require an expert investigation, witnesses are heard at a court hearing.

2.4. *Witness Evidence*

One of the aspects of Dutch civil procedure that shows that Dutch judges have a rather active role (especially in comparison with common law systems) is illustrated by the way witnesses are examined. Here the court plays a leading role.

The witnesses to be heard are selected by the parties, but examining the witnesses is primarily the work of the court. In theory it is even the judge who determines the order in which the witnesses are to be heard, but this is usually left to the party that called the witnesses.[16] Parties can testify on their own behalf, but this cannot lead to evidence to the parties' advantage, unless the party testimony is used to supplement incomplete evidence.[17] It is common practice that the party testifying on his own behalf is heard first.

Certain persons, such as notaries, attorneys and doctors, specific family members or persons who could incriminate themselves, can invoke the privilege to refuse to give testimony or to answer specific questions.[18] The court decides whether the privilege applies or not. If no privilege applies, a witness has to appear in court to testify and has to answer all questions according to 'the truth, the whole truth and nothing but the truth'. The witness promises to do so with an oath or vow and can be punished for perjury when lying or omitting something on purpose.[19]

The judge should start the witness examination with some formalities. The judge has to ask the witness to state last and first name, age, current occupation and residence and also has to check whether there is a family relationship with one of

14 De Bock 2011, p. 144.
15 Art. 150 CCP; De Bock 2011, p. 144-145.
16 Thoe Schwartzenberg 2011, p. 170.
17 Art. 164(2) CCP.
18 Art. 165 CCP.
19 Art. 177(2) CCP and Art. 207 CC (Criminal Code).

the parties.[20] After these formalities, the court should inform the witness about his rights and obligations during the interrogation. In the absence of a single term in English, the German word *Rechtsbelehrung* will be used for this notification of rights and obligations. This *Rechtsbelehrung* has not been codified, but is a result of the requirements developed to ensure due process and a fair trial.[21]

Questioning the witnesses is primarily the task of the court.[22] Parties and their lawyers can only ask questions when the judge has nothing more to ask. The testimony of the witness is not recorded in any particular way, but is summarized by the judge and dictated to the court clerk; the clerk has no independent function regarding the contents of the witness testimony as part of the court minutes. The testimony is thus summarized and sometimes even transformed into phrases that are used by lawyers, not by the witness himself. The testimony is read out loud by the clerk or the judge, and the witness is asked to sign it. In the end, the court decides on the witness's costs, which the parties will have to pay.[23]

3. Four Indicators to Assess Witness Examination

The principal goal of the investigation was to see whether Dutch civil procedure is efficient with respect to witness testimony in civil cases without sacrificing quality to efficiency. It should be noted that efficiency is not only about time, but also about ensuring that the necessary information is gathered effectively. In order to assess witness examination, we approached witness examinations from four different points of view, using the following indicators:

1. The length of witness testimony.
2. The way that time is spent.
3. The way the witness is informed of his position.
4. The participation of the parties in the examination of the witness.

The first and second indicators tell more about the degree of efficiency that is reached. The second indicator is also used to check whether the formalities (see section 2.4 above) are taken seriously by the court. The third indicator shows whether the court is not over-efficient when it comes to the *Rechtsbelehrung*. The fourth indicator reveals whether or not the system is in need of ongoing correction by means of the intervention of the parties and their lawyers.

The indicators have been operationalized by using several parameters. In addition, other factors that could affect the way witnesses are heard were examined, such as the gender and age of the judge, location of the court, gender and age of the witness, and gender and age of the lawyers. Differences between these groups could

20 Art. 177(1) CCP.
21 Fernhout 2004, p. 291-296.
22 Art. 179(1) CCP.
23 Art. 182 CCP.

indicate that the procedure functions less well with certain groups – which could imply that the model should be optimized.

4. Research Design

To investigate the indicators introduced above it was necessary to observe witness examinations in different courts in the Netherlands. Due to limited capacity, not all courts and not all witness examinations could be visited. To take a representative sample, a selection was made. The court locations chosen were The Hague, Heerlen, Utrecht, Arnhem, Eindhoven, Den Bosch, Roermond, Rotterdam, Maastricht, Breda, Amsterdam and Zutphen, belonging to the District Courts of Den Haag, Oost-Brabant, Zeeland-West Brabant, Midden-Nederland, Amsterdam, Rotterdam, Gelderland and Limburg.

This sample is representative because these locations include small, medium and large courts, as well as courts from industrialized, urbanized and more rural areas. Only the courts in the north of the Netherlands were not visited. This does not affect the representativity of the sample, since the northern area is quite comparable to the eastern and south-western areas of the Netherlands.

An observation form was used to keep track of everything observed during the hearing. To avoid a coding bias, the form was tested by having the complete hearing attended by all researchers together.[24] Apart from some minor aspects, it appeared that the parameters were interpreted in the same way by all researchers. Some parts of the form appeared not to be useful. Those were removed, while other aspects were added.

The form used was split into two subforms, a general subform and a witness subform. On the general subform, all facts were noted that were related to the entire hearing, such as the names and functions of the persons present (including the judge), the length of the hearing and the length of adjournments. On the witness subform all data were noted related to the witness interrogation, such as the length of the examination, any interruptions, the formalities, the *Rechtsbelehrung*, the type of questions (open or closed), what happened with regard to the dictations, any objections made to the dictations and the number of questions that were asked.

The *Rechtsbelehrung* should include all the rights and duties of a witness. It is the task of the judge to make sure that witnesses are aware of these rights and duties. Therefore the *Rechtsbelehrung* was split into nine separate parameters. These included parameters such as the duty to answer the questions of the judge, the duty to answer truthfully and the right not to answer in case of a privilege.

The research design relied on the possibilities created by Article 121 of the Dutch Constitution that states that except for cases as specified by law each hearing will be held in public, thus guaranteeing free entrance to all courtrooms for everyone. There is no exception in the law for witness hearings in civil cases, which should imply that these hearings are accessible to the public, including researchers.

24 As advised in Lawless, Robbenholt & Ulen 2010, p. 175-180.

This does not only mean that those interested must be able to visit the hearings, but also that information about the hearings must be open to anyone.

Contrary to what the law prescribes, information about witness hearings was not easily obtainable from court employees. Many courts were not willing to communicate the starting time of witness hearings. Sometimes it was even stated that these hearings were not open to the public at all. Some good arguments were necessary to convince court employees of the contrary. In Den Haag and Maastricht the situation was even worse, since the court employees working there did not even know what a witness hearing was.

Entrance to the courtrooms was another obstacle that had to be overcome. In Rotterdam, court employees refused to let the researcher enter the court building. It took an hour of arguing to convince them to let the researcher pass, which was long after the hearing had started. Whether they did it intentionally or not, the next problem was that the researcher was sent to the wrong room several times and eventually had to abandon the project for that day. In Amsterdam, court employees were not very cooperative either. However, in Eindhoven, Zutphen and Roermond court employees were very interested and helpful.

5. Results

The researchers visited and observed 40 hearings where 108 witnesses were interrogated. Of those witnesses 32 were party witnesses and 76 were non-party witnesses. The sample group of witnesses consisted of 84 male and 24 female witnesses. The results are presented separately for each indicator mentioned in section 3 above.

5.1. *Length of Witness Testimony*

The indicator that probably gives the most valuable information on how efficient the Dutch witness hearings are is the time a witness hearing lasts on average. In fact, this is where the combination of the post-defence hearing model and the sieve model should bear fruit more than anywhere else in civil procedure.

For each hearing, 2.70 witnesses are heard on average. The length of each hearing is shown in Figure A. It was found that the mean length of a hearing is 115 minutes. With an average of only 36 minutes per witness examination, including all formalities such as dictating, printing and signing the minutes of the examination, it can be said that the Dutch judge is rather fast.[25] Since the data showed that 'lost time'[26] during a hearing is not more than 18 minutes on average (which means less

25 Unfortunately, similar research in other countries could not be found so a solid, quantitative comparison could not be made.

26 This refers to the time used for other activities than hearing the witness, such as inviting parties to take their seats, short breaks, looking for a witness who is not inside the courtroom, etc.

than 7 minutes per witness), we can draw the conclusion that an overall efficient result is achieved, provided that all information the witness could give has been obtained. This shows how efficient the combination of the post-defence hearing model and the sieve model actually works.

Figure A: Length of all hearings in minutes

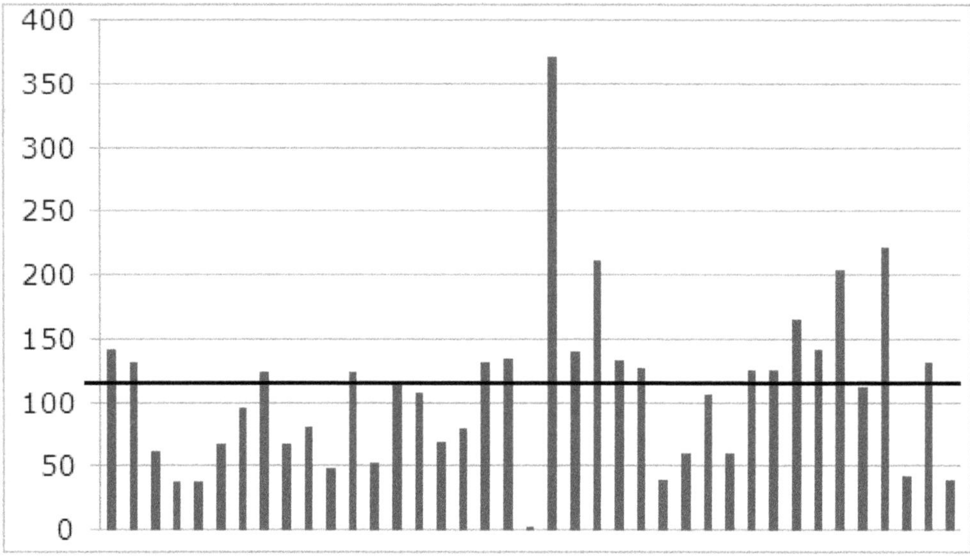

Another aspect which shows that the Dutch system is functioning properly can be found in the delays from the schedule set for the hearings. Our data show that the delay with which the hearings started was on average not more than a trifling six minutes. Sometimes courts, parties and witnesses started even before the time that was scheduled. This shows that the system assures the predictability of the length of the hearing, which allows planning the hearings in an accurate way.

Some variation in the length of the witness examination was due to the fact that Dutch procedural law allows parties to take the stand as a witness. It is to be expected that examining a party witness will take more time than examining other witnesses. The party witness will know about all aspects of the case, he will be eager to tell the judge all he knows and he will also be invited to comment (as a witness) on the allegations of the other party. The survey showed that indeed there is a significant difference between the two types of witnesses. The average length of the examination of a party witness is 49 minutes against 30 minutes for the other witnesses (Figure B). Since the courts know which witnesses are party witnesses, this difference can be and is taken into account when planning the hearings.

Figure B: Examination of party witnesses and other witnesses in minutes

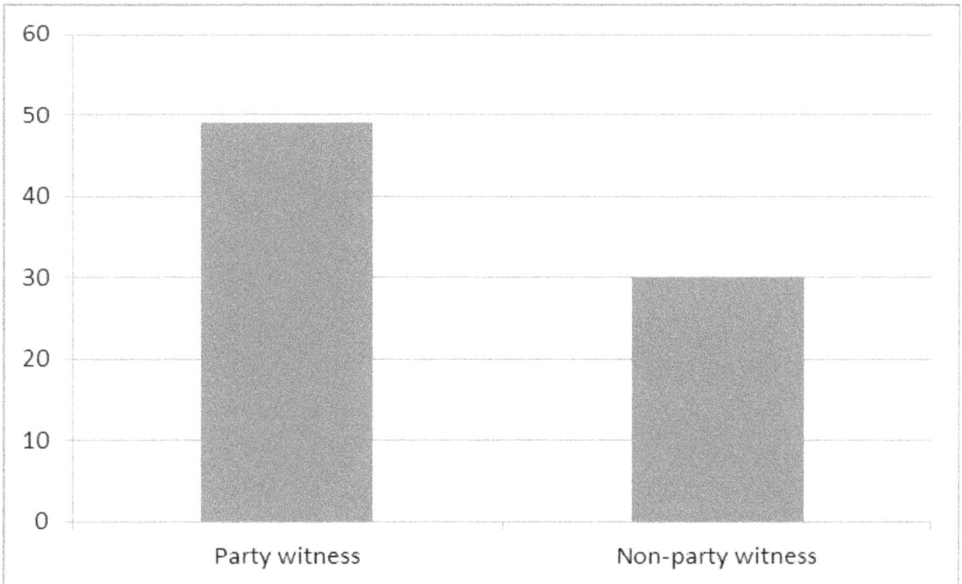

Dutch civil procedural law distinguishes between small claims and other claims, for which the limit is set at a litigation value of € 25,000. Below that amount, legal representation is not mandatory and there is a slight relaxation of procedural requirements. These cases are dealt with by a single judge with the name of 'cantonal judge'. Supposing that cantonal cases are on average a bit less complex than non-cantonal cases, it was worth investigating whether hearing witnesses in those cases takes less time. Actually, there is a slight difference, but this difference has no statistical meaning and is therefore due to chance.

Other factors that were investigated to see whether they influence the length of the witness examination are the time of the day, the geographical location, the age of the judge and the gender of the witness. However, no relevant differences were found regarding these factors. A slight (and statistically significant) difference in length was found related to the gender of the judge, but this difference might be explained by the fact that the female judges turned out to hear relatively more party witnesses. It can therefore be concluded that only the witness category (party witness or other witness) affects the length of a witness hearing, which is perfectly confirmed by the accurate planning of witness hearings.

5.2. *The Way in which the Time of a Hearing was Spent*

To examine the way the 36 minutes used to hear witnesses are spent, three distinctions have to be made: the actual questioning of the witness, the dictation for the court minutes and the reading of the dictation to the witness. It turns out that 51 per cent of the time is used for the interrogation, whereas 37 per cent of the time is used for the dictation and 12 per cent for reading the dictation out loud to the witness (Figure C).

Figure C: Distribution of time used to examine a witness

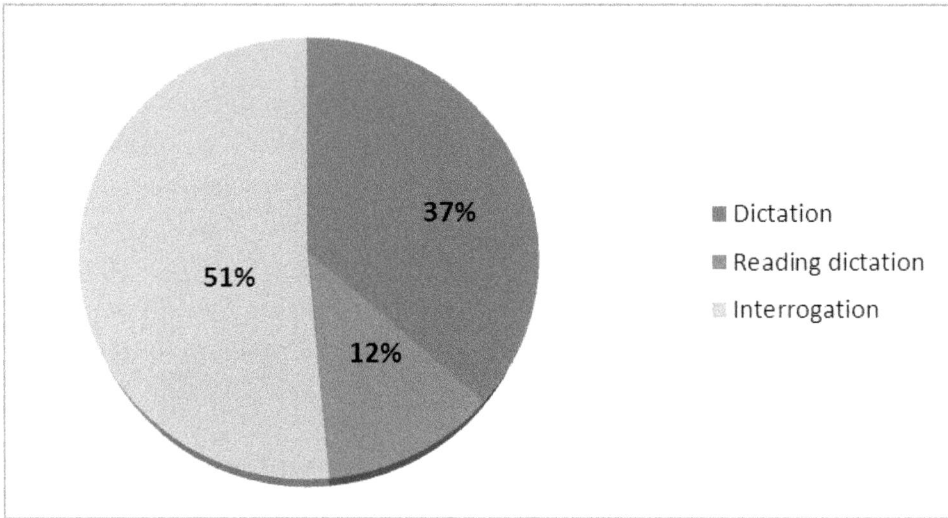

One interesting result of the survey is that male judges spent significantly more time on the dictation (dictating and reading it out loud; 49 per cent of the time) than female judges (43 per cent of the time). This is the more striking since female judges heard relatively more party witnesses. The explanation could be that male judges are more open to later developments and are therefore more liberal in their selection of the relevant parts of the witness testimony. The gender of the witness and the location of the court could not account for differences found in the length of dictating activities.

Although on average 49 per cent of the time is used for the dictation (37 per cent on drafting it, 12 per cent on reading it), which seems a bit long, in fact this modus operandi is quite efficient. Another possibility would be to record the questioning of the witness on video. However, even though it may not take much time to do the actual recording, it does take a lot of time to go through it later, especially for those judges who want to be sure of what has been said. The time saved will therefore be lost exponentially in a later stage.

But more important, from the Dutch perspective working with summaries is mandatory. Human speech is imperfect, sometimes unclear and often contradictory. That means that a witness has to be helped to express what he really means. The summary of the judge, often construed on the basis of later corrections and interventions of the witness and the parties, provides for this. The witness himself, but also parties and their lawyers, can raise objections to the dictation. It is for the judge to decide whether he will make a change to the minutes or not. The number of objections found in this research – two for each witness examination on average –

shows that summarizing the statement of the witness in court is really an interactive event. This could never be replaced by a recording on DVD.

Judges have different dictation styles. Some start dictating after every question asked, while others summarize everything at the end of the witness examination. Striking is that both techniques take (on average) the same amount of time, whereas we expected that summarizing the whole statement at the end of the examination would be far more efficient. No difference was found in dictation style between male and female judges.

Another aspect of the survey concerned the formalities the judge has to go through to identify the witness before the actual examination starts. He has to ask for the witness's name, his residence, age, profession, kinship with the parties, whether he is an employee of one of the parties or not and whether he chooses to swear the oath or take a vow.[27] These formalities are included in the 51 per cent interrogation time. In a system that is designed to be efficient, it is not excluded that these formalities, some of which go back to 1838 and do not have a real function any more,[28] might be skipped now and then. It is interesting to see that this is indeed the case, but that it can sometimes be explained in terms of reasoned efficiency.

However, the overall conclusion is not very positive. Of all the formalities, the question regarding the kinship with the parties is skipped most: almost 60 per cent of the time. This is peculiar, because this question is important both to determine the reliability of the statement and to identify a potential privilege. However, it is not excluded that sometimes the judge already knows from the file how the witness is linked to the case and therefore does not ask about it. The same may apply to the question whether the witness is an employee of one of the parties.

The questions regarding the age of the witness and his profession are seldom skipped by the judge. Likewise, the question as to where the witness lives is only omitted in less than 5 per cent of the witness examinations. This question is part of the identification of the witness, so it is obvious that the judge will ask for that. There is a slight difference between the party witness and the regular witness. This might be a consequence of the fact that the residence of a party witness is already clear in most cases. That is what was meant by 'reasoned efficiency': what is already known is not asked.

Only in 33.6 per cent of the witness examinations did the judge actually ask all obligatory questions. That is an alarmingly low number, but is mainly due to the fact that the questions regarding kinship and employment are skipped so often. The distribution of laxness over the ages of the judges seems to be random (Figure D).

[27] Art. 177 CCP.

[28] Fernhout 2004, p. 339.

Figure D: Obligatory questions correlated to the age of the judge[29]

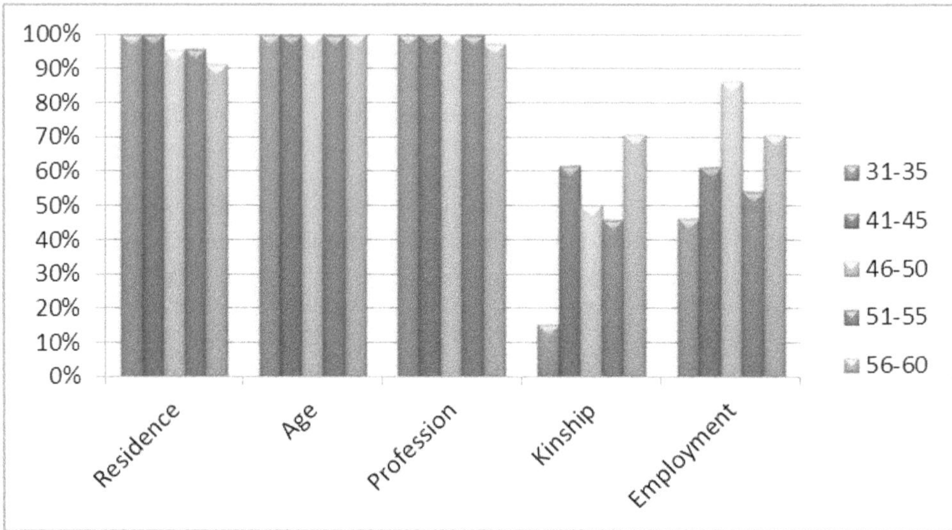

Another parameter that was tested is the part of the country where the hearing was held. A distinction was made between courts in urbanized (and industrialized) areas and courts in rural areas. It turned out that judges in the urbanized areas are significantly keener on asking about the employment of the witness than judges in rural areas. A cause for this might be that in urbanized areas more companies are involved in litigation. This may trigger the interest of the judge to know more about the position of the witness.

After these formalities, the judge asks the witness to swear the oath or take a vow. There was only one case in which this question was not asked. Usually, religious people swear the oath, since doing so involves appealing to a supreme being. It turns out that 58 per cent of the Dutch witnesses choose to swear the oath, which is in keeping with the data published by the Dutch Central Office for Statistics about religion in the Netherlands.[30] The assumption of some authors that the connection between swearing the oath and the religious experience of the witness himself – the need to ask God's help by promising to tell the truth – has faded over the course of time thus could not be confirmed.[31]

Another parameter that was investigated regards the questioning itself. It was not excluded that the post-defence hearing model would cause an information deficiency on the side of the court, which would appear from a low number of

29 The category 36-40 is missing since the number of judges in that part of the sample was too low (only one).

30 CBS 2014, p. 4, which states that in 2013 53 per cent of the population saw itself as a member of a religion.

31 Rammeloo 2005, p. 2.

questions asked by the court and a virtual absence of closed questions. However, this was not the case. On average, the judge asks 25 questions per witness examination. No significant difference could be found between male and female judges. Almost 65 per cent of the questions are closed, mainly because the judge usually starts asking questions about what the witness knows (open questions) to stimulate him to tell the judge his own story (Figure E). After this, the judge asks for details about the statement by asking more specific questions that can often be answered with 'yes' or 'no' only. The gender of the judge and of the witness or the length of the examination turned out to have no influence on the type of questions asked. Therefore, no traces of an information deficiency caused by the post-defence hearing model were found.

Figure E: Type of questions asked, average in absolute numbers

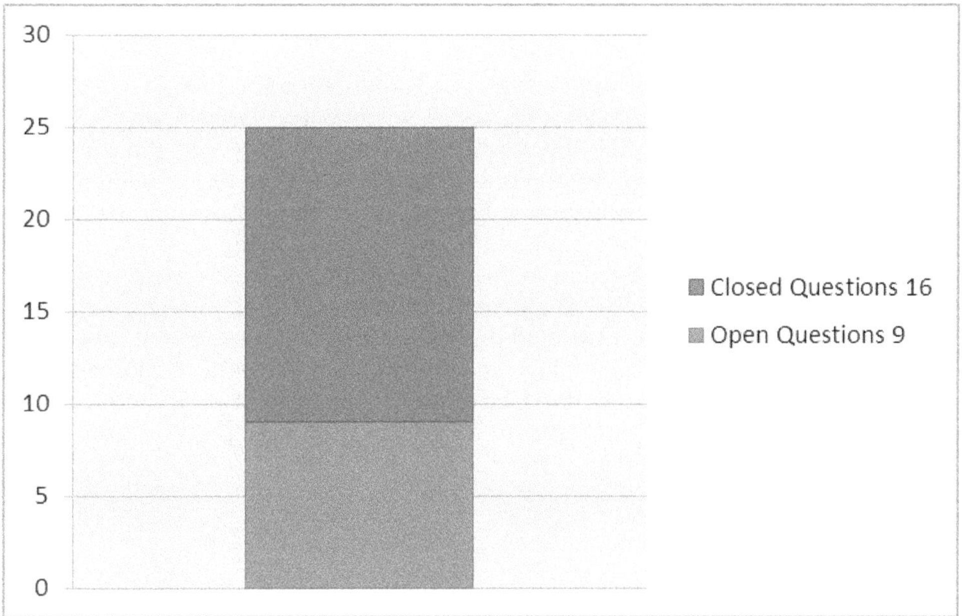

5.3. *The Way a Witness is being Informed (Rechtsbelehrung)*

A more important indicator of the effect of the Dutch model is the way the courts inform the witnesses about their rights and obligations: the *Rechtsbelehrung*. The *Rechtsbelehrung* of the witness should include the obligation to answer and to answer completely and truthfully, the difference between the oath and a vow, what perjury is, that civil arrest is a possible sanction for non-complying witnesses, whether kinship or a professional privilege can be invoked, what the privilege against self-incrimination exactly is and what it means to invoke a privilege. The duty of the judge to inform the witness about those rights and obligations is not a duty that can be found in Dutch civil law, but follows from the general requirements of due process.[32] Thus it can be seen as a consequence of Article 6 of the European Convention for the Protection of Human Rights and Fundamental Freedoms, which provides the right to a fair trial.

The judges score very badly when it comes to this *Rechtsbelehrung* (Figure F). The obligation to answer is skipped in more than half of the cases, but that the witness needs to answer completely and truthfully is stated by the judge in almost 90 per cent of the hearings. This is still alarming, since not answering or answering incorrectly or incompletely can have far-reaching consequences. When it comes to the explanation of the difference between the oath and a vow, the judge does not do better. In more than half of the cases, the judge leaves out this part of the *Rechtsbelehrung*. An even higher percentage was found when it comes to the possibility of a prosecution for perjury: in 68 per cent of the cases the judge does not mention this. The sanction of civil arrest and the privilege against self-incrimination were not mentioned one single time, and the possibility of a privilege was only mentioned incidentally. It is to be feared that this sloppiness is inspired by the desire to be efficient.

No statistically relevant differences were found regarding parameters such as the gender of the witness, witness type (party or non-party), part of the country or time of the day. One factor that did seem to have an influence was the age of the witness. The judge informs younger witnesses more than three times as often as the older witnesses about their obligation to answer. A reason for this could be that the judge expects that older people have more respect for a higher authority than the younger generation. The obligation to answer truthfully as well is explained to the younger generation much more often than to older people.

On the whole, it can be concluded that the *Rechtsbelehrung* in Dutch civil courts leaves much to be desired. Changing the current practice would do no harm. An efficient *Rechtsbelehrung* would not take more than one or two minutes, which would prevent the right of witnesses to be informed of their position from being violated for reasons of efficiency.

32 Fernhout 2004, p. 291-296.

Figure F: Rechtsbelehrung

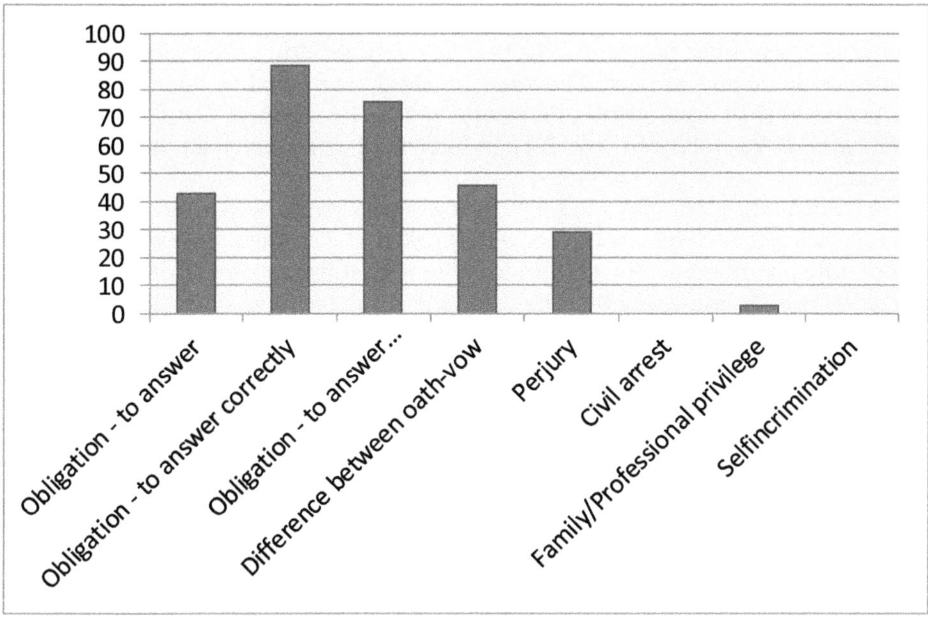

5.4. *Participation in a Witness Hearing*

The fourth indicator is used to check whether the procedural framework within which witnesses are heard is too optimistic with regard to the actual possibilities for the judge to play a leading role in a witness examination. This could occur when the other participants (the parties and their lawyers) are more dominant than the court.

It was easy to establish that this was not the case. The average number of questions asked by the lawyers of plaintiff and defendant lies between three and four. That is much less than the 25 mentioned above for the court. The questions on behalf of the parties do not show a specific distribution between open and closed questions. There is even no correlation with the party that proposed the witness. Apparently, the information about the case is sufficiently communicated between the parties and the court before the examination starts, which is exactly what the procedural model aims at.

6. Conclusion

The Dutch procedural model aims at narrowing down the facts that are relevant for the outcome of the case in only four steps (writ of summons, statement of defence, post-defence hearing, interlocutory judgment). The workings of this model were explored by investigating the actual practice of witness examinations in Dutch courts. This was done using four indicators.

The first indicator is the time a witness examination takes on average. This turned out to be 36 minutes, of which half is spent on dictating and finalizing the court minutes. Since it can be assumed that within this time indeed all information the witness has to offer has been obtained, we conclude that the procedural model functions well in this respect. The time invested in finalizing the court minutes could be diminished significantly by recording the examination, but this initial time benefit would be followed by higher losses of time in later stages of the proceedings.

A confirmation for the model functioning correctly was found in the way witness hearing schedules are respected in practice. The data showed an average delay of only six minutes. The system leads to a high predictability of the length of witness examinations, especially when the difference between party and non-party witnesses is taken into account.

Studying the patterns of interrogation, no indication was found that the courts were hampered by an information deficiency. Given the Dutch model, where the judge leads the interrogation and is the first to ask questions, the patterns of interrogation confirmed that the court was fully informed about the case and that the parties did not have to take over the interrogation.

When it comes to the formalities and the *Rechtsbelehrung* – informing the witness of his rights and obligations – the conclusions are less favourable. The desire to work efficiently seems to be the deeper cause of a certain sloppiness on the side of the Dutch courts, especially when it comes to acquiring initial information regarding the witness (occupation, kinship with the parties) and informing the witness about possible privileges. The privilege against self-incrimination was not even mentioned once, while professional and kinship privileges were only mentioned incidentally.

A possible cause for these last findings could be that the *Rechtsbelehrung* follows from Article 6 ECHR and has not been codified in Dutch law. Reviewing the formalities at the start of the witness examination would help judges to be more precise and to avoid the trap of sacrificing fundamental rights to efficiency.

A last recommendation regards the accessibility of court hearings to the public. As discussed above, quite a number of problems occurred when researchers attempted to visit the courts. This is embarrassing for the administration of justice in the Netherlands. The public should be motivated to visit the courts in order to see with their own eyes how the justice system works. A better instruction and training of court employees could certainly improve the transparency that the Judiciary claims to aim at.

Bibliography

CBS 2014
De religieuze kaart van Nederland 2010-2013 [The religious map of the Netherlands 2010-2013], Den Haag: CBS, 2014.

De Bock 2011
De Bock, R.H., *Tussen waarheid en onzekerheid: over het vaststellen van feiten in de civiele procedure* [Between truth and uncertainty: On determining the facts in civil procedure], Deventer: Kluwer, 2011.

Fernhout 2004
Fernhout, F.J., *Het verschoningsrecht van getuigen in civiele zaken* [Witness privileges in civil procedure], Maastricht: Gianni, 2004.

Frissen 2012
Frissen, P., *Reputatie op afstand, Rechtspraaklezing 2012* [Reputation from a distance, Justice lecture 2012], Den Haag: SDU, 2012.

Lawless, Robbenholt & Ulen 2010
Lawless, R.M., Robbenholt, J.K. & Ulen, T.S., *Empirical Methods in Law*, New York: Aspen Publishers, 2010.

Rueb 2011
Rueb, A.S., *Compendium van het burgerlijk procesrecht* [A compendium of civil procedure], Deventer: Kluwer, 2011.

Snijders 2011
Snijders, H.J., *Inleiding Nederlands burgerlijk procesrecht* [Introduction to Dutch civil procedure], Deventer: Kluwer, 2011.

Rammeloo 2005
Rammeloo, L., 'Het risico van chicanes, "Zo waarlijk helpe mij God almachtig"' [The risk of quibbling, 'So help me God'], *Advocatenblad special* 2005, p. 2.

Thoe Schwartzenberg 2011
Thoe Schwartzenberg, H.W.B., *Civiel bewijsrecht voor de rechtspraktijk* [The law of evidence for civil practitioners], Apeldoorn: Maklu, 2011.

Van der Linden 2008
Van der Linden, J., *Zitten, luisteren en schikken, Rechtvaardigheid en doelbereik bij de comparitie na antwoord* [Sitting, listening and settling, Justice and efficiency at the post-defence hearing], Den Haag: Raad voor de Rechtspraak, 2008.

Van Rhee 1997
Van Rhee, C.H., 'De traagheid van de civiele procedure: een eeuwenoud fenomeen' [Slowness of civil litigation: a phenomenon of all ages], in Jacobs, B.C.M. (ed.), *De rechtspraktijk in beeld. Van Justinianus tot de Duitse bezetting* [Focus on legal practice. From Justinian to the German occupation], Tilburg: Tilburg University Press, 1997.

Verschoof 2004
Verschoof, R.J., 'De praktijk van de comparitie na antwoord' [The post-defence hearing in practice], *Trema,* 2004, p. 339-345.

Wemmers 1995
Wemmers, J.-A., *Doorlooptijden in de civiele rechtspraak* [Process time in civil procedure], Den Haag: WODC, 1995.

P.C.H. Chan
U.-U. Rehman

CURBING ADVERSARIAL EXCESSES: AN EVALUATION OF THE EXPERT EVIDENCE REGIME IN HONG KONG AFTER THE CIVIL JUSTICE REFORM (WITH A FOCUSED STUDY ON PERSONAL INJURY LITIGATION)[1]

1. Introduction

While the court is the ultimate finder of facts, a case may involve such highly technical issues that the court is unable to discharge its fact-finding function unless qualified persons assist in the process. As the learned Hong Kong district judge in *Chan Shu Wing v. Link Management Ltd*[2] said: 'Expert evidence is relevant if it will assist the court to resolve one or more relevant issues in dispute in the cause or matter and the issue is not one which the court can come to an informed decision without such expert evidence.'[3]

The Hong Kong expert evidence regime in the past was highly adversarial. It was not uncommon that experts were instructed as 'hired guns'. Instead of assisting the court to find the truth, adversarial experts acted more like advocates than witnesses. Part A of this contribution seeks to expound the procedural framework for the use of expert evidence in civil lawsuits, highlighting those changes made pursuant to the Civil Justice Reform to tackle the adversarial excesses in the system. Part B of this contribution explores expert evidence within the context of personal injury litigation in Hong Kong (which is governed under a set of specialist rules). Given the nature of personal injury disputes, the use of expert evidence is essential in the fact-finding process. The way expert evidence is deployed and managed under the specialist rules in personal injury litigation provides invaluable insight for further reform in the general procedural regime.

1 This contribution repeats a number of points made (and reproduces parts of the content) in Chan, 2012, p. 231-260.

2 (unreported) DCPI 1883/2011, 26 November 2013.

3 DCPI 1883/2011, para 14.

Part A: An overview of the expert evidence regime after the Civil Justice Reform in Hong Kong

2. The Role of the Expert in Civil Litigation

The role of the expert in civil litigation is clear under the law. An expert witness, in assisting the court, should give independent and unbiased opinions on matters within his own expertise.[4] It is not the function of the expert witness to usurp the role of the court in the fact-finding process or to assume the role of an advocate. By definition, expert witnesses are authorities in specialist areas where no layman (including the judge) is capable of navigating by himself. While it is sound in theory that the court decides the ultimate issue of the proceedings (and therefore the expert is only giving 'evidence' and not offering an opinion on the ultimate issue of the proceedings), in practice this can be difficult if the fundamental question turns on a very technical factual point that can only be answered with the assistance of an expert. It is therefore important to devise a procedural regime that promotes expert independence and accountability.

The traditional common law approach on expert evidence encouraged excessive use of experts. Expert witnesses tend to be partisan and adversarial, at times acting more like advocates than witnesses. 'Expert shopping', if taken to the extreme, distorts the intended function of expert evidence and threatens procedural fairness in the fact-finding process. The party that engages in expert shopping may suffer as well. As Judge Toulmin CMG Q.C. puts it in *Anglo Group Plc v. Winther Brown & Co Ltd*:[5]

> 'It needs to be recognised that a failure to take such an independent approach is not in the interest of the clients who retain the expert, since an expert taking a partisan approach, resulting in a failure to resolve before trial or at trial issues on which experts should agree, inflates the costs of resolving the dispute and may prevent the parties from resolving their disputes long before trial.'[6]

In this connection, the *Civil Justice Reform: Interim Report and Consultative Paper* (the preliminary report that proposes reform measures leading to the Civil Justice Reform) (*Interim Report*), made the following observations:

> 'The two major deficiencies which the civil justice system needs to address are therefore:

4 *Ibidem.*

5 [2000] EWHC Technology 127 (8 March 2000).

6 *Anglo Group Plc v. Winther Brown & Co Limited, BML (Office Computers) Limited; Winther Brown & Co Limited v. Anglo Group Plc, BML (Office Computers) Limited* [2000] EWHC Technology 127 (8 March 2000), at para 112.

> The inappropriate or excessive use of experts, which increases costs, the duration of proceedings and their complexity.
>
> Partisanship and a lack of independence amongst experts, devaluing their role in the judicial process.'[7]

Even before the Civil Justice Reform (**CJR**), the expert witness owed a 'special duty' to the court and should never assume the role of an advocate.[8] In the well-known case *The Ikarian Reefer*,[9] the court canvassed the parameters of the duties and responsibilities of expert witnesses. Principles of independence[10] and impartiality were entrenched in such parameters. Among other duties, an expert witness must limit his opinion to the areas of his expertise, provide the facts and assumptions on which his opinion is based and assist the court by providing unbiased and objective opinions.[11]

7 Interim Report 2001, para 489, p. 184.

8 *Stevens v. Gullis* [2000] 1 All E.R. 527 (per Lord Woolf MR). For earlier judicial views on an expert's duty to the court, see *Graigola Merthyr Co Ltd v. Swansea Corp* [1928] Ch. 31, 38 (per Tomlin J):
'Of late years cases involving expert evidence appear to have increased in number and in length. Having regard to the complexity of modern life and the widened field over which science ranges, this is perhaps inevitable, but the overloading of these cases in the preparation of them is becoming not infrequent. Long cases produce evils; they place the parties with the lesser resources at a grave disadvantage, and they delay the course of the general business of the Courts and thereby inflict serious hardship on other litigants. In every case of this kind there are generally many "irreducible and stubborn facts" upon which agreement between experts should be possible, and in my judgment the expert advisers of the parties, whether legal or scientific, are under a *special duty* to the Court in the preparation of such a case to limit in every possible way the contentious matters of fact to be dealt with at the hearing. That is a duty which exists not-withstanding that it may not always be easy to discharge.' (emphasis provided)

9 [1993] 2 Lloyds Rep 68, 81.

10 It appears that the mere fact that an expert acted in a partisan capacity for a party does not automatically disqualifies him from being instructed by that party in a subsequent lawsuit: *Helm Hong Kong Ltd v. Au Tat Kei*, (unreported) Court of First Instance, HCA 1517/2006, 4 June 2010.

11 It is worth setting out the duties of the expert witness as expounded in *The Ikarian Reefer*:
'1. Expert evidence presented to the court should be, and should be seen to be, the independent product of the expert uninfluenced as to form or content by the exigencies of litigation: *Whitehouse v. Jordan* [1981] 1 W.L.R. 246 at 256, *per* Lord Wilberforce.
2. An expert witness should provide independent assistance to the court by way of objective, unbiased opinion in relation to matters within his expertise: *Polivitte Ltd. v. Commercial Union Assurance Co. plc* [1987] 1 Lloyd's Rep. 379 at 386, Garland J. and *Re J* [1990] F.C.R. 193, Cazalet J. An expert witness in the High Court should never assume the role of an advocate.
3. An expert witness should state the facts or assumptions upon which his opinion is based. He should not omit to consider material facts which could detract from his concluded opinion (*Re J, supra*).
4. An expert witness should make it clear when a particular question or issue falls outside his expertise.

→

The independent nature of expert evidence in civil litigation is perhaps most clearly explained in Lord Wilberforce's dictum in *Whitehouse v. Jordan*:[12]

> 'While some degree of consultation between experts and legal advisers is entirely proper, it [is] necessary that expert evidence presented to the court should be, and should be seen to be, the independent product of the expert, uninfluenced as to form or content by the exigencies of litigation. To the extent that it is not, the evidence is likely to be not only incorrect but self-defeating.'[13]

This position of the law in England in relation to expert evidence did not change after the implementation of the CPR.[14]

3. The Civil Justice Reform and the Modification of the Expert Evidence Regime

The CJR, which came into effect in April 2009, fundamentally changed the landscape of civil litigation practice in Hong Kong, including a significant shift of case-management powers from the parties to the judge. The exercise of these powers by the judge has significant implications for fact-finding. Civil procedure in Hong Kong is governed by the Rules of the High Court (Cap 4A) (**RHC**). The RHC have been amended to effect the changes of the CJR.[15]

The CJR not only conferred extensive procedural case-management powers to the judge but also substantive case-management powers. For instance, RHC Order 1A, rule 4(2)(c) provides that 'Active case-management includes ... deciding promptly which issues need full investigation and trial and accordingly disposing summarily of the others' and RHC Order 1B, rule 1(2)(j) provides that the court may 'exclude an issue from consideration'.

5. If an expert's opinion is not properly researched because he considers that insufficient data is available, then this must be stated with an indication that the opinion is no more than a provisional one (*Re J, supra*). In cases where an expert witness, who has prepared a report, could not assert that the report contained the truth, the whole truth and nothing but the truth without some qualification, that qualification should be stated in the report: Derby & Co. Ltd. and others v. Weldon and others, The Times, 9 November 1990, *per* Staughton L.J.
6. If, after exchange of reports, an expert witness changes his view on a material matter having read the other side's expert's report or for any other reason, such change of view should be communicated (through legal representatives) to the other side without delay and when appropriate to the court.
7. Where expert evidence refers to photographs, plans, calculations, analyses, measurements, survey reports or other similar documents, these must be provided to the opposite party at the same time as the exchange of reports (see 15.5 of the Guide to Commercial Court Practice).' (*The Ikarian Reefer* [1993] 2 Lloyds Rep 68, 81.) Also see *The Ikarian Reefer* [1995] 1 Lloyd's Rep 455, which is the English Court of Appeal decision of the same case.

12 [1981] 1 WLR 246.

13 [1981] 1 WLR 246, 256-257.

14 *Stevens v. Gullis* [2000] 1 All ER 527; also see Final Report 2004, p. 322 (FN 509).

15 The amendments were set out in the Rules of the High Court (Amendment) Rules 2008 (L.N. 152 of 2008).

The CJR does not seek to transform the adversarial system into an inquisitorial one. Parties are still actively involved in a civil lawsuit. The principle of party presentation is securely entrenched and the court has no *ex officio* power to investigate. What the CJR has done is to curtail the excesses of the adversarial system and concurrently retain the best features of the adversarial system.[16]

Reform in the system of civil fact-finding was premised on empowering the court to take an active role in case-management. It was identified that the traditional non-interventionist role of the judge has made litigation very inefficient, both in terms of time and cost.[17] Armed with extensive case-management powers, the judge today is expected to manage proceedings in a way that gives effect to the underlying objectives of the reform, including the objectives to promote procedural expediency and increase cost-effectiveness. This development has great implications for the fact-finding process in Hong Kong, particularly in the enhancement of efficiency in fact-finding.

Among other goals, the underlying objectives to promote procedural efficiency, proportionality and cost-effectiveness in litigation impacted the way expert evidence is deployed in practice.[18]

While clear principles that govern the use of expert evidence were laid down in case law before the CJR, many of these principles were not rigorously enforced. Expert evidence frequently took the form of an adversarial opinion that sought to pitch the best case for the instructing party. This situation is aptly summarised in the Interim Report as follows:

> 'Experts are supposed to assist the court, yet adversaries use them to excess and often as partisan "hired guns"... Where experts are used as "hired guns" the consequences are counter-productive and unacceptable. Far from helping the court to resolve expert issues, competing partisan experts tend to make resolution of such issues more difficult and confusing. The court may sometimes be compelled to try to evaluate to some degree the credibility of each expert - an exercise that should have no place in the assessment of expert evidence.'[19]

The distortion of expert evidence called for an overhaul of the system. The following reform measures were proposed in the Interim Report:

> 'To counter these problems, possible reforms aim:-
> __to give the court control over the introduction and scope of any expert evidence sought to be adduced;

16 First Year Report 2010, p. 1 (para 3(a)). An example of this philosophy at work is discovery, which is still fundamentally a party-driven exercise. Consider the Working Party's recommendation that a modified regime of discovery should focus on improving case-management instead of narrowing the scope of discovery: *see* Final Report 2004, p. 246 (para 478).

17 Wilkinson, Cheung & Booth 2011, p. 5-6.

18 RHC O. 1A, r. 1.

19 Interim Report 2001, paras 34.3 and 494, p. 13 and 186.

__to emphasize the expert's primary duty to the court which overrides his duty to his client by requiring the expert to acknowledge that duty and to agree to adhere to a specified code of conduct which promotes independence and impartiality;
__to allow the expert to approach the court for guidance as to his function in his own capacity without giving notice to the parties; and
__to allow the court to require the parties to appoint a single joint expert.'[20]

The Chief Justice's Working Party on Civil Justice Reform (**Working Party**) recommended the adoption of the following rules, which became the reform highlights of the CJR in relation to expert evidence:

1. A rule along the lines of CPR 35.3 ('declaring that expert witnesses owe a duty to the court which overrides any obligation to those instructing or paying the expert');[21]
2. A rule that in order for the reception of any expert report or oral testimony it is required that '(a) the expert declares in writing (i) that he has read the court-approved Code of Conduct for Experts and agrees to be bound by it, (ii) that he understands his duty to the court, and (iii) that he has complied and will continue to comply with that duty; and (b) that his expert report is verified by a statement of truth'.[22]
3. A code of conduct for expert witnesses.[23]

Following the Woolf Reforms in England, a significant change in the court's power in relation to its control over expert evidence was CPR 35.4, which gave the court general discretionary powers to exclude expert evidence altogether:

'35.4
(1) No party may call an expert or put in evidence an expert's report without the court's permission.
(2) When parties apply for permission they must provide an estimate of the costs of the proposed expert evidence and identify –
(a) the field in which expert evidence is required and the issues which the expert evidence will address; and
(b) where practicable, the name of the proposed expert.
(3) If permission is granted it shall be in relation only to the expert named or the field identified under paragraph (2). The order granting permission may specify the issues which the expert evidence should address.'

It was proposed that the same change should be made in Hong Kong. The Working Party, however, rejected the proposal to give the court greater discretionary powers to exclude expert evidence along the lines of CPR 35.4 in England (i.e. that 'No party may call an expert or put in evidence an expert's report without the court's

20 Interim Report 2001, para 98 of the Executive Summary, p. 23.
21 Final Report 2004, Recommendation 102, p. 324.
22 Final Report 2004, Recommendation 103, p. 324.
23 Final Report 2004, Recommendation 104, p. 325.

permission').[24] The Working Party based its rejection on three key grounds: (1) that the legal profession and the majority of stakeholders were against the proposal;[25] and (2) there were already sufficient procedural tools for the court to manage the use of expert evidence in such a way that prevents the excessive and inappropriate use of expert evidence (the problem is the lack of enforcement, not the lack of authority);[26] and (3) the adoption of the proposal would effectively allow the court to exclude relevant and admissible expert evidence.[27]

Regarding the sufficiency of current procedures to manage expert evidence, the Working Party wrote:

> 'It will be evident from the foregoing discussion that the court already enjoys considerable powers to exclude inappropriate or excessive use of expert evidence. If the evidence sought to be adduced involves subject-matter not properly susceptible to expert evidence, or if the witness is not qualified as an expert in the field, or if the evidence is not relevant, it may be excluded as inadmissible. If a party is inclined to call a string of experts where this is not justified, O 38 r 4 allows the court to restrict him to the appropriate number. Parties are not permitted to adduce expert evidence unless its substance has first been the subject of pre-trial disclosure. The existing rules are therefore quite apt to filter out expert evidence which is inappropriate or excessive. The problem appears to be that the existing rules are not sufficiently invoked by the parties or applied by the courts ... If the existing rules were to be applied more assiduously, it is difficult to see what useful role there would be for a general discretionary power to exclude expert evidence in respect of evidence which has not been excluded under the present rules.'[28]

Two further proposals were considered but ultimately rejected by the Working Party.

Proposal 39(d): (requiring expert reports prepared for use by the court to state the substance of the instructions forming the basis of such reports, abrogating legal professional privilege to the extent necessary for this purpose). Since expert evidence could possibly be swayed by the way instructions are drafted (e.g. instructions may contain rhetorical questions aimed to influence the opinion of an expert), disclosure of the instructions could help the court in assessing the weight to be given to the expert evidence. However, the Working Party was concerned about the arguable unconstitutionality of the proposed rule in respect of its constitutionality.[29] After

24 Final Report 2004, Recommendation 101, p. 320.
25 Final Report 2004, para 593, p. 314.
26 Final Report 2004, paras 594–601, p. 314-318.
27 Final Report 2004, para 593, p. 314.
28 Final Report 2004, paras 602 and 603, p. 319-320.
29 Potential constitutional challenge may be lodged pursuant to Article 35 of the Basic Law of Hong Kong:
'Hong Kong residents shall have the right to confidential legal advice, access to the courts, choice of lawyers for timely protection of their lawful rights and interests or for representation in the courts, and to judicial remedies.
Hong Kong residents shall have the right to institute legal proceedings in the courts against the acts of the executive authorities and their personnel.'

considering possible arguments for and against the proposed rule,[30] as well as other factors,[31] the Working Party rejected the proposal on the following basis:

> 'One might add that in relation to civil proceedings, the constitutional protection afforded to confidential legal advice by BL 35 is rather more specific than the general rights to a fair trial and privacy conferred by ECHR 6 and ECHR 8. Even accepting (for the reasons which attracted those in support of *Proposal 39(d)*) that such a rule pursues a legitimate purpose, there would appear to be room for argument as to whether such a measure is reasonably proportionate to that purpose and as to the extent of impairment to the essence of the right to confidential legal advice.
> The Working Party does not seek to resolve those questions. However, the arguable constitutionality of the proposed rule, taken together with the points made in opposition to such a rule have led the Working Party to conclude that *Proposal 39(d)* should not be adopted.'[32]

Proposal 39(e) (for permitting experts independently to approach the court for directions). The Working Party was of the view that the disadvantages outweighed the advantages and rejected the proposal:

> 'The proposal was thought objectionable because:-
> (a) it would inject distrust between a party and his lawyers on the one hand and the experts on the other, exacerbated by making the parties bear the costs of the expert's approach to the court;
> (b) it espouses a procedure that is not transparent and prevents impartial justice from being seen to be done;
> (c) it is likely to erode legal professional privilege;
> (d) it would promote the use (and expense) of a second set of advisers to monitor the expert engaged in the court proceedings;
> (e) professional experts would in any event be reluctant to take the step in question as they might never be instructed again;
> (f) it is in any event an unnecessary procedure since an expert in a difficult position could simply raise the point with the party or his legal advisers and have them, if necessary, approach the court for directions, resigning or threatening resignation if they refuse to address the difficulty.'[33]

4. The Procedural Rules Governing Expert Evidence and Analysis

When an expert assumes the role of a 'hired gun', the evidence he gives is likely to distort fact-finding. Justice cannot be done without fairness and accuracy in the fact-finding process. Codifying the expert's overriding duty to the court (meaning that the duty 'overrides any obligation to the person from whom the expert witness has received instructions') therefore promotes independence of an expert.[34] Furthermore, an expert report is inadmissible unless the report contains a

30 Final Report 2004, paras 616-620, p. 327-328.
31 Final Report 2004, paras 614-615, p. 326.
32 Final Report 2004, paras 620-621, p. 328-329.
33 Final Report 2004, para 622, p. 329-330.
34 RHC O. 38, r. 35A.

'declaration' by the expert witness that he has read the code of conduct for expert witness and agrees to be bound by it, has understood his overriding duty to the court and has complied with (and will continue to comply with) that duty.[35] An expert report must also be verified by a statement of truth.[36]

This section examines key procedural rules on expert evidence (including those rules introduced by the CJR).

4.1. *Restrictions on Adducing Expert Evidence and Court's Power to Limit the Number of Expert Witnesses*

Expert evidence can only be adduced at trial or any hearing: (a) with the leave of the court; (b) where all parties agree; or (c) a party has applied to the court for directions and has complied with such directions under RHC Order 38, rule 37 or 41.[37] A party may also adduce expert evidence by way of affidavit if so permitted.[38]

In practice, parties should apply for court's direction to adduce expert evidence at trial. This is usually (and ideally) done during the Timetabling Questionnaire stage. As a general rule (i.e. unless there are special reasons), the direction requires that the substance of the evidence be disclosed in the form of a written report (i.e. 'expert report')[39] to such other parties and within such period as the Court may specify.[40]

If the parties are able to reach agreement on the directions on expert evidence, a consent summons should be filed containing the agreed directions for the court's consideration and approval.[41] Under such circumstances (and assuming there is no other disagreements on procedure), the parties can indicate in the Timetabling Questionnaire that a Case Management Conference (**CMC**) is not necessary. Provided that the court agrees, no CMC is needed.

35 RHC O. 38, r. 37C.

36 RHC O. 38, r. 37A.

37 RHC O. 38, r. 36(1)(a) imposes restrictions on adducing expert evidence:
'(1) Except with the leave of the Court or where all parties agree, no expert evidence may be adduced at the trial or hearing of any cause or matter unless the party seeking to adduce the evidence – (a) has applied to the Court to determine whether a direction should be given under rule 37 or 41 (whichever is appropriate) and has complied with any direction given on the application'.

38 RHC O. 38, r. 36(2).

39 In practice, even where no court directions are given, a party must produce an expert report if leave is given to adduce expert evidence at trial (or if expert evidence is adduced by way of consent summons).

40 RHC Order 38, rule 37(1) provides:
'(1) Subject to paragraph (2), where in any cause or matter an application is made under rule 36(1) in respect of oral expert evidence, then, unless the Court considers that there are special reasons for not doing so, it shall direct that the substance of the evidence be disclosed in the form of a written report or reports to such other parties and within such period as the Court may specify.'
For what constitutes the 'substance' of the expert evidence, see Lau 2014, p. 243.

41 Practice Direction 5.2, para 13.

If there is no agreement on the directions on expert evidence, each party could propose a set of directions to be determined by the court at the CMC (the proposed directions should be attached to the Timetabling Questionnaire).[42]

The proposed directions (whether agreed or not) should attach a list of issues to be addressed by the expert in the report.[43] The proposed direction must contain the following: (a) leave to be given to the party to adduce expert evidence on the issues set out in the attached list of questions (i.e. the proposed directions incorporates the leave to adduce the expert evidence); (b) the date of filing and exchange of the respective final expert reports. Directions carry a time limit (e.g. the exchange of provisional report must be done within 21 days from the exchange of factual witness statements). The types of directions may vary depending on the circumstances of the case.

If the name of the expert cannot be confirmed at the Timetabling Questionnaire stage, the party can simply indicate 'to be confirmed' in the questionnaire and specify the field of the expertise needed.[44]

If no directions are sought at the Timetabling Questionnaire stage, then a party seeking to adduce expert evidence at trial must issue a summons for leave to adduce expert evidence (or by way of consent summons) in a timely manner.

The White Book notes, 'The sanction for failure to apply for the direction of the court to adduce expert evidence at trial is the effective exclusion of the expert evidence of that party.'[45]

If no directions are given on the exchange of expert reports, a party should either file a consent summons[46] or apply for leave from the court for adducing expert evidence.

Parties should plan ahead and only incur such costs that are necessary for the case when instructing an expert. The court has discretion to determine the extent of the expert costs recoverable having considered proportionality and necessity. As a matter of practice, a party must refrain from incurring costs in instructing experts unless the above procedural requirements are complied with (i.e. confirming that expert evidence can be adduced).[47]

42 The plaintiff should take out a Case Management Summons: Practice Direction 5.2, para 16.

43 The list of issues should be very specific with references made to the pleadings where necessary.

44 Item E11, Sample Timetabling Questionnaire, Appendix A, Practice Direction 5.2. The party should also indicate in the questionnaire the number of experts it proposes to call at trial if this is confirmed at the Timetabling Questionnaire stage.

45 White Book 2014, [38/36/1].

46 Consent summons is used if parties agree that the expert evidence in question should be adduced at trial. Consent order is reserved for only a handful of situations set out under RHC O. 42, r. 5A.

47 See Practice Direction 5.2 (the Case Management Practice Direction), para 20(2): 'A party who obtains expert evidence before obtaining leave does so at his own risk as to costs, except where he obtained the evidence in compliance with a pre-action protocol.'

The court has general case management powers to limit the number of expert witnesses who may be called at trial.[48] For instance, the court may limit the number of expert witnesses that a party may call on a particular issue at trial.[49] In giving the direction or order to limit the number of experts, the court will look at a number of relevant factors, for instance, the time limited for a trial must be reasonable.[50] This power, however, is not a discretionary power to exclude all expert witnesses (i.e. discretionary power to exclude admissible and relevant expert evidence).[51]

It is important for parties and their legal representatives to bear in mind that expert reports must be necessary and proportionate, and that 'costs for the preparation of unnecessary or over elaborate expert reports should be expected to be disallowed as being disproportionate, even if the party relying on it wins the case'.[52]

4.2. *Expert's Overriding Duty to the Court*

The rule on an expert's overriding to the court is RHC Order 38, rule 35A:

> '35A. *Expert witness's overriding duty to the Court (O. 38, r. 35A)*
> (1) It is the duty of an expert witness to help the Court on the matters within his expertise.
> (2) The duty under paragraph (1) overrides any obligation to the person from whom the expert witness has received instructions or by whom he is paid.'

Expert independence goes to the heart of the fact-finding process. It is therefore important to ensure that experts are there to serve the greater good of overall justice and not to further pure partisan interests. This can only be achieved when the expert owes an overriding duty to the court. By nature, an adversarial process driven by partisan interests is prone to abuse. Such potential abuse is profoundly detrimental to justice especially in those cases where the main issue of the proceedings turns on a specialist matter. The only way to promote independence is for the expert to be accountable to the chief case manager - the court, and placing that duty above the expert's duty to his instructing party.

The court attaches little to no weight to expert evidence if it is of the view that the experts are partisan or biased.

48 RHC O. 38, r. 4: 'The Court may, at or before the trial of any action, order that the number of medical or other expert witnesses who may be called at the trial shall be limited as specified by the order'. Also see RHC O. 35, r.3A.

49 RHC O. 35, r.3A(1)(b); also see White Book 2014, [38/4/1].

50 RHC O. 35, r.3A(2).

51 White Book 2014, [38/4/1], referring to *Sullivan v. West Yorkshire Passenger Transport Executive* [1985] 2 All ER 134, CA.

52 White Book 2014, [38/4/7].

4.3. *Statement of Truth and its Effect on Expert Evidence*

The CJR introduced a requirement that if the maker of an expert report fails to verify the expert report by a statement of truth, the expert report is not admissible in evidence unless otherwise ordered by the Court.[53] The effect of the statement of truth is that the maker of the witness statement or expert report believes that the facts stated in the document are true and (if applicable) the opinion expressed in it is honestly held.[54] The statement of truth must be signed by the maker of the report (i.e. the expert himself).[55] Proceedings for contempt of court may be brought against a person if he makes a false statement in a document verified by a statement of truth without an honest belief in its truth,[56] though costs sanctions are more commonly used (and are considered more proportionate) to deal with such situations.[57]

The verification requirement serves two important functions that are conducive to efficient fact-finding. Firstly, if an expert is required to certify his belief in the accuracy and truth of the matters put forward in the expert report, his opinion is less likely to be speculative.[58] It is also more likely that the expert report is drafted more carefully and comprehensively to avoid any potential accusation that the report is incomplete (i.e. by deliberately omitting material matters) or misleading. Secondly, the possibility of contempt proceedings being brought against the maker of an expert report puts pressure on the expert to act honestly and truthfully as his reputational risk is directly at stake.

4.4. *Code of Conduct of Expert Witness*

After the CJR, every expert must be supplied a copy of the Code of conduct for expert witness:

> '*37B. Duty to provide expert witness with copy of code of conduct*
> (O. 38, r. 37B)
> (1) A party who instructs an expert witness shall as soon as practicable provide the expert witness with a copy of the code of conduct set out in Appendix D.
> (2) Where the Court has under rule 4A(1) ordered that 2 or more parties shall appoint a single joint expert witness, paragraph (1) applies to each of the parties.
> (3) If the instruction is in writing, it must be accompanied by a copy of the code of conduct set out in Appendix D.'

53 RHC O. 41A, r. 7; also see RHC O. 38, r. 35A.
54 RHC O. 41A, r. 4(1)(b). The standard wording of a statement of truth for expert report is provided under RHC O. 41A, r. 5(2): "I believe that the facts stated in this [name document being verified] are true and (if applicable) the opinion expressed in it is honestly held."
55 RHC O. 41A, r. 3(1)(a).
56 RHC O 41A, r. 9(1).
57 White Book 2014, [38/37A/1].
58 Final Report 2004, p. 111 (para 221), quoting the White Book [published in 2003], [22/0/2].

Among other principles, the code of conduct for expert witness specifically prohibited an expert from acting as the advocate for a party.[59]

In *Singh Arjun v. Secretary for Justice*,[60] the Court of Appeal highlighted the following principles underlying the code of conduct for expert witness:

> 'Under the Code, the expert witness owes a paramount duty to the court to render his *professional* assistance in areas in which his expertise is required. He should not act as an advocate for a party. Two important touchstones for expert evidence can be highlighted: (a) it has to be professional; and (b) it has to be independent and impartial. Thus, an expert witness should not allow his personal preconceptions or prejudice to taint his professional opinions rendered to the court. The court takes this duty seriously as a departure from this standard can undermine the integrity and effectiveness of the judicial process.'[61]

4.5. *Expert Witness's Declaration of Duty to the Court*

Another condition to admission of expert evidence is the making of a declaration by the expert witness in relation to the following:

> '*37C. Expert witness's declaration of duty to Court (O. 38, r. 37C)*
> (1) An expert report disclosed under these rules is not admissible in evidence unless the report contains a declaration by the expert witness that –
> (a) he has read the code of conduct set out in Appendix D and agrees to be bound by it;
> (b) he understands his duty to the Court; and
> (c) he has complied with and will continue to comply with that duty.
> (2) Oral expert evidence is not admissible unless the expert witness has declared, whether orally or in writing or otherwise, that –
> (a) he has read the code of conduct set out in Appendix D and agrees to be bound by it;
> (b) he understands his duty to the Court; and
> (c) he has complied with and will continue to comply with that duty.
> (3) Paragraph (1) does not apply to a report that was disclosed under rule 37 before the commencement of this rule.'[62]

As a matter of practice, the declaration is always incorporated in the expert report.

A leading practice manual on the CJR noted the following, which succinctly and accurately summarised the intention behind the revision of RHC Order 38: 'These amendments address the concern of partisan experts and are intended to bring home individually to each expert every time an expert report is issued or expert testimony given that the expert's overriding duty is to assist the court.'[63]

The White Book has the following note regarding the effect of this rule: 'The purpose of this requirement is to remind the expert preparing the report that his

59 RHC Appendix D, para 4.
60 [2014] 2 HKLRD 678.
61 [2014] 2 HKLRD 678, 684.
62 RHC O.38, r. 37C.
63 Chan & Rogers 2010, para 8.41, p. 199.

duty to assist the court overrides any obligation to the person from whom he has received instructions or by whom he is paid. Full compliance with this duty would include ensuring that the report contains everything which the expert regards as being relevant to the opinion which he has expressed, and that any matter which would affect the validity of that opinion has been drawn to the attention of the court.'[64]

4.6. *Procedural Efficacy and Fairness*

Expert reports must be exchanged in a timely manner. The court does not allow a party to furnish an expert report at the final stage that effectively leaves no time for the other side to respond. In *Chok Yick Interior Design & Engineering Co Ltd v. Lau Chi Lun*,[65] a late interlocutory application was made by the plaintiff to put in an expert report. Lam J (in chambers) rejected the application on the following grounds:

> 'Such forensic manoeuvre [i.e. the late deployment of an expert report] is not in line with the duty of a party and his legal representative under Order 1A Rule 3. As the Defendant pointed out, if I were to allow the Plaintiff to put in the report of Mr Cheung [the expert] at this late stage, fairness requires that a chance be given to the Defendant to respond to the same. And there is simply not enough time between now and the commencement of the trial for that to be done ... In the circumstances, I do not think it is in the interest of the fair and expeditious resolution of the dispute to grant leave to the Plaintiff to use the expert report of Mr Cheung.'[66]

The expert report, by setting out the substance of the expert evidence, serves a number of functions from the perspective of procedural efficacy: (a) it provides the other party ample opportunity to study the contents of the expert evidence prior to trial and prepare his case accordingly, thereby saving trial time; (b) it delineates the scope of the expert's testimony (a function consistent with the principle of party presentation) and focuses the testimony on only the contentious issues (i.e. issues that the experts do not agree on); (c) as the expert report is filed with the court, it allows the court to manage the case being fully aware of the main contents of the expert evidence before trial.

4.7. *What is the Exact Realm of an Expert's Expertise?*

The Code of conduct for expert witness made it a requirement that an expert report must (in the body of the report or in an annexure) specify, if applicable, that a particular question or issue falls outside his field of expertise.[67] Even where the

64 White Book 2014, [38/37C/1].
65 *Chok Yick Interior Design & Engineering Co Ltd v. Lau Chi Lun*, (unreported) HCA 1480/2008, 5 May 2010.
66 *Ibidem*, see paras 49 and 51 of the decision.
67 RHC Appendix D, para 8(d).

expert witness is opining on a question well within his expertise, the Code of conduct requires that 'If an expert witness considers that his opinion is not a concluded opinion because of insufficient research or insufficient data or for any other reason, this must be stated when the opinion is expressed.'[68]

These requirements essentially mimicked the practice direction governing expert evidence in England:

> '2.4
> Experts should make it clear –
> (a) when a question or issue falls outside their expertise; and
> (b) when they are not able to reach a definite opinion, for example because they have insufficient information.'[69]

While being a criminal appeal, the decision of the Court of Final Appeal in *Fu Kor Kuen Patrick v. HKSAR*[70] sheds light on the remit of an expert witness's expertise generally (i.e. principles that the court would consider for both criminal and civil cases). The following *obiter* (per Litton and Gleeson NPJJ) are of particular relevance:

> 'I would add here this postscript. It is important that expert witnesses adhere to their code of conduct. When they express an opinion they must state clearly the facts, matters and assumptions on which such opinion is based, thus enabling the court to see whether such expression of opinion is within their field of expertise.'[71]

> 'The propensity of some expert witnesses to express opinions not wholly or substantially based on their specialised knowledge, but based upon inferences of fact outside their field of particular training or experience is well understood. The danger for the proper process of fact-finding at civil or criminal trials is obvious. When, in 1782, Lord Mansfield said that "the opinion of scientific men upon proven facts may be given by men of science, within their own science" [*Folkes v. Chadd* (1783) 3 Doug KB 157, 99 ER 589, cited in *Clark v. Ryan* (1960) 103 CLR 486, 502], he made an important point about both form and substance. An opinion, resting upon transparent factual assumptions, based upon a branch of knowledge in which the witness is an expert, may be of legitimate assistance to a finder of fact. It is when a witness goes beyond those bounds and expresses a judgment on a matter outside his area of specialised knowledge that the danger arises.'[72]

68 RHC Appendix D, para 10.
69 (CPR) Practice Direction 35 (Experts and Assessors), para 2.4.
70 (2012) 15 HKCFAR 524
71 (2012) 15 HKCFAR 524, para 25 (per Litton NPJ).
72 (2012) 15 HKCFAR 524, para 51 (per Gleeson NPJ).

5. Single Joint Expert

The CJR also conferred powers to the court in relation to the appointment of a single joint expert (**SJE**). The court may order two or more parties to appoint a SJE.[73] The court may make this order notwithstanding that a party disagrees with the appointment as long as such an appointment is in the interest of justice taking into account all the circumstances of the case and that the objecting party has been given reasonable opportunity to present to the court the reasons for the objection.[74] Where the parties cannot agree on who should be the SJE, the court may select the expert witness from a list prepared by the parties or direct that the SJE be selected in such manner as the court may direct.[75] Appointing a SJE has many benefits. As the Working Party observed, 'all the parties and the court may benefit significantly from the services of a well-chosen and intelligently employed SJE. The appointment of SJEs, even if only in a minority of cases, may place a professional premium on impartiality and so generally raise expert standards.'[76] The Second Year Report observed that '[When] a SJE is appointed in an appropriate case, partisan conflicting views are avoided and only one set of fees and expenses incurred.'[77]

The number of appointments of SJEs in the District Court (**DC**) has increased sharply in the second year of the CJR when compared with the first year.[78] The Second Year Report 2011 gave a promising account on the use of SJEs in the DC:

> 'Further analysis reflects that more than half of these cases were personal injuries claims and the majority of SJE orders were made pursuant to filing of consent summons. As was the case in the first year, no special efforts were made by judges and judicial officers to encourage the appointments in the DC. It is believed that more SJEs were appointed because of the change in litigation culture and the relatively small amount of claims involved in the DC.'[79]

While sharp increases of SJE cases was noted in both the second and third years,[80] the Fourth Year Report observed that this trend has changed in the fourth year: 'In the DC, after a significant increase in the numbers of SJEs in the second and third years of the Post-CJR Periods, there was a drop in the fourth year mainly attributable to PI actions. Some parties indicated their preference of using their own

73 RHC O. 38, r. 4A(1). The order may be set aside if the court is satisfied that it is inappropriate. In such an event, the parties are free to appoint their own expert witnesses: RHC O. 38, r. 4A(7).

74 RHC O. 38, rr. 4A(4) and 4A(6). A non-exhaustive list of relevant circumstances is set out in RHC O. 38, r. 4A(5).

75 RHC O. 38, r. 4A(2).

76 Final Report 2004, para 630, p. 333.

77 Second Year Report 2011, para 78, p. 37.

78 Compare the two appointments of SJEs in the DC during the period between 2 April 2009 and 31 March 2010 to the 80 appointments during the period between 1 April 2010 and 31 March 2011: *see* Second Year Report 2011, p. 38 (Table 23.2 and para 79).

79 Second Year Report 2011, para 79, p. 38.

80 Third Year Report 2012, para 99, p. 41.

expert particularly if the expert was nominated by the other side. For PI cases involving smaller sums, parties might agree not to have any expert evidence at all in order to save costs. We need to observe for a longer period to see if the use of SJEs indeed becomes more commonly accepted in the DC.'[81]

Despite being an innovative measure, the use of SJEs remains very limited. In practice, it is seldom used in commercial cases. This is partly due to fact that many cases are too complex to be suitable for SJE. As a leading practice manual puts it 'Reasons why separate experts may be more appropriate include: (i) the case is large and complex, (ii) the expert issues are contentious and requires the Court to sample a range of expert opinions rather than being confined to the view of a single expert.'[82]

Part B: Expert Evidence in the Context of Personal Injury Litigation

6. Expert Evidence and Personal Injury Claims

The most germane elements of a personal injury (**PI**) case are the issues of liability and quantum. Given that a large number of such cases involve actions by individual litigants against large commercial entities such as insurance companies, the need for the resolution of such disputes in a fair, just and economical manner is of overriding importance. In personal injury litigation, the courts are sometimes faced with the undesirable intermingling of the legal principles of tort law and the emotional sufferings of the injured litigants. It is on these occasions that the neutral and detached testimony of expert witnesses can greatly assist the court in dealing with the difficult questions concerning liability and quantum.

In Hong Kong, the protocol for commissioning expert reports is contained in Section I of the Practice Direction 18.1 on the Personal Injuries List (**PD 18.1**). PD 18.1 came into effect in April 2009 and gives effect to the changes brought about by the CJR. Whilst not meant to supersede or substitute the rules relating to expert evidence that are contained in the RHC, PD 18.1 provides practical guidance for practitioners engaged in personal injury practice in Hong Kong.

7. An Overview of the Process

The most common type of opinion evidence that is commissioned by parties in personal injury cases is evidence in the form of written reports from medical experts. According to PD 18.1, leave of the court or consent of the parties is required before any expert evidence can be adduced at trial and as soon as a party becomes aware of the need to present such evidence at trial, permission should be sought from the court. The aim of this rule is not to stifle the right of a party to adduce expert evidence but rather to allow the court to assess the necessity of the expert

81 Fourth Year Report 2013, para 119, p. 43.
82 Chan & Rogers 2010, para 8.29, p. 197.

evidence. In furthering the underlying objectives of the CJR, the courts are duty bound to ensure procedural economy in the conduct of proceedings and avoid the escalation of excessive costs. If after hearing the arguments for the inclusion of the expert evidence, the court decides that such evidence will not aid in the determination of the issues, then the application should be denied. Although a party whose application has been denied is still free to commission the expert report, the party should proceed with the knowledge that it does so at its own risk in terms of costs and that it would be highly unlikely that the court would subsequently allow that report to be used at the trial.

In personal injury litigation, the need to obtain an expert medical report becomes evident at an early stage and often even before the commencement of proceedings. Once a claimant becomes aware of the need for this type of evidence, one of the first issues to determine is whether a single joint expert should be appointed or whether the examination should be carried out by an expert who can then conduct a joint examination and prepare a joint report with an expert retained by the defendant. In most cases, claimants prefer the latter course of action as it grants the claimant and its legal representatives the freedom to choose the expert of their choice and it presents an opportunity for them to independently assess the strengths and weaknesses of the medical evidence.

The settlement of disputes in an efficient manner is one of the underlying objectives of the RHC and the CJR and the courts are continually mindful of the need to manage cases in order to further that objective. In that respect, the protocol for commissioning expert reports as stated in PD 18.1 provides clear guidelines for practitioners and parties to the litigation. In order to avoid any disruptions to the case management timetable, the experts who are chosen by the parties should be informed that they must be able to produce the expert report (whether by a single joint expert or jointly by the experts of each side) in a timely manner. The experts also have to be conscious of the fact that the fixture of the case management timetable will be dependent on the assessment by the court of the reasonable time that would be required for the preparation of the case rather than the availability of the experts. In order to avoid any disruptions to the case management timetable, the courts are generally averse to vary the dates that have previously been fixed. If a party which has instructed a medical expert subsequently discovers that a date for the examination of the injured claimant has to be changed, it is incumbent upon that party to inform the PI Master at once (but no later than 5 days). The Master can then assess the situation and decide whether any extensions of the time can be granted. PD 18.1 makes it clear that no such extensions are to be granted as a matter of course and only the provision of sufficient grounds would make the application for extension successful. Where the court finds the reasons to be below the acceptable standard, it can impose peremptory orders stipulating sanctions in the case of further non-compliance.

8. Joint Examination and Joint Report

Whilst the CJR may have formally documented and instituted the judicial mechanisms to achieve greater efficiency and speedier resolution of civil disputes, judges in personal injury cases had already been moving towards the adoption of the use of the joint examinations and the joint report approach even prior to the implementation of the CJR. Whereas in the past when each party would retain its own expert and each expert would prepare his own report, PD 18.1 now mandates the use of joint examinations and reports (except cases involving single joint experts as discussed below). In *Mok King Sun v. Turn Round Company Limited,*[83] Fung J listed the benefits of the joint approach:

> '(1) avoidance of different observations on different occasions, or disputes on observations under single examination;
> (2) discussions amongst the experts to narrow down the issues;
> (3) specifying matters agreed and matters not agreed and the reasons for any non-agreement;
> (4) avoidance of numerous supplemental reports commenting on the reports of the other side; and
> (5) minimizing the need to call the experts to deal with matters which could have been dealt with under (1) to (4) above.'[84]

PD 18.1 has been drafted in a pragmatic manner because it states that if one of the experts is unwilling to conduct a joint examination or prepare a joint report with the expert of the other party, each party shall then nominate new experts to conduct the joint examinations and prepare the joint report. If there is still disagreement on this issue, the parties can seek directions from the court. Also, any party that unreasonably fails to cooperate in instructing a joint examination or arranging for the preparation of a joint examination report of an injured person risks the imposition of sanctions by the court including the refusal by the court to grant leave to adduce the medical evidence prepared by the infringing party's own expert and/or refusal by the court to allow costs for obtaining such a report.

When instructing experts for the preparation of a joint examination and a joint report, parties should also ensure that the instructions provided to the experts are clear and the matters to be investigated by the experts are defined in a cogent manner. The purpose of this stipulation is to avoid the multiplicity of reports and supplemental examinations of the experts that can result from initial failures of the legal advisors to delineate the issues, which in turn defeats the purposes of cost efficiency and timely resolution of disputes.

For their part, the experts also have a duty to clearly state the issues on which they have reached a common opinion and what that opinion is so that the court can formulate its own views on the issues. Likewise, if there are any issues on which the

83 (unreported) HCPI 865/2007, 25 March 2009.
84 *Ibidem*, para 26.

experts have failed to reach a common consensus, they have to voice their reasons for disagreement and state their personal views. Again, this exercise can allow the court to discern the incongruities between the experts and adopt the most convincing position.

9. Single Joint Expert in PI Cases

One of the more innovative changes brought about by the CJR, as already briefly alluded to above, has been the notion of the single joint expert (**SJE**). The new RHC Order 38, rule 4A states that any action in which the parties to litigation are of the view that a SJE should be appointed or any action in which the court is satisfied that such an arrangement would be in the interests of justice, the court may appoint a SJE to provide his opinion.

Though the list is not exhaustive, the court will consider the following factors when deciding upon the appointment of a SJE:

> '(a) whether the issues requiring expert evidence can readily be identified in advance;
> (b) the nature of those issues and the likely degree of controversy attaching to the expert evidence in question;
> (c) the value of the claim and the importance of the issue on which expert evidence is sought, as compared with the cost of employing separate expert witnesses to give evidence;
> (d) whether any party has already incurred expenses for instructing an expert who may be asked to give evidence as an expert witness in the case; and;
> (e) whether any significant difficulties are likely to arise in relation to –
> (i) the choosing of the joint expert witness;
> (ii) the drawing up of his instructions; or
> (iii) the provision to him of the information and other facilities needed to perform his duties.'[85]

There is no doubt that the idea of a SJE offers an attractive alternative when compared with the appointment of separate experts by individual parties engaged in personal injury litigation. One of the more intuitive arguments for the adoption of the system is that it can lead to a significant reduction in time and costs as opposed to the two-party appointed system. It is not difficult to comprehend the reduction in costs because in almost all cases, the appointment of one expert is going to be more cost-effective than the appointment of two experts. Also, in personal injury cases, one factor that in some instances can lead to delay is the lack of qualified experts in certain medical specialties. The highly sought after experts are booked well in advance and it can be difficult to arrange a joint examination if both experts are popular in their field. The appointment of a SJE can greatly assuage this difficulty, as parties need only be concerned with the timetable of one expert.

Proponents of SJEs also argue that it cures other deficiencies of the two-party appointed system. Since both parties are paying the SJE, there is no pressure on the

85 RHC O. 38, r. 4A(5).

SJE to compulsorily embrace the position of either party and he can dispense his opinion in an objective and unbiased manner. This not only assists in the court in seeing a clearer picture of the issues but also fosters a less adversarial environment that in turn encourages settlement between the parties.

Though it may appear to be an attractive alternative, in personal injury litigation, the SJE approach is suitable for a very limited number of cases. Firstly, given the technical nature of the practice, it is often incumbent upon claimants to have their injuries assessed by a healthcare expert before the commencement of proceedings. When one party has already instructed its own expert, it is unlikely that the opposing side will subsequently agree to the appointment of the same expert as the SJE. Also, by the time the decision to appoint a SJE is made in most cases, the costs for the appointment of two experts have usually been incurred. Since most parties retain the services of their own experts even before the proceedings are begun, the cost benefits of a SJE approach are most often not realized.

Another argument against the adoption of a SJE in personal injury litigation is the limited information that is available to the court in forming a conclusion on the issues. The obvious advantage of having two or more experts is that each expert can bring his ideas and conclusions that are based on his individual assessment of the injuries. Though the set of facts may be identical, each expert scrutinizes them from his own unique perspective and forms an opinion that is based on his accepted school of thought. The court has the benefit of hearing different competing theories and the onus is on each expert to persuade the court to accept his conclusions. When there is only one expert, the court is deprived of the chance to test the multiplicity of conclusions and select the most suitable conclusion after a careful and deliberate examination of the facts. The danger is more acute in cases involving highly technical matters as the opinion of the SJE can effectively decide the case and take the decision making power away from the tribunal. To avoid this undesirable result, the use of SJE is best confined to low value and low complexity cases where the medical knowledge is relatively controversial and the judges have sufficient experience to make their decisions without over-reliance on the opinion of the SJE.

10. Critical Review of the Case Law on Expert Evidence in PI Cases

Cost effectiveness, expeditiousness, reasonable proportion and procedural economy in the conduct of civil proceedings are the stated objectives of the CJR. Although the initial analysis of the perceived deficiencies in a system and the subsequent implementation of reforms to offset the supposed flaws are imperative stages in the quest to achieve sustainable progress, all this groundwork is futile unless there are some measurable and meaningful changes brought about by the reforms. So far, no comprehensive study to assess the effectiveness of the CJR in the area of expert evidence has been carried out. However, there are some encouraging signs in the law relating to the use of expert evidence that suggest that the reforms are achieving the intended results.

In *Tang Tak Ping v. Kai Shing Construction Company and Another,*[86] the court highlighted the relevant principles to be followed in personal injury and medical negligence cases when considering the appointment of experts. In that case, the parties had obtained a joint report from two orthopaedic experts. In the report, both experts agreed that no further expert reports were necessary. Nonetheless, the plaintiff obtained an additional report from a psychiatrist who diagnosed the plaintiff to have suffered from a mild depressive episode. Subsequently, the plaintiff's solicitors wrote to the defendants' solicitors to propose a joint psychiatric examination to be conducted by a SJE or by two experts. The defendants' solicitors replied that previous reports were sufficient but if the plaintiff intended to adduce a further expert report, the correct course of action was to seek leave from the court. The plaintiff ignored the suggestion and appointed its own expert. In its decision, the court first emphasized the general rule stated in PD 18.1 that a party wishing to adduce expert evidence at trial must either obtain leave of the court or seek consent from the opposing side. The mandatory nature of the general rule in PD 18.1 means that failure to obtain the court's permission or the consent of the other party puts the party wanting to adduce the evidence at risk of adverse cost consequences and/or refusal by the court to allow the admission of the said evidence. The court also took the opportunity to restate the factors it would take into consideration when exercising its judicial discretion in granting leave for the admission of expert evidence. The overriding element is that of necessity of the evidence. In light of the underlying objectives of the CJR, if the court deems that the evidence of the proposed expert will assist it in determining the contentious issues between the parties, the court may allow the evidence. It is only then that the court should move onto considering the suitability of appointing a SJE or the appointment of two experts to prepare a joint report or even the appointment of each party's own experts to prepare their separate reports. Finally, the court pointed out that if the expert evidence is required only for issues related to quantum, the general rule in PD 18.1 is to be applied and any party that commissions a report without leave of the court or the consent of the other party risks adverse cost consequences. However, the court also highlighted the fact that in medical negligence cases where the issues are related to liability only, sequential exchange of expert reports remains the norm and parties are free to commission evidence from experts without the need to seek leave of the court or consent from the other party. Unless there are some exceptional circumstances in the case that would warrant a joint report on liability, the parties would not face any adverse cost consequences as stated in PD 18.1.

In *Tang Tak Ping,*[87] the plaintiff tried to persuade the court to appoint its own psychiatric expert and another expert to be nominated by the defendants to carry out a joint examination and prepare a joint report. The court held that in the interest of saving time and reducing costs, the appointment of a SJE was adequate. The

86 (unreported) HCPI 539/2011, 6 February 2012.

87 *Ibidem.*

court also disqualified the plaintiff's expert from being appointed as the SJE as the plaintiff had appointed him without the leave of the court or the consent of the defendants. In terms of costs, the court held that the costs incurred by the plaintiff in its unilateral appointment of the expert would not form any part of the plaintiff's costs of the action and the plaintiff would have to pay 50 per cent of the costs of the hearing on the expert evidence to the defendant in any event.

Given the divergent needs to keep practice directions as clear and concise as possible whilst striving to address as many of the complexities that can arise in civil litigation, it is not surprising that PD 18.1 does not cover every facet of personal injury litigation. One issue that PD 18.1 fails to address is the proper procedure to be followed when parties wish to clarify issues expressed by experts in joint expert reports. The issue arose *in Liu Ka Chun v. Hong Kong Airport Services Limited and Others.*[88] As the court noted in this case, where experts have been appointed by each party to produce a joint report, the experts need to set out clearly for the benefit of the court the issues and areas on which they agree. Similarly, if there are any areas of disagreement between the experts, they need to highlight those areas and each expert should then give his opinion on the disagreed issues and provide sufficient reasons for holding such an opinion. At times, a party may wish to seek further clarification of the differing opinion expressed by the opposing party's or even their own expert. In handing down its decision, the court restated the proper procedure that it had enunciated in *Chan Yuet Keung v. Harmony International Knitting Factory Limited.*[89] In the first instance, the party seeking the clarification should write to the other party and seek the other party's consent for the question to be put to the expert. If the other party disagrees with the question that has been raised, the other party can then propose a different question for the consideration of the first party. The parties should only seek the assistance of the court in resolving the matter if they cannot reach any consensus.[90] If the matter does indeed have to be adjudicated by the court, the court retains the discretion to impose sanctions on any party that raised a matter for clarification that ought not to have been raised or on the party that unreasonably refused to agree to questions being put to the expert to clarify genuine issues. The possible imposition of adverse cost orders or other sanctions is consistent with the underlying objectives of the CJR and it compels each party to act reasonably and judiciously in seeking clarifications or agreeing to the questions being posed by the other party.

In *Chan Yuet Keung,*[91] the court also made it clear that the same procedure is to be adopted whether a SJE produces the joint report or whether two or more experts appointed by each party produce the report. The court further stated that where two or more experts have been appointed, even though the party seeking clarification is posing the question to one of the experts for further explanation,

88 (unreported) HCPI 416/2009, 11 November 2011.
89 (unreported) HCPI 144/2009, 2 November 2010.
90 HCPI 416/2009, paras 5-7.
91 HCPI 144/2009.

since the exercise is a joint one, the other expert should be apprised of the question also. If the other expert thinks that it is appropriate for him to comment on the clarification provided by the expert being questioned, he ought to do so. This joint exercise only comes to an end when the judge decides that the difference of opinion between the experts is so great that they have to give oral evidence at the trial. At this juncture, the parties can resume private discussions with their own experts. In the instant case, the plaintiff had tried to adduce a supplemental report from its expert as evidence at trial to clarify certain issues in the joint report. In seeking the leave of the court, the plaintiff also proposed that the defendants be granted leave to seek comment on the clarification from their own expert. The court found that the plaintiff had adopted the wrong procedure. In any event, the court found the additional views of the plaintiff's expert to be of no assistance to the court and held that there were no areas in the joint report that required further clarification. The court awarded the costs of the hearing to the defendants.[92]

In Hong Kong personal injury cases, the practice of adducing evidence from non-medical experts such as occupational therapists or rehabilitation experts at trial is pervasive. Even before the commencement of CJR, the court routinely reminded litigants of not only the importance of identifying the name and field of the expert whose evidence they wished to adduce but also the issues which the expert would address at trial. In *Lam So Chai v. Cheung Sai Lui trading as Hoi Fung Stevedore and Transportation Company*,[93] Fung J. observed that non-medical experts often relied on medical reports to form their opinions and the contents of the reports prepared by them were frequently too long. It was counter-productive for these experts to extensively repeat the contents of the medical reports and such a practice went against the spirit of cost effectiveness and efficiency that was advocated by the CJR. Emphasizing the necessity for quality as opposed to quantity, Fung J. suggested the capping of costs on the preparation of reports by non-medical needs experts in certain cases.[94]

This issue came to a head again in *Wong Siu Tong v. So Man Che and Another*.[95] The plaintiff made an application to adduce expert evidence of a rehabilitation consultant. The court held that the majority of the relevant evidence in this case was to be adduced from the neurological experts and the only issues for the consideration of the rehabilitation expert were related to the resources required and the costs of home care for the plaintiff. Although the judge ultimately decided to grant leave to the plaintiff to adduce the report of the rehabilitation expert, the court reiterated the fact that in appropriate cases, a judge was well within his discretion to cap the costs for the preparation of such reports.[96] Also, the court sounded a warning to the plaintiff that if any costs were unreasonably incurred during the commission of the rehabilitation consultant report, the defendants would be at

92 *Ibidem*.

93 (unreported) HCPI 360/2007, 3 July 2009.

94 *Ibidem*, para 17.

95 (unreported) HCPI 506/2009, 24 December 2009.

96 *Ibidem*, para 20.

liberty to ask the judge to disallow the costs pursuant to RHC Order 62 rule 5(2).[97] This decision is again an encouraging sign of the shift in judicial attitude that reflects the intentions of the court and spells out to personal injury litigants in a very unambiguous manner that many of the previously tolerated practices are going to undergo much stricter scrutiny in the post-CJR era.

This is not to say that every post-reform decision has been an example of the definite and unmistakable validation by the court to adopt the goals of the CJR. A case in point is the recent decision in *Daimler AG (formerly known as Mercedes-Benz AG) v. Helge Herbert Leiduck and Another.*[98] Whilst this was not a personal injury case, it nevertheless involved the appointment of a SJE to assess the physical and mental capacities of the first defendant and the case provides useful guidance in personal injury litigation. At issue was whether the plaintiff could adduce evidence from its own expert to contradict the evidence of the SJE.

Since 2000, a number of English authorities have clearly affirmed the principle that the appointment of a SJE does not necessarily limit the right of a party to adduce additional expert evidence. The most cited example is the judgment of Neuberger J (as he then was) in *Cosgrove v. Pattison*[99] in which he cited nine factors for consideration in allowing a second expert:

(1) the nature of the dispute;
(2) the number of disputes on which the expert evidence is relevant;
(3) the reason for requiring the second report;
(4) the amount at stake or the nature of the issues at stake;
(5) the effect of permitting a second expert report on the conduct of the trial;
(6) the delay in making the application;
(7) the delay that might be caused in the conduct of the proceedings;
(8) any other special features;
(9) the overall justice to the parties.[100]

In *Cosgrove,*[101] Neuberger J (as he then was) had based his decision on the earlier case of *Daniels v. Walker,*[102] in which Lord Woolf MR (as he then was) had held that if the party that wished to adduce the additional evidence had reasons that were 'not fanciful', it ought to be allowed to do so. In a later case, Lord Woolf himself intimated, *obiter*, a stricter test requiring 'good reasons'.[103]

97 *Ibidem*, para 23.
98 (unreported) HCA 4089/1994, 17 April 2014.
99 [2001] CPLR 177; [2001] CP Rep 68.
100 *Ibidem.*
101 *Ibidem.*
102 [2000] 1 WLR 1382 (CA).
103 *Peet v. Mid-Kent Healthcare Trust* [2002] 1 WLR 210 (CA).

In *Daimler*,[104] Recorder L. Wong, SC considered all the above cases before reaching her decision. When commenting on the nine factors proposed by Neuberger J (as he then was) in *Cosgrove*, she added that the list was not exhaustive and two additional factors were relevant to the case. One was whether the SJE's report could be challenged without the need for a further report and the other was whether the parties had already engaged own-party experts. Recorder L. Wong, SC ultimately preferred the 'not fanciful reasons' test and gave leave to the plaintiff to adduce evidence of its own expert. In resisting the application, the defendants' lawyers had expressed strong concern that additional time and costs would be incurred if the plaintiff's application were successful. Whilst the judge accepted the possibility that an application for reciprocal leave by the defendants and the recall of the SJE would inevitably lead to increased costs and time, she held that both sides would suffer the prejudice equally. Also, she stated that the additional costs should be 'viewed and weighed in perspective of the magnitude of costs that has no doubt already been incurred in this matter'.[105] As for the timetable, Recorder L. Wong, SC again conceded that it would slip but she was of the opinion that had the defendants' lawyers acted more quickly in bringing the matter of the 1st defendant's competency to the attention of the court, the preparation work for the additional evidence could have been carried out much earlier.[106] Undoubtedly, the complexity of the medical issues involved and the delay in bringing the matter to the attention of the court by the defendants played significant roles in the final decision of the court. Whilst the decision itself appears to be correct, the reasons given by the court in relation to the issues of delay and increased costs are not entirely persuasive. It remains to be seen whether this case will be interpreted as suggesting that as long as the reasons for wanting to adduce additional evidence from your own expert are 'not fanciful', hurdles such as cost and delay can be overcome without too much difficulty. In this new era when costs and the timely resolution of disputes have taken on a greater significance in the progress of cases through the court, the ideas that the costs of an application should be viewed in perspective of the totality of the costs or that both sides would suffer the prejudice equally are not the most resounding endorsements of the CJR and arguably run contrary to the aims of the underlying objectives.

11. Further Reforms and Concluding Remarks

On 1 April 2013, Lord Justice Jackson's cost reforms (**Jackson Reforms**) came into effect in England and Wales. Though the primary focus of the reforms is on personal injury litigation, they will also have an impact on other areas of civil litigation. In respect of expert evidence, an amendment to the practice direction to

104 (unreported) HCA 4089/1994, 17 April 2014.
105 (unreported) HCA 4089/1994, 17 April 2014, para 47.
106 *Ibidem*, paras 48-49.

Civil Procedure Rule 35[107] now allows a judge to order expert witnesses to give concurrent evidence. The practice, also known colloquially as 'hot-tubbing' originated in Australia and was described by The Hon Justice Peter McLellan (writing extra-judicially) as:

> '... a discussion chaired by the judge in which the various experts, the parties, the advocates and the judge engage in a cooperative endeavor to identify the issues and arrive where possible at a common resolution of them. Where resolution of issues is not possible, a structured discussion, with the judge as chairperson, allows the experts to give their opinions without the constraints of the adversarial process and in a forum which enables them to respond directly to each other. The judge is not confined to the opinion of one advisor but has the benefit of multiple advisors who are rigorously examined in public.'[108]

The process bears some similarity to the preparation of a joint expert report in that the experts retained by the parties prepare their individual reports that are later exchanged between the experts. The experts then meet and discuss the areas of agreement and issues on which they differ. After the discussion, they prepare a Joint Statement in which they state a list of issues they disagree on and this Joint Statement is subsequently passed onto the judge. At trial, the experts are heard together at the witness table and the judge directs a discussion of the issues in disagreement. The experts can question each other's opinion in the open court setting and the lawyers of the parties also get a chance to challenge the opinion of the opposing expert.[109]

The most obvious advantage of this approach is that it allows all the expert evidence to be heard at the same time. In a traditional trial, significant time can elapse between the testimonies of different experts and in cases involving complex issues, it can become difficult for judges to keep track of the evidence given by each expert. Concurrent evidence overcomes this difficulty by ensuring that both experts give their opinions at the same time and it enables the judge to compare and contrast the testimonies of the experts at the same time.

Only one year has passed since the implementation of the Jackson Reforms and it may be too early to assess the viability of implementing a similar concurrent evidence procedure in Hong Kong. However, if the England and Wales experience can demonstrate that the practice can lead to a narrowing of issues and a resultant reduction in time and costs, a similar procedure could prove beneficial in Hong Kong personal injury practice as well as civil litigation practice generally.

107 PD 35.11 (of CPR 35).

108 McClellan 2010, p. 264.

109 The procedure described here is specific to PI litigation. In general civil litigation, the usual procedure starts with the exchange of provisional expert reports, followed by a without prejudice meeting of the experts to determine the issues that they can agree on and issues they cannot agree on. Then a joint expert report is filed with the court setting out the issues that they can agree on. The process ends with the filing of the final expert reports on issues that they cannot agree on.

On the whole, the CJR measures have been effective in expediting the fact-finding process where expert evidence is used. Adversarial excesses in the deployment of expert evidence are exposed and generally rectified partly through the codification of principles of expert independence and impartiality, and partly by way of conferring extensive case management powers on the court to regulate the use of expert evidence.

Bibliography

Chan 2012
Chan, P.C.H., 'Efficiency and Truth in Civil Fact-finding: The Evolving Role of the Judge in Mainland China and Hong Kong and the Effect of the Policy Preference for Court Mediation on Fact-finding in the People's Courts', in Van Rhee C.H. & Uzelac, A. (eds.), *Truth and Efficiency in Civil Litigation: Fundamental Aspects of Fact-finding and Evidence-taking in a Comparative Context*, Antwerp: Intersentia, 2012, p. 231-260.

Chan & Rogers 2010
Hon. Justice Chan, P. & Rogers, M., (eds.), *Hong Kong Civil Justice Reform Practice Manual*, 2nd edn., Hong Kong: Sweet & Maxwell, 2010.

Final Report 2004
Chief Justice's Working Party On Civil Justice Reform, *The Final Report of the Chief Justice's Working Party on Civil Justice Reform*, 3 March 2004.

First Year Report 2010
Legislative Council Panel on Administration of Justice and Legal Services, '*The First Year's Implementation of the Civil Justice Reform from 2 April 2009 to 31 March 2010*', LC Paper No. CB(2)591/10-11(06), December 2010.

Fourth Year Report 2013
Legislative Council Panel on Administration of Justice and Legal Services, '*Statistics on the First Four Years' Implementation of the Civil Justice Reform from 2 April 2009 to 31 March 2013*', December 2013. Available at: <http://www.civiljustice.gov.hk/-eng/implement.html>.

Interim Report 2001
Chief Justice's Working Party On Civil Justice Reform, '*Civil Justice Reform: Interim Report and Consultative Paper*', 21 November 2001.

Lau 2014
Lau, D., *Civil Procedure in Hong Kong: A Guide To The Main Principles*, 3rd edn., Hong Kong: Sweet & Maxwell, 2014.

McClellan 2010
Hon. Justice McClellan, P., 'New Method With Experts - Concurrent Evidence', *Journal of Court Innovation*, 2010, Vol. 3(1), p. 259-268.

Second Year Report 2011
Legislative Council Panel on Administration of Justice and Legal Services, 'The First Two Year's Implementation of the Civil Justice Reform from 2 April 2009 to 31 March 2011', LC Paper No. CB(2)713/11-12(01), December 2011.

Third Year Report 2012
Legislative Council Panel on Administration of Justice and Legal Services, '*Statistics on the First Three Years'* Implementation of the Civil Justice Reform from 2 April 2009 to 31 March 2012', December 2012 (see <www.civiljustice.gov.hk/eng/implement/-CJR_First_3Year_Implementation.pdf>).

White Book 2014
Justice Chan, P. & Rogers, M. (eds.), *Hong Kong Civil Procedure 2014*, Vol. 1, Hong Kong: Sweet & Maxwell, 2014.

Wilkinson, Cheung & Booth 2011
Wilkinson, M., Cheung, E.T.M. & Booth, C.N., *A Guide to Civil Procedure in Hong Kong*, 4th edn., Hong Kong: LexisNexis, 2011.

T. Zoroska-Kamilovska

THE NEW RULES OF EXPERT EVIDENCE IN MACEDONIAN CIVIL PROCEDURE: ARE THEY A FAILED EFFORT AT REFORM?

1. Introduction

For decades now, it has been claimed that as regards civil procedural law the Republic of Macedonia belongs to the Continental tradition and more precisely to the so-called 'Germanic legal circle'. Just as in the other ex-Yugoslav republics, the fundamentals of Macedonian civil procedure are deeply rooted in the Roman law tradition within the Germanic circle. It was the Austrian Code of Civil Procedure of 1895 that traditionally provided the inspiration and model solutions for civil procedural issues. However, this practice was discontinued beginning about ten years ago. A striking trend of convergence between the common law and Continental legal systems spread to Macedonia, resulting in a completely different approach to the concept of civil proceedings in general, and particularly with regard to the rules of evidence. The changed position of expert evidence as a particular means of evidence in Macedonian civil procedure seems to be one of the best examples of shifting from the typically Continental approach to the more adversarial approach.[1]

This contribution aims to analyse the altered rules of expert evidence in Macedonian civil procedure and also to reflect on the extent to which the changed position of expert evidence has not lived up to the expected improvement in efficiency and cost cutting, which were the prime reasons for the change.

1 Some additional elements of the adversarial approach were also announced in the last proposed amendments of the Macedonian Civil Procedure Act (still pending in Parliament), such as cross-examination and discovery.

2. A Summary of the Regime of Expert Evidence in Macedonian Civil Procedure before 2010

Following the independence of Macedonia in 1991, the Yugoslav Civil Procedure Act of 1976 continued to apply until 1998, when the first Macedonian Civil Procedure Act came into force. Although at that time the country went through a period of fundamental changes in its political and economic order, this did not imply a re-evaluation of its system of civil justice. Therefore, the first Macedonian Civil Procedure Act did not depart from the former Yugoslav Act. In the field of fact-finding and evidence-taking, Macedonian civil procedure was a mixture of adversarial and inquisitorial elements, with emphasis on the latter.[2]

The discussions concerning the possible reforms of civil procedure started several years later, when the Macedonian Judiciary was hampered by extensive backlogs of civil cases. All the analyses and debates (although modest) indicated that in Macedonian civil procedure there was a tension between efficiency and the pursuit of truth, to the detriment of efficiency. There was a general consensus that reform was needed, which very soon resulted in the new Macedonian Civil Procedure Act (MCPA) of 2005.[3] Several important novelties were introduced with this Act, but the crucial one was a more passive role of the judge concerning fact-finding and evidence-taking, as it became the responsibility of the parties to assert facts and to present means of evidence.[4] This was followed by restrictions with regard to the time frames limiting the parties' rights to assert new facts and evidence (preclusions). The parties could assert facts and propose means of evidence in a statement of claim and in a statement of defence, then in the preparatory briefs, at the preparatory hearing, and at the first session of the main hearing at the latest.[5]

The power of the court to introduce facts and take evidence not proposed by the parties was abolished.[6] The only exception was the possibility for the court to take expert evidence and order an inspection *ex officio*. The exception concerning expert evidence will be examined in more detail below. In fact, it implies the need for a full analysis of the regime of expert evidence in Macedonian civil procedure until 2010.

2 Janevski & Zoroska-Kamilovska 2012, p. 89.

3 Official Gazette of the Republic of Macedonia, No. 79/2005.

4 Art. 7(1) MCPA 2005.

5 Arts. 176, 270 and 272 MCPA 2005.

6 Nevertheless, it should be stressed that the rules regarding the parties' initiative in fact-finding and evidence-taking were (and still are) notably softened by the rules on active judicial case management in terms of the so-called 'substantive procedural guidance' of a judge. Namely, even though the judge is bound by the factual allegations and evidence proposed by the parties, he has a right and duty to stimulate the parties in order to amend and clarify their factual allegations, and to propose additional means of evidence (e.g. with questions, hints, etc.). If necessary, the judge also needs to openly review his legal viewpoint with the parties. See Art. 283 MCPA.

First, it is very important to highlight that just as in other Continental civil procedures, the person providing expert evidence in Macedonian civil procedure is not referred to as an 'expert witness' but simply called an 'expert'. This is due to the fact that on the Continent expert evidence is considered to be fundamentally different from the testimony of witnesses. Namely, unlike the witness, the expert is also appointed to draw conclusions (or to give an opinion) on the basis of the available and relevant facts (findings). While a witness may only give evidence of facts within his own knowledge, the fundamental characteristic of expert evidence is that it is opinion evidence[7] based on the specialized knowledge of an expert. This opinion evidence is (or more precisely was) given on scientific and technological matters which are beyond the knowledge and experience of judges.

The MCPA of 2005 (like its predecessors) does not explicitly define the notion of expert evidence, although it refers to its fundamental features. It appears in Article 235 (named 'experts'), which states:

> (1) The court shall take expert evidence on the party's request, when professional knowledge, which the court does not have, is necessary in order to determine or clarify any fact.
>
> (2) By exception, the court shall take expert evidence, without the party's proposal, if during the taking of evidence of a disputed fact, professional knowledge, which the court does not have, is needed.

From the cited article it becomes evident that under the MCPA of 2005 the notion of expert evidence required matters at issue (factual questions) which necessitate expertise for their observation, description or analysis. And this could be provided by a person who has professional knowledge (or who is qualified) to give expert evidence on any relevant matter (a so-called expert). On the contrary, expert evidence was not necessary where on the relevant facts of the case the judge could form his own conclusions without the help of an expert. Procedural theory defines experts as 'persons invited before the court, by using their expert knowledge, to state their current observations (findings) and an opinion on a fact that may be of importance for determining the validity of the statements that are subject of proof'.[8]

Another important element of the regime of expert evidence under the MCPA of 2005 is the principle of party presentation of expert evidence. However, this principle was significantly softened by the judicial power to introduce this means of evidence *ex officio,* without any proposal of the parties. Although this was supposed

7 Due to this, Remme Verkerk justifiably observes that 'although most modern Continental systems list the expert amongst the means of evidence, it is from an historic point of view disputed whether or not the expert provides evidence'. Furthermore, he acknowledges that 'many Austrian authors have argued that the expert is primarily an "assistant" of the court although his findings may also, secondly, constitute evidence'; Verkerk 2009, p. 170.

8 Janevski & Zoroska-Kamilovska 2012, p. 335; also Triva & Dika 2004, p. 526.

to be an exception in introducing this kind of evidence,[9] the inquisitorial element gave the court broad discretion to turn to experts in order to resolve complex or difficult factual questions, whenever professional knowledge was needed.

Furthermore, according to the MCPA of 2005 in both situations - when expert evidence is proposed by a party or ordered by the court on its own motion - the expert was appointed by the court. The MCPA of 2005 adhered to the Continental tradition pursuant to which the expert is selected and commissioned by the court (the so-called court-appointed expert). The court itself selected and appointed a neutral expert, who was treated as the judge's aide.[10] [11] There were, of course, mechanisms for protecting the parties' interests: the parties needed to be heard before the appointment of an expert[12] and also they could challenge the expert for bias, on the same grounds as judges.[13] Experts were appointed primarily from the list of permanent court experts on a certain type of expertise.[14] The appointed experts were obliged to answer the summons of the court and to prepare their findings and an opinion. The court was empowered to impose a fine on the expert if he failed to perform the duty to provide expertise,[15] and also to release him from said duty.[16]

Finally, the court itself instructed the expert in terms of formulating the expert's task. Just as John H. Langbein has observed for German civil procedure, the court that selected the expert instructed him in the sense of propounding the facts that he was to assume or to investigate and in framing the questions that the court wished the expert to address.[17] The expert was instructed to prepare written findings and an opinion within a time limit set by the court. In order to be truly of assistance to the court, the expert should not only give an opinion, but also support it, showing the court that it was well substantiated.

9 Before 2005, this inquisitorial element was even more emphasized - a court might decide to appoint an expert against the will of the parties, or not to appoint an expert although both parties would like the court to do so.

10 For the same position of expert evidence in other Continental systems, see Verkerk 2009, p. 168-169.

11 Triva & Dika 2004, p. 527.

12 Nevertheless, the MCPA of 2005 allowed the judge to decide not to hear the parties in emergency cases in order to avoid excessive costs or delay. See Art. 236 MCPA 2005.

13 See Art. 239 MCPA 2005.

14 Until 2005, the courts kept and updated lists of so-called permanent court experts. These lists were a primary tool for the courts to find experts. However, judges were not bound by these lists and the court might appoint an expert who was not on the list.

15 See Art. 240 MCPA 2005.

16 Upon the expert's request, the court was empowered to release him from a duty to provide expertise based on the same grounds that the witness may refuse to testify or answer a particular question, or if there were any other valid grounds (Art. 238 MCPA 2005).

17 Langbein 1985, p. 839. Compare with Arts. 243 and 244 MCPA 2005. It is noteworthy that although the parties might, with the court's approval, put questions to the expert during the hearing, there was no specific provision that allowed the parties to put questions to the expert prior to the expert's investigations.

The MCPA of 2005 took the written findings and the opinion of the expert as a starting point. Although it has been argued that due to the principle of immediacy the hearing of the expert in open court is preferable, the MCPA of 2005 prescribed the oral testimony of the expert just as a possibility. It did not even impose a strict obligation on the court to circulate the written findings and the opinion to the parties before the hearing at which they would be the subject of discussion. Instead, the court was to circulate the written findings and the opinion - if possible. At the hearing scheduled for discussion on the written findings and the opinion, the court on its own motion might request the expert to amplify his findings and his opinion. Upon the court's approval, the parties as well had the right to interrogate the expert.[18]

Within the old regime of expert evidence, the expertise was taken from one expert as a rule, but in cases of complex expertise the court had the power to appoint two or more experts. In the latter case, the experts could prepare a joint report (findings and an opinion) if they agreed on the issues. Otherwise separate reports were submitted to the court. The MCPA of 2005 had also foreseen the mechanisms for correcting inaccurate, sloppy, partial or contradictory reports by repeating the expertise with the same or other experts.[19]

According to the Continental tradition, once the expert had reported, the court freely evaluated his findings and opinion.[20] The expert's findings did not bind the court and the court had a duty to weigh the expert's opinion against other available evidence. Nevertheless, in practice, the courts were not inclined to assess the findings and the opinion of the expert critically. On the contrary, the judge always took a decision in line with the expert's findings and opinion. It was often argued that in Macedonian civil procedure the court-appointed expert was too influential, and it was almost impossible for the litigants to convince the judge not to base his decision on the expert's report. Many saw the court-appointed expert as the *de facto* decision maker.[21]

On the other hand, despite the legally accepted concept of the court-appointed expert, in the practice of Macedonian civil procedure it was not uncommon for the parties to engage their own experts in order to rebut the court-appointed expert. Being traditionally sceptical about the benefits of party-appointed experts, both theory and practice attributed only limited evidentiary value to expert opinions put forward by the parties. It was argued that:

> Certain findings and opinions can be considered as expertise only when they are given by the persons who were entrusted by the court to perform such a task, and not findings and opinions of a person who has been engaged by one of the parties,

18 See Arts. 244 and 245 MCPA 2005.

19 Art. 246 MCPA 2005.

20 See Art. 8 MCPA, which governs the principle of free evaluation of evidence by the court.

21 Of course, one can argue that this is legitimate because the judge does not have the same level of scientific or professional knowledge as the expert, thus limiting the judge's control over the expert.

> regardless whether he/she is a permanent court expert. Findings and opinions of a person, who was engaged by one of the parties, even if that person is a permanent court expert, have no such meaning - it is private findings and opinions. It should be taken that as regards proof, such private findings and an opinions may be taken into account as private documents that verify the professional knowledge of their compilers. In the assessment of the evidentiary value of such a document, the circumstance whether the expertise was ordered by one of the parties, and which of the parties paid for the expertise, has to be taken into consideration.[22]

To summarize: even though the arguments against the inquisitorial domination of fact-finding and evidence-taking were so compelling in 2005, they were not sufficient for radical changes of the regime of expert evidence. Hence, the MCPA of 2005 still reflected a certain divide which exists between the common law approach and the Continental approach to expert evidence. The court still played a pivotal role in the involvement of expertise in civil proceedings. The MCPA of 2005 did not recognize the concept of party-appointed experts.

3. Voices for a More Adversarial Approach, and Some Facts Against This

Despite the fact that the MCPA of 2005 nominally strengthened the principle of party presentation of expert evidence, the judicial practice concerning the use of the court-appointed expert remained unchanged. The use of the court-appointed expert has become a routine aspect of civil proceedings: whether presented by the parties or not, expert evidence appeared in almost all proceedings. The proliferation of this means of evidence was obvious, but it was nothing new in daily court practice. It remained expert-prone, just as before, causing in that way excessive expenses and delays. Even in the new procedural context, the courts were hardly refusing the parties' proposals for expert evidence. It is not far from the truth to say that the courts granted the parties' requests to order expertise almost automatically, without assessing whether in the particular dispute expertise was really needed. The underlying reason for this conduct on the part of the judges cannot be determined with certainty, but it may be assumed that it was based on the reasoning that it is easier to order expertise than to explain the rejection of a request for expertise. Therefore, it was evident that there was no benefit from the rules on the manner in which expert evidence enters the proceedings: primarily on a party's initiative, and as the exception on the court's own motion.

In these circumstances an opinion developed that the MCPA of 2005 did not address the expectations concerning the use of expert evidence and at the same time asked for a more adversarial approach. Still, it is noteworthy that this opinion was more the result of the speculative discussions on the merits of party-appointed and party-driven experts than on minimal comparative or empirical research. Indeed, it showed a complete ignorance of emerging trends and practices concerning expert

22 Dika 2009, p. 46.

evidence and also a serious lack of knowledge with regard to the historical origins and tradition of this procedural tool. More detailed analysis of the common law counterpart certainly would have discouraged the proponents of a 'more adversarial approach'. So here let me put forward some more details on the evolving rules of expert evidence in common law jurisdictions.

It is the common law tradition for the parties to present their case and propose evidence, a tradition built on the notion of a fully adversarial system. The courts have traditionally refrained from intervening in the parties' conduct and presentation of their case. This means that the court should address only such evidence as may be placed before it by one or more of the parties and should not seek out other evidence that may occur to the court to be relevant. This also applies to expert evidence, known as 'expert witness' testimony.

As a matter of fact, the rules governing the use of expert evidence in common law jurisdictions have changed considerably in the last two decades. The genesis of these changes dates back to 1996 when Lord Woolf in his *Access to Justice Reports*[23] considered expert evidence as a major source of difficulties in the civil justice system in England. Lord Woolf deemed that the need to engage experts was a source of excessive expense, delay and, in some cases, increased complexity through the excessive or inappropriate use of experts. Apprehension was also expressed as to the failure of experts to maintain their independence from the parties by whom they had been engaged and instructed. Lord Woolf noted:

> Most of the problems with expert evidence arise because the expert is initially recruited as part of the team which investigates and advances a party's contentions and then has to change roles and seek to provide the independent expert evidence which the court is entitled to expect.[24]

Hence, the principal recommendation made in the Woolf Reports was that the use of expert evidence should be subject to the complete control of the court through the exercise of the court's case management powers. From this recommendation, three years later - on 26 April 1999 - the new Civil Procedure Rules were enacted. Opting for the term 'expert' rather than 'expert witness', the CPR has significantly increased the role of the court regarding this evidence, as the permission of the court is needed to present expert evidence.[25] The court is not to grant this permission too readily as the court has a duty to restrict the use of expert evidence - in line with the overriding objective - to that which is reasonably required to resolve the dispute.[26] Apart from this, one of the biggest innovations within the adversarial system was the introduction of the 'single joint expert'.[27] Aiming to limit the use of expert

23 See Lord Woolf 1995, Chapter 23; and Lord Woolf 1996, Chapter 13.

24 See Lord Woolf 1995, Chapter 23.

25 Rule 35.4 CPR - 'No party may call an expert or put in evidence an expert's report without the court's permission.'

26 Rule 35.1 CPR.

27 In this occasion, it is interesting to mention that Lord Woolf addressed the possibility of court-appointed experts without proceeding to recommend this.

evidence and to strengthen objectivity, the CPR prescribes that if both parties wish to present expert evidence on the same matter, the court may determine that evidence on that issue be given by one expert only.[28] If possible this single expert is chosen by the parties. Still, the court may impose a single expert against the will of both parties.

Apprehensions regarding the experts were (and still are) present in other common law countries as well. For example, in the USA even though it is considered that 'the inherent power of a trial judge to appoint an expert of his own choosing is virtually unquestioned',[29] in practice the judges rarely, if ever, exercise such power. Undoubtedly, John Henry Wigmore's proposal in his 1904 *Treatise on the Anglo-American System of Evidence in Trials at Common Law* that 'the State, not the party, shall be the one to pay his fee, and ... the Court, not the party, shall be the one to summon him'[30] has never been realized. Furthermore, while the rules govern that the court should act as a gatekeeper to prevent the admission of irrelevant or unreliable evidence,[31] expert evidence in the practice of US courts is largely party-driven, and thus not fully independent, nor impartial. Many surveys conducted in the USA have found that adversarial bias was the single most important problem with expert evidence in US courts.[32] In his provocative article regarding 'The German Advantage in Civil Procedure' Professor John H. Langbein used the slang 'saxophones' to describe the position of experts in US civil proceedings. He considers:

> The idea is that the lawyer plays the tune, manipulating the expert as though the expert were a musical instrument on which the lawyer sounds the desired notes ... Nobody likes to disappoint a patron; and beyond this psychological pressure is the financial inducement. Money changes hands upon the rendering of expertise, but the expert can run his meter only so long as his patron litigator likes the tune. Opposing counsel undertakes a similar exercise, hiring and schooling another expert to parrot the contrary position. The result is our familiar battle of opposing experts. The more measured and impartial an expert is, the less likely he is to be used by either side.[33]

The same conclusions have been reached in Australia and Canada, as basis for legislative changes that have been introduced in these countries in order to place limits on the allowable scope of expert evidence, and particularly to define the expert's duty to the court. For example, the legislative changes in Australia have

28 See Rule 35.2 CPR.

29 Langbein 1985, p. 840, at f. 58, who refers to the advisory committee note on Rule 706(a) of the Federal Rules of Evidence.

30 As cited by Sonenshein & Fitzpatrick 2013, p. 26-27.

31 See Rule 702 of the Federal Rules of Evidence, as amended on 1 December 2000.

32 See 'Judge and Attorney Experiences, Practices and Concerns Regarding Expert Testimony in Federal Civil Trials', Federal Judicial Center, Carol Kafta *et al.*, 2002, available at: <https://bulk.resource.org/courts.gov/fjc/judattex/pdf> (last consulted on 6 April 2014). See also the papers by Sonenshein & Fitzpatrick 2013, p. 1-64; and Timmerbeil 2003, p. 163-187.

33 Langbein 1985, p. 835.

also codified that an expert has an 'overriding duty to assist the court' and have explicitly granted the court the power to appoint an expert.[34]

To sum up: the regulation and use of expert evidence obviously has been one of the hottest topics of civil procedure regarding fact-finding and evidence-taking, whether speaking of common law or civil law countries. It constantly calls for legislative changes in order to create rules that will provide the most suitable concept of expert evidence. Emerging trends and practices concerning expert evidence show that in recent times legislators in common law jurisdictions have encouraged the use of court-appointed experts while Continental jurisdictions gradually have recognized the merits of hearing party-appointed experts.[35] This gives us the right to assume that if the perceived problems in the use of expert witnesses within the adversarial system were taken into consideration, it would certainly lead to the question of whether it is necessary for Macedonia to shift towards a more adversarial approach regarding expert evidence or whether improvements can be made within the current system. Unfortunately, it seems that this question was never asked and, hence, the issue was not addressed in the legislative changes introduced in the MCPA in 2010.

4. The New Concept of Expert Evidence under the Amendments of the MCPA of 2010

The amendments of the MCPA of 2010[36] changed the above-mentioned Article 235 (now named 'expertise'), which states:

> (1) The Court shall take expertise as evidence if the party in his statement of claim or in his statement of defence has submitted expert findings and an opinion.
>
> (2) If a party proposes expertise, but can prove that there are facts or circumstances for which it cannot provide expert findings and an opinion, the court shall determine expertise by a written order. In the order the court will state on which facts or circumstances the expertise will be performed and upon the party's proposal will determine who is entrusted with the expertise.

Comparing Article 235 as presently formulated with the previous version, the first aspect which deserves attention is that the legislator has changed the name of this means of evidence from 'experts' to 'expertise'. By this renaming, it becomes clear that the aim is to put the emphasis on the activity, i.e. the method of carrying out proof by experts - which is expertise - and not on the persons who perform it. Indeed, the real reason for this renaming was the fact that the amendments of the MCPA of 2010 came about due to the fact that the Act on expertise[37] which regulates

34 For more details, see Edmond 2003, p. 139-143.
35 Verkerk 2009, p. 167.
36 Official Gazette of the Republic of Macedonia, No. 116/2010.
37 Official Gazette of the Republic of Macedonia, No. 115/2010.

the expertise in a substantive sense as a separate activity performed by experts was not applied in practice.[38] This Act introduced a 'certified' or 'licensed' expert,[39] instead of the previous so-called permanent court expert.

A further conclusion that may be drawn is that by the amendments of 2010 in the Macedonian civil procedure the court-appointed expert is replaced by a party-appointed expert. Several features clearly reflect the essence of the new concept of expert evidence and in the following I will briefly analyse them.

The first feature is connected with the manner in which expert evidence can enter into the proceedings - only upon the parties' proposal. The court is no longer empowered to take expert evidence *ex officio*: it has no discretion to turn to experts in order to resolve difficult factual questions which are beyond the knowledge and experience of a judge. The new procedural rules have removed from the discourse the traditional consideration of expert evidence as a means of evidence that presupposes the matters at issue require expertise for their comprehension based on specialized knowledge which the court does not have. Under the new rules, the court has the power to determine expertise by written order, but only upon the party's request, and if the party proves that there are facts or circumstances for which he cannot provide expert findings and an opinion. Still, this does not mean taking expert evidence *ex officio.*

Second, the new procedural rules empower the parties to engage and appoint experts by themselves. The court has no discretion to determine how many experts should be appointed and who should be appointed as an expert.[40] The parties can appoint only a certified expert.[41] Of course, although the expert is engaged by the party, he should be objective and neutral. This is not explicitly expressed in the MCPA, but in the new Act on expertise it is.[42]

Third, the use of experts has come to be recognized as a necessity for the parties in order to put forward the most convincing case and is actually explicitly required by law. That is to say, each party, if he deems it necessary so as to verify his factual assertions, can provide expert findings and an opinion. The plaintiff should provide an expert report before filing a statement of claim to the court and attach the report to the statement of claim. The defendant should submit expert findings and an opinion in a written statement of defence. The submittal of the statement of claim and the statement of defence are actually the last moments in

38 According to the Act on expertise, '… an expertise is the preparation of expert findings and an opinion based on the application of scientific and professional methods, technical developments, professional knowledge and experience in the areas defined, in all cases determined by law or at the request of an interested party' (Art. 2).

39 'Expert is a person who has a license for expertise in the relevant field (issued by the Ministry of Justice) and registered in the register of experts' - Art. 2 of the Act on expertise.

40 This applies even in cases where the court orders expertise in writing.

41 Art. 236 MCPA as amended in 2010.

42 See Art. 3 of the Act on expertise regarding the basic principles of providing expertise.

which the parties cannot just propose, but also submit, expert findings and an opinion to the court.[43]

The court now has no power to restrict expert evidence in terms that it is not reasonably required to resolve the subject matter.[44] Yet, the court will not accept the expertise as evidence if the opposing party challenges the expert for bias (on the same grounds as judges), and the court is of the opinion that this challenge is justified.[45]

Even though the amendments of the MCPA of 2010 have basically a common law orientation, analysing the new rules in more detail one can conclude that the new concept of expert evidence is not purely adversarial as it also has some features of the Continental tradition, as well as some other original and exceptional features.[46] Let me briefly offer some comments on these.

As the expert is hired by the parties, the court has no power to instruct the expert in terms of deciding which issues should be examined by the expert. The only exception is when the court determines expertise by written order, as mentioned above. Nevertheless, the court may still order the expert to appear in court to explain the written opinion. Thus, the duty to provide expertise remains the public duty of the expert to participate in the proceedings before the court, based on the court's invitation. It is not just the obligation that the experts have towards the party who hired them. Consequently, the sanctions for violation of this duty have a public, not a private, nature: they are determined and implemented by the court,[47] not by the parties themselves.

On the other hand, the expert may still be released from a duty to provide expertise, and the provisions for release remain unchanged. Yet, one issue remains legally unanswered: How will the court treat the written findings and the opinion if afterwards (when summoned by the court) the expert seeks release from providing expertise?

Under the amendments of the MCPA of 2010, in an open court hearing the expert explains his written opinion and then the court may ask him questions.

43 Indeed, due to legal inconsistency, it is disputed whether the submittal of a statement of claim and statement of defence are the last moments for submitting expert reports. Namely, the MCPA governs that the parties are obliged to present all facts and evidence on which they base their findings, and to submit the documents and objects that they intend to use as evidence in the proceedings, at the preparatory hearing at the latest (Art. 271). It is questionable whether this applies to expert evidence, too.

44 Contrary to this, the MCPA still contains the provision which empowers the court to select evidence. It is Art. 285 which states: 'The presentation of evidence shall be determined by a court decision, indicating the contentious fact on which the evidence should be taken and the means of evidence. The court shall reject the proposed evidence not considered relevant to the merits and shall specify the reason for the rejection.'

45 See Art. 239 MCPA as amended in 2010.

46 Therefore, it is claimed that indeed Macedonia has implemented a 'mixed' model of expert evidence.

47 The amendments of 2010 empower the court not just to fine the expert, but also to order that the expert be forcibly brought to court and that he bear the cost of this order. See Art. 240 MCPA as amended in 2010.

Afterwards, the parties have the opportunity to examine the expert as well, but only upon the court's approval. There is no cross-examination, the traditional adversarial tool for discrediting the expert's testimony, casting doubt upon his scientific conclusions and, perhaps, revealing the expert's bias.

Furthermore, whenever ordering expertise by written order, the court will set time limits for the expert to prepare and submit the written report to the court, which may not be longer than 45 days, and in more complex cases not longer than 60 days. Otherwise the court will revoke the expertise and impose a fine on the expert.[48] The court is obliged to communicate the written findings and the opinion to the parties not later than eight days prior to the hearing scheduled for discussion of them.

Finally, the exceptional feature of the new concept of expertise is the possibility to determine so-called super-expertise. Although the idea of super-expertise is to provide a higher degree of expertise or critical expertise of two conflicting expert opinions (which can be performed by a team composed of at least three experts in the relevant field), the normative framework of super-expertise does not fully and consistently reflect this idea. Namely, according to the amendments of the MCPA of 2010, the court is not expressly empowered to order super-expertise in cases of two conflicting expert opinions submitted by the plaintiff and the defendant, although this should be the typical situation for it. Instead, under the new rules the court is empowered to determine super-expertise only when the judge had ordered expertise in a written order and entrusted the expertise to two or more experts, who afterwards submit vague, incomplete or contradictory reports, and these drawbacks cannot be eliminated by a re-examination of the same experts.[49] In order to provide guarantees for fair and objective expertise, the amendments of 2010 lay down that the court determines super-expertise electronically by using the rule of random selection from the register of experts, in the presence of either the parties or their attorneys. The super-expertise should be executed within the time limits mentioned above.

5. Criticism of the New Concept of Expert Evidence

As it was stated in the explanatory memorandum to the draft amendments of the MCPA of 2010, the general idea of the new concept of expert evidence is to introduce a procedural tool that will raise the capability of civil litigation to deliver a simple, cost-effective and prompt resolution of disputes, so that the court system will be fair and accessible to all. But, what does experience suggest?

At first glance, the new concept of expert evidence seems to be very fair in the sense that it provides both parties sufficient and equal legal opportunities to try to convince the court on the merits of their position. Still, the new concept is not without its critics. Although a relatively short period of time since the

48 Art. 245 MCPA as amended in 2010.

49 Art. 246 MCPA as amended in 2010.

implementation of the new rules has passed, some substantive concerns with regard to expert evidence based on the new adversarial approach have already been expressed.

The criticism is primarily addressed against the rule that the plaintiff and defendant should submit the expert report in a statement of claim and a statement of defence, respectively.[50] This criticism derives from the inconsistency of the rule for submitting the expert report at the very beginning of the proceedings with some other procedural rules. As the MCPA still requires the court to identify the facts that need evidence-taking, and that evidence be taken for disputed facts,[51] it is questionable as to how the new concept of expert evidence can go along with this. At the very beginning of the proceedings, it is almost impossible to identify which facts are disputed and need evidence-taking, more precisely expertise. Furthermore, since the experts preparing the reports have been instructed by the parties and not by the court, it is to be expected that the expert reports will have a different focus than the court has. The experts instructed by the parties may develop points which are not decisive from the court's point of view. Finally, when both parties appoint an expert to give an opinion on the same subject matter, it is likely that much of the work done by one expert is also done by the other expert. This seems to be a serious drawback compared with the court-appointed expert. Macedonian judges and attorneys have already addressed the problem of unnecessary proof or cumulative evidence on the same subject matter, while at the same time a number of relevant factual questions remain unanswered.[52]

A second and closely related concern concerns the abolition of the power of the court to take expert evidence *ex officio*.[53] This clearly reflects the fact that Macedonian procedural practice is deeply rooted in the Continental tradition. The following question raised by judges is illustrative of the point: Is it not the role of experts to assist the court, in a fair and impartial manner, in specific fields in which the judges do not themselves have the relevant knowledge?

Complaints have also been made as to the evidentiary value of the expert reports because they advocate too heavily in the interest of the party presenting them. Although the experts should be independent and objective, under the new system experts are inevitably to an extent partisans. The experts give opinions favourable to the respective party because, at least financially, they depend on the parties and this, of course, influences their objectivity. This often leads to distrust of expert evidence in general and subsequently to the devaluation of expert opinion. The attorneys have also connected this phenomenon with the lack of rules which oblige the party to present documentation and other evidence that the opposing party expert needs in order to prepare full and objective expertise. Therefore, the

50 Dimovska 2013, p. 128; also Popovski-Buloski 2013, p. 141.

51 Arg. ex. Arts. 206 and 207 MCPA 2005.

52 Dimovska 2013, p. 128; also Popovski-Buloski 2013, p. 140-141.

53 Dimovska 2013, p. 128; also Popovski-Buloski 2013, p. 141.

expert report is always one-sided and directly confirms the position of the party presenting it.[54]

Furthermore, since within the new system the experts of both parties always reach diametrically opposite and hardly reconcilable conclusions, the court is faced with the problem of deciding between the opinions of opposing experts. This is a rather unsatisfactory situation for the court: it is difficult, if not impossible, for the court to bridge the gap between the opposing reports without another expertise. Thus, the problem of multiple expert opinions is addressed by super-expertise, which becomes a regular part of almost every proceedings. But super-expertise is not just time-consuming, it is also a very expensive evidentiary means. With regard to this, Judge Antoaneta Dimovska[55] has pointed out the following:

> Almost every judge will confirm that even in a small claims procedure there is a necessity to order super-expertise and this leads to the absurd situation where in a dispute of 50,000 denari[56] we have 150,000 denari of costs.

This leads us to another drawback of the new system: the use of party-appointed experts seems to be more expensive than the use of a single court-appointed expert. Obviously, the costs outweigh the benefits of involving party-appointed experts.

Finally, it should not be overlooked that the new system of expert evidence creates an unfavourable situation for the defendant.[57] Having in mind that the defendant should attach the expert report to the written statement of defence, which he is obliged to submit within a time limit determined by the court (not shorter than 15 days, nor longer than 30 days from the delivery of the statement of claim),[58] it is questionable as to whether the defendant is able to provide the expert findings and an opinion within this short period of time. On the other hand, the plaintiff has practically unlimited time for getting such a report before the commencement of the proceedings. The procedural inequality of the parties is more than evident.

6. Conclusion

The question of how to regulate the use of expert evidence in civil proceedings is certainly not a new one. The debate concerning expert evidence has been going on intensively over the last few decades, in both common law and civil law countries, resulting in the adoption of different models of this evidentiary means, without giving a clear preference to one of them. Between a pure-adversarial and pure-inquisitorial model of expert evidence, there are variations of a mixed model, which are nowadays more and more attractive and generally more promising.

54 Popovski-Buloski 2013, p. 141.
55 Dimovska 2013, p. 128.
56 Approximately € 800.
57 Zoroska-Kamilovska 2011, p. 859.
58 Compare this time limit with the time limits set for preparing the expert report when the expertise is ordered by the court.

For those who seek to modernize their legal systems, the comparative lessons are of great importance, as they provide a rich variety of experiences and practices. But these lessons should be taken as a whole, with both the advantages and the shortcomings. That is the way to adopt best practices. Otherwise the results of the reforms will run counter to the general normative expectations.

The latest legislative changes in Macedonian civil procedure as regards expert evidence clearly support the above. These changes were introduced with almost no debate and with no opportunities for criticism from the Macedonian legal profession. The reactions have come *post festum*, and they are very doubtful whether party-driven experts are the best solution for Macedonian civil procedure. They reflect the widespread opinion that any real attempt to bring the two concepts into closer unity would involve changing, not only the positive law, but also deeply rooted cultural traditions.[59] Up to now, it is obvious that the new approach to expert evidence has no merit either in accelerating the proceedings or in cutting costs. Rather, it seems that the new concept of the party-appointed expert has become an even bigger source of increased complexity because of the excessive and inappropriate use of experts, and thus of excessive expenses and delays.

59 Reitz 1990, p. 988.

Bibliography

Dika 2009
Dika, M., 'O vještacima i vještačenju u hrvatskom parničnom postupku', in *Zbornik na Pravniot fakultet 'Justinijan Prvi' vo čest na Stefan Georgievski*, Skopje: Praven fakultet 'Justinijan Prvi', 2009, p. 41-69.

Dimovska 2013
Dimovska, A., 'Pregled na rešenijata koi sozdavaat problemi vo primenata na Zakonot za parničnata postapka so osvrt na najnoviot Predlog-zakon za izmeni i dopolnuvanja na Zakonot za parničnata postapka', in *Delovno pravo, Izdanie za teorija i praktika na pravoto*, Godina XIV, 2013, Br. 29, p. 123-137.

Edmond 2003
Edmond, G., 'After Objectivity: Expert Evidence and Procedural Reform', *Sydney Law Review, 2003, Vol. 25, p.* 131-163.

Janevski & Zoroska-Kamilovska 2012
Janevski, A. & Zoroska-Kamilovska, T., *Građansko procesno pravo, kniga prva, parnično pravo, vtoro izmeneto i dopolneto izdanie*, Skopje: Praven fakultet 'Justinijan Prvi', 2012.

Krafka *et al.* 2002
Krafka, C., Dunn, M.A., Johnson, M.T., Cecil, J.S. & Miletich, D., 'Judge and Attorney Experiences, Practices and Concerns Regarding Expert Testimony in Federal Civil Trials', 2002. Available at: <https://bulk.resource.org/courts.gov/-fjc/judattex.pdf>.

Langbein 1985
Langbein, J.H., 'The German Advantage in Civil Procedure', *The University of Chicago Law Review*, 1985, Vol. 52(4), p. 835-841.

Lord Woolf 1995
Lord Woolf, *Access to Justice: Interim Report to the Lord Chancellor on the Civil Justice System in England and Wales*, June 1995.

Lord Woolf 1996
Lord Woolf, *Access to Justice: Final Report to the Lord Chancellor on the Civil Justice System in England and Wales*, July 1996.

Popovski-Buloski 2013
Popovski-Buloski, T., 'Koi problemi se javuvaat pri primenata na ZPP?', in *Delovno pravo, Izdanie za teorija i paktika na pravoto, Godina XIV*, 2013, Br. 29, p. 139-152.

Reitz 1990
Reitz, J.C., 'Why we probably cannot adopt the German Advantage in Civil Procedure', *Iowa Law Review*, 1990, Vol. 75, p. 987-1009.

Sonenshein & Fitzpatrick 2013
Sonenshein, D. & Fitzpatrick, C., 'The Problem of Partisan Experts and the Potential for Reform through Concurrent Evidence', *The Review of Litigation*, **2013, Vol. 32(1),** p. 1-64.

Timmerbeil 2003
Timmerbeil, S., 'The Role of Expert Witnesses in German and U.S. Civil Litigation', *Annual Survey of International & Comparative Law*, 2003, Vol. 9(1), p. 163-187.

Triva & Dika 2004
Triva, S. & Dika, M., *Građansko parnično procesno pravo*, Zagreb: Narodne Novine d.d., 2004.

Verkerk 2009
Verkerk, R., 'Comparative Aspects of Expert Evidence in Civil Litigation', *The International Journal of Evidence & Proof*, 2009, Vol. 13(3), p. 167-197.

Zoroska-Kamilovska 2011
Zoroska-Kamilovska, T., 'Osvrt na noviot koncept na veštačenje vo parničnata postapka vo Republika Makedonija', in *Zbornik na Pravniot fakultet 'Justinijan Prvi' vo čest na prof.dr. Nikola Matovski*, Skopje: Praven fakultet Justinijan Prvi, 2011, p. 847-867.

EVIDENCE IN ARBITRATION AND NATIONAL CIVIL LITIGATION

P. Oberhammer

EVIDENCE: LEARNING FROM ARBITRATION

1. General

As is generally known, there are major differences between the fact-finding processes of arbitration and litigation proceedings.[1] This is not only true from a civil law, but also from a common law perspective: Today's practice with respect to the taking of evidence in arbitration proceedings results from a combination of approaches of lawyers with different backgrounds, in particular, from lawyers from civil and common law jurisdictions.[2] In particular, this combination of approaches is reflected in the International Bar Association Rules on the Taking of Evidence in International Arbitration.[3] Different from many other 'principles', 'rules' etc. which only play a role in the discussion of academic or practitioners' conferences, these rules have gained significant acceptance in arbitration practice and serve as guideline for the decision of fact-finding issues in many arbitration proceedings all over the world today.[4]

The reason for asking about what litigation can learn from arbitration with respect to evidence-taking is obvious. Arbitration is market-made and, therefore, concepts developed in arbitration practice and accepted by parties and arbitration practitioners might be effective and user-friendly. Therefore, one might argue that arbitration could be a laboratory for best practices in civil procedure not only, but also when it comes to evidence. I do not suggest that, therefore, arbitration is

1 See, e.g., Koller 2011, p. 80; Schumacher 2011, p. 3 *et seq.*; Smit 1994, p. 164; Waincymer 2012, p. 40 *et seq.*

2 Born 2014, p. 2127; Smit 1994, p. 164.

3 Cf. Kühner 2010, p. 667; Raeschke-Kessler 2001, p.45; von Segesser 2010, p. 735; Zuberbühler *et al.* 2012, p. 1 *et seq.*

4 According to a study on 'Current and Preferred Practices in the Arbitral Process' conducted by the School of International Arbitration at Queen Mary, University of London, the IBA Rules are used in 60 per cent of arbitrations (available at: <http://www.arbitration.qmul.ac.-uk/research/2012/index.html> (last consulted in September 2014); see also Webster & Bühler 2014, p. 5; Rivkin 2011, p. 212.

superior to litigation. As is generally known, not all results of market-driven processes are in the best interests of all stakeholders. This contribution, however, is not about criticizing arbitration practice where there might be shortcomings,[5] but simply asks which lessons can be learnt from arbitration with respect to evidence-taking.

My approach is, of course, based on my personal experience resulting from my academic and practical work in civil procedure in the German speaking countries on the one hand and in international commercial arbitration on the other. Therefore, some of the aspects which I will address where litigation might learn lessons from arbitration are based on my 'Germanic' litigation experience and might, therefore, not apply to the civil procedure of other jurisdictions to the same extent. Moreover, I would like to clarify that user-friendliness and efficiency, of course, are not necessarily the only relevant factors for identifying the best approaches in the field of evidence – it is just one very important perspective, and it is the one perspective which I will focus on in the following.

In addition, it is, of course, also true that arbitration can learn a lot from litigation. However, one must be cautious in order to avoid 'importing' overly formalistic or doctrinal concepts into the field of arbitration, simply because the low degree of regulation of procedural issues in arbitration proceedings and, as a consequence, the procedural discretion of the arbitral tribunal are important factors for the functioning and acceptance of the arbitration process today. In this context, it has often been stated in the debate of recent years that arbitration is undergoing a process of a 'judicialization' today.[6] This, however, is a rather problematic label from a Continental European perspective. The 'judicialization' criticized by many arbitration practitioners and businesses as 'users' of the arbitration process rather refers to the fact that, to some extent, arbitration has tended to become more and more like litigation in particular in the USA which is indeed a problematic development given the costs and duration of litigation in the USA.[7] From a Continental European or civil law perspective, there is no such 'judicialization' of arbitration. On the contrary: from this perspective, litigation and arbitration practices are differentiated much more strongly today. It is generally known that younger arbitrators with an international outlook conduct arbitration proceedings in Continental European jurisdictions in a fashion which is much less similar to litigation proceedings than the practices adopted by an earlier generation of arbitrators which still strongly drew upon their respective civil procedure as model.

Finally, the arbitration practice I am referring to is the one tailored to large-scale business-to-business disputes, i.e., the arbitration I am confronted with in my practice as an arbitrator (different from what is the practice in other jurisdictions such as the USA[8] – both the law and the practice of the German speaking countries

5 For a critical assessment see Hanotiau 2011, p. 89 *et seq.*

6 See, e.g., Carbonneau 1994, p. 115; van Houtte 2010a, p. 525; Stipanowich 2010, p. 1.

7 See Alford 2003, p. 69 *et seq.*; Bergsten 2006, p. 294; Grenz 2014, p. 2; Strong 2013, p. 117.

8 See, e.g., Schmitz 2013, p. 81.

do not embrace consumer arbitration and I believe rightly so). Accordingly, I am not suggesting that arbitration might serve as a model for small claims proceedings and/or proceedings involving issues such as consumer law, family law or tenancy law disputes. I only suggest solutions for larger and more complex commercial cases before the courts.

In this context, I would like to identify several features of evidence in arbitration proceedings which might be worth discussing as a model for litigation. It should be noted that this contribution is based on a lecture which was primarily intended to trigger debate (which it actually did).

2. Preparation of the Oral Hearing

Arbitration proceedings usually involve much more thorough preparation of the evidentiary hearing than court proceedings: In addition to the procedural rules of the institution, specific rules and a time-table for the proceedings in a first procedural order on the basis of a first procedural hearing or conference call are common practice;[9] documents need to be submitted before the hearing;[10] the same is true for a request for document production; and written witness statements which allow both the parties and the arbitral tribunal to prepare detailed questions for the examination of such witnesses in the course of the oral hearing.[11] In most arbitration proceedings the cut-off-date for new allegations and new evidence will normally be before the oral hearing,[12] so that, as a principle, no new facts and evidence are admitted at the hearing stage. Before the hearing, another preparatory conference call takes place in most cases which results in a detailed schedule for the hearing.[13] In some cases, tribunals ask the parties to submit skeleton arguments immediately before the hearing or to submit a hearing bundle with the most important documents.[14]

This allows arbitral tribunals to master even highly complex cases in one single hearing which, of course, might take a couple of days or even weeks. Different from that, many systems of litigation do not provide for such a degree of preparation of the oral hearing and/or allow new facts and evidence also in the course of the oral hearing, some only in the beginning, some also at a later stage of the oral hearing. As a consequence, a case very often cannot be heard in one single hearing, but hearings must be adjourned for months and months and are held in a succession of rather short meetings within a relatively long period of time. This process encourages parties to file additional submissions and to present additional

9 See, e.g., Arts. 23 and 24 of the ICC Arbitration Rules; *cf.* Böckstiegel 2013, p. 3; Born 2014, p. 2233; Koller 2011, p. 86.

10 See Böckstiegel 2013, p. 4; Redfern *et al.* 2009, para 6.101.

11 *Cf.* Van den Berg 2008, p. 159; Born 2014, p. 2256 *et seq.*

12 See, e.g., Hoffmann & Shetty 2013, p. 199 *et seq.*; Waincymer 2012, p. 728 *et seq.*

13 See Van den Berg 2008, p. 167; Waincymer 2012, p. 722.

14 See Grierson & van Hooft 2012, p. 187; Kerr 1997, p. 125.

allegations and evidence in the course of this piece meal hearing which has an obvious tendency to make things even more complicated.

Therefore, legislators should give procedural powers to the courts (and impose the respective duties upon them) allowing them to prepare the oral hearing more thoroughly in the written proceedings prior to the oral hearing and to preclude new facts and evidence at a later stage - and, of course, courts should actively use such powers.

3. Document Production

Arbitration may have found a reasonable approach to document production. That is, neither 'US style fishing expeditions' apply, nor the German approach that - to put it very simplistically - it is simply bad luck for the claimant if he does not know the facts from the outset.[15] In particular, the IBA Rules on the Taking of Evidence in International Arbitration provide for a very well-balanced system drawing upon the 'best of both worlds'.[16] This might be a model for court proceedings in both worlds.

4. Experts

As is generally known, party-appointed experts play an important role in arbitration proceedings.[17] Different from that, many courts in civil law countries rely on court-appointed experts only. Before I became acquainted with the system of party-appointed experts in international arbitration, I thought that such experts would simply be 'hired guns' who would not tell the truth while a court-appointed expert would always strive to present a true and correct account of his insights to the court and, therefore, relying on a court- (or tribunal-) appointed expert is the better solution.

However, after becoming acquainted with arbitration practice I found out that court-appointed or tribunal-appointed experts often have a significant lack of motivation, hidden prejudices and a certain bias for the 'easy way out'; moreover, they are hard to examine from the parties' perspective because they always are to some extent on the court's or tribunal's 'side' as an 'assistant' in the fact-finding process; therefore, a tough examination of such an expert always runs a certain risk of insulting the court or tribunal. Different from that, party-appointed experts have a strong motivation as they compete to convince the tribunal; they have no hidden agenda as it is plain to see that they are there to help the party that has hired them; and they normally have much broader access to the facts and much more time for their work than court-appointed or tribunal-appointed experts, if necessary.

15 See, e.g., Born 2014, p. 2319 *et seq.*; Hoffmann & Shetty 2013, p. 201; Kaufmann-Kohler & Bärtsch 2004, p. 14; Schroeder 2007, p. 231 *et seq.*; Varga 2006, p. 123 *et seq.*; Waincymer 2012, p. 833 *et seq.*

16 *Cf.* Ashford 2013, p. 41 *et seq.*; D'Allaire & Trittman 2011, p. 124; Kneisel & Lecking 2013, p. 150; Vercauteren 2012, p. 355; Zuberbühler *et al.* 2012, p. 23 *et seq.*

17 Schwarz & Konrad 2009, para 21-006; Waincymer 2012, p. 931; *cf.* Freyer 2008, p. 430.

Therefore, it might be worth thinking about relying on party-appointed experts in the first place also in court proceedings and to have court-appointed experts only if it turns out that the party-appointed experts do not yet provide a sufficient basis for the court's decision with respect to specific issues. In many cases, however, a confrontation of experts ('expert conferencing')[18] might lead to very reliable results without the involvement of a court-appointed expert. (I hope the reader notes that I do not talk about small claims proceedings here!)

5. Witness Examination

It is a truly remarkable fact that almost all arbitration practitioners prefer a more or less simplified American style cross-examination over the traditional ways of interrogating experts and witnesses in their domestic systems. Today, cross-examination practices are even used in domestic arbitration cases within the German speaking countries where no tradition of cross-examination existed.[19] The difference between litigation and arbitration proceedings is particularly obvious in Austria: while the examination of witnesses and experts before a court is normally always performed by the judge and counsel will only be permitted to ask a few follow-up-questions, it becomes more and more normal even in domestic arbitration practice that counsel will examine experts and witnesses in a kind of cross-examination.

There are, however, at least three important differences between the actual cross-examination process in e.g. US litigation practice and what happens before arbitral tribunals in civil law countries: First, a simplified and less formalistic way of cross-examination is applied; second, there is often much space for direct examination; and third - and most important - the tribunal is allowed to ask anything anytime and in practice becomes involved in the examination process very actively. Nevertheless, the parties will always have the lead in the examination process while it is typically the arbitral tribunal which asks follow-up questions.

This might also be an effective system for court proceedings. I come from a jurisdiction which is famous for the stronger role of the judge in the fact-finding process[20] - and I am still convinced that it is a good approach for small and simple cases. When it comes to complex issues and when parties are represented by experienced counsel, there is, however, no way to deny the fact that the parties know much more about the facts of the case than the judge and are, therefore, much better prepared to ask the right questions. However, also in complex litigation, an additional active role of a judge is very desirable. While the parties might be better

18 See, e.g., Hunter 2007, p. 820; Sachs & Schmidt-Ahrendts 2011, p. 141; Waincymer 2012, p. 966.

19 Köllensperger 2011, p. 161; Wirth 2003, p. 9 *et seq.*; *cf.* Schütze 2006, p. 2 (criticizing a case where the tribunal ordered the application of such practices relying on its procedural discretion).

20 See, e.g., Fasching 1988, p. 102; Fucik 1998, p. 196; Kralik 1988, p. 91; *cf.* Oberhammer & Domej 2005, p. 295.

aware of the details of the case, it is, after all, finally the judge who knows first what will become relevant for his or her decision, and I believe that this should be communicated actively to the parties. This, however, is already done in many arbitration cases today; and this does not exclude starting the process with a cross-examination type of examination.

6. Party Examination and Witness Examination

Most civil law systems still have complicated differentiations between witness evidence and party testimony although there has been a certain tendency over the last decades to lessen the differences between these two means of evidence.[21] The arbitration practice I know has completely done away with this differentiation some time ago, drawing upon the Anglo-Saxon model.[22] This is based on a simple practical observation: It is true that one should not trust parties giving testimony because they might have a certain tendency to lie in their own interest. Nothing, however, indicates that third party witnesses are any better. Therefore, I suggest that completely abandoning such differences might also be a good choice for the courts. Courts should simply listen to all people that might have relevant information and then make up their mind on whether they believe what has been stated or not.

7. Witness and Expert Conferencing

Many courts have a tendency to simply interrogate one witness and one expert after the other. Confrontations of experts and witnesses might be admissible but do not take place very often, at least in the practice I am aware of. Different from that, many arbitrators avail themselves of witness and especially expert conferencing techniques. In particular, expert conferencing is a very powerful fact-finding tool. In this process, both party-appointed experts will discuss their findings before the tribunal, and, of course, the tribunal and the parties are free to ask questions. Sometimes, a tribunal-appointed expert will also be involved in such discussions. I am convinced that this system of 'expert testimony' is a much more efficient way of fact-finding than interrogation of experts by counsel and/or judges 'one after the other'. I suggest that this should play a much more important role in litigation as well. (Of course, one has to embrace the system of party-appointed experts in the first place in order to have partners for such a discussion.)[23]

21 See Coester-Waltjen 2000, p. 269 *et seq.*; Oberhammer 2000, p. 295 *et seq.*

22 See, e.g., Born 2014, p. 2274 *et seq.*; Waincymer 2012, p. 895 *et seq.*

23 See above point 4 and footnote 18.

8. Confidentiality

Finally, arbitration practice has developed interesting approaches to dealing with confidentiality[24] issues while at least most civil law systems still struggle to do so. The issue is multifaceted. In the following, I can only give two examples.

It is striking that most civil law arbitral tribunals have adopted the common law approach to privileges, at least in principle.[25] I have heard German lawyers referring to the 'attorney-client-privilege' in cases involving no jurisdiction that actually provides for such a privilege for documents in civil cases. The reason for that simply is that many practitioners have accepted that the protection of such privileges is a reasonable approach to fair play in commercial disputes. These experiences suggest that civil procedure in the civil law countries should also develop a much more refined and far-reaching system of privileges, and the US approach to such issues imported and both modified and simplified by arbitral tribunals could serve as a model for such a development.

Arbitral tribunals have adopted promising approaches for the protection of confidential information by availing themselves of specific experts for such issues. For example, Article 3(8) of the IBA Rules provides for a 'confidentiality advisor' to the tribunal.[26] These rules state that in exceptional circumstances, if the propriety of an objection can be determined only by the review of the document, the arbitral tribunal may determine that it should not review the document. In that event, the IBA Rules provide that the arbitral tribunal may, after consultation with the parties, appoint an independent and impartial expert, bound to confidentiality, to review any such document and to report on the objection. To the extent the objection is upheld by the arbitral tribunal, the expert shall not disclose to the arbitral tribunal and the other parties the contents of the document reviewed according to this provision. Similar tools are applied in intellectual property cases before the courts even today in some jurisdictions.[27] It might be worth thinking about whether the introduction of such tools in other cases might be desirable. Of course, one must not forget about the right to be heard in this respect, and, therefore, there will always be limits to such approaches based on fundamental due process notions.

24 See, e.g., de Ly, Friedman & Radicati di Brozolo 2012, p. 355; Haas 2012, p. 315; Hwang & Thio 2012, p. 137; Noussia 2010, p. 37 *et seq.*; Oberhammer 2003, p. 1149; Pryles 2008, p. 501; Smeureanu 2011, p. 26 *et seq.*

25 See, e.g., Berger 2006, p. 503 *et seq.*; Born 2014, p. 2375 *et seq.*; Heitzmann 2008, p. 216.

26 See, e.g., van Houtte 2010b, p. 1148; Schwarz & Konrad 2009, para 20-144.

27 See, e.g., Bornkamm 2006, p. 906; Schneider 2013, p. 152; Siebert 2011, p. 346; Stadler 2010, p. 261 *et seq.*

Bibliography

Alford 2003
Alford, R., 'The American Influence on International Arbitration', *Ohio State Journal on Dispute Resolution*, 2003, p. 69-88.

Ashford 2013
Ashford, P., *The IBA Rules on the Taking of Evidence in International Arbitration*, Cambridge: Cambridge University Press, 2013.

Berger 2006
Berger, K.-P., 'Evidentiary Privileges: Best Practice Standards versus/and Arbitral Discretion', *Arbitration International*, 2006, p. 501-520.

Bergsten 2006
Bergsten, E., 'The Americanization of International Arbitration', *Pace International Law Review*, 2006, p. 289-298.

Böckstiegel 2013
Böckstiegel, K.H., 'Party Autonomy and Case Management - Experiences and Suggestions of an Arbitrator', *Zeitschrift für Schiedsverfahren*, 2013, p. 1-5.

Born 2014
Born, G., *International Commercial Arbitration*, 2nd edn., The Hague: Kluwer Law International, 2014.

Bornkamm 2006
Bornkamm, J., 'Der Schutz vertraulicher Informationen im Gesetz zur Durchsetzung von Rechten des geistigen Eigentums - In-camera-Verfahren im Zivilprozess?', in Ahrens, H.-J. *et al.* (eds.), *Festschrift für Eike Ullmann*, Saarbrücken: Juris, 2006, p. 893-912.

Carbonneau 1994
Carbonneau, T., 'National Law and the Judicialization of Arbitration: Manifest Destiny, Manifest Disregard, or Manifest Error', in Lillich, R. & Brower, C. (eds.), *International Arbitration in the 21st Century: Toward 'Judicialization' and Conformity?: Towards 'Judicialization' and Uniformity - Twelfth Sokol Colloquium*, New York: Transnational Publishers, 1995, p. 115-132.

Coester-Waltjen 2000
Coester-Waltjen, D., 'Parteiaussage und Parteivernehmung am Ende des 20. Jahrhunderts', *Zeitschrift für Zivilprozeß*, 2000, p. 269-294.

D'Allaire & Trittman 2011
D'Allaire, D. & Trittman, R., 'Disclosure Requests in International Commercial Arbitration: Finding A Balance Not Only Between Legal Traditions But Also Between the Parties' Rights', *The American Review of International Arbitration*, 2011, p. 119-132.

de Ly, Friedman & Radicati di Brozolo 2012
de Ly, F., Friedman, M. & Radicati di Brozolo, L., 'International Law Association International Commercial Arbitration Committee's Report and Recommendations on Confidentiality in International Commercial Arbitration', *Arbitration International*, 2012, p. 355-396.

Fasching 1988
Fasching, H.-W., 'Die Weiterentwicklung des Zivilprozessrechts im Lichte der Ideen Franz Kleins', in Hofmeister, H. (ed.), *Forschungsband Franz Klein*, Wien: Manz, 1988, p. 97-118.

Freyer 2008
Freyer, D., 'Assessing Expert Evidence', in Newman, L. & Hill, R. (eds.), *The Leading Arbitrators' Guide to International Arbitration*, 2nd edn., New York: Juris Publishing, 2008, p. 429-443.

Fucik 1998
Fucik, R., 'Die Rolle des Richters in der ZPO - Eine ökonomische Analyse', in Bundesministerium für Justiz, Lewisch, P. & Rechberger, W. (eds.), *100 Jahre ZPO – Ökonomische Analyse des Zivilprozesses*, Wien: Manz, 1998, p. 191-202.

Grenz 2014
Grenz, C., 'US-amerikanische Beweismethoden: Ein Hindernis in Schiedsverfahren?', *Zeitschrift für Deutsches und Amerikanisches Recht*, 2014, p. 2-6.

Grierson & Van Hooft 2012
Grierson, J. & Van Hooft, A., *Arbitrating under the 2012 ICC Rules*, The Hague: Kluwer Law International, 2012.

Haas 2012
Haas, U., 'Vertraulichkeit im Zusammenhang mit Schiedsverfahren', in Geimer, R. & Schütze, R. (eds.), *Festschrift für Athanassios Kaissis*, München: Sellier European Law Publishers, 2012, p. 315-331.

Hanotiau 2011
Hanotiau, B., 'International Arbitration in a Global Economy: The Challenges of the Future', *Journal of International Arbitration*, 2011, p. 89-103.

Heitzmann 2008
Heitzmann, P., 'Confidentiality and Privileges in Cross-Border Legal Practice: The Need for a Global Standard?', *ASA Bulletin*, 2008, p. 205-240.

Hoffmann & Shetty 2013
Hoffmann, A. & Shetty, N., 'Evidence and Hearings', in Van den Berg, A. (ed.), *International Arbitration: The Coming of a New Age?*, The Hague: ICCA Congress Series, 2013, p. 197-219.

Hunter 2007
Hunter, M., 'Expert Conferencing and New Methods', in Van den Berg, A. (ed.), *International Arbitration 2006: Back to Basics?*, ICCA Congress Series, 2006 Montreal, The Hague, Kluwer Law International, 2007, p. 820-828.

Hwang & Thio 2012
Hwang, M. & Thio, N., 'A Proposed Model Procedural Order on Confidentiality in International Arbitration: A Comprehensive and Self-Governing Code', *Journal of International Arbitration*, 2012, p. 137-169.

Kaufmann-Kohler & Bärtsch 2004
Kaufmann-Kohler, G. & Bärtsch, Ph., 'Discovery in International Arbitration: How much is too much?', *Zeitschrift für Schiedsverfahren*, 2004, p. 13-21.

Kerr 1997
Kerr, M., 'Concord and Conflict in International Arbitration', *Arbitration International*, 1997, p. 121-144.

Kneisel & Lecking 2013
Kneisel, S. & Lecking, C., 'Verteidigungsstrategien gegen die Anordnung der Document-Production - insbesondere nach den IBA-Regeln zur Beweisaufnahme in der internationalen Schiedsgerichtsbarkeit', *Zeitschrift für Schiedsverfahren*, 2013, p. 150-158.

Köllensperger 2011
Köllensperger, B., 'Beweis durch Zeugen und Parteien', in Schumacher, H. (ed.), *Beweiserhebung im Schiedsverfahren*, Wien: Manz, 2011, p. 83-191.

Koller 2011
Koller, C., 'The Role of Judges and Arbitrators in Contemporary Dispute Resolution', in Dahlberg, M. (ed.), *Party Autonomy – Civil Procedural Views on Party Autonomy, Franz Klein, EU Law and more*, Uppsala: Iustus Förlag, 2011, p. 79-98.

Kralik 1988
Kralik, W., 'Die Verwirklichung der Ideen Franz Kleins in der Zivilprozessordnung von 1895', in Hofmeister, H. (ed.), *Forschungsband Franz Klein*, Wien: Manz, 1988, p. 89-96.

Kühner 2010
Kühner, D., 'The Revised IBA Rules on the Taking of Evidence in International Arbitration', *Journal of International Arbitration*, 2010, p. 667-677.

Noussia 2010
Noussia, K., *Confidentiality in International Commercial Arbitration: A Comparative Analysis of the Position under English, US, German and French Law*, Berlin/Heidelberg: Springer, 2010.

Oberhammer 2000
Oberhammer, P., 'Parteiaussage und Parteivernehmung am Ende des 20. Jahrhunderts', *Zeitschrift für Zivilprozeß*, 2000, p. 295-326.

Oberhammer 2003
Oberhammer, P., 'Zur Vertraulichkeit von Schiedsverfahren', in Nakamura, H. *et al.* (eds.), *Festschrift für Kostas E. Beys*, 2003, p. 1139-1166.

Oberhammer & Domej 2005
Oberhammer, P. & Domej, T., 'Powers of the Judge - Germany, Austria, Switzerland', in Van Rhee, C.H. (ed.), *European Traditions in Civil Procedure*, Antwerp/Oxford: Intersentia, 2005, p. 295-304.

Pryles 2008
Pryles, M., 'Confidentiality', in Newman, L. & Hill, R. (eds.), *The Leading Arbitrators' Guide to International Arbitration*, 2nd edn., New York: Juris Publishing, 2008, p. 501-552.

Raeschke-Kessler 2001
Raeschke-Kessler, H., 'Die IBA Rules über die Beweisaufnahme in Internationalen Schiedsverfahren, in Böckstiegel, K.-H. (ed.), *Beweiserhebung in internationalen Schiedsverfahren, Schriftenreihe der Deutschen Institution für Schiedsgerichtsbarkeit*, Vol. 14, Cologne/Berlin/Bonn/Munich: Carl Heymanns, 2001, p. 41-75.

Redfern *et al.* 2009
Redfern, A., Hunter, M., Blackaby, N. & Partasides, C., *Redfern and Hunter on International Arbitration*, Oxford: Oxford University Press, 2009.

Rivkin 2011
Rivikin, D., 'The Revised IBA Rules on the Taking of Evidence', in Rovine, A. (ed.), *Contemporary Issues in International Arbitration and Mediation: The Fordham Papers 2011*, Leiden: Koninklijke Brill, 2012, p. 212-219.

Sachs & Schmidt-Ahrendts 2011
Sachs, K. & Schmidt-Ahrendts, N., 'Protocol on Expert Teaming: A New Approach to Expert Evidence', in Van den Berg, A. (ed.), *Arbitration Advocacy in Changing Times*, ICCA Congress Series, The Hague: Kluwer Law International, 2011, p. 135-148.

Schmitz 2013
Schmitz, A., 'American Exceptionalism in Consumer Arbitration', *Loyola University Chicago International Law Review*, 2013, p. 81-103.

Schneider 2013
Schneider, B., 'Rechtsdurchsetzung und Geheimnisschutz - ein Widerspruch?', *Österreichische Juristenzeitung*, 2013, p. 149-154.

Schroeder 2007
Schroeder, H.-P., *Die lex mercatoria arbitralis – Strukturelle Transnationalität und transnationale Rechtsstrukturen im Recht der internationalen Schiedsgerichtsbarkeit*, Frankfurt am Main: Sellier, 2007.

Schumacher 2011
Schumacher, H., 'Grundsätze der Beweiserhebung im Schiedsverfahren', in Schumacher, H. (ed.), *Beweiserhebung im Schiedsverfahren*, Wien: Manz, 2011, p. 3-51.

Schütze 2006
Schütze, R., 'Die Ermessensgrenzen des Schiedsgerichts bei der Bestimmung der Beweisregeln', *Zeitschrift für Schiedsverfahren*, 2006, p. 1-5.

Schwarz & Konrad 2009
Schwarz, F. & Konrad, C., *The Vienna Rules: A Commentary on International Arbitration in Austria*, The Hague: Kluwer Law International, 2009.

Siebert 2011
Siebert, M., *Geheimnisschutz und Auskunftsansprüche im Recht des Geistigen Eigentums – Der Konflikt mit dem Schutz von personenbezogenen Daten und Geschäftsgeheimnissen – Eine Analyse des europäischen und deutschen Rechts*, Tübingen: Mohr Siebeck, 2011.

Smeureanu 2011
Smeureanu, M., *Confidentiality in International Commercial Arbitration*, The Hague: Kluwer Law International, 2011.

Smit 1994
Smit, H., 'Roles of the Arbitral Tribunal in Civil and Common Law Systems with Respect to Presentation of Evidence', in Van den Berg, A.J. (ed.), *Planning Efficient Arbitration Proceedings: The Law Applicable in International Arbitration*, ICC Congress Series, No. 7, The Hague: Kluwer Law International, 1994, p. 161-172.

Stadler 2010
Stadler, A., 'Geheimnisschutz im Zivilprozess aus deutscher Sicht', *Zeitschrift für Zivilprozess*, 2010, p. 261-282.

Stipanowich 2010
Stipanowich, T., 'Arbitration: the "New Litigation"', *University of Illinois Law Review*, 2010, p. 1-58.

Strong 2013
Strong, S.I., 'Increasing Legalism in International Commercial Arbitration: A New Theory of Causes, A New Approach to Cures', *World Arbitration and Mediation Review*, 2013, p. 117-130.

Van den Berg 2008
Van den Berg, A., 'Organizing an International Arbitration: Practice Pointers', in Newman, L. & Hill, R. (eds.), *The Leading Arbitrators' Guide to International Arbitration*, 2nd edn., New York: Juris Publishing, 2008, p. 149-170.

Van Houtte 2010a
Van Houtte, H., 'Arbitration Guidelines: Straitjacket of Compass?', in Hober, K. *et al.* (eds.), *Between East and West: Essays in Honour of Ulf Franke*, Huntington, New York: Juris, 2010, p. 515-528.

Van Houtte 2010b
Van Houtte, H., 'The Document Production Master and the Experts' Facilitator: Two Possible Aides for an Efficient Arbitration', in Fernández-Ballesteros, M. & Arias, D. (eds.), *Liber Amicorum Bernardo Cremades*, Wolters Kluwer España: La Ley, 2010, p. 1147-1159.

Varga 2006
Varga, I., *Beweiserhebung in transatlantischen Schiedsverfahren*, Baden-Baden: Nomos, 2006.

Vercauteren 2012
Vercauteren, L., 'Disclosure Requests in International Commercial Arbitration: Finding a Balance Not Only Between Legal Traditions But Also Between The Parties' Rights', *The American Review of International Arbitration*, 2012, p. 341-364.

von Segesser 2010
von Segesser, G., 'The IBA Rules on the Taking of Evidence in International Arbitration: Revised version, adopted by the International Bar Association on 29 May 2010', *ASA Bulletin*, 2010, p. 735-752.

Waincymer 2012
Waincymer, J., *Procedure and Evidence in International Arbitration*, The Hague: Kluwer Law International, 2012.

Webster & Bühler 2014
Webster, Th. & Bühler, M., *Handbook of ICC Arbitration*, 3rd edn., London: Sweet & Maxwell, 2014.

Wirth 2003
Wirth, M., 'Ihr Zeuge, Herr Rechtsanwalt! - Weshalb Civil-Law-Schiedsrichter Common-Law-Verfahrensrecht anwenden', *SchiedsVZ*, 2003, p. 9-15.

Zuberbühler *et al.* 2012
Zuberbühler, T., Hofmann, D., Oetiker, C. & Rohner, T., *IBA Rules of Evidence – Commentary on the IBA Rules on the Taking of Evidence in International Arbitration*, Zurich/Basel/Geneva: Schulthess & Sellier, 2012.

C.H. van Rhee

EVIDENCE IN CIVIL PROCEDURE IN THE NETHERLANDS: TRADITION AND MODERNITY[1]

In order to fully understand the law of evidence in any procedural system, one needs to have knowledge of the wider procedural context in which it is used. Therefore, this contribution on evidence in Dutch civil procedure will start by providing some basic details of the Dutch procedural system.[2] The discussion will be limited to civil matters, since evidence law in the Netherlands is not generic for all types of litigation. A specific law of evidence for civil matters exists and since 1988 it can be found (for the largest part)[3] in the Code of Civil Procedure.[4] It will appear that the Dutch law of evidence in civil matters is still (to a certain extent at least) based on traditions, often derived from its French 19th century model, but that especially since 1988 important innovations have been introduced which have resulted in rules that - when considered within the wider procedural framework - have prepared Dutch civil evidence law well for some of the challenges of the 21th century.

In this contribution I will mainly concentrate on the procedure initiated by writ of summons (contentious litigation). The other type of civil action, i.e. the procedure started by way of a petition (originally only for non-contentious matters,

1 The present contribution is based on a national report on Dutch civil evidence law written by the author within the context of the project Dimensions of Evidence in European Civil Procedure, JUST/2011-2012/JCIV/AG/3434. The author would like to thank Dr. F.J. Fernhout for his comments on an earlier version of this contribution.

2 See also Van Hooijdonk & Eijsvoogel 2012.

3 Sometimes we find rules on civil evidence elsewhere. This is for example true for presumptions, rules on which cannot be found in the current Code of Civil Procedure. Examples of specific presumptions can, however, be found elsewhere, for example in Article 7:610a of the Dutch Civil Code (presumption as to the existence of a labour contract).

4 For the legislative history of the 1988 Dutch evidence law in civil matters, see Rutgers, Flach & Boon 1988. Before 1988, the 'substantive' aspects of the law of evidence in civil matters could be found in the Dutch Civil Code; this was in line with the 19th century French example of the Dutch law of civil evidence.

especially family matters) will be addressed incidentally. In the future, the differences between the two types of procedure will remain even though it is the intention of the Dutch Legislature to introduce a single document for bringing a civil court action. The single introductory document is not aimed at removing procedural differences, but is mainly introduced for reasons of simplification and digitalisation of litigation.[5]

Like so many other jurisdictions in Europe, the Netherlands has embraced the concept of judicial case management in civil matters (especially since the reforms of the Code of Civil Procedure in 2002).[6] This means that the traditional Dutch principle of the 'passivity of the judge' (in Dutch: *lijdelijkheid*) in civil matters has faded away to a considerable extent.[7] The case management powers of the modern Dutch judge concern in the first place procedural issues, but they may to a certain extent also concern the merits of the case. For example, the judge has to guard against undue delay and if necessary take measures to prevent such delay.[8] He makes sure that the proceedings unfold in an orderly manner and may deny further postponements for the submission of statements of case.[9] The judge also has extended powers as regards the factual basis of the case and evidence. He may order the parties whenever necessary during the proceedings to provide information, orally or by way of documents.[10] The judge may, *ex officio*, investigate the facts of the case by way of a court hearing at which the parties themselves have to appear.[11] The judge may also *ex officio* order a party to supply proof by way of witnesses (he may not nominate witnesses though),[12] and he may, *ex officio*, investigate the truth of contested facts by way of a local inspection (*descente sur les lieux*)[13] or an expert report[14] (although for practical reasons this only happens to a limited extent). In cases where the procedure is initiated by way of a petition, the possibilities to collect evidence *ex officio* are more extended in the sense that the judge may also call witnesses selected by himself.[15] The extended powers of the

5 See *Voorstel tot Wijziging van het Wetboek van Burgerlijke Rechtsvordering en de Algemene wet bestuursrecht in verband met vereenvoudiging en digitalisering van het procesrecht* (Legislative proposal for amendment of the Code of Civil Procedure and the General Administrative Law Act in relation to the simplification and digitalisation of the law of procedure) (Kamerstukken 34 059).

6 In 2002, the 'post-defence hearing model' – an important tool in judicial case management – was formalized in the Code of Civil Procedure. On this model, see below.

7 On the principle of 'passivity' and its history, see Chorus 1987.

8 Art. 20(1) Dutch Code of Civil Procedure (hereafter CCP).

9 Art. 133 CCP.

10 Art. 22 CCP. The parties may refuse this for serious reasons to be assessed by the judge. When the judge decides that no serious reasons exist, he may derive the conclusions he deems fit from the party's refusal to supply information (which conclusions, however, should be related to this information).

11 Art. 88 CCP.

12 Art. 166(1) CCP.

13 Art. 201 CCP.

14 Art. 194 CCP.

15 Art. 284(2) CCP.

judge as regards evidence are in line with the approach in many civil law jurisdictions on the European Continent.[16]

Traditionally, and especially before the 2002 reforms,[17] a Dutch civil action unfolded through a series of separate hearings (cause-list sittings) for the performance of the necessary procedural acts. This was in line with the model of civil procedure provided by the Romano-canonical example as it had developed on the European Continent since the medieval period.[18] Procedural acts could be performed throughout litigation until final judgment (with some exceptions, such as submitting procedural defences (exceptions) which had (and still have) to be submitted in an early stage, an innovation dating from the 1890s).[19] The court could (and can), for example, order the submission of additional evidence whenever needed.

Since the start of the third millennium and especially since 2002, the 'concentration' of civil litigation has been an issue in Dutch civil proceedings. This has given rise to what may be termed the 'post-defence hearing model'.[20] Although Dutch civil procedure does not know a main hearing as in German civil procedure (*Haupttermin*), this model nevertheless prescribes that in the majority of cases the judge should order an oral hearing after the submission of the statement of defence.[21] This hearing is ordered by an interlocutory judgment that may indicate which issues are on the agenda of the hearing.[22] Parties may be ordered to submit supplementary documents and are usually ordered to appear in person. The hearing may be used for various purposes, e.g. for establishing the relevant facts and for attempting an amicable settlement.[23] If the judge is satisfied that the case can be decided after this hearing, he may do so without allowing any further statements or procedural acts. If more information is needed, he will issue an interlocutory judgment elaborating on the burden of proof and ordering the submission of witness evidence, the appointment of an expert or announcing a visit to a locality by the court.[24] The court cannot go back on its decisions regarding evidence in the interlocutory ruling, unless new circumstances occur after the decision. It may also

16 See, for example, the contributions of Uzelac and Zoroska in the present volume.

17 On these reforms, see Van Rhee 2008, p. 191-212.

18 On the Romano-canonical procedure, see e.g. Nörr 2012.

19 Art. 128(3) CCP. See also *Voorstel van wet tot wijziging van het Wetboek van Burgerlijke Regtsvordering van Mr. A.F.K. Hartogh*, The Hague: Belinfante, 1895-1898, and Hartogh & Cosman 1897.

20 See also the contribution of Hoogers *et al.* in the present volume.

21 Art. 131 CCP.

22 Art. 4.1 *Landelijk procesreglement voor civiele dagvaardingszaken bij de rechtbanken* (National procedural directions for civil summons cases at the general court of first instance) and Art. 4.3 *Landelijk procesreglement voor de civiele rol van de kantonsectoren* (National procedural directions for the civil cause-list of the cantonal section of the general first instance court).

23 Art. 131 jo. Arts. 87 and 88 CCP.

24 Art. 232 CCP.

happen that events after the interlocutory judgment ordering the submission of evidence lead to a new decision on the burden of proof.[25]

Recent reform plans aim at the introduction of digital litigation[26] and these reforms will give rise to further changes in civil procedure. As stated, the present distinction between the introduction of a civil case by way of a writ of summons or a petition will be abolished even though several of the existing differences in procedure will remain, the (currently already digital) general cause list for scheduling purposes and for the execution of procedural acts will be replaced by a simplified, individual case calendar in an individual digital environment (referred to as 'Mijn Zaak', i.e. 'My Case'), whereas the post-defence hearing will gain in importance as an instrument for the judge to promote celerity.[27]

At present, procedural acts are, as a rule, rendered in writing.[28] Since no audio or video recordings are made of court hearings including the hearing of witnesses, the case file has great significance. Where parties are allowed to submit their statements in oral form,[29] the records of the hearing will summarize those statements in written form. The current reform plans aim at changing this situation, by facilitating the use of audio and video recordings of hearings, including the administration of witness evidence.[30]

Special mention should be made here of proceedings on appeal. Generally speaking, when compared to other European jurisdictions,[31] Dutch law is very liberal as regards what procedural acts may be performed on appeal (in practice, this does not cause significant delays). On appeal, litigants may correct mistakes

25 HR 20-01-2006, NJ 2006, 78.

26 In the legislative proposal, the use of the terminology 'electronic litigation' is discouraged, since due to wireless systems of data processing not all digital litigation can be referred to as 'electronic' anymore. See *Voorstel tot Wijziging van het Wetboek van Burgerlijke Rechtsvordering en de Algemene wet bestuursrecht in verband met vereenvoudiging en digitalisering van het procesrecht* (Legislative proposal for amendment of the Code of Civil Procedure and the General Administrative Law Act in relation to the simplification and digitalisation of the law of procedure) (Kamerstukken 34 059).

27 See *Voorstel tot Wijziging van het Wetboek van Burgerlijke Rechtsvordering en de Algemene wet bestuursrecht in verband met vereenvoudiging en digitalisering van het procesrecht* (Legislative proposal for amendment of the Code of Civil Procedure and the General Administrative Law Act in relation to the simplification and digitalisation of the law of procedure) (Kamerstukken 34 059).

28 With some exceptions, e.g. where witnesses are heard by the court of first instance in cases where no appeal is possible; in these cases the court may decide not to make a written record of the testimonies of witnesses but include a short summary of the testimonies in the judgment only (Art. 181(1) CCP).

29 This happens in cases dealt with by the small claims and specialized section of the first instance court ('cantonal section' or in Dutch: *Sector Kanton*, Art. 82(2) CCP).

30 See *Voorstel tot Wijziging van het Wetboek van Burgerlijke Rechtsvordering en de Algemene wet bestuursrecht in verband met vereenvoudiging en digitalisering van het procesrecht* (Legislative proposal for amendment of the Code of Civil Procedure and the General Administrative Law Act in relation to the simplification and digitalisation of the law of procedure) (Kamerstukken 34 059).

31 See, e.g. the contribution of Aras in the present volume.

made at first instance and may introduce new arguments, new facts, new defences and new evidence.[32] However, defences that have been expressly abandoned at first instance (in Dutch: *gedekte weren*) cannot be brought forward on appeal.[33]

Various fundamental principles are observed in Dutch civil litigation. Court hearings are public,[34] and this is obviously in line with the requirements of Article 6 of the European Convention of Human Rights. The *Dispositionsmaxime*, which lays down that the parties determine whether or not to bring a court action as well as the content of this action, is observed since the court is not allowed to go beyond the facts stated by the parties to justify their claims and defences.[35] The court will not help a party to complete its statements. The same holds for evidence: the court assesses the evidence after it has been submitted. If the evidence is incomplete, the party concerned will learn about this from the judgment. The court is not under an obligation to initiate evidentiary proceedings itself when the evidence is incomplete, even though the court may exercise *ex officio* powers in this respect as indicated above. The principle of equality is also observed, and this entails that both parties should be heard by the judge equally (either orally and/or in writing).[36] The judge may not obtain information from a party without allowing the other party to comment on this information,[37] and he may only decide the matter on the basis of documents and information of which both parties have been able to obtain knowledge during the proceedings and on which they have been allowed to comment.[38] Furthermore, it can be claimed that in the Netherlands a principle comparable to the German *Wahrheitspflicht* (duty of truth) exists, codified by Article 21 of the Dutch Code of Civil Procedure. This Article provides that the parties have the duty to provide all facts that are relevant for the decision of the case fully and truthfully. If they do not observe this duty, the judge may draw the conclusions with regard to the facts he deems fit. The relevance of the duty of Article 21 is, however, limited in value since it only aims at preventing deliberate lies, whereas facts that are advanced by one party and that are not disputed by the other party do not have to be proven; the judge may not investigate such facts even though he may feel that there are problems as regards the truth. This is only different if these facts give rise to legal consequences which are not at the free disposition of the parties.[39] In addition, Dutch law recognizes the principle of *ius curia novit*.[40] The principle means that positive law does not need to be pleaded and proven since the court is supposed to know the law. Even foreign law does not need proof (although the

32 Art. 353(1) jo. Art. 130 CCP; HR 16-12-1926, *NJ* 1927, p. 263, W 11612; HR 03-09-1993, *NJ* 1993, 714; HR 01-03-2002, *NJ* 2003, 355 (HJS).

33 Art. 348 CCP.

34 Art. 27 CCP.

35 Art. 24 CCP.

36 Art. 19 CCP (*audi et alteram partem*). See also Asser 1992.

37 Art. 19 CCP. See also Art. 12 Act on Judicial Organisation (*Wet op de Rechterlijke Organisatie*, hereafter: RO).

38 *Cf.* Art. 85(4) CCP.

39 Art. 149(1) CCP.

40 Art. 25 CCP.

judge may be required to obtain information on foreign law)[41] since the court is supposed to know foreign law if the parties state that foreign law applies.[42] The free assessment of evidence is sometimes also mentioned as a fundamental principle of civil procedure[43] (see below for further details).

1. Dutch Evidence Law in General

Facts that need proof

As in other modern systems of civil procedure,[44] not all facts alleged by a party need proof in Dutch civil litigation. This is true for facts that are not disputed or not sufficiently disputed by the opponent party,[45] and obviously this is different from the approach in socialist systems of civil procedure where the court may establish the truth of uncontested facts if doubts about their truthfulness arise.[46] No proof is needed either for facts that are expressly recognized by the opponent party.[47] Notorious facts and general empirical rules (rules of experience) do not need to be put forward by the parties and do not need proof either,[48] just as procedural facts that are observed by the judge in the court action.[49] The same is true for positive law according to the principle of *ius curia novit* that prevails in Dutch law[50] (see above).

Burden of proof

The parties are in charge of proving contested facts according to the burden of proof as established by the court. The main doctrine on burden of proof in Dutch civil litigation is provided by Article 150 of the Code of Civil Procedure: The party who invokes the legal consequences of the facts or rights posed by him has the burden of proof of these facts or rights, unless a specific legal rule or the requirements of equity or fairness require a different distribution of the burden of proof. A party who has the burden of proof and who does not provide the required evidence will suffer the detrimental consequences of not having proven the facts that are relevant for his case since the burden of proof produces what in Dutch is called the 'evidentiary risk' (*bewijsrisico*). There is not, however, a duty (in German: *Pflicht*) to submit evidence in the sense that a party can be forced to submit it.

41 This procedure is regulated in Arts. 67-68 CCP.
42 HR 22-02-2002, *NJ* 2003, 483.
43 Art. 152(2) CCP.
44 Nagel & Bajons 2003. For an older but still relevant study see Nagel 1967.
45 Art. 149(1) CCP.
46 See e.g. the contribution of Uzelac in the present volume.
47 Art. 154 CCP.
48 Art. 149(2) CCP.
49 Hugenholtz & Heemskerk (continued by W. Heemskerk in collaboration with J.M.L. van Duin, R.S.I Lawant and I.C. Blomsma) 2015, No. 78.
50 Art. 25 CCP.

Evidentiary agreements
Under certain circumstances, the parties may conclude a so-called 'evidentiary agreement' (in Dutch: *bewijsovereenkomst*). In this agreement, they may deviate from the applicable rules of evidence pending litigation or exclude their application in view of future litigation. The agreement may concern issues such as the burden of proof and the exclusion of certain means of proof. The court is bound by this agreement, unless the agreement concerns proof of facts which according to the law give rise to legal consequences that are not at the free disposition of the parties.[51] The general rules of contract law of the Civil Code apply to 'evidentiary agreements'.

Offers of proof
The party with the burden of proof has to offer proof of the facts on which the claim or defence is based (apart from some rare exceptions where proof of the contrary has to be provided by the opponent party). Quite often this proof can be found in the documentary evidence or assumptions accepted by the court. In those cases, the opponent party will have to offer counter-proof. The judge may ignore an offer to provide proof if it is, for example, too vague, not serious or irrelevant for the decision of the case.[52] However, a judge may never deny the administration of evidence based on the chances of whether or not a party will succeed in providing the proof that is required for his case.[53] An offer to provide counter-proof cannot be rejected.[54]

Submission of evidence
As in most other modern European systems, the *Eventualmaxime* does not exist in Dutch civil procedure (this is an example of 19th century French influence; the *Eventualmaxime* was a feature of the German *gemeines Recht*),[55] and there are no strict rules on when new facts and evidence should be introduced at first instance or on appeal. However, apart from documentary evidence, which may be submitted without a court order, other evidence can only be introduced when the court issues an interlocutory judgment to this end and therefore the court is in control of evidence taking.[56] In the Netherlands, it is not exceptional that even appellate courts take evidence. Appeal is a complete rehearing of the aspects of the first instance judgment that are brought before the appellate court. On appeal, the same rules on the introduction of facts and the submission of evidence apply as at first instance. Both at first instance and on appeal a party should not abuse his procedural rights

51 Art. 153 CCP.
52 For appeal, see HR 09-07-2004, *NJ* 2005, 270; HR 28-01-2011, *NJ* 2012, 603; HR 27-05-2011, *NJ* 2011, 512; HR 31-10-2014, ECLI 3075.
53 See conclusion of Advocate-General Biegman-Hartogh, *NJ* 1986, 766.
54 Art. 168 CCP.
55 E.g. Schulte 1980, p. 3 *et seq*.
56 Art. 353(1) jo. Arts. 130 and 149 *et seq*. CCP.

by submitting facts and evidence at a late point in the court action.[57] Article 133(4) of the Code of Civil Procedure provides that procedural acts (including the submission of evidence) that have not been executed within the period of time fixed for them by the judge (if such time period has indeed been fixed by him) cannot be executed anymore.[58]

Even though the parties have a lot of freedom in determining when they submit documentary evidence, the way in which litigation is framed in the Netherlands results in the parties having an interest in introducing facts and indicating their evidence at an early stage, i.e. in the statement of claim (which is part of the summons)[59] and in the statement of defence,[60] respectively. After all, the standard procedure requires the judge to order the parties to make an appearance before him after submission of the statement of defence (unless the case is unsuitable for such a hearing).[61] At the end of this court hearing, where the parties may introduce additional facts and arguments and where the judge should make sure that the principle of *audi et alteram partem* is sufficiently observed, the judge may decide that he has acquired enough information to decide the matter without giving the parties an opportunity to introduce additional statements of case and evidence.[62] Since the litigants may not be given an opportunity to submit further statements and evidence after the hearing, they have an incentive to be as complete as possible in their respective statements of claim and defence and at the court hearing.

Interlocutory judgments relating to information and proof

If a court thinks that the information given by the parties is lacking clarity, an interlocutory judgment is used to invite the parties to give the clarifications that are needed. The clarification can be given in written form or at an oral hearing following the decision of the court. The interlocutory judgment is also used to order one or both parties to submit proof or counter-proof of facts explicitly described in that judgment.[63] The actual submission of evidence is entirely up to the parties. The court is not even under an obligation to request the deposition of documentary evidence that has been mentioned by a party without actually submitting it (although it may do so; see below).[64] The parties will not get a second chance if they do not submit evidence following an interlocutory judgment to this extent.

57 Art. 353(1) jo. Art. 130 CCP; HR 16-12-1926, *NJ* 1927, p. 263, W 11612; HR 03-09-1993, *NJ* 1993, 714; HR 01-03-2002, *NJ* 2003, 355 (HJS).

58 However, in HR 18-03-2011, *NJ* 2012, 315 the Dutch Supreme Court states that disregarding the time-limit has to be evaluated in light of the efficient and speedy administration of justice.

59 Art. 111(3) CCP.

60 Art. 128(5) CCP.

61 Art. 131 CCP

62 Art. 132 CCP.

63 Art. 232 CCP.

64 HR 09-03-2012, *LJN* BU9204.

If the court orders the submission of a specific piece of evidence (for instance when a party claims to be in possession of the original contract, but does not produce it), not complying with this order will give the court the power to draw the conclusions regarding this piece of evidence it deems fit.[65]

Judge in charge of taking evidence
Evidence can only be taken by the judge, a judge-commissioner or a panel of judges (three judges). There are no specific conditions for taking evidence before a judge-commissioner. As a rule, the judge-commissioner hears witnesses if the case is decided by a panel (in that event, the judge-commissioner has to be part of the panel deciding the case, unless serious reasons exist why this cannot be done; these reasons need to be expressed in the judgment).[66] If the case is decided by a single judge, this single judge will hear the witnesses himself.

Ex officio powers of the judge
Although the collection of evidence is a task of the parties, the judge may (to a certain extent) also *ex officio* be active in this respect (see the introduction above), but he is restricted by the statements put forward by the parties.[67] Collection of evidence beyond the contested facts submitted by the parties is not allowed. That is why it may be held that in Dutch civil litigation only the formal, not the material truth is relevant, although the duty of truth expressed in the Dutch Code of Civil Procedure may act as a counterbalance in this respect.

Presence of the parties during proof proceedings
The parties have the right to be present when evidence is taken, and this is in line with fundamental principles of civil procedure. Article 167 of the Code of Civil Procedure determines that the judge can even order parties to be personally present when witnesses are heard. In the case of the appointment of an expert, the expert will be instructed to invite the parties to assist at his activities. The expert also has to give the parties the opportunity to ask questions and to make remarks.[68]

No limitations on the means of proof
As in most modern systems of civil procedure, evidence can be administered by all means; there are only a few exceptions. An example of an exception can be found in Article 1:78 of the Dutch Civil Code: a marriage that has been concluded in the Netherlands can in principle only be proven by way of the official certificate of marriage or an official document in which a civil partnership has been commuted into a marriage. Furthermore, in some cases, proof is only possible by producing proof in written form (as is the case with jurisdiction clauses).[69]

65 Art. 22 CCP.
66 Art. 155 CCP.
67 Art. 24 CCP.
68 Art. 198(2) CCP.
69 Art. 8(5) CCP.

In some instances the law provides that witness or documentary evidence is only allowed when other types of evidence have been destroyed. This is for instance the case in Article 1:79 of the Dutch Civil Code that allows proof of a marriage by witness evidence if the register of marriages has been destroyed.

There is no mandatory sequence in which evidence has to be taken in the Netherlands. Documentary evidence is submitted before and after the post-defence hearing, whereas witnesses can only be heard after an interlocutory judgment to this end (the latter is also true for hearing experts and a local inspection).

Counter-proof

Counter-proof is obviously allowed in civil matters. Occasionally, however, counter-proof is excluded by law. Article 8:48 of the Dutch Civil Code, for example, does not allow counter-proof against a signed and dated document specifying the goods that have been received for transportation ("CT document") issued to the sender of goods by a carrier that uses more than one means of transport, at least if the document has been transferred to a third party who acts in good faith. As regards third parties, further examples can be found in Articles 8:414 and 921 of the Dutch Civil Code, and in the ruling of the Supreme Court that against a third party no counter-proof is allowed where it concerns a document that has been registered in the public register of mortgages.[70] Moreover, if the facts of the case are such that the law instructs the court to assume a legal fiction (which is *not* the same as a legal presumption), counter-proof is never possible.

Free evaluation of evidence and limitations

There is no hierarchy of evidence in the Netherlands, with a few exceptions. The judge is free in assessing the evidence, and obviously this means that the Netherlands has broken with the Romano-canonical tradition in this respect.[71] This principle is deeply entrenched in Dutch civil procedural law. It can be found in Article 152(2) of the Code of Civil Procedure. The exception is where the law provides otherwise, e.g. where the judge has to consider the case proven by a certain means of proof unless counter-proof is produced (i.e. 'compulsory proof'). Public and private evidentiary documents (these should be distinguished from ordinary documents; see below), for example, provide in principle full proof between the parties and their heirs as regards the statements of the parties recorded in these documents if they are drafted in order to provide proof of these statements.[72] Counter-proof is allowed.[73] Perhaps the best definition of the principle of the free assessment of evidence in Dutch civil procedural law is that the judge decides on proof according to his 'intimate conviction' (in this – as in other respects – Dutch law follows the French example).

70 HR 22-10-2010, *NJ* 2011, 111.
71 See e.g. Lévy 1965, p. 137-168.
72 Art. 157(2) CCP.
73 Art. 151(2) CCP.

No standards of proof are formulated in Dutch civil procedural law. As just stated, the judge decides the case based on his intimate conviction, but within the boundaries set by the parties in their statements of facts. The judge freely evaluates the evidence and needs to be convinced that the facts have been proven, unless specific proof rules apply such as those concerning 'compulsory proof'[74] (see above). The Dutch legal system does not provide methodological guidance for judges on the free assessment of evidence.

Apart from this, it should be pointed out that, although Dutch law does not have a minimum standard of proof, the country does have a minimum standard of counter-proof. This standard depends on the way the facts have been proven by the party with the burden of proof. In case of compulsory proof, for counter-proof what is needed is to 'knock the bottom out of' the proof submitted.[75] This is a rather high standard. In the case of the existence of presumptions, the other party only has to make a reasonable case of his refutations.[76] In case witnesses are heard on both sides, the judge takes his decision on the basis of his intimate conviction regarding the credibility of the witness testimonies.

Early gathering of evidence

Pre-trial discovery in the technical, common law sense does not exist in the Netherlands. However, there are some means available in the Dutch Code of Civil Procedure to acquire information before the action is brought into court. According to Articles 186 *et seq.* of the Code, a preliminary hearing of witnesses may be ordered by the court at the request of an interested party before an action has been brought. The court cannot order such a hearing *ex officio,* and the request must be submitted by a party who has an interest in the preliminary hearing of witnesses. In the specific case for which the preliminary hearing is asked, the administration of proof by way of witnesses needs to be allowed, otherwise a preliminary hearing of witnesses is not allowed.

The aims of a preliminary hearing of witnesses can be manifold. One may think of the need to hear witnesses quickly after the relevant facts have occurred, or to safeguard evidence that may be lost otherwise (witnesses may, for example, die), to allow the parties to evaluate whether bringing a civil action will be appropriate, to prevent litigation by way of a settlement based on the information obtained by way of a preliminary hearing of witnesses,[77] to determine who should be summoned to court as the defendant, to stimulate a subsequent efficient hearing of the case, and to prevent interlocutory proceedings during the action for the hearing of witnesses (since the necessary witnesses have already been heard before the action was brought).

74 Art. 152(2) CCP.
75 See HR 02-05-2003, *NJ* 2003, 468.
76 For instance in HR 23-11-2012, *NJ* 2012, 669.
77 Art. 191(1) CCP.

The judge needs to take care that the preliminary hearing will not be used as a fishing expedition, or in order to uncover business secrets. He may not deny a preliminary hearing of witnesses based on a prediction of the outcome of the future civil action.[78] In general, a request for a preliminary hearing of witnesses can only be rejected on very limited grounds, which all come down to the lack of sufficient interest on the side of the requesting party.[79] This could be the case when the evidence has already been produced.[80]

Since 1988, the Dutch Code of Civil Procedure also allows a preliminary expert report and a preliminary local inspection to be ordered by the court.[81] The rules applying to a preliminary expert report and local inspection are roughly the same as the rules applying to the preliminary hearing of witnesses.

A preliminary hearing of witnesses to secure evidence can also be ordered when the action has already been commenced.[82] The same is true for an expert report and a local inspection.[83]

Illegal evidence

In the Netherlands, the concept of illegal evidence or illegally obtained evidence is of limited relevance in civil litigation. In 1988, the Legislature decided not to regulate this issue in the Code of Civil Procedure but to leave the development of it to case law.[84]

In Dutch legal literature, we read that the duty to litigate in a fair manner and not with the help of information that has been obtained illegally has to be weighed against the duty of truth of the parties in a civil lawsuit and the interest of finding the truth in civil litigation in general. In the literature, there seems to be consensus about the fact *that* illegally obtained evidence *may* result in the exclusion of this material in civil litigation. There is, however, no agreement about the question of *when* illegally obtained evidence may be excluded (i.e. left out of consideration by the judge).[85]

In practice and as a general rule, the judge may use any means of proof in civil litigation. Unfortunately, relevant case law usually deals with the question *whether* or not evidence has been obtained illegally, and *not* with the question whether it may be excluded.

Examples of cases concerning possibly illegally obtained evidence are:[86]

78 HR 06-06-2008, *NJ* 2008, 323.
79 Art. 189 jo. 166(1) CCP. Criteria have been set in HR 13-09-2002, *NJ* 2004, 18.
80 See HR 22-10-2010, *NJB* 2010, 2000.
81 Arts. 202-207 CCP.
82 Art. 186(2) CCP.
83 Art. 202(2) CCP.
84 See Rutgers, Flach & Boon 1988.
85 See Asser Procesrecht/Asser 3 2013/145.
86 All mentioned in Asser Procesrecht/Asser 3 2013/146.

1. A recording without notification of a business call by telephone *cannot* be qualified as illegally obtained;[87]
2. Camera observations of the house of someone entitled to welfare and made by civil servants in the execution of their legal duty to uncover fraud are *not* illegally obtained;[88]
3. Video recordings of the check-out counter of a shop made by an employer without informing his employees indeed causes a breach of the right to privacy but this does *not* hinder the use of these recordings in a civil lawsuit since in the case at hand there existed a presumption of criminal acts being committed which could only be uncovered with video recordings;[89]
4. Secretly taken pictures and video recordings by an insurer of the victim of a traffic accident in order to uncover whether the victim was limited in his movements due to the whiplash resulting from the accident are in principle illegally obtained (the right to privacy is at stake here). There may be circumstances, however, which justify obtaining the information in the manner mentioned above, but this can only be decided by taking into consideration the circumstances of the case, by weighing the gravity of the contravention of the right to privacy, on the one hand, and the interests that are served by the contravention of this right, on the other (i.e. finding the truth in the civil lawsuit). In the case at hand, the Supreme Court did not answer the question whether indeed there was a justification;[90]
5. The submission in a civil action of a report made in a criminal lawsuit may be in contravention of the right to privacy of the opponent party, but this is *not* necessarily the case.[91]

A recent case might be of interest too, since in it the use of illegally obtained evidence was refused by the court of appeal.[92] The Dutch Supreme Court did not quash this decision and thus considered the decision on appeal *not* in contravention of the law. In the case, an insurer had obtained evidence by contravening the right to privacy of the insured (this was concluded by also taking into consideration a Code of Conduct for insurers holding specific rules on the matter). The insurer submitted this illegally obtained evidence in a civil lawsuit. Due to the fact that alternatives were available to obtain the necessary information for the insurer, and due to the fact that there was no reason to assume fraud on the side of the insured person, and since the insured person had not refused to cooperate with the insurer, the court of appeal refused to take into consideration the illegally obtained evidence contravening the right to privacy.

87 HR 16-10-1987, *NJ* 1988, 850.
88 HR 11-11-1994, *NJ* 1995, 400.
89 HR 27-04-2001, *NJ* 2001, 421.
90 HR 31-05-2002, *NJ* 2003, 589.
91 HR 11-09-1998, *NJ* 1999, 664.
92 ECLI:NL:HR:2014:942.

Parties against whom illegally obtained evidence is used may consider whether an action in tort can be brought against the opponent party who makes use of the illegally obtained evidence. Using illegally obtained information in a civil lawsuit may constitute a tort, e.g. due to the contravention of the right to privacy or because the information used had to remain secret for other reasons (e.g. evidentiary privileges).

Perhaps the safest way to express the situation in the Netherlands is that in a civil lawsuit illegally obtained information may be used, unless... The aim of the norm that has been contravened when obtaining the evidence must be weighed against the duty of truth of the parties and the interest of establishing the truth in civil cases. For example, stealing information will not lead to the exclusion of this information as evidence unless the theft also results in the contravention of a norm that excludes the information for publication by all means, e.g. where the evidence is privileged or where the safety of the state is at stake.[93]

2. Types of Evidence

Article 152(1) of the Dutch Code of Civil Procedure provides that proof may be administered by all means unless the law determines otherwise. Accordingly, in most cases there are no limitations as regards the means by way of which evidence may be administered, i.e. Dutch law does not know a *numerus clausus* in this respect.

Some means of proof are specifically regulated by the Code of Civil Procedure: documentary evidence (including proof by way of accounts),[94] witness testimony (including the testimony of party-witnesses),[95] expert reports[96] and a local inspection.[97] An example of a means of proof that is not regulated in the Code of Civil Procedure is presumptions.

2.1. *Documentary Evidence*

General

While there is no definition of documents in the Code of Civil Procedure, or elsewhere, a document in Dutch civil procedure is seen as an entity capable of carrying legible characters that express an idea when considered in relation to each other. Electronic documents obviously meet the requirement and are therefore regarded as documents.[98] Video or audio recordings, on the other hand, do not meet the requirement, so they cannot be regarded as documents proper. Since there is no *numerus clausus* as regards means of proof, however, they are nevertheless means of

93 See Asser Procesrecht/Asser 3 2013/143-148.
94 Arts. 156 *et seq.*
95 Arts. 163 *et seq.*
96 Arts. 194 *et seq.*
97 Arts. 201 *et seq.*
98 See e.g. Arts. 843a(1) and 843b(1) CCP. See also Asser Procesrecht/Asser 3 2013/154.

proof (although not documents), and no negative consequences result from their not being qualified as documents.

Article 160(1) of the Code of Civil Procedure provides that the force of documentary evidence resides within the original document. Copies may be submitted in court but the opponent party may ask to see the original.[99] Article 160(2) lays down that authenticated and full copies of public evidentiary documents (on these, see below) that need to be archived by the relevant authorities according to the relevant legal rules may also serve as evidence. In this case, the original document does not have to be produced in court.

As a general rule, the parties are free to submit documentary evidence (in the broadest sense of the word) in any stage of the proceedings (see above). Documentary evidence is, as a rule, submitted to the court by the parties and does not have to be read at a court hearing.

Three types of documents are distinguished in Dutch civil procedural law as means of proof: ordinary documents, private evidentiary documents (in Dutch: *onderhandse akten*) and public evidentiary documents (in Dutch: *authentieke akten*).[100]

Ordinary documents, in the sense of documents which cannot be considered as 'evidentiary documents' (*akten*), do not have specific evidentiary value. The judge determines whether or not such documents can serve as proof of the facts regarding which a party has the burden of proof. They can be the sole evidentiary basis of a judgment.[101]

Article 156(1) of the Code of Civil Procedure defines 'evidentiary documents' (*akten*) as signed documents drafted in order to provide proof. Although this is not mentioned in the Code, this should be read as 'to provide proof in civil matters'. Thus documents governed by public law (like driving licences) are not considered to be 'evidentiary documents' for the purpose of civil procedure (they can, however, be produced in court as proof; they are classified as 'ordinary documents'). According to Article 156(2), public evidentiary documents are documents that are drafted in the required manner by an official who is competent to do so according to the law, aiming at recording what the official has perceived or what he has executed. Private evidentiary documents are defined as documents which are not public in nature.[102]

Private and public evidentiary documents enjoy a specific status in proof-taking since they will be considered to provide full proof ('compulsory proof') when certain requirements are met (see below).

According to Article 159(1) of the Code of Civil Procedure, a document that has the appearance of a public evidentiary documents will be considered as such until it has been proven that it is not a public evidentiary document. There are no

99 Art. 85 CCP and HR 22-11-2013, ECLI 1384.
100 Art. 156 CCP.
101 Art. 152 CCP.
102 Art. 156(3) CCP.

limitations as regards the manner in which it can be proven that a document is not a public evidentiary document.

According to Article 157(1) of the Code of Civil Procedure, public evidentiary documents provide full proof as regards the perceptions or acts which the competent official has recorded. Article 157(2) states in addition that public and private evidentiary documents provide in principle full proof between the parties and their legal successors as regards the statements of the parties recorded in these documents if they are drafted in order to provide proof of these statements.

Article 158 of the Code of Civil Procedure provides specific rules for private evidentiary documents in which the obligation of a party to pay a money debt is recorded without specifying obligations for the other party. In that event, the rule of Article 157(2) (i.e. full proof) only applies if the debtor has written the whole document manually or if he has written his approval on a typed document mentioning the amount in words. This requirement does not need to be met as regards a bond loan or if the debtor acts in the exercise of his profession or in a business context.

If the signature under a private evidentiary document is expressly contested by the party against whom it would serve as full proof, such a private evidentiary document cannot serve as proof unless the origin of the signature under the document can be proven by the party who uses the document as evidence.[103] There are no limitations as regards the manner in which the origin of the signature can be proven.

If the character of a public evidentiary document or the signature under a private evidentiary document is not contested, but the content of these documents is, counter-proof is available without limitations unless excluded by law.[104] However, there is a high minimum standard for this counter-proof.[105]

Judicial decisions in civil disputes have the status of documentary evidence (public evidentiary document), and often result in the judge having to consider certain procedural facts to be proven unless counter-proof is produced ('compulsory proof').[106] If a criminal judgment in which the Dutch judge has decided that it is proven that a person has committed a certain crime is submitted as proof in a civil case, the judge has to consider the crime as proven unless counter-proof is produced (even though the criminal judgment can only be classified as an ordinary document in civil proceedings).[107] Administrative decisions are also mere ordinary documents and do not constitute any form of 'compulsory proof'.

[103] Art. 159(2) CCP.

[104] Art. 151(2) CCP.

[105] Knocking out the bottom. See HR 02-05-2003, *NJ* 2003, 468.

[106] Arts. 156 *et seq.* CCP.

[107] Art. 161 CCP. This rule does, however, not apply to any other decision in the criminal judgment than the one concerning the crime itself. See HR 27-03-2015, ECLI 760.

Electronic documents and electronic signature

In the Netherlands, electronic documents may be used for evidentiary purposes. The probative value of electronic documents is, just as the probative value of other means of proof, left to the free evaluation of the judge.[108] To be considered as a legal instrument with a special evidentiary status, electronic documents have to meet the relevant requirements (i.e. they should qualify as private or public evidentiary documents). In practice, electronic public or private evidentiary documents are non-existent.

Electronic documents can be signed by way of an electronic signature. The electronic signature is regulated by Article 3:15a of the Dutch Civil Code. This article specifies that in order for an electronic signature to have the same value as an ordinary signature, the method of authentication used for the electronic signature should be sufficiently reliable given the specific circumstances of the case at hand. Reliability is presumed if the signature meets the following requirements: a) the signature is exclusively related to the person having signed the document; b) it allows identification of the person having signed; c) the signature has been executed by means which are exclusively available to the person having signed; d) the signature is related in such a manner to the signed document that any later changes in this document can easily be detected; e) it is based on a qualified certificate as regulated in the Dutch Law on Telecommunications (*Telecommunicatiewet*, 1998); and f) it has been generated by way of a safe means for generating electronic signatures as provided by the same Law. The parties may, however, agree to deviate from the above requirements.

Duty to submit accounts

Litigating legal persons or non-legal persons being professionals or involved in commercial activities must, at the orders of the court, provide their accounts for consultation in court proceedings to which they are a party.[109] If the court's orders are not complied with, the judge may conclude as he deems fit with regard to the facts in question. In cases concerning annual accounts, the court may *ex officio* fortify its orders by way of *astreinte*.[110]

Evidence in possession of the opponent or a third party

If a party wants to use evidence in the possession of his opponent or a third party, he may ask the judge to order the opponent or the third party to make such evidence available. The evidence must be identified sufficiently and without such identification a party cannot get hold of documents in the possession of an opponent or a third party. The relevant articles in the Dutch Code of Civil Procedure are Articles 843a and 843b.

108 Art. 152 CCP.
109 Art. 162(1) CCP.
110 Art. 162(3) CCP.

The first mentioned Article provides that he who has a justifiable interest can ask the court to allow him, at his own expense, to consult or acquire a copy or excerpt of documents (including electronic documents) concerning a legal relationship in which he himself or those to whom he has succeeded are a party. Consultation must be made possible or the copy or excerpt must be provided by the person who has the relevant document at his disposal. The judge determines, if necessary, the manner in which the document can be consulted, or the manner in which a copy or excerpt can be obtained. Those who can claim a privilege do not have to provide the necessary information. Others do not have to cooperate if there are serious reasons for not doing so or if the required information is not necessary for the proper administration of justice.

Article 843b lays down that a party who has lost a certain means of proof can ask the court to order those who have evidentiary material proving the fact concerning which the lost means of proof would have provided proof to allow him to consult this material or to provide a copy or excerpt of it.

An attachment or garnishment order can be issued against the person who is in possession of the necessary documents.[111] The only purpose of a subsequent seizure of the documents by a bailiff (who is allowed to access every place, including private residences) is to secure its preservation. To obtain a right to consult the document or a copy of it, the procedure of Article 843a of the Code of Civil Procedure has to be followed.[112]

A proposal for new, more elaborate legislation is pending in Parliament and, if introduced, will result in new articles in the Code of Civil Procedure.[113] However, it seems that the proposal for new legislation will be repealed.

2.2. *Witnesses*

General

The judge orders the hearing of witnesses when a party offers proof by way of witnesses if this type of proof is allowed in the case at hand and if the court finds that proof of contested facts is indispensable for the final judgment.[114] The right to present witness evidence only comes into being after a court decision regarding the burden of proof.

It should also be noted that the court in the summons procedures is not allowed to nominate witnesses of its own motion. Only in petition procedures

111 Asser Procesrecht/Asser 3 2013/201.

112 HR 13-09-2013, *LJN* BZ9958.

113 Proposed Arts. 162a-162c. See *Wetsvoorstel Aanpassing van het Wetboek van Burgerlijke Rechtsvordering in verband met de wijziging van het recht op inzage, afschrift of uittreksel van bescheiden* (Legislative proposal for amendment of the Code of Civil Procedure in relation to a change in the entitlement to consult, obtain a copy or an excerpt of documents) (33 079). See also Asser Procesrecht/Asser 3 2013/200.

114 Art. 166(1) CCP.

(originally only meant for non-contentious matters) has this power been attributed to the courts.[115]

Witnesses have to be called to court by the interested party. In doing so, the party needs to indicate the facts as regards which proof has been ordered by the court and the consequences of failing to appear.[116] The interested party may use a registered letter for this purpose, but also the services of a bailiff.[117] The advantage of summoning a witness to court by way of a bailiff is that witnesses who do not make an appearance after being summoned may be taken to court with the help of the public authorities (i.e. the police) in order to testify if this is ordered by the court.[118] Refusing to appear as a witness is a criminal offence.[119]

The interested party needs to communicate the names and places of residence of the witnesses he wants to have heard at least one week in advance to the opponent party and to the court.[120] If the list of witnesses has not been submitted in time, this may lead to the ordering of a new hearing at the expense of the party concerned.[121]

In principle, witnesses indicated by a party must be heard by the judge if that party has been ordered to provide proof or counter-proof.[122] The court fixes a date and time for the hearing of witnesses.[123] Outside of the hearing, no witnesses can be heard, unless a new hearing is ordered.

The interlocutory judgment ordering a witness hearing will include decisions regarding date and place and will set time limits for the specification of the personal details of the witnesses.[124]

The general rule applies that witness testimony should be about facts that have been perceived by the witness himself.[125] Hearsay evidence is allowed.[126]

A statement in writing submitted by a party containing the depositions of a witness cannot be regarded as witness evidence but should be classified as documentary evidence.

Capability to serve as a witness

No one is deemed to be unfit to serve as a witness in the Netherlands. Article 177(3) of the Code of Civil Procedure, however, determines that those persons who cannot understand the significance of the oath (or promise) to speak the truth will not be allowed to take the oath. The same is true for witnesses who have not reached the

115 Art. 284(2) CCP.
116 Art. 170 CCP.
117 Art. 170(1) CCP.
118 Art. 172 CCP.
119 Art. 444 Dutch Criminal Code.
120 Art. 170(1) CCP.
121 Art. 237(1) CCP.
122 Art. 166(1) CCP.
123 Art. 166(2) CCP.
124 Art. 166(2) CCP.
125 Art. 163 CCP.
126 Asser Procesrecht/Asser 3 2013/171.

age of 16 years. These witnesses are admonished to tell nothing but the truth. If the judge makes use of the testimony of such witnesses, he has to give reasons for this in the judgment.[127]

Duty to testify
Article 165(1) of the Dutch Code of Civil Procedure provides that everyone who has been summoned to court in the required manner has the duty to testify in court. This duty was introduced as it is a societal interest that in litigation the truth can be uncovered.

A witness who refuses to provide witness testimony is subject to civil imprisonment if such is asked for by the interested party. The expenses of such imprisonment have to be paid by the interested party, and the civil imprisonment may not last longer than 1 year.[128] The judge will only order civil imprisonment if he is of the opinion that this is justified in light of establishing the truth.[129] Civil imprisonment is rarely ordered in the Netherlands. Criminal prosecution[130] and an *astreinte* are also possible if a witness refuses to testify;[131] this does not apply to party-witnesses.[132]

Information provided by the parties and party-witnesses
The courts in the Netherlands routinely order a court appearance after the statement of defence has been submitted (unless this is deemed superfluous).[133] This hearing may be used for several purposes. One of these purposes is to obtain information from the parties.[134] The judge questions the parties and the parties may also ask each other questions unless the judge rules that a specific question is not allowed. Such a hearing may be ordered later in the proceedings too and is an effective means of obtaining the required information, including an elaboration of the claim and an opinion on any factual or legal matter. When witnesses are heard, the court has the power to ask the parties questions as well.[135]

Parties are also allowed to serve as witnesses in their own case. The testimony of a party may not serve as proof for the facts that that party needs to prove, unless the party's testimony serves to complement incomplete proof.[136] This last provision does not apply in cases where the party-witness is providing counter-proof in a situation where his opponent has the burden of proof and proof has indeed been delivered by this opponent; in that event his testimony may serve as proof for facts

127 Art. 177(3) CCP.
128 Art. 173(1) CCP.
129 Art. 173(2) CCP.
130 Arts. 192 and 444 Dutch Criminal Code.
131 HR 18-05-1979, *NJ* 1980, 213.
132 HR 06-04-2012, *LJN* BV3403.
133 Art. 131 CCP.
134 Art. 88 CCP.
135 Art. 179(3) CCP.
136 Art. 164(2) CCP.

advanced by him.[137] The same is true for written depositions of party-witnesses.[138] The restriction does, however, apply in case of two party-witnesses whose depositions support each other.[139]

As regards party testimony, part of the general rules relating to witness testimony apply. Article 166(1) of the Code of Civil Procedure provides that witness testimony (and therefore party testimony) can be offered by the parties, but it may also be ordered *ex officio* by the court. Testifying parties are under oath, since the ordinary rules on witnesses apply to them in this respect.[140]

A party-witness has a duty to testify, just like other witnesses. He cannot excuse himself from testifying, and this is different from, for example, his spouse or family members (see below). Nevertheless, he may excuse himself if there is a risk of a criminal judgment for felony (in Dutch: *misdrijf*) against him if he would testify (*nemo tenetur*).[141] The legality of a refusal of a party-witness to testify is evaluated by the judge. Civil imprisonment is not available if a party-witness refuses to testify (as stated, civil imprisonment is allowed where other witnesses are concerned).[142] However, a refusal to testify allows the judge to draw the conclusions he deems fit as regards the particular facts at stake.[143]

Privileged witnesses[144]

Article 165 of the Dutch Code of Civil Procedure provides that certain groups of witnesses can excuse themselves from providing witness testimony in a court of law. Witnesses who can excuse themselves are certain family members, including previous spouses and registered partners, and those who need to keep information secret as a result of their office or profession (e.g. notaries,[145] lawyers,[146] legal staff of legal aid bureaus,[147] medical doctors[148] and clergy).[149] Staff and other persons working for such privileged witnesses may also claim the privilege not to testify derived from the privilege of the originally privileged witness, including secretaries[150] and external experts.[151] The question as to who may claim to be privileged due to his profession has to a large extent been determined in case law.

137 HR 17-01-2003, *NJ* 2003, 176; HR 20-01-2009, *RvdW* 2009, 243.
138 HR 24-01-2003, *NJ* 2003, 166.
139 HR 14-04-2005, *NJ* 2005, 272.
140 Art. 177(2) CCP.
141 Art. 165(3) CCP.
142 Art. 173(1) CCP.
143 Art. 164(3) CCP.
144 On this topic in depth: Fernhout 2004.
145 HR 13-01-2006, *NJ* 2006, 480.
146 HR 22-06-1984, *NJ* 1985, 188.
147 HR 25-10-1985, *NJ* 1986, 176.
148 HR 14-12-1948, *NJ* 1949, 95.
149 *Ibidem.*
150 BRvC 8 November 1948, *NJ* 1949, 66.
151 HR 29-03-1994, *NJ* 1994, 552.

A privilege against self-incrimination (*nemo tenetur*) is recognized in Dutch civil procedure.[152] A witness may refuse to answer a question if doing so would subject himself or certain family members to the risk of a criminal sentence for felony (in Dutch: *misdrijf*).

As a rule, witnesses who claim to be privileged have to appear in court to invoke their privilege orally. The Dutch Supreme Court has accepted an exception in the sense that witnesses may file a petition asking the court to decide in advance on their claim to the privilege not to testify.[153] The judge hearing the witnesses decides on this issue by way of a judgment (in the summons procedure) or a court order (in the petition procedure). The interested party may file an appeal against the decision of the judge that a witness has rightfully claimed to be privileged.[154] The parties cannot appeal against a decision assuming an exception to the privilege or deciding that the privilege does not apply; in that event only the witness himself may file an appeal.[155]

Professional witnesses claiming a privilege are only allowed to refuse to testify if it concerns information that is provided to them within the context of their profession. This means that they cannot claim to be privileged in general.[156]

In principle, the privilege for witnesses exercising a profession involving confidentiality is absolute. An exception can only be made in 'extremely exceptional circumstances'. Such circumstances only occur when the privileged witness himself is involved in criminal activities of a severe nature with those who share confidential information with him.[157]

Let us look at professional privilege and professional secrets in further detail now.

The first category of secrets that are recognized in Dutch law and that can affect the taking of evidence are the professional secrets of those professions for the exercise of which secrecy (confidentiality) is essential. In this category we find doctors, notaries, clergy and advocates (see above).

The second category of secrets depends on specific regulations. State secrets and military secrets can be such that the law specifies that there is no obligation to testify in court. State secrets in general are not recognized as a category of information about which no questions can be asked.[158] If the secret is covered by the Act on the Intelligence and Security Services (*Wet op de inlichtingen- en veiligheidsdiensten*, 2002), Articles 85 and 86 of that Act give a privilege to everyone who is involved in the enforcement of the Act. Members of local boards and Parliament, parties in a procedure, study advisors in certain specified circumstances, the secret services, whistle-blowers, judges in chambers, the King

152 Art. 165(3) CCP.
153 HR 19-09-2003, *NJ* 2005, 454 (although the Supreme Court has not repeated this decision).
154 HR 17-01-1986, *NJ* 1987, 352.
155 HR 17-11-1967, *NJ* 1968, 164.
156 Art. 165(2)b CCP.
157 HR 14-06-2005, *NJ* 2005, 353.
158 HR 22-12-1989, *NJ* 1990, 779.

and threatened witnesses in criminal cases are also privileged based on specific regulations.[159]

The third category of secrets is based on the general obligation of the court to balance the interest of finding the truth in civil proceedings against the interest claimed by the witness not to reveal the information concerned. Here the circumstances of the case are decisive. In this way, for instance, the privilege of journalists who do not want to reveal their sources is protected. Only in exceptional circumstances, to be invoked by the party who called the witness, is the journalist under an obligation to answer questions regarding his sources.[160] This happens when the general principle of the interest of finding the material truth outweighs the privilege of journalists regarding their sources. This can be the case when there are no other means of establishing the truth.[161]

The Netherlands do not have bank secrecy, whereas business secrets can be protected, but only if they fall within the third category above. When a CEO (or general manager of a juridical person) refuses to testify about a certain fact, claiming that it represents a company's business secret, the court will not accept this excuse, but the circumstances of the case can be such that specific questions will not have to be answered. When the company is a public law entity or a holder of concession or public service, this is one of the circumstances that have to be considered by the court.[162]

Immediacy

In Dutch civil procedure the principle of immediacy is not strictly observed where it concerns witnesses. The hearing of witnesses is often entrusted to a judge-commissioner, who usually summarises the testimony to a court clerk. This summary is read to, approved by and signed by the witnesses,[163] and it becomes part of the case file. Article 155 of the Code of Civil Procedure states that the main rule is that the judge before whom evidence has been administered should as much as possible be the judge by whom the final judgment is rendered or that he should be a member of the panel entrusted with rendering a final judgment. The reason for not following this rule has to be expressed in the final judgment. No means of recourse are available against the decision not to follow the main rule.[164]

Video

The current Code of Civil Procedure clearly assumes that witnesses are heard by the judge in a hearing where both parties are present. The law does not provide for any possibility to hear witnesses at a distance, either by telephone or by

159 Fernhout 2004, p. 241-271.
160 HR 10-05-1996, *NJ* 1996, 578.
161 HR 09-11-1999, *NJ* 2000, 461.
162 HR 17-03-1981, *NJ* 1981, 382.
163 Art. 180 CCP.
164 However, HR 13-10-2014, NJ 2015, 181 seems to indicate that the Dutch Supreme Court has changed its view on this matter, allowing recourse against this decision.

videoconferencing. However, when all interested parties, including the witness, agree, 'teletestimony' is possible,[165] but the statement of the witness will not be a witness's testimony as described in the Code of Civil Procedure. This does not matter at all, since there is no *numerus clausus* as regards the means of proof: the court is entirely free to evaluate all evidence provided and therefore 'teletestimony' may be taken into consideration by the judge as well. Currently, a legislative proposal has been introduced in Parliament that will regulate this matter in more detail.[166]

Oath and perjury

Witnesses normally take an oath or make a promise to tell nothing but the truth. They themselves choose whether to take an oath or make a promise.[167] A witness cannot be forced to take an oath or make a promise. According to Article 178 of the Code of Civil Procedure, a witness who makes an appearance in court and who refuses to take the oath (or make a promise) will be liable for costs, and will also have to pay damages if there are reasons for this. Refusing to take the oath or make a promise is a criminal offence.[168]

Perjury is a criminal offence and can be prosecuted under the Criminal Code.[169] The maximum penalty is imprisonment for a maximum of six years or a fourth category money penalty (currently € 20,250 max.). In practice, perjury is usually punished with a three-month term of imprisonment.

Judge questions witnesses

Witnesses are questioned by the court (in the case of a panel, usually before a judge-commissioner).[170] The parties and their counsel are also allowed to ask questions.[171] The judge may determine that a specific question or questions do not have to be answered by the witnesses.[172] It is not necessary for the parties to adduce a witness deposition before the witness provides oral testimony.

Article 179(1) of the Code of Civil Procedure provides that witnesses are heard individually in the sense that witnesses who have not been heard yet should not be present when a fellow witness is being questioned (unless the latter witness is a party-witness; a party-witness may be present, for which reason party-witnesses are

165 District Court Rotterdam 4 June 2009, *LJN* BJ8571.

166 *Voorstel tot Wijziging van het Wetboek van Burgerlijke Rechtsvordering en de Algemene wet bestuursrecht in verband met vereenvoudiging en digitalisering van het procesrecht* (Legislative proposal for amendment of the Code of Civil Procedure and the General Administrative Law Act in relation to the simplification and digitalisation of the law of procedure) (Kamerstukken 34 059).

167 Art. 177(2) CCP.

168 Art. 192 Dutch Criminal Code.

169 Art. 207 Dutch Criminal Code.

170 Art. 155 CCP.

171 Art. 179(2) CCP.

172 *Ibidem*.

always heard first). Witnesses who have already testified may attend the hearing of a later witness, unless the court orders otherwise.

Witness testimony is summarized by the judge, and this written record is read to and if necessary amended and then signed by the witnesses, the judge and the court clerk.[173] This document becomes part of the case file and is used in the decision of the matter. If the case is not subject to appeal, no separate record of the hearing of witnesses needs to be made. In that event, mention of the witness testimony will be made in the judgment.[174]

Preparing witnesses before the hearing in the sense of rehearsing their statement at a lawyer's office is considered to be unethical in the Netherlands.

Counter-Proof
After the hearing of witnesses, the judge determines the date and time for what is called a *contra-enquête,* i.e. hearing witnesses for the other party.[175] In the Netherlands, cross-examination in the Anglo-American sense does not occur. The parties (including the opponent party) and their counsel may ask the witnesses questions, but the major part of the questioning is done by the judge.

2.3. *Experts*

General
Expert reports are only ordered when proof by witnesses does not seem to be possible (which is especially the case in disputes of a technical nature, for instance about the proportion of minerals in certain food supplements). The court is not limited to, for example, public interest issues for ordering expert evidence.

Appointment of the expert and the expert report
When the court expresses its intention to appoint an expert, first the parties are asked to make a proposal regarding the number and the person of the experts. If the parties agree on the experts, usually the court follows their choice. Otherwise the expert is (or the experts are) selected from a list of experts informally kept by the court. Recent initiatives from the Ministry of Justice have led to a national registration of experts, but until now the register is only relevant for criminal cases.[176] The parties do not have the right to reject a court appointed expert. However, immediately after the report has been submitted, the parties are allowed to raise objections against the report on the ground that the expert was not impartial.[177]

173 Art. 180 CCP.
174 Art. 181(1) CCP.
175 Art. 168 CCP.
176 See <www.nrgd.nl> (last consulted on 18 May 2015).
177 HR 02-05-2014, *NJ* 2014, 310.

The judge appoints the expert.[178] Obviously, the parties may suggest issues that the expert should report on, but the final decision on hearing an expert is the judge's and the parties do not have the possibility to file an appeal against this part of his decision. The interlocutory judgment ordering the taking of expert evidence will include detailed instructions for the procedure to be followed by the expert, including a list of questions that has to be answered in his final report.[179] This part of the decision is in principle open to appeal. Since 1 January 2002 the Dutch Code of Civil Procedure provides that the judge may also allow a party himself to have experts who are not appointed by the judge heard in court. Whether or not such experts will be heard is decided by the judge.[180] As regards party experts, various articles of the Code of Civil Procedure dealing with hearing witnesses have been declared equally applicable.[181] The Dutch Code of Civil Procedure does not provide for written party expert reports, although it is up to the parties to submit such reports as (ordinary) documents. These reports do not have any special evidentiary status, but will be taken into consideration by the court.

Article 197 of the Code of Civil Procedure provides that the judge establishes the time period for the submission of an expert report.

Procedure

To a large extent, the same procedure is followed in hearing witnesses and experts. The judge is in charge of the hearing of experts and may decide - either *ex officio* or at the request of a party - to ask additional questions.[182] If the court wishes, the activities of the expert will be supervised by a judge.[183]

The parties have the right to be present when the expert conducts his activities, and then they have the right to ask questions and to make remarks.[184] They have a duty to cooperate with the expert.[185]

Written or oral report

The expert can be ordered to deliver a written report. He can also be ordered to deliver his report orally, and this will happen during a court hearing.[186] Whether an expert will produce a written or oral opinion is decided by the judge.[187] A distinction between the two types of expert evidence from the perspective of their evidentiary value is not made.

178 Art. 194(2) CCP.
179 Art. 194(1) CCP.
180 Art. 200 CCP.
181 Art. 200(5) CCP.
182 Art. 194(5) CCP.
183 Art. 198(2) CCP.
184 *Ibidem.*
185 Art. 198(3) CCP.
186 Art. 197(2) CCP.
187 Art. 194(2) CCP.

Usually, a written report is added to the case file and will be debated by the parties. An oral report has to be presented at a court hearing and is recorded by the court clerk. This document has to be signed by the judge, the clerk and the expert.[188] It has to be mentioned, however, that this is highly exceptional; in practice, all experts are ordered to submit a written report, of which a draft has to be submitted to the parties first.

In the Netherlands, the judge is not bound by written expert opinions.

2.4. *Local Inspection*

A local inspection (*descente*) can be ordered *ex officio* by the judge by way of an interlocutory judgment. The court determines the place, date and time for a local inspection in the interlocutory judgment. The parties may be present and may make comments and requests. The judge may hear witnesses at the site of the local inspection. A report is made of the inspection. A local inspection is not needed when physical objects can be shown in court during the hearing.[189]

2.5. *Presumptions*

Presumptions are sometimes classified as indirect means of proof. In the Netherlands, presumptions are not dealt with in the Code of Civil Procedure anymore as a separate category of means of proof. As in other European jurisdictions,[190] it has been argued that presumptions are actually not even a means of proof but part of an intellectual exercise by the judge or a particular method of legislation.[191] We encounter presumptions nevertheless at some particular places in legislation outside the Code of Civil Procedure. In practice, presumptions are an important means for the court to shift proof for the party with the burden of proof to counter-proof for the other party. According to the case law of the Dutch Supreme Court, under specified circumstances the causal relationship between damage and either tort or a breach of contract even has to be assumed by means of a presumption.[192] In other cases as well, presumptions may be useful.[193]

3. Language

The official languages in Dutch courts are Dutch and Frisian.[194] However, not all documents in other languages have to be translated. The court may accept

188 Art. 198(5) CCP.
189 Art. 201(2) CCP.
190 Nagel 1967, p. 98 *et seq.*
191 On this topic, see Van Rhee 2009, p. 85-101.
192 HR 19-03-2004, NJ 2004, 307.
193 See e.g. HR 12-09-2003, NJ 2005, 268.
194 *Cf.* Parliamentary Proceedings I 2007-2008, 31 513, C, p. 2, and see Act on the Use of the Frisian Language (*Wet gebruik Friese taal*) (Stbl. 2013, 382).

documents in foreign languages. In most cases, English, French and German texts do not have to be translated. If a translation is required, it should be done by a translator who has been sworn in under the Act on sworn interpreters and translators (*Wet beëdigde tolken en vertalers*, 2007). The statements of case themselves, petitions and writs have to be in Dutch.

The court may accept testimony in a foreign language, which is then translated into Dutch by the judge hearing the witness. It is up to the court to decide on this, which is done with caution. The parties producing witnesses do not have a right to interpreter and translation services. If no interpreter has been provided by the party who called the witness and if the court has indicated that translation by an interpreter is needed, the witness is simply not heard.

Interpreters are not mentioned in the Code of Civil Procedure. Accordingly, they are not sworn in by the court, but, as stated, the interpreters used by the court are 'sworn interpreters'.

4. Costs

In the Netherlands, two types of legal expenses are distinguished. Legal expenses either concern judicial expenses generated by making use of the court system (in Dutch: *proceskosten*) or so-called extra-judicial expenses (in Dutch: *buitengerechtelijke kosten*), e.g. costs for legal advice. The two types of costs have a different legal basis and follow different rules. Again, here we may note French influence.

Judicial expenses are limited to lawyer's fees, court fees, the costs of a bailiff, the costs of experts and the costs of witnesses and interpreters. In cases in which legal representation is not mandatory, the unrepresented party can also claim travel expenses and a compensation for the time lost while attending court hearings.[195]

Extra-judicial expenses are the costs made for recovery of the claim and costs made to establish the extent of the damages and liability of the other party.[196] Expenses can only be extra-judicial when they have *not* been made for the 'instruction' of the proceedings or the preparation of the pleadings.[197] These extra-judicial expenses are treated as compensation for damages.

The general rule in the Netherlands is that the loser also pays the full costs of his opponent (except for costs made for legal representation which in practice are only partially recoverable).[198]

When evidence by witnesses is ordered, the party who is bringing forward the witness will have to pay the costs of the witness. These costs are determined by the judge at the witness hearing after the witness has been heard.[199] The party's lawyer has to guarantee that these costs will be paid.[200] A costs order against the losing

195 Art. 238(1) CCP.

196 Art.6:96 Dutch Civil Code.

197 Art. 241 CCP.

198 Art. 237 CCP.

199 Art. 182 CCP.

200 Art. 32 Code of Conduct for Lawyers (*Gedragsregels voor Advocaten*, 1992).

party will include the court-determined costs of the witnesses of the winning party.[201] There is no obligation for a party to pay the witnesses more than has been determined by the court.

The compensation for the appearance of a witness includes travel expenses and compensation for the time lost.[202] Reasonable travel expenses will be included for the full amount. For the time of the witness a fixed tariff is set at a mere € 6.81 per hour.[203] The court has the freedom to use another tariff when both parties agree (which happens quite often).

When the costs are contested, the witness needs to submit proof of the costs he has made.[204] In practice, however, reasonable costs of the witness are hardly ever contested. Costs of witnesses are paid after they have been heard.

The costs of an expert are determined by the court.[205] The main rule is that the claimant has to deposit the expenses for the expert with the court, although the judge may, for specific reasons (usually related to the burden of proof), decide that costs should be deposited by the defendant or by both parties instead (in case of litigants of limited means, no deposit will be ordered, since the costs are covered by the state).[206] The court is not liable for the costs and does not take any responsibility for them. For that reason, the experts are always instructed only to commence their activities when the court-determined deposit has been paid. A costs order against the losing party will include the court-determined costs of the experts advanced by the winning party.[207] When the expert has submitted his report, he will send in his bill. The court will determine the expert's compensation (which can be less than the bill), which compensation will have to be paid by the party who had to pay the deposit.

When the court orders a local inspection, the costs of the court and the court clerk are fully covered by the state.[208]

Where the hearing of witnesses is concerned, the costs of interpreter services can be part of a costs order against the losing party. These costs may be awarded if they are considered to be reasonable. Costs of interpreters are paid afterwards, but the costs of the translation of documents cannot be recovered.[209]

201 Art. 182 jo. 237 CCP.
202 Art. 182 CCP.
203 Art. 2(1) Decree on Tariffs in Civil Cases (*Besluit tarieven burgerlijke zaken*) in conjunction with Art. 8(1) Decree on Tariffs in Criminal Cases (*Besluit tarieven strafzaken*).
204 Art. 150 CCP.
205 Art. 199 CCP.
206 Art. 195 CCP.
207 Art. 244 CCP.
208 Art. 201(6) CCP.
209 HR 13-09-2013, *LJN* BZ5688.

5. Final Remarks

The above discussion of the Dutch law of evidence in civil matters clearly shows that it is based on a tradition dating back to the 19th century and that its roots in French civil procedure (e.g. the proof standard of the 'intimate conviction' of the judge) and, through this procedure, in Romano-canonical law can still be noted. However, since the time of its introduction in 1838 in the Code of Civil Procedure and the Civil Code, various reforms have changed the outlook of Dutch evidence law in civil matters, especially as a result of law reforms in 1988 and 2002.

In 1988, it was decided that the traditional distinction between substantive evidence law, which could be found in the Civil Code, and procedural evidence law, which was part of the Code of Civil Procedure, should be abolished. Since that time, the Dutch law of evidence in civil matters has been firmly based in the Code of Civil Procedure. This reform did not, however, reduce the powers of the judge in the evidentiary proceedings. In line with the continental European approach, the Dutch judge has extended powers as regards evidence. The judge may, *ex officio*, order a party to supply proof by way of witnesses although he may not nominate witnesses himself. The same approach is chosen as regards documents: the judge may order the parties to submit documents, but he may not search for relevant documents himself. He may, however, appoint an expert *ex officio* and define the issues on which the expert has to report, and he may investigate the truth of contested facts by way of a local inspection at his own motion (although this does not happen very often in practice). Currently, and this is an innovation dating from 2002, party-appointed experts may also provide expertise, and obviously this is a sign of modernity which brings Dutch civil procedural law in line with other European systems.

It is a matter of debate whether or not the Dutch law of civil evidence aims at establishing the material truth. Some authors hold that only the formal truth is aimed at, since the collection of evidence beyond the contested facts submitted by the parties is not allowed. However, the *ex officio* powers of the judge in the area of evidence as regards contested facts may help to provide a certain balance between the material and formal truth. Obviously, when the parties agree about the facts, the court has no powers to establish whether this agreement is based on true facts. This is only different if these facts give rise to legal consequences which are not at the free disposition of the parties. This is not changed by the rule of Article 21 of the Dutch Code of Civil Procedure that the parties should provide all facts that are relevant for the decision of the case fully and truthfully. The duty of Article 21 is limited in value since it only aims at preventing deliberate lies, whereas facts that are advanced by one party and that are not disputed by the other party do not have to be proven.

The Dutch system also shows its origins in 19th century French law where it is very liberal as regards the moment documentary evidence may be introduced. In principle, the parties may provide documentary evidence throughout the proceedings, and may even do so on appeal. Nevertheless, the 'post-defence hearing model' introduced in the Dutch Code of Civil Procedure in 2002 and explained above, results in concentration. So here, without introducing a formalistic and unworkable *Eventualmaxime* or preclusions aimed at concentration, the Dutch Legislature has achieved concentration by framing the civil lawsuit in a specific and innovative manner.

Important reforms in the Dutch Code of Civil Procedure, which are currently being prepared, will result in innovation and bring the text of the law in line with developments in modern technology, and will also extend the use of modern technology in court proceedings. Actually, the planned changes will mean an overhaul of the existing procedural model and will do away with institutions of venerable antiquity such as the 'cause list' (rôle). Each case will get its own digital environment accessible by litigants called 'Mijn Zaak' (i.e. 'My Case'). Within this environment, all kinds of evidence may be introduced, ranging from electronic documents to other types of evidence in electronic format. Hearing witnesses through video link, although already possible, will be officially regulated. These and other reforms in the Dutch system of civil evidence lead me to the conclusion that tradition and innovation currently complement each other in providing a modern evidence law that will be able to face several of the challenges of the 21st century. Whether it is a good decision to abolish the cause list, replacing it with a 'My Case' environment, is, however, subject to debate. This is due to the fact that the cause list is public whereas 'My Case' is accessible for a limited group of people only, while it has also been claimed that a central cause-list offers the court better possibilities to monitor and handle its case load.

Bibliography

Asser 1992
Asser, W.D.H., *Salomo's wijsheid. Hoor en wederhoor: een rechterlijk oor voor partijen*, Nijmegen: Gouda Quint, 1992.

Chorus 1987
Chorus, J.M.J., *De lijdelijkheid van de rechter: Historie van een begrip*, Deventer: Kluwer, 1987.

Fernhout 2004
Fernhout, F.J., *Het verschoningsrecht van getuigen in civiele zaken*, Deventer: Kluwer, 2004.

Hartogh & Cosman 1897
Hartogh, A.F.K. & Cosman, C.A., *De wet van 7 Juli 1896 (Stbl. no 103) tot wijziging van het Wetboek van burgerlijke regtsvordering, toegelicht door ...*, The Hague: Belinfante, 1897.

Hugenholtz & Heemskerk 2015
Hugenholtz, W. & Heemskerk, W.H. (continued by W. Heemskerk in collaboration with J.M.L. van Duin, R.S.I Lawant and I.C. Blomsma), *Hoofdlijnen van Nederlands burgerlijk procesrecht*, Dordrecht: Convoy Uitgevers, 2015.

Lévy 1965
Lévy, J.-Ph., 'La preuve dans les droits savants au Moyen Âge', in: Lévy, J.Ph., *La Preuve* (Recueils de la Société Jean Bodin pour l'histoire comparative des institutions 17: Moyen âge et temps modernes), Brussels: Editions de la librairie encyclopédique, 1965, p. 137-168.

Nagel 1967
Nagel, H., *Die Grundzüge des Beweisrechts im europäischen Zivilprozess*, Baden-Baden: Nomos, 1967.

Nagel & Bajons 2003
Nagel, H. & Bajons, E.M. (eds.), *Beweis - Preuve - Evidence: Grundzüge des zivilprozessualen Beweisrechts in Europa*, Baden-Baden: Nomos, 2003.

Nörr 2012
Nörr, K.W., *Romanisch-kanonisches Prozessrecht. Erkenntnisverfahren erster Instanz in civilibus*, Heidelberg: Springer, 2012.

Rutgers, Flach & Boon 1988
Rutgers, G.R., Flach, R.J.C. & Boon, G.J. (eds.), *Parlementaire geschiedenis van de nieuwe regeling van het bewijsrecht in burgerlijke zaken: Parlementaire stukken systematisch gerangschikt*, Deventer: Kluwer, 1988.

Schulte 1980
Schulte, J., *Die Entwicklung der Eventualmaxime*, Cologne etc.: Carl Heymanns, 1980.

Van Hooijdonk & Eijsvoogel 2012
Van Hooijdonk, M. & Eijsvoogel, P.V., *Litigation in the Netherlands: Civil Procedure, Arbitration and Administrative Litigation*, The Hague: Kluwer Law International, 2012.

Van Rhee 2008
Van Rhee, C.H., 'Dutch Civil Procedural Law in an International Context', in: Deguchi, M. & Storme, M. (eds.), *The reception and transmission of civil procedural law in the global society. Legislative and Legal Educational Assistance to Other Countries in Procedural Law*, Antwerp/Apeldoorn: Maklu, 2008, p. 191-212.

Van Rhee 2009
Van Rhee, C.H., 'Presumptions in Dutch Private Law (19th and 20th Centuries) within a European Context', in: Helmholz, R.H. & Sellar, W.D.H. (eds.), *Law of Presumptions. Essays in Comparative Legal History* (Comparative Studies in Continental and Anglo-American Legal History, 27), Berlin: Duncker & Humblot, 2009, p. 85-101.

S. Aras Kramar

TAKING OF EVIDENCE IN CROATIAN APPELLATE COURTS: WHY NO FACT-FINDING AT SECOND INSTANCE?

1. Introduction

The regular form of appeal proceedings in countries of the European continental legal tradition involves review of facts and law. The appellate court re-examines the evidence and legal arguments advanced at first instance with a view to correct errors in adjudication and procedure. In some European legal systems, parties may introduce facts and evidence which were not addressed in the original judgment, and the appellate court may examine them at a new hearing. Often, however, litigation on appeal does not involve an actual second *de novo* hearing in which all evidence is introduced anew. The review may be limited to the examination of the first instance files. Based on the review of documents and protocols of the first instance court, the appellate court may (or may not) make its own independent findings of fact.[1]

In a number of countries of the European continental legal tradition it is quite common and normal to hold oral hearings before appellate courts with the purpose of establishing facts and reviewing the findings of the first instance court.[2] This contribution will, however, present as a contrast one example where this regularly

1 Americans are more familiar with appeal 'on the record' in which the court reviews only the matters of law, leaving the questions of fact to the trial judge and/or jury. Thus the appellate court looks at only those portions of the record relevant to the trial court's legal rulings rather than fully re-examining all the evidence in order to reach its own independent findings of fact. For two basic forms of appellate proceedings in the various legal systems of the world see Shapiro 1980, p. 645-649. For a comprehensive discussion of the purposes of review *de novo* in European (Continental) legal systems see Kaplan, von Mehren & Schaefer 1958, p. 1453-1454; Langbein 1985, p. 856-857.

2 This is particularly the case in Germany and the Netherlands. In general, this applies also to Austria, though to a lesser extent. For Austria and Germany see Secs. 6.1 and 6.2 below. For the Netherlands see Sec. 6.3 below.

does not happen: in post-Yugoslav countries. As a particular example of this procedural style, we will use the law and practice in the Republic of Croatia.

2. Oral Hearings in Croatian Appellate Courts: From a Theoretical Option to a Legal Impossibility (and Back)

The story about the introduction and abolition of oral hearings in the Croatian appellate courts is one of trial and error. Initially, until the 2003 Amendments to the Civil Procedure Act,[3] the option of holding oral hearings for the purpose of re-examination of evidence in the appellate courts existed, but it was dependant on the discretionary decision of the appellate courts. The courts almost never made use of this option, so the 2003 Amendments abolished this option entirely. However, the 2008 CPA Amendments[4] reintroduced the facultative possibility of holding oral hearings before the appellate court. The option of appellate evidentiary hearings was strengthened further in the latest 2013 CPA Amendments.[5] Namely, following several decisions of the European Court of Human Rights that declared the practice of successive remittals to be one of the systemic problems of Croatian civil procedure,[6] the CPA amendments over the last five years progressively introduced a prohibition of multiple remittals of first instance judgments.

Thus, following the changes in 2008 and 2013, after the first remittal it became mandatory that the appellate courts conduct the proceedings in such a way that sending the case to the first instance court for rehearing was avoided. This, most likely, means that an oral hearing at the second level may become indispensable.

Despite the reintroduction and recodification of oral hearings at the appellate level, the Croatian reality is still the same: the appellate courts continue not to hold any oral hearings, and thus they avoid any autonomous fact-finding. This trend is also present in the neighbouring post-Yugoslav countries.

3. The Origins of the Reluctance to Hear Evidence at the Appeals Level: An Outline of Arguments

Why is there no fact-finding at the second level of adjudication? To answer this question, I will first analyse the Croatian system of obligatory and facultative oral hearings and evidence-taking in the courts of second instance, bearing in mind the historical

3 *Zakon o izmjenama i dopunama Zakona o parničnom postupku* (Act on Amendments to the Civil Procedure Act) from 2003 (*Službeni list RH* (Official Gazette of the RC) 117/03).

4 *Zakon o izmjenama i dopunama Zakona o parničnom postupku* (Act on Amendments to the Civil Procedure Act) from 2008 (*Službeni list RH* (Official Gazette of the RC) 84/08).

5 *Zakon o izmjenama i dopunama Zakona o parničnom postupku* (Act on Amendments to the Civil Procedure Act) from 2013 (*Službeni list RH* (Official Gazette of the RC) 25/13).

6 See e.g. *Vajagić v. Croatia,* No. 30431/03 § 44, 20 July 2007: '... delays in proceedings were caused mainly by the successive remittals. ... The Court considers that the repetition of such orders within one set of proceedings discloses a deficiency in the procedural system.' See also Uzelac 2014, p. 243-244.

context.[7] The purpose of this exercise is to find reasons for the reluctance of appellate courts to hold oral hearings and conduct fact-finding proceedings, even when it is mandatory under the current law and procedural rules.[8]

Taking into account the same starting point of development, and to outline the trends of convergence and divergence, I will analyse the system of obligatory and/or facultative oral hearings and their function in the fact-finding process in the courts of second instance of other post-Yugoslav countries.[9] I will then consider the same issue in Austrian and German law, mainly because of the strong historical influence of the law of these countries on Croatian civil procedure.[10] Following that, I will analyse the Dutch law to show another extremely permissive system in regard to oral hearings, evidence-taking procedures and fact-finding at the second level of adjudication.[11]

Finally, I will evaluate the current Croatian rules on fact-finding in the courts of second instance, and indicate certain projections of its further development.[12] Although this paper primarily concerns Croatia, my concluding remarks on the current situation in Croatia[13] apply *mutatis mutandis* to other post-Yugoslav countries as well.

4. Fact-Finding at Second Instance: Historical Remarks and Current Law

The newly found duty of appellate courts to hold oral hearings and conduct fact-finding proceedings is actually not very new. Already under the 1956 Civil Procedure Act of the Federal People's Republic of Yugoslavia[14] it was possible to hold oral hearings and take evidence at the second level of adjudication. The CPA 1956 required that the oral hearing be preceded by a closed session of the appeals panel, which was entitled to decide whether the appeal was to be handled *in camera* or at a hearing with the parties where evidence could be taken.[15] The appellate court would schedule an oral hearing if the appeals panel had assessed that it was necessary for the proper determination of the facts, either because new evidence

7 See Sec. 4 below.

8 See Sec. 7 below.

9 See Sec. 5 below.

10 See Sec. 6 below.

11 See Sec. 6 below. The legal institutions of the Netherlands more often follow the French example than the German. However, in substantive matters the Dutch are closer to the Germanic family. Thus many Dutch judicial institutions form a compromise between the French and the German traditions. See Blankenburg 1998, p. 1-2 (discussing the two related families of the 'Romanic' and 'Germanic' traditions).

12 See Secs. 7 and 8 below.

13 *Ibidem.*

14 *Zakon o parničnom postupku* (Civil Procedure Act) from 1956 (*Službeni list FNRJ* (Official Gazette of the FPRY) 4/57; hereinafter: CPA 1956).

15 Art. 350(2) CPA 1956.

should be heard or because of the need to re-hear already presented evidence.[16] A separate procedural order of the appeals panel on the need to hold an oral hearing had to be delivered in all cases.[17]

At the appellate hearing, the parties could present new facts and introduce new evidence not presented on appeal (and in response to the appeal).[18] Facts and evidence brought to light after the issuance of the first instance judgment were admissible as well.[19] Therefore, the appellate court could have the opportunity to decide on the basis of material significantly different from that which was heard before the first instance court. During the hearing, the appellate court did not have the straightforward task to review the first instance judgment, but had to discuss *de novo* on the merits and make decisions independent of the proceedings before the first instance court, addressing directly all procedural material. Thus, the hearing before the appellate court essentially turned into a new hearing in which the appellate court had the same function as the court at first instance (which was criticised as 'second-turning-into-first-instance').[20]

Essentially the same regime continued in the next Yugoslav CPA of 1976, but with some exceptions.[21] [22] An important change consisted in the fact that appellate courts lost their power to hear on appeal new evidence not presented before the first instance court. At the second instance hearing the parties were still allowed to present new facts and introduce new evidence not adduced before the first instance court or in the appeal memoranda. But, if the appellate court assessed that the new evidence was relevant, it had to quash the first instance judgment and remit the case to the first instance court for rehearing. Therefore, after 1976 the appellate courts could rule on the merits of the appeal only on the basis of facts and evidence that were already presented before the first instance court.[23] Consequently, the actual use of appellate oral hearings was limited, and they became increasingly rare.

16 *Ibidem.*

17 See Triva 1964, p. 579; Triva 1972, p. 586.

18 Art. 351(5) CPA 1956.

19 Art. 341(1) CPA 1956.

20 See Triva 1964, p. 580; Triva 1972, p. 586-587. Given that the decision of the appellate court in this procedural situation – especially when it was based on new facts and evidence – essentially took on all the hallmarks of a decision of the first instance court, the doctrine of that time suggested that the appellate courts were not supposed to opt for a hearing at the second level of adjudication when against second instance decisions appeal on points of law ('revision') was not allowed – i.e. the third level of adjudication. In cases in which adjudication was only allowed at two levels, the revision of judgments based on new factual findings formed in the appeal proceedings led in fact to the deprivation of the constitutionally guaranteed right to appeal against any of the judgments. According to previous Yugoslav doctrine, it was therefore more appropriate that the appellate court in such cases quash the first instance judgment and remit the case to the first instance court for rehearing. Triva 1972, p. 587.

21 *Zakon o parničnom postupku* (Civil Procedure Act) from 1976 (*Službeni list SFRJ* (Official Gazette of the SFRY) 4/77; hereinafter: CPA 1976).

22 See Art. 362(2) CPA 1976.

23 See Poznić 1980, p. 299; Triva 1983, p. 547.

Following Croatia's independence, the CPA 1976 continued to apply, subject to numerous amendments.[24] Some of the amendments dealt with appeal proceedings. The 2003 CPA Amendments abandoned the option of public oral hearings for the taking of evidence at the second level. This change was justified by the fact that 'such option was not confirmed in practice'.[25] Instead, the 2003 Amendments allowed the appellate court to invite the parties and their representatives to the otherwise closed session of the appeals panel.[26] At the same time, the law introduced a ban on the presentation of new facts and evidence in the appeal proceedings.[27]

After 2003, the appellate courts in Croatia decided on the appeal without holding an oral hearing,[28] regularly in a closed session of the panels of appellate judges, attended only by the members of the panel and the court typist. Optional invitation of the parties or their representatives for the purpose of clarification was seldom used.[29] The judgments and other decisions on appeal were also made *in camera*.[30] In most of the cases where factual errors were claimed by the appellants, the appellate courts would, if they considered that errors existed, quash the first instance judgment and remit it to the first instance court for rehearing.

In the context of an attempt to reduce the number of judgments that would be quashed and remitted, the 2008 Amendments to the Civil Procedure Act (AACPA 2008) reintroduced the facultative possibility of holding oral hearings before the appellate court.[31] Yet, as this option continued to depend on the discretion of the appellate courts, it was by and large ignored until the next legislative changes in 2011.

The 2011 CPA Amendments introduced for the first time the prohibition of multiple remittals of first instance judgments. In other words, if a case had already been remitted to the first instance court upon appeal, the next time the options of the appellate court were limited. If the appeals panel held that some facts still needed to be clarified, it would in principle have the duty to conduct an evidentiary hearing itself. However, from 2011 to 2013 the prohibition of double remittals

24 *Zakon o parničnom postupku* (Civil Procedure Act) (*Službeni list SFRJ* (Official Gazette of the SFRY) 4/77 - 35/91; *Narodne novine RH* (Official Gazette of the RC) 26/91, 53/91, 91/92, 112/99, 88/01, 117/03, 88/05, 2/07, 84/08, 96/08, 123/08, 57/11, 148/11, 25/13, 43/13; hereinafter: CPA).

25 See Triva & Dika 2004, p. 703. See also for case law in the period of the former Yugoslavia Poznić 1980, p. 299.

26 See Art. 362(2) CPA.

27 See Art. 352(1) CPA.

28 Art. 362(1) CPA.

29 *Ibidem*, para 2.

30 Art. 363(1) CPA.

31 After the 2008 Amendments, when the panel of the appellate court assesses that, for the proper determination of the facts, it is necessary to rehear evidence already taken, a hearing shall be scheduled (facultative oral hearings at the second level - Art. 373(b)(2) CPA).

applied only to some litigation proceedings (proceedings in family,[32] commercial[33] and labour disputes).[34]

In 2013, the prohibition of double remittals was extended to all types of litigation. Thus, under the new law, after the first remittal it would be absolutely necessary that appellate courts conduct the proceedings in a way that would avoid sending the case to the first instance court for rehearing.[35]

The oral hearings at the second instance, however, had their price. Simultaneously with these changes, it was provided that all decisions of the appellate court made on the basis of second-instance oral hearings be widely open to re-examination before the Supreme Court by way of 'ordinary revision' (appeal on points of law),[36] regardless of the value of the dispute.[37]

5. Taking of Evidence in Appeal Proceedings in the Law of Other Post-Yugoslav Countries[38]

After the dissolution of the Socialist Federal Republic of Yugoslavia in 1992, all post-Yugoslav countries amended former Yugoslav law or adopted new acts on civil procedure.[39] One common element remained the same in all of these countries:

32 See former Art. 266(a) of the Family Act (*Obiteljski zakon*) from 2003 (*Narodne novine RH* (Official Gazette of the RC) 116/03, 17/04, 136/04, 107/07, 57/11 - see Art. 52 AACPA 2011, 61/11).

33 See former Art. 497(b) CPA.

34 See former Art. 437(a) CPA.

35 Art. 366(a) CPA.

36 In the Croatian procedural system, 'ordinary revision' against the second instance decision is allowed if the value of the dispute exceeds a certain amount (Art. 382(1), pt. 1 CPA), or in case of a judgment against which the law always allows it (Art. 382(1), pt. 2 CPA), or with respect to the procedure that preceded the second instance decision - that is, if the appellate court holds a hearing before delivering the second instance decision (Art. 382(1), pt. 3 CPA). If 'ordinary revision' would not be allowed under any of the above criteria, the parties could lodge 'extraordinary revision' against the second instance decision if the decision in dispute depended on the resolution of a substantive or a procedural issue important to ensure uniform application of the law and equality of all in its application (Art. 382(2) CPA). 'Ordinary' and 'extraordinary' revisions are extraordinary means of recourse against the second instance decision that acquired the status of *res iudicata*. On these recourses in Croatian law see more in Dika 2010, p. 258 *et seq*.

37 Art. 382(1), pt. 3 in conjunction with Art. 366(a)(3), Art. 373, Art. 373(b) CPA; Art. 373(b) CPA.

38 The comparative law research includes Montenegro, the Federation of Bosnia & Herzegovina, the former Yugoslav Republic of Macedonia, Slovenia and Serbia. Taking into account the fact that in this area the systems of the Federation of Bosnia & Herzegovina, the Republic of Srpska and the District of Brčko are very similar (for some of the issues they are identical), only the system of the Federation of Bosnia & Herzegovina will be analysed. From the post-Yugoslav countries only Kosovo - the youngest post-Yugoslav country - is excluded in order to avoid unnecessary repetition in the comparative law review of the post-Yugoslav countries.

39 Following independence, all post-Yugoslav countries adopted the CPA 1976 as a piece of their legislation, subject to numerous amendments, which applied until they adopted (new) →

appeal is continually permitted as a matter of right against all first instance judgments.[40] Also, the dogmatic position on the purpose of appeals remained the same: the aim of appeal proceedings is a review of first instance judgments, not a full rehearing.[41]

Under the civil procedure acts of (other) post-Yugoslav countries the court either decides on the appeal in a closed session of the appeals panel (which is still the dominant and general approach)[42] or on the basis of an optional evidentiary hearing.[43]

In addition to the general principle according to which priority is given to deciding on an appeal in a closed session, some post-Yugoslav laws determine the cases in which the appellate courts decide on the basis of hearings. According to the Slovenian, Bosnian-Herzegovinian and Macedonian CPAs, the appellate court must schedule a hearing if it assesses that, for the proper determination of the facts, it is necessary to re-hear all or some of the already heard evidence[44] or if procedural errors can be eliminated due to their nature by the procedural actions undertaken before the appellate court.[45] A similar, though slightly different formulation is to be found in the Serbian and Montenegrin CPAs, stipulating that in such cases the appellate court is empowered to schedule a hearing if it finds it necessary to do so.[46] Serbian, Montenegrin and Macedonian law contain the prohibition of double remittals. Consequently, the appellate court has the obligation to schedule a hearing

acts on civil procedure. In 1998 Macedonia adopted a Civil Procedure Act (*Službeni vesnik RM* (Official Gazette of the RM) 33/98), and then in 2005 adopted a new Civil Procedure Act (*Službeni vesnik RM* (Official Journal of the RM) 79/05; hereinafter: MCPA). The Federation of Bosnia & Herzegovina adopted a Civil Procedure Act in 1998 (*Službene novine FBH* (Official Gazette of the FBH) 42/98), and then in 2003 adopted a new Civil Procedure Act (*Službene novine FBH* (Official Gazette of the FBH) 53/03; hereinafter: BHCPA). Slovenia adopted a Civil Procedure Act in 1999 (*Uradni list RS* (Official Gazette of the RS) 26/99; hereinafter: SloCPA). Serbia adopted a Civil Procedure Act in 2004 (*Službeni glasnik RS* (Official Gazette of the RS) 125/04), and then in 2011 adopted a new Civil Procedure Act (*Službeni glasnik RS* (Official Gazette of the RS) 72/11; hereinafter: SerCPA). Montenegro adopted a Civil Procedure Act in 2004 (*Službeni glasnik CG* (Official Gazette of Montenegro) 22/04; hereinafter: MNCPA). Croatia still applies the adopted CPA from 1976, subject to numerous amendments.

40 See Čizmović & Đuričin 1997, p. 261; Čalija & Omanović 2000, p. 273-274; Triva & Dika 2004, p. 672-673; Zobec 2009, p. 216; Poznić & Rakić-Vodinelić 2010, p. 390, 392; Dika 2010, p. 107-108.

41 Čizmović & Đuričin 1997, p. 260; Čalija & Omanović 2000, p. 273-274, 280; Zobec 2009, p. 226-227; Dika 2010, p. 1-3.

42 Art. 347(1) SloCPA; Art. 383(1) SerCPA; Art. 351(1) MCPA.

43 Art. 375(1) MNCPA; Art. 217(1) BHCPA.

44 Besides Croatia, only Macedonia excludes the possibility of presenting new facts and proposing new evidence on appeal (Art. 341(1) MCPA; Art. 352(1) Croatian CPA).

45 Art. 347(2) and (3) SloCPA; Art. 217(2) BHCPA; Art. 351(2) MCPA.

46 Art. 383(3) SrbCPA, Art. 375(4) MNCPA. According to the Montenegrin CPA, the appellate court must set a hearing in those cases when it comes to new facts and evidence which are allowed under certain conditions (Art. 375(2), Art. 365(1) and (2) MNCPA).

if it assesses for the second time that the first instance judgment needs to be remitted for rehearing.[47]

The laws of post-Yugoslav countries have different attitudes towards the right to present new facts and evidence on appeal. The Macedonian CPA, just as the Croatian CPA, are under the influence of the Austrian model[48] and contain preclusions regarding the introduction of new facts and evidence upon appeal (the only exceptions relate to procedural errors that may be proven by new evidence).[49] Slovenian, Serbian and Montenegrin law follow the German model[50] and contain the *beneficium novorum* – the right to present new facts and evidence on appeal, but only if such evidence was not adduced at first instance without fault on the part of the appellant.[51] The Bosnian-Herzegovinian law is the most permissive: the parties may present in the appeal proceedings new facts and evidence without any limitations.[52]

The laws of other post-Yugoslav countries generally do not extend the options for launching an appeal on points of law with the Supreme Court ('revision') for cases in which the appellate court ruled on the basis of an oral hearing.[53]

Despite the legislative efforts to encourage independent and direct fact-finding at the second level of adjudication, in reality the appellate courts of post-Yugoslav countries still more often than not use their cassation powers: they quash first instance judgments and remit the cases to the first instance courts for rehearing rather often.[54] Consequently, oral hearings at the second level of adjudication are rare beasts in the practice of post-Yugoslav litigation.[55]

47 Art. 383(3) SrbCPA; Art. 375(3) MNCPA; Art. 351(3) MCPA.

48 See Sec. 6.1 below.

49 Art. 341(1) MNCPA; Art. 352(1) Croatian CPA.

50 See Sec. 6.2 below.

51 Art. 337(1) SloCPA; Art. 372, Art. 384(5) SrbCPA; Art. 365(1) and (3) MNCPA. In Serbian and Montenegrin practice (and theory) this rule is interpreted such that by new facts are to be understood not only the facts that the party did not present although they existed before the conclusion of the hearing at first instance (subjective *nova facta*), but also the facts that have arisen after the conclusion of the hearing at first instance (objective *nova facta*). Poznić & Rakić-Vodinelić 2010, p. 399; Čizmović & Đuričin 1997, p. 262. In Slovenian theory and practice this rule is interpreted such that by new facts are to be understood only subjective new facts – that is, only those facts that have occurred before the conclusion of the hearing at first instance. Zobec 2009, p. 228.

52 Art. 334(1) BHCPA. In Bosnian-Herzegovinian theory this rule is interpreted such that by new facts are to be understood not only the facts that the party did not present although they existed before the conclusion of the hearing at first instance (subjective *nova facta*), but also the facts that have arisen after the conclusion of the hearing at first instance (objective *nova facta*). Čalija & Omanović 2000, p. 279.

53 See for Serbia: Poznić & Rakić-Vodinelić 2010, p. 403-404.

54 Poznić & Rakić-Vodinelić 2010, p. 409; see also Zobec 2009, p. 393 *et seq.*

55 Omanović 2003, p. 92-93; Poznić & Rakić-Vodinelić 2010, p. 403; Zobec 2009, p. 378 *et seq.* (who argues that the Slovenian Legislature, despite having prescribed obligatory hearings at the second level of adjudication, does not prescribe any direct recourse where the appellate court has not set a hearing and used its reformatory (revision) powers).

6. Comparative Models - Appeals and Evidence-Taking in the Western Neighbourhood of Croatia

6.1. *Austria*

Civil law matters in Austria are governed by general rules of civil procedure.[56] There are, in principle, two different branches of civil courts, each of which may be divided into three instances.[57] The manner of proceeding is affected by this distinction.

Under the Austrian CPA, there are two means of recourse against the decisions delivered by the first instance courts: appeal (*Berufung*)[58] and complaint (*Rekurs*).[59] [60] I will analyse only the appeal.

The appellate court reviews the correctness of the first instance judgment. This means that in principle the court decides the matter only on the basis of the claims and facts which existed at the moment of the conclusion of the hearings at first instance.

Questions of law, questions of fact and procedural issues (especially nullity, if fundamental procedural principles have been violated) may be raised on appeal.[61]

56 Civil Procedure Act (*Gesetz über das gerichtliche Verfahren in bürgerlichen Rechtsstreitigkeiten, Zivilprozessordnung* (RGBl 1895/113) of Austria from 1895 (available at: <http://www.-jusline.at/Zivilprozessordnung_(ZPO).html>, last consulted in June 2013>); hereinafter: ACPA.

57 At first instance disputes are assigned to either the local courts (*Bezirksgerichte*) or the regional courts (*Landesgerichte*). Local courts have jurisdiction in cases involving a value in dispute of up to € 15,000 (Art. 49(1) Jurisdiction Act (*Gesetz über die Ausübung der Gerichtsbarkeit und die Zuständigkeit der ordentlichen Gerichte in bürgerlichen Rechtssachen, Jurisdiktionsnorm*) (RGBl 1895/111); hereinafter: JA) and subject-matter jurisdiction in most disputes relating to family law or tenancy agreements (Art. 49(2) JA). An appeal on points of fact and law (*Berufung*) goes to the regional court (*Landesgerichte*) (Art. 3(1) JA), where an appeals panel decides the appeal (Art. 7(1) JA). In particularly important cases concerning legal issues of fundamental importance, a further recourse (*Revision*) against the result of the first appeal is available at the Supreme Court of Justice (*Oberster Gerichtshof*) (Art. 3(2) JA). Regional courts (*Landesgerichte*) have jurisdiction in cases involving a value in dispute of over € 15,000 and subject-matter jurisdiction in disputes pursuant to the Austrian Nuclear Liability Act (*Atomhaftpflichtgesetz*), Public Liability Act (*Amtshaftungsgesetz*), Data Protection Act (*Datenschutzgesetz*) and in cases of unfair competition and breach of copyright (see Art. 50 JA; and Fasching 1990, p. 135). An appeal on points of fact and law (*Berufung*) goes at the second instance to the Higher Regional Court (*Oberlandesgericht*) (Art. 4 JA).

58 The procedure on appeal (*Berufung*) is governed by Art. 461 *et seq.* ACPA.

59 The procedure on complaint (*Rekurs*) is governed by Art. 514 *et seq.* ACPA.

60 A complaint (*Rekurs*) is the mode of attacking orders and rulings other than judgments delivered at first and second instance (Art. 514(1) ACPA). Such orders and rulings are known as *Beschlüsse*. A complaint is also applicable to specific kinds of interlocutory rulings and to court orders issued in matters of non-contentious jurisdiction under the Austrian Non-Contentious Proceedings Act (*Außerstreitgesetz*) from 2003. For recourse against decisions under the Austrian CPA, see Fasching 1990, p. 841 *et seq.*

61 See Art. 477, Art. 503, pt. 4 ACPA. See Fasching 1990, p. 887 *et seq.*

In general, the first instance court's factual findings are appealable, except in certain special proceedings, and in all cases where the amount in dispute is less than € 2,700.[62]

In general, the rules applying to the procedure before the courts of first instance are applicable in the procedure on appeal as well.[63] Nevertheless, the Austrian procedural system strictly holds that the introduction of new facts and evidence, just as any change of the claim in the procedure on appeal, is not admissible.[64]

The appellate court decides on appeal, within the framework defined by the motions and submissions presented at first instance. Oral hearings are held if the complexity of the case demands it; otherwise, the appellate court decides on appeal in a closed session of the appeals panel,[65] in particular when only to correct certain procedural errors.[66] The appellate court should, in principle, decide the case under consideration itself.[67] The court may quash the judgment and remand the case only in exceptional cases specified in the CPA, in particular if the court of first instance failed to decide on substantive claims or if grave procedural errors committed in the first instance prevented a thorough examination of the claims. The case may also be remitted if the first instance court did not address relevant factual allegations of the parties.[68] However, the decision whether the case should be remitted or finally decided by the appellate court depends on the assessment of whether a particular course of action would contribute to the saving of time and expenses.[69] To that extent, even in exceptional cases where it is not necessary to decide on the merits of the case, the court of second instance has broad discretion and may, in all cases where it would enhance the efficiency of the proceedings, schedule an oral hearing and take the evidence itself.

6.2. *Germany*

Under the German Civil Procedure Act[70] there are two methods of recourse against decisions delivered by the first instance courts: appeal (*Berufung*) and complaint subject to a time limit (*sofortige Beschwerde*).[71] I will analyse only the former.[72]

62 An appeal may be lodged in all cases on the grounds of invalidity or legal errors. Factual errors may only be raised in cases where the amount in dispute is greater than € 2,700, and in some other special categories of cases (Art. 501, Art. 502(4) and (5) ACPA). See also Hofmann 2006, p. I/38.

63 Art. 463(1) ACPA.

64 Art. 482(1) ACPA.

65 Art. 480(1) ACPA.

66 Art. 471, Art. 473(1) ACPA.

67 Art. 497 ACPA.

68 Art. 494, Art. 495, Art. 496 ACPA.

69 Art. 496(3) ACPA.

70 Civil Procedure Act (*Zivilprozessordnung* (RGBl S 83) of Germany from 1877 (available at: <http://www.gesetze-im-internet.de/bundesrecht/zpo/gesamt.pdf>, last consulted in June 2013); hereinafter: GCPA.

Unlike Croatian law and the laws of other post-Yugoslav countries, in German law the right of appeal is not without limits. Appeal is in principle not admissible in small claims cases.[73]

After the significant reform of German civil procedure in 2001, the purpose of procedure on appeal changed. Originally, appeal included a full rehearing of the case and a *de novo* procedure on all issues; after the reform, the appeals process was converted into a review procedure, limited to the correction of errors in the first instance judgment.[74] Currently, all preclusions at first instance apply also at second instance, so that the procedure on appeal no longer offers a second chance to the parties to significantly alter or complement their claims and views on the substantive issues in dispute.[75]

Therefore, bringing forward new facts, raising new issues and introducing new evidence is in principle not permissible in the appeals process.[76] New facts and arguments are now only allowed under strict conditions.[77] New arguments are

71 A complaint subject to a time limit (*sofortige Beschwerde*) is the mode of attacking orders and rulings other than judgments, and certain judgments (e.g. a decision on costs in a judgment on the basis of a confession). Such orders and rulings are known as *Beschlüsse*. Not every *Beschluss* is reviewable. Reviewable are only those decisions delivered by the local courts (*Amtsgerichte*) and regional courts (*Landgerichte*) in proceedings before them as courts of first instance if this has been expressly determined by law or the decisions so being challenged did not require a hearing for oral argument and dismissed a petition concerning the proceedings (Art. 567(1) GCPA). Complaint (*Beschwerde*) is also applicable to specified kinds of interlocutory rulings and to court orders issued in matters of non-contentious jurisdiction under the Act on Proceedings in Family Matters and in Matters of Voluntary Jurisdiction (*Gesetz über das Verfahren in Familiensachen und in den Angelegenheiten der freiwilligen Gerichtsbarkeit*) from 2008 (BGBl I S 2587). For recourses against decisions under the German CPA, see Rosenberg, Schwab & Gottwald 2010, p. 769 *et seq*.

72 The procedure for contentious jurisdiction is governed by Art. 253 *et seq*. GCPA (at first instance), by Art. 511 *et seq*. GCPA (on appeal, *Berufung*) and by Art. 542 *et seq*. GCPA (on appeal on points of law, *Revision*).

73 An appeal is allowed only if the value of the subject matter of the appeal is greater than € 600, or if in its ruling the first instance court has granted leave to appeal (Art. 511(2) GCPA). The first instance court will allow an appeal in cases in which the legal matter is of fundamental significance or wherever the further development of the law or the interests in ensuring a uniform adjudication require a decision to be handed down by the appellate court, and wherever the judgment does not adversely affect the party by an amount greater than € 600 (Art. 511(4) GCPA). The appellate court also has the power to deny leave to appeal if all of its members are satisfied that: the appeal manifestly has no chance of success, the legal matter is not of any fundamental significance, the further development of the law or the interests in ensuring uniform adjudication do not require a decision to be handed down by the appellate court, and that no hearing for oral argument is mandated (Art. 522(2) GCPA).

74 Since the reform of civil appeals (*Zivilprozessreformgesetz ,2001*) the appeals process is no longer meant to be a second hearing. It is meant to be a review of the first instance judgment, although in practice the appeal proceedings offer in most cases more of a rehearing than a review. See for an evaluation of the appellate system Barendrecht, Bolt & de Hoon 2005, p. 11.

75 See Rosenberg, Schwab & Gottwald 2010, p. 769-770, 804.

76 See Art. 531, Art. 533 GCPA.

77 Rosenberg, Schwab & Gottwald 2010, p. 769-770, 804.

allowed if the first instance court has obviously disregarded or erroneously held as irrelevant important issues; if the failure to introduce these arguments is due to a procedural error of the first instance court; or, if the appellant failed to introduce an argument at first instance without fault on its part.[78]

The German appellate courts decide appeals in principle on the basis of an oral hearing.[79] Evidence on appeal is produced in essentially the same manner as at first instance. In general, the rules applying to the procedure before the regional courts (*Landgerichte*) as courts of first instance are to be applied *mutatis mutandis* to procedure on appeal.[80]

The appellant may amend his original claim, raise a set-off claim and introduce counterclaims only with the permission of the opposing party, or if the court holds this to be expedient. However, the amendments and new claims have to be based on facts that would in any case have to be established before the appellate court (i.e. the claims should not be based on new facts that would otherwise be inadmissible).[81]

Courts of second instance are bound by the facts established at first instance, except if there is serious doubt regarding the correctness or completeness of the factual findings at first instance.[82] In practice, this means that the appellate court is often not bound by the determination of the facts at first instance.[83]

Where the appellate court holds the appeal is founded, it should decide in principle the case under consideration itself.[84] The court may quash the judgment and remit the case to the first instance court for rehearing only under very limited conditions specified in the German Civil Procedure Act. Remitting of the case to the first instance court may essentially take place only if, due to grave procedural errors committed at first instance, the proceedings were so deficient that extensive or complex taking of evidence is necessary for the proper determination of the case.[85] In some special proceedings – e.g. in labour cases – remittals are prohibited altogether.[86]

78 Art. 531(2) GCPA.

79 Art. 523(1) GCPA. See Rosenberg, Schwab & Gottwald 2010, p. 804.

80 Art. 525 GCPA.

81 Art. 533 GCPA. See Rosenberg, Schwab & Gottwald 2010, p. 802.

82 Art. 529(1) GCPA.

83 Barendrecht, Bolt & de Hoon 2005, p. 25.

84 Art. 538(1) GCPA. See Rosenberg, Schwab & Gottwald 2010, p. 767-770, 813.

85 See Art. 538(2) GCPA. Other options from that paragraph are not important in this context, as they generally relate to cases in which no fact-finding took place before the first instance court.

86 Art. 68 of the Law on Labour Courts (ArbGG).

6.3. *The Netherlands*

Under the Dutch Civil Procedure Act[87] there are two main types of civil actions: the 'procedure commenced by writ of summons' (writ procedure or *dagvaardingsprocedure*) and the 'procedure commenced by petition' (*verzoekschriftprocedure*). Both at first instance and on appeal the manner of the proceedings is affected by this distinction.[88] (It should be noted here that in the near future a single document for the initiation of both types of actions will be introduced, but at the procedural level the existing differences between the actions will largely remain).

The most important procedure for contentious litigation is 'the procedure commenced by writ of summons'.[89] [90] For voluntary jurisdiction (e.g. in noncontentious divorce cases and in cases for the appointment of a guardian for a minor after the parents' death) the 'petition procedure' is the essential one.[91] The appeal proceedings are essentially a 'second first instance'.[92]

Both errors of fact and law may be corrected on appeal.[93] On appeal the Dutch courts are obliged (within boundaries) to check whether the arguments introduced at the first instance are relevant in the appeal proceedings.[94]

The parties are entitled to plead their case orally before the court, a right which is used relatively more often in appeal proceedings than in proceedings before the court of first instance.[95]

In actions commenced by writ of summons, the appellant who acted as plaintiff at first instance may change his original claim. The adverse party may oppose the change on the grounds that it would unreasonably hinder his defence or delay the proceedings. A new counterclaim, however, cannot be introduced on appeal. In general, procedural legal steps that may be taken at first instance are also allowed on appeal.[96]

87 Civil Procedure Act (*Wetboek van Burgerlijke Rechtsvordering*) of the Netherlands (available at: <http://www.st-ab.nl/wetten/0471_Wetboek_van_Burgerlijke_Rechtsvordering_Rv.htm>, last consulted in June 2013); hereinafter: DCPA.

88 See Van Rhee 1999, p. 241; Chorus, Gerver & Hondius 2006, p. 255, 258 *et seq.*

89 As far as it concerns proceedings at first instance provided for in Title II of Book I of the DCPA. However, there is a trend in Dutch legislation to prescribe the proceedings commenced by petition for contentious cases as well, e.g. contentious divorce proceedings and some types of employment cases. Chorus, Gerver & Hondius 2006, p. 255, 258.

90 The rules for an appeal in cases commenced by writ of summons are laid down in Arts. 332-356 DCPA and the rules for cassation in a procedure commenced by writ of summons are laid down in Arts. 398-425 DCPA. See Chorus, Gerver & Hondius 2006, p. 260-261.

91 The proceedings commenced by petition are governed by Art. 261 *et seq.* DCPA at first instance, by Art. 358 *et seq.* DCPA on appeal and by Art. 426 *et seq.* DCPA on appeal in cassation. See Chorus, Gerver & Hondius 2006, p. 258.

92 Art. 347(1) DCPA. See Van Rhee 1999, p. 243.

93 Van Rhee 1999, p. 243; see also Chorus, Gerver & Hondius 2006, p. 261.

94 Barendrecht, Bolt & de Hoon 2005, p. 28.

95 Chorus, Gerver & Hondius 2006, p. 261.

96 See Art. 353 DCPA. See Van Rhee 1999, p. 243; Chorus, Gerver & Hondius 2006, p. 261.

The procedure on appeal in cases commenced by petition is virtually identical to the petition procedure at first instance. The claim may only be changed with the court's consent. A counter-petition on appeal is excluded.[97]

Evidence on appeal is produced in essentially the same manner as at first instance.[98] In principle, the adverse party may introduce a new defence on the merits in proceedings on appeal.[99] A litigant who failed to produce witnesses at first instance can do this on appeal, with the exception of those witnesses who at first instance he formally declared he would not produce.[100] As a result of the above rules, the appellate court will sometimes entertain questions which were not raised during litigation at first instance.[101]

7. Why Croatian Civil Procedure Fears Fact-Finding at Second Instance

There are several reasons why oral hearings are so rare in Croatian appellate courts, even after the legislative changes that tried to encourage them:

I. Unclear and incomplete provisions in the current procedural legislation
When a case has already been remitted to the first instance upon appeal, the appellate court no longer has the option to quash the judgment and remit it back since a remittal is allowed only once. Consequently, the appellate court has the duty to conduct an evidentiary hearing itself if this is necessary to eliminate errors (prohibition of multiple remittals). The procedure is then *per analogiam* governed by the rules applicable to the first instance courts.

What does it mean to hold an oral hearing before the appellate court in accordance with the rules applicable to the first instance procedure? Some issues arise in this respect:

1. Does it mean that second instance proceedings, as well as first instance proceedings, consist of preliminary proceedings, within which it is necessary to set a preliminary hearing at which the judge will decide which evidence is to be heard, and a (main) hearing at which evidence will be taken?[102]

2. Does it mean that the parties may present new facts and propose new evidence on appeal because this is allowed at first instance (*beneficium novorum*)? It seems that this question should have a negative answer, because presenting new facts and

97 See Art. 362 DCPA. See Chorus, Gerver & Hondius 2006, p. 261.
98 Art. 353(1) DCPA. See Chorus, Gerver & Hondius 2006, p. 261.
99 Art. 348 DCPA.
100 Van Rhee 1999, p. 244.
101 *Ibidem*, p. 243-244; see also Chorus, Gerver & Hondius 2006, p. 261.
102 See for the first instance procedure Art. 277 CPA.

proposing new evidence is not allowed on appeal;[103] this applies also to the hearing before the appellate court.

3. Does it mean that the parties may admit or waive their claim at the hearing before the appellate court, as they may at first instance?

After the CPA amendments in 2011, court settlements in appeal proceedings became permissible.[104] Therefore, the parties may settle their case on appeal. They may also withdraw their claim on appeal, since this is still possible until the decision acquires the status of *res iudicata*.[105]

Would it then be possible to deliver at this point a judgment based on an admittance or a waiver of the claim? The CPA provides that the claim may be admitted or waived only up until the conclusion of the hearings at first instance.[106] If the appellate court 'holds the hearing in accordance with the rules of the first instance procedure',[107] it is doubtful whether judgments based on admittance or waivers may be delivered on appeal.[108] *De lege ferenda*, I think that this should be allowed for reasons of economy and acceleration of the proceedings.

4. Does it mean that the parties may modify the claim at the appellate court, as they may at first instance?

Pursuant to Article 190(1) CPA, the plaintiff may only modify the claim up until the conclusion of the preliminary proceedings. Later modifications are not allowed, even at the (main) hearing at first instance. Despite the rule that the appellate court has to conduct the hearing in accordance with the rules of the first instance procedure,[109] it seems that the possibility of a modification of a claim at second instance should be denied, in particular due to the fact that new facts and new evidence may not be introduced on appeal.[110]

II. Logistics – lack of hearing rooms at the appellate courts

In public discussions, judges often blamed the lack of space at the appellate courts as the main reason for the non-implementation of the provisions on second instance hearings. But, it is a fact that courtrooms of the first instance courts in Croatia are also not very numerous, large or well-equipped. Space for the parties and counsel is lacking (and even more so for the general public). Nevertheless, first instance judges hold hearings regularly and the lack of space at the first instance courts has never

103 Art. 352(1) CPA.
104 Art. 321(6) CPA.
105 Art. 193(3) CPA.
106 Art. 331(1), Art. 331(1) CPA.
107 Art. 366(2) CPA.
108 *Argumentum ex* Art. 331(1) CPA.
109 Art. 366(2) CPA.
110 See in this Sec., question 2 above.

been regarded as a sufficient reason to withhold the parties' right to an oral and public hearing.

The lack of space at the appellate courts may easily be overcome if the appellate judges would follow the example of their first instance colleagues and hold hearings in a similar manner.

III. A lack of understanding of the principles underlying second instance hearings

The 2013 CPA Amendments allowed the appeals panel to decide that, during the course of appeal proceedings, evidence is to be taken before a single judge of the first instance court.[111] In addition, the appeals panel may decide that evidence is to be taken before the reporting judge of the appellate court in the courtroom of the first instance court.[112] Most importantly, when evidence is taken in such a manner, the appeals panel decides on the appeal without holding a full hearing. Instead, the court will hold a closed session to which the parties will be invited.[113]

Taking into account the prohibition of introducing new facts and evidence on appeal, we may doubt whether there is any essential difference between the (erroneous or incomplete) findings of the first instance court in the proceedings at first instance, and the findings that the same court would make for the second time upon request of the appellate court. Moreover, it seems that fact-finding by the appellate court will more likely be less accurate than the findings of the first instance court. Namely, when a judge of the lower court or a judge rapporteur hears witnesses for the second time, and then transmits the protocol to the appeals panel, witness testimony will certainly lose its original flavour (not to mention the lack of an opportunity for the parties to question the quality and credibility of such 'improved' and 'corrected' second-hand evidence).

8. Concluding Remarks

Five general tendencies underlie the appellate systems of Austria, Germany and the Netherlands. First, there is a widespread tendency to limit the right of appeal, i.e. to limit appeal to cases with a relevant (monetary or social) value. The second trend is partly connected with the first: the judgments become increasingly final and binding already at first instance (especially in Germany and Austria). Third, there is a less widespread but at least as important change of the aim of the appeal proceedings from *de novo* hearing of the case to review of the correctness of the adjudication at the first instance (true for Germany and Austria, but not true for the Netherlands).[114] Fourth, appellate courts (if they have both powers) exercise their reformatory (revision) powers more often than their powers to quash a decision and send the case back to the lower court. Fifth, appellate courts hold oral hearings and,

111 Art. 373(b)(3) CPA.

112 *Ibidem.*

113 *Ibidem*, para 4.

114 See also Barendrecht, Bolt & de Hoon 2005, p. 3.

despite some limitations regarding the introduction of new facts (Austria and Germany), conduct fact-finding proceedings at the second level of adjudication.

Despite the strong historical influence of Austrian and German models on civil procedural law and doctrine of the successor states of former Yugoslavia,[115] the study of the development of the appellate systems of the post-Yugoslav countries shows that trends and tendencies are definitively different.

The right to appeal is guaranteed against every first instance judgment and imposed as a constitutional right.[116] Consequently, the appeals are widespread and the judgments are very rarely final and binding at first instance. Appellate courts (still) tend to use their cassation powers and, more often than not, remit cases for rehearing instead of passing their own decisions on the merits. The legislative provisions that aim at reversing this situation are resisted in practice, and the appellate courts in Croatia (as well as in other post-Yugoslav countries) generally avoid oral hearings and independent fact-finding proceedings.

It seems that Croatian appellate courts have no serious intention to start using the provisions introduced in the 2008 CPA Amendments on appellate oral hearings. Furthermore, it is likely that the 2013 Amendments opened another way to circumvent the wishes of the Legislature. Namely, the desire to encourage oral hearings before the appellate courts has been put in jeopardy due to the new option of ordering that evidence be taken in appeal proceedings before a judge-commissioner – a first instance or reporting judge of the appellate court – in the courtroom of the lower court.[117] In such cases, the appellate court decides on the appeal without holding a hearing and without giving the right to the parties to fully present their case, which may cause further issues connected to the right to a fair trial.[118]

115 See Triva & Dika 2004, p. 34-47. For the influence of the German and Austrian codes of civil procedure in continental Europe, see Cappelletti 1971, p. 854-855.

116 On the right to appeal as a human and constitutional right, see Triva & Dika 2004, p. 672-673; Dika 2010, p. 107-108.

117 Art. 373(b)(3) CPA.

118 *Ibidem*, para 4.

Bibliography

Barendrecht, Bolt & de Hoon 2005
Barendrecht, J.M., Bolt, K.F. & de Hoon, M.W., *Appeal Procedures: Evaluation and Reform*, 2005. Available at: <https://www.wodc.nl/images/appeal-procedures_tcm44-59294.pdf> (p. 1-47).

Blankenburg 1998
Blankenburg, E., 'Patterns of Legal Culture: The Netherlands Compared to Neighboring Germany', *The American Journal of Comparative Law*, 1998, Vol. 46(1), p. 1-41.

Cappelletti 1971
Cappelletti, M., 'Social and Political Aspects of Civil Procedure: Reforms and Trends in Western and Eastern Europe', *Michigan Law Review*, 1971, Vol. 69(5), p. 847-886.

Čalija & Omanović 2000
Čalija, B. & Omanović, S., *Građansko procesno pravo*, Sarajevo: Univerzitet u Sarajevu, Pravni fakultet, 2000.

Chorus, Gerver & Hondius 2006
Chorus, J., Gerver, P.H. & Hondius, E., *Introduction to Dutch Law*, 4th edn., The Hague/London/Boston: Kluwer Law International, 2006.

Čizmović & Đuričin 1997
Čizmović, M. & Đuričin, B., *Građansko procesno pravo*, 4th edn., Podgorica: Kulturno prosvjetna zajednica, 1997.

Dika 2010
Dika, M., *Građansko parnično pravo; X. knjiga; Pravni lijekovi*, Zagreb: Narodne novine, 2010.

Fasching 1990
Fasching, H.W., *Lehrbuch des österreichischen Zivilprozeßrechts*, 2nd edn., Wien: Manzsche Verlags- und Universitätsbuchhandlung, 1990.

Hofmann 2006
Hofmann, L., 'Austria', in Campbell, C. (ed.), *International Civil Procedure*, Vol. I, Salzburg: Yorkhill Law Publishing, 2006, p. I/23-40.

Kaplan, von Mehren & Schaefer 1958
Kaplan, B., von Mehren, A.T. & Schaefer, R., 'Phases of German Civil Procedure II', *Harvard Law Review*, 1958, Vol. 71(8), p. 1443-1472.

Langbein 1985
Langbein, J.H., 'The German Advantage in Civil Procedure', *The University of Chicago Law Review*, 1985, Vol. 52(4), p. 823-866.

Omanović 2003
Omanović, S., *Draft novog Zakona o parničnom postupku Federacije Bosne i Hercegovine sa komentarom*, Sarajevo: Magistrat, 2003.

Poznić 1980
Poznić, B., *Građansko procesno pravo*, 7th edn., Belgrade: Savremena administracija, 1980.

Poznić & Rakić-Vodinelić 2010
Poznić, B. & Rakić-Vodinelić, V., *Građansko procesno pravo*, 16th edn., Belgrad: Savremena administracija, 2010.

Rosenberg, Schwab & Gottwald 2010
Rosenberg, L., Schwab, K.H. & Gottwald, P., *Zivilprozessrecht*, 17th edn., München: C.H. Beck, 2010.

Shapiro 1980
Shapiro, M., 'Appeal', *Law & Society Review, Contemporary Issues in Law and Social Science*, 1980, Vol. 14(3), p. 629-661.

Triva 1964
Triva, S., *Građansko procesno pravo I; Parnično procesno pravo*, Zagreb: Narodne novine, 1964.

Triva 1972
Triva, S., *Građansko procesno pravo I; Parnično procesno pravo*, 2nd edn., Zagreb: Narodne novine, 1972.

Triva 1983
Triva, S., *Građansko parnično procesno pravo*, 5th edn., Zagreb: Narodne novine, 1983.

Triva & Dika 2004
Triva, S. & Dika, M., *Građansko parnično procesno pravo*, 7th edn., Zagreb: Narodne novine, 2004.

Uzelac 2014
Uzelac, A., 'Features and Shortcomings of Appellate Review in Civil and Administrative Cases in Croatia', in Uzelac, A. & Van Rhee, C.H. (eds.), *Nobody's Perfect. Comparative Essays on Appeals and other Means of Recourse against Judicial Decisions in Civil Matters*, Cambridge/Antwerp/Portland: Intersentia, 2014, p. 243-244.

Van Rhee 1999
Van Rhee, C.H., 'Recourse against Judgments in the Netherlands', in Jolowicz, J.A. & Van Rhee, C.H. (eds.), *Recourse against Judgments in the European Union,* The Hague/London/Boston: Kluwer Law International, 1999, p. 239-260, (also available at: <http://arnop.unimaas.nl/show.cgi?fid=1038> (p. 1-16).

Zobec 2009
Zobec, J., 'Redna pravna sredstva', in Ude, L. & Galič, A. (eds.), *Pravdni postopek; Zakon s komentarjem; 3. knjiga,* Ljubljana: Uradni list: GV Založba, 2009, p. 209-520.

D. van Loggerenberg

EVOLUTION OF THE POWERS OF THE JUDGE AND THE POWERS OF THE PARTIES REGARDING THE TAKING OF EVIDENCE IN SOUTH AFRICA

1. Introduction

The word 'procedure' inherently means 'going forward'.[1] Viewed as such, civil procedure not only aims at moving forward the dispute between the parties up to the point of its eventual determination by a court, but also aims at reflecting the evolution (i.e. change) of society and its needs. Since all legal systems are closely linked to the historical, cultural, socio-economic and political milieu in which they have developed and find application, the degree of the powers of the judge and the powers of the parties regarding the taking of evidence in a given system must necessarily depend upon a variety of factors, juridical and non-juridical, that determine its character. With regard to this, as far back as 1975 Jolowicz[2] stated the following:

> The essential question, to which each country must work out its own answer, concerns the extent to which the powers of the court can be increased without thereby sacrificing other values which are held to be vital to the due administration of civil justice.

In this contribution, the focus will be directed at the South African adversarial system of civil procedure which owes its origin to that of England.[3] It has, however,

1 Bernhardt 1968, correctly states that a legal procedure is 'als Lebensvorgang betrachtet, ein *Verfahren*. Daher kommt auch der Name: processor (procedure - *vorwärtschreiten*)'.

2 Cappelletti & Jolowicz 1957, p. 272.

3 See Erasmus 1991, p. 108, p. 265, where, *inter alia*, the following is stated: 'South African civil procedure "owes its origin to and is essentially that of England". The forms of procedure devised under the First and Second Charters of Justice of 1828 and 1834 for the Supreme Court of the Colony of the Cape of Good Hope displayed the fundamental features characteristic of proceedings at common law, namely, the adversary character of the system and the predominant role of the parties in the conduct of the litigation, the passive and neutral role of the court, and the "morality, immediacy and publicity of its proceedings".'

materially steered an independent course in its development since its implementation by the English in 1828.[4]

In terms of Sec. 166 of the Constitution of the Republic of South Africa, 1996,[5] the courts in South Africa consist of:

a. The Constitutional Court;[6]
b. The Supreme Court of Appeal;[7]
c. The High Court;[8]
d. The Magistrates' Courts.[9]

4 South African law is *sui generis*: its substantive law is of civil law (i.e. Roman-Dutch) origin whereas its civil procedural law is mainly of common law origin. In other words, it is a mixed legal system.

5 As amended by the Constitution Seventeenth Amendment Act of 2012 which came into operation on 23 August 2013.

6 In terms of Sec. 167(3) of the Constitution of the Republic of South Africa, 1996, the Constitutional Court –
(a) is the highest court of the Republic; and
(b) may decide –
(i) constitutional matters; and
(ii) any other matter, if the Constitutional Court grants leave to appeal on the grounds that the matter raises an arguable point of law of general public importance which ought to be considered by that court; and
(c) makes the final decision whether a matter is within its jurisdiction.
In terms of section 167(5) of the Constitution, the Constitutional Court makes the final decision whether an Act of Parliament, a provincial Act or conduct of the President is constitutional, and must confirm any order of invalidity by the Supreme Court of Appeal, the High Court of South Africa, or a court of similar status, before that order has any force.

7 In terms of section 168(3)(*a*) of the Constitution of the Republic of South Africa, 1996, the Supreme Court of Appeal may decide appeals in any matter arising from the High Court of South Africa or a court of a status similar to the High Court of South Africa, except in respect of labour or competition matters to such extent as may be determined by an Act of Parliament.
In terms of section 168(3)(*b*) of the Constitution, the Supreme Court of Appeal may decide only –
(i) appeals;
(ii) issues connected with appeals; and
(iii) any other matter that may be referred to it in circumstances defined by an Act of Parliament.

8 In terms of section 169(*a*) of the Constitution of the Republic of South Africa, 1996, the High Court of South Africa may decide -
(a) any constitutional matter except a matter that –
(i) the Constitutional Court has agreed to hear directly in terms of section 167(6)(*a*) of the Constitution; or
(ii) is assigned by an Act of Parliament to another court of a status similar to the High Court of South Africa; and
(b) any other matter not assigned to another court by an Act of Parliament.

9 In terms of Sec. 170 of the Constitution of the Republic of South Africa, 1996, a Magistrate's Court may not enquire into or rule on the constitutionality of any legislation or any conduct of the President.

Although courts of appeal are entitled, on the hearing of an appeal, to receive further evidence,[10] the focus in this contribution will be placed on the taking of evidence in courts of first instance and, in particular, the High Court as court of first instance in contradistinction to its being a court of appeal also.

2. Civil Procedure in the High Court: A Traditional Perspective

In this regard the presentation is confined to the action procedure.[11]

The civil procedure in the High Court distinguishes clearly between the pre-trial and trial stages. The pre-trial stage is subdivided into the pleading, discovery and preparation for trial stages. The trial, in turn, is a continuous process which is characterised by the immediate (direct) and, mainly, oral presentation of evidence.

2.1. *Commencement of Proceedings and the Determination of Issues: The Pleadings*

The plaintiff institutes the action by issuing a summons that is normally accompanied by an annexure containing all the material facts upon which the plaintiff relies to support his claim. These facts should be set out with sufficient particularity to enable the defendant to reply thereto,[12] otherwise the defendant

10 Section 22(*a*) of the former Supreme Court Act 59 of 1959, provided as follows:
'The appellate division or a provincial division, or a local division having appeal jurisdiction, shall have power -
(a) on the hearing of an appeal to receive further evidence, either orally or by deposition before a person appointed by such division, or to remit the case to the court of first instance, or the court whose judgment is the subject of the appeal, for further hearing, with such instructions as regards the taking of further evidence or otherwise as to the division concerned seems necessary.'
The Supreme Court Act 59 of 1959 was repealed by the Superior Courts Act 10 of 2013 with effect from 23 August 2013. Sec. 19 of the Superior Courts Act 10 of 2013 now provides as follows:
'19 Powers of court on hearing of appeals
The Supreme Court of Appeal or a Division exercising appeal jurisdiction may, in addition to any power as may specifically be provided for in any other law -
(a) dispose of an appeal without the hearing of oral argument;
(b) receive further evidence;
(c) remit the case to the court of first instance, or to the court whose decision is the subject of the appeal, for further hearing, with such instructions as regards the taking of further evidence or otherwise as the Supreme Court of Appeal or the Division deems necessary; or
(d) confirm, amend or set aside the decision which is the subject of the appeal and render any decision which the circumstances may require.'

11 The rules of the High Court also make provision for an application procedure, namely a procedure where the cause of action and defence, respectively, are set out in affidavits supported by the necessary and relevant factual evidence.

12 Rule 18 of the rules of the High Court, *inter alia*, provides as follows:

→

may except thereto or apply to court to have it set aside as an irregular step. The summons is served upon the defendant, who must thereupon, if he wishes to defend the action, deliver a notice of intention to this effect. Thereafter the defendant must, within a stated time, deliver a plea in which he must answer all the allegations of the plaintiff and set out all the material facts upon which he relies. Once again, these facts must be set out in sufficient particularity to enable the plaintiff to reply thereto, if necessary. Although the rules of court make provision for pleadings other than the plaintiff's particulars of claim (contained in the annexure attached to the summons) and the defendant's plea, these two are the most important. The purpose of the pleadings is to apprise each party of the nature of his opponent's case, while their function is to determine the issues which are to be tried by the court. The pleading stage is, therefore, traditionally characterised by party control.

2.2. *The Discovery Stage*

After the close of pleadings, the action proceeds through the next stage where the emphasis is on discovery of documents,[13] the procedural requirements in regard to

'(4) Every pleading shall contain a clear and concise statement of the material facts upon which the pleader relies for his claim, defence or answer to any pleading, as the case may be, with sufficient particularity to enable the opposite party to reply thereto.
(5) When in any pleading a party denies an allegation of fact in the previous pleading of the opposite party, he shall not do so evasively, but shall answer the point of substance.
(6) A party who in his pleading relies upon a contract shall state whether the contract is written or oral and when, where and by whom it was concluded, and if the contract is written a true copy thereof or of the part relied on in the pleading shall be annexed to the pleading.
(7) ...
(8) ...
(9) ...
(10) A plaintiff suing for damages shall set them out in such manner as will enable the defendant reasonably to assess the quantum thereof: Provided that a plaintiff suing for damages for personal injury shall specify his date of birth, the nature and extent of the injuries, and the nature, effects and duration of the disability alleged to give rise to such damages, and shall as far as practicable state separately what amount, if any, is claimed for –
(a) medical costs and hospital and other similar expenses and how these costs and expenses are made up;
(b) pain and suffering, stating whether temporary or permanent and which injuries caused it;
(c) disability in respect of -
  (i) the earning of income (stating the earnings lost to date and how the amount is made up and the estimated future loss and the nature of the work the plaintiff will in future be able to do);
  (ii) the enjoyment of amenities of life (giving particulars);
  (iii) and stating whether the disability concerned is temporary or permanent; and
(d) disfigurement, with a full description thereof and stating whether it is temporary or permanent.'

13 The object of discovery was stated in *Durbach v. Fairway Hotel Ltd* 1949 (3) SA 108 (SR) at 1083 to be 'to ensure that before trial both parties are made aware of all the documentary evidence →

expert evidence,[14] the steps to be taken by the parties in order to obtain statements of witnesses in support of their respective cases,[15] and steps to be taken in order to

that is available. By this means the issues are narrowed and the debate of points which are incontrovertible is eliminated.' Discovery has been set to 'rank with cross-examination as one of the mightiest engines for the exposure of the truth ever to have been devised in the Anglo-Saxon family of legal systems. Properly employed where its use is called for, it can be, and often is a devastating tool. But it must not be abused or called in aid lightly in situations for which it was not designed or it will lose its edge and become debased' (*The MV Urgup: Owners of the MV Urgup v. Western Bulk Carriers (Australia) (Pty) Ltd* 1999 (3) SA 500 (C) at 513G-I). The essential feature of discovery is that the person requiring discovery is *in general* only entitled to discovery once the battle lines are drawn and the legal issues established. It is not a tool designed to put a party in a position to draw the battle lines and establish the legal issues. Rather, it is a tool used to identify factual issues once legal issues are established (*The MV Urgup: Owners of the MV Urgup v. Western Bulk Carriers (Australia) (Pty) Ltd,* above, at 513I). Discovery is not intended to be used as a sniping weapon in preliminary skirmishes (*The MV Urgup: Owners of the MV Urgup v. Western Bulk Carriers (Australia) (Pty) Ltd, ibidem*). The underlying philosophy of discovery of documents is that the party in possession or custody of documents is supposed to know the nature thereof and thus carries the duty to put those documents in proper order for both the benefit of his adversary and the court in anticipation of the trial action (*Copalcor Manufacturing (Pty) Ltd v. GDC Hauliers (Pty) Ltd (formerly GDC Hauliers CC)* 2003 (3) SA 181 (W) at 194I). Discovery assists the parties and the court in discovering the truth and, by doing so, helps towards a just determination of the case. It also saves costs (*Air Canada v. Secretary of State for Trade* [1983] 2 AC 394 at 445-446; *Santam Ltd v. Segal* 2010 (2) SA 160 (N) at 162E-F).

14 Rule 36(9) of the rules of the High Court provides as follows:
'No person shall, save with the leave of the court or the consent of all parties to the suit, be entitled to call as a witness any person to give evidence as an expert upon any matter upon which the evidence of expert witnesses may be received unless he shall -
(a) not less than fifteen days before the hearing, have delivered notice of his intention so to do; and
(b) not less than ten days before the trial, have delivered a summary of such expert's opinion and his reasons therefor.'
In essence, the function of an expert is to assist the court to reach a conclusion on matters on which the court itself does not have the necessary knowledge to. In *Schneider NO v. AA and Another* 2010 (5) SA 203 (WCC) at 211E--214B the following was stated as regards the role of an expert:
'In this connection it is necessary to deal with the role of an expert. In Zeffertt, Paizes & Skeen 2003, p. 330, the learned authors, citing the English judgment of *National Justice Compania Naviera SA v. Prudential Assurance Co Ltd (The "Ikarian Reefer")* [1993] 2 Lloyd's Rep 68 at 81, set out the duties of an expert witness thus:
"1. Expert evidence presented to the court should be, and should be seen to be, the independent product of the expert uninfluenced as to form or content by the exigencies of litigation.
2. An expert witness should provide independent assistance to the court by way of objective, unbiased opinion in relation to matters within his expertise. ... An expert witness should never assume the role of an advocate.
3. An expert witness should state the facts or assumptions upon which his opinion is based. He should not omit to consider material facts which could detract from his concluded opinion.
4. An expert witness should make it clear when a particular question or issue falls outside his expertise.

→

ensure the presence of witnesses at the trial. Traditionally the preparatory stage is also dominated by the parties. It is for the parties to take the initiative in regard to all these procedures.[16] As a general rule the court exercises no control over the development of this phase of the proceedings, except in so far as it may be called upon to resolve a dispute relating to one or the other of the procedures involved.

2.3. *The Pre-trial Conference*

Traditionally, the parties must hold a pre-trial conference in order to endeavour to limit the issues between them, in other words, to curtail the duration of the trial, narrow down issues, cut costs and facilitate settlements.[17] The pre-trial conference is not meant to be a full preparation for trial; it is a stocktaking of possible co-operation in steps which will limit or prevent avoidable effort and costs.[18]

5. If an expert opinion is not properly researched because he considers that insufficient data is available, then this must be stated with an indication that the opinion is no more than a provisional one. In cases where an expert witness who has prepared a report could not assert that the report contained the truth, the whole truth and nothing but the truth without some qualification, that qualification should be stated in the report.
In short, an expert comes to court to give the court the benefit of his or her expertise. Agreed, an expert is called by a particular party, presumably because the conclusion of the expert, using his or her expertise, is in favour of the line of argument of the particular party. But that does not absolve the expert from providing the court with as objective and unbiased an opinion, based on his or her expertise, as possible. An expert is not a hired gun who dispenses his or her expertise for the purposes of a particular case. An expert does not assume the role of an advocate, nor gives evidence which goes beyond the logic which is dictated by the scientific knowledge which that expert claims to possess."'
Expert evidence is only as sound as the factual evidence on which it is based. The less fixed (or more variable) the assumption and the fewer hard facts available to the expert, the greater the scope for alternative conclusions (*Harrington NO v. Transnet Ltd t/a Metrorail* 2010 (2) SA 479 (SCA) at 494B-C).
It is not the mere opinion of the witness which is decisive but his ability to satisfy the court that, because of his special skill, training or experience, the reasons for the opinions he expresses are acceptable (*Menday v. Protea Assurance Co Ltd* 1976 (1) SA 565 (E) at 569B).
The notice pursuant to rule 36(9) of the rules of the High Court has no evidential value. Accordingly, the failure of the witness to give evidence about his qualifications and expert knowledge *in court*, is fatal, as his evidence in relation to the matter before the court remains mere opinion evidence that is irrelevant (*Mkhize v. Lourens* 2003 (3) SA 292 (T) at 299C-G).

15 The witness statements are privileged and are not disclosed to the court or the other party/parties.

16 See, in general, Hurter 2007, p. 240. Hurter 2007, at p. 242, *inter alia*, states:
'The parties interview witnesses (including experts) and alone decide which of these will be called upon to testify and in what order. The preparation and presentation of the case before and at the trial are thus in the hands of the parties.'
Hurter 2007, at p. 243 states:
'To summarise: under the adversarial system it is the parties who dictate at all stages the form, content and pace of proceedings.'

17 *Road Accident Fund v. Krawa* 2012 (2) SA 346 (ECG) at 353H-354A.

18 *Lekota v. Editor*, 'Tribute' Magazine 1995 (2) SA 706 (W) at 709A.

Traditionally the parties are in control of the pre-trial conference.[19]

2.4. *The Trial*

The trial is a 'single continuous drama' where the parties present all the evidentiary material at their disposal to establish their respective cases. As a general rule, evidence is given orally and each witness is subject to cross-examination by the legal representative of the other party, whereafter the judge gives a judgment based upon such material. During the trial the judge is constrained to adopt a passive and neutral attitude lest it be seen that the judge 'descends into the arena and be liable to have his vision clouded by the dust of the conflict'.[20] The judge may, however, put questions to a witness in order to clarify obscure points and it is the judge's duty to see to it that the legal representatives appearing on behalf of the parties behave themselves seemly and comply with the prescribed procedure. The judge is not allowed to go beyond this by, for example, putting questions to witnesses in the form of cross-examination or out of his own accord calling witnesses not called by the parties.

3. The Action Procedure in the High Court: A Developmental Perspective

The greatest historical and contemporaneous challenge facing South African civil procedure is that of making litigation less costly and the courts more accessible to a far greater number of people. Throughout the years the legislators, in attempts to address this challenge, have framed various rules of court and/or practice directives. Each of these attempts mainly focussed on a more active role of the court in the preparation for trial stage, in other words, was aimed at enhancing the concept of judicial activism or, as it is called lately, judicial oversight. The following are examples of such attempts:

During January 1994 the rules of the High Court were amended by the inclusion, in the rule dealing with pre-trial conferences,[21] of, *inter alia*, the following provisions:

> '(8)(a) A judge, who need not be the judge presiding at the trial, may, if he deems it advisable, at any time at the request of a party or *mero motu*, call upon the attorneys or advocates for the parties to hold or to continue with the conference before a judge in chambers and may direct a party to be available personally at such conference.
>
> (b) ...

19 Hurter 2007, p. 243.

20 Per Lord Greene in *Yuill v. Yuill* 1945 All ER 183 (CA); and see *Hamman v. Moolman* 1968 (4) SA 340 (A) at 344E-G.

21 Rule 37.

> (c) The judge may, with the consent of the parties and without any formal application, at such conference or thereafter give any direction which might promote the effective conclusion of the matter ...'

It is clear from the wording of the rule that a judge can give a direction only with the consent of the parties, i.e. party control prevails. If there is no agreement between the parties in respect of, for example, factual admissions or expert evidence, a judge has no power to compel a party to agree to any matter in that regard.

During April 1996 practice directives in respect of commercial actions were issued in the then Witwatersrand Local Division of the High Court.[22] The practice directives empower parties to jointly apply for an action to be designated a commercial action and have same decided by the commercial court of the Witwatersrand Local Division. Rules 8 to 10 of the practice directives read as follows:

> '8 Any party to a commercial action may upon notice to all other parties, apply to the nominated judge in chambers, for an order for directions. Upon such an application, the nominated judge may make such order as he deems appropriate to ensure the just, expeditious and satisfactory determination of the issues between the parties. It may where appropriate *inter alia* provide for and regulate the following matters:
>
> 8.1 A written statement of the issues between the parties.
>
> 8.2 The separation of issues in terms of rule 33(4).
>
> 8.3 The discovery and exchange of documents.
>
> 8.4 The exchange of expert summaries or reports.
>
> 8.5 The identification of witnesses of fact and the exchange of statements or summaries of their evidence.
>
> 8.6 The order in which the parties are to present their evidence at the trial.
>
> 8.7 Any other matters required to be dealt with at a pre-trial conference in terms of rule 37.
>
> 9 The nominated judge may at any time of his own accord or on application by any party, issue, supplement or amend an order for direction, if he deems it appropriate to do so.
>
> 10 No order that witnesses' statements be exchanged will be made without the consent of all parties to the action.'

22 Now the Gauteng Division of the High Court, Johannesburg.

As far as the taking of evidence is concerned, party control clearly prevails. The nominated judge has no power to take evidence and may not make an order that witness statements be exchanged without the consent of all the parties to the action. These practice directives are hardly used by parties to a commercial action nowadays.

During the recent past numerous divisions of the High Court have adopted practice directives dealing with pre-trial conferences and case management.[23] Except for requiring that summaries of expert witnesses must be properly and sufficiently prepared by the parties, these practice directives lack provisions dealing with the taking of evidence by the court and/or the parties. Thus the traditional position in respect of party control in the taking of evidence prevails.

During 2010 the South African government, via the Office of the Chief Justice, embarked upon an attempt to address the need for reform. In a statement on the Cabinet Meeting that was held on 5 May 2010 the following is said:

> 'Cabinet discussed the Civil Justice Reform Project that seeks to improve the efficiency of the civil justice system. The primary objective of the project is to provide a speedy, affordable and simple process for resolution of civil disputes. The terms of reference for the project will entail investigation of the following elements: increasing the effectiveness of the civil courts; the impact and effectiveness of the current legislation on the civil justice system, simplification of court procedures and processes, modernisation of the court's system; effective case management; and harmonisation of the court rules.'

In pursuance of the aforesaid a judicial Case Flow Management Committee was established consisting of senior judges of the Constitutional Court, the Supreme Court of Appeal and the various divisions of the High Court.

The Committee has overseen the drafting of a practice directive which was disseminated to the various heads of court of the respective divisions of the High Court for their input. A copy of the draft practice directives (dated 1 October 2012) is annexed hereto, marked 'A'. The draft practice directive, *inter alia*, makes provision for the following:

An initial case management conference to be held before a judge where, amongst other matters, the admission of facts and other evidence by consent of the parties must be discussed. The judge may from time to time schedule, or the parties may

23 See, in this regard, the Consolidated Practice Notes of the Western Cape Division of the High Court, Cape Town; the Eastern Cape Rules of Practice; the Gauteng Division of the High Court, Pretoria, *Practice Manual*; the Gauteng Division of the High Court, Johannesburg, *Practice Manual*; the *Practice Manual* of the KwaZulu-Natal Division of the High Court, Pietermaritzburg and Durban; the Practice Directives of the North West Division of the High Court, Mahikeng and the Practice Directives of the Limpopo Division of the High Court, Thohoyandou.

from time to time request, additional case management conferences where, amongst other matters, the admission of facts and other evidence by consent of the parties could be discussed and agreed upon. Prior to the trial in any case the judge must hold a final pre-trial conference at which the parties must table a joint proposed final pre-trial order in which the following must be addressed:[24]

a. All issues of fact to be resolved at the trial;
b. All issues of law to be resolved at the trial;
c. All relevant common cause facts;
d. All exhibits to be introduced into evidence during the trial, identified by the party that intends to introduce the exhibit;
e. All objections to exhibits.

Issues and objections not specified in the final pre-trial order are not available to the parties at the trial.

Although the draft practice directive extensively makes provision for judicial oversight, the taking of evidence and the limitation of issues of facts are still in the hands of the parties, in other words, party control prevails. This is, further, illustrated by para *(b)* of the standard draft case management order, which reads as follows:

> 'All documents contained in the trial bundle are what they purport to be, without either party necessarily thereby admitting the correctness of the content thereof, but no document may be relied on as proof of a fact or facts unless the document was pertinently referred to either in an opening address or in the course of evidence.'

The draft practice directive was met with opposition from the Bar (i.e. the advocates profession) as well as the side Bar (the attorneys profession). Amongst the criticism is that the proposals may threaten judicial independence and impartiality since, on the one hand, they will require judges to adopt a more administrative and managerial role (for which they are not suited by the nature of their office), whilst, on the other hand, trial judges will be required to delve into the merits of the dispute at an early stage, thereby substantially increasing the possibilities that the parties and the issues may be pre-judged. In short, judges are primarily there to hear and decide cases and are by and large not supposed to be involved in the developing of the litigation process.

In its response to the draft practice directive, the Pretoria Society of Advocates raised various issues. It, *inter alia,* stated:

24 This is a far cry from civil procedure rule 32.1 in England which empowers the court to 'control evidence' by giving directions on the issues on which it requires evidence, on the nature of the evidence that it requires to determine those issues, and on the manner in which the evidence is to be placed before the court.

'... Both the previous draft Practice Directive and the 2012 Practice Directive provide in paragraph 15 thereof as follows:

"If a party or his or her legal representative fails without lawful cause to attend an initial case management conference, additional case management conference or final pre-trial conference, fails to participate in the preparation of a case management report or proposed final pre-trial order, fails to adhere to the terms of a case management order or final pre-trial order, or fails to participate in the case management or final pre-trial processes in good faith, the Judge may issue such orders as are just, including but not limited to the following -

(a) an order refusing to allow the defaulting party to advance or oppose designated claims or offences, or prohibiting that party from introducing designated issues in evidence;

(b) an order striking out pleadings or parts thereof;

(c) an order dismissing a claim or entering final judgment;

(d) an order requiring the defaulting party or his or her legal representative to pay the other party's costs caused by the default."

9.

In our submission such powers are draconian and cannot, in law, be acquired by means of a mere ad hoc Practice Directive. The constitutionality or otherwise of the powers also needs to be carefully considered. Furthermore, material questions such as the following arise:

9.1 Would the trial court be bound by an order contemplated in, for example, paragraphs 15(a) or (b)?

9.2 What remedies will a party against whom any of the orders contemplated in paragraph 15 have if, for example, the case management judge has not exercised his or her discretion in a judicial manner or if it appears that such judge has been influenced by wrong principles or a misdirection on the facts, etc?

9.3 Is there a right of appeal in the aforesaid circumstances, or not?

9.4 If there is, how does the exercise of such a right enhance the principle of procedural economy[25] and access to justice?

9.5 If there is not such a right, why not?

25 In terms of this principle cases must be disposed of within a reasonable time and with reasonable costs.

10.

> A further question that arises is whether the case management judge may, in view of the active role that he or she played in the arena of case management, ultimately hear the case. In our view, this is not desirable.
>
> 11.
>
> Lastly, we submit that it is common knowledge that the judges in the ... Gauteng High courts have a very heavy workload. In our view they should not be unnecessarily burdened with case administration over and above their primary role as adjudicators. If they are, a real danger exists that it could have a detrimental effect on their primary role, for example, it may hamper their reading time in preparation for cases and it may cause judgments not to be delivered within a reasonable time.'

The draft practice directive has not, as yet, been put into operation.

4. The Power of the Parties in Taking of Evidence

Over the years the 'powers' of the parties in taking and presenting evidence[26] have indirectly evolved through actions taken by the Legislature and the courts. Examples of this evolution include the following:[27]

> Whenever a commercial bank claims payment of money said to be owed to it by a customer who enjoys overdraft facilities, on a current account, which fluctuates, possibly from day to day, it must rely on its books of account and other records of transactions in order to establish the amount due to it by the customer or by a person who bound himself as surety and co-principal debtor. To prove every one of the many entries in the books, which may have been made from time to time by a large number of different employees, might for obvious reasons sometimes be extremely difficult. It has, therefore, become customary for commercial banks to include in their agreements with customers and sureties a clause to the effect that a certificate purportedly signed by any manager of the bank would constitute *prima facie* evidence of the nature of the debt and of the amount due by the debtor to the bank and, further, that such certificate would on its mere production in a court constitute such evidence. In *Senekal v. Trust*

26 The South African law of evidence is based on that of England as at 30 May 1961. See, in this regard, Zeffertt & Paizes 2009, p. 13 *et seq*.

27 Sec. 35(5) of the Constitution of the Republic of South Africa, 1996, which provides as follows, does not pertain to civil proceedings but only to criminal proceedings:
'Evidence obtained in a manner that violates any right in the Bill of Rights must be excluded if the admission of that evidence would render the trial unfair or otherwise be detrimental to the administration of justice.'

> *Bank of Africa Ltd*[28] the Appellate Division (now the Supreme Court of Appeal) approved of the use of such certificates.[29]

The Electronic Communications and Transactions Act 25 of 2002,[30] *inter alia*, provides[31] that a data message[32] made by a person in the ordinary course of business, or a copy or printout of or an extract from such data message certified to be correct by an officer in the service of such person, is on its mere production in any civil proceedings admissible in evidence against any person and rebuttable proof of the facts contained in such record, copy, printout or extract. Pursuant to this provision commercial banks are, for example, empowered to prove bank statements by means of their mere production in civil proceedings.

Sec. 3 of the Law of Evidence Amendment Act 45 of 1988 has empowered the parties to take and present hearsay evidence under certain conditions. It has revolutionised the approach to hearsay evidence.[33] Sec. 3 reads as follows:

> '3.(1) Subject to the provisions of any other law, hearsay evidence shall not be admitted as evidence at criminal or civil proceedings, unless -
>
> (a) each party against whom the evidence is to be adduced agrees to the admission thereof as evidence at such proceedings;
>
> (b) the person upon whose credibility the probative value of such evidence depends, himself testifies at such proceedings; or
>
> (c) the court, having regard to -
>
> (i) the nature of the proceedings;
>
> (ii) the nature of the evidence;
>
> (iii) the purpose for which the evidence is tendered;
>
> (iv) the probative value of the evidence;

28 1978 (3) SA 375 (A).
29 It is upon the debtor to rebut the *prima facie* evidence. If the *prima facie* evidence remains unrebutted at the close of the case, it becomes sufficient proof of the facts set out in the certificate.
30 The Act came into force on 30 August 2002. For a more comprehensive treatment of the law, see Hoffmann 2007.
31 In Sec. 15 thereof.
32 Sec. 1 of the Act defines 'data' as meaning 'electronic representation of information in any form' and a 'data message' as meaning 'data generated, sent, received or stored by electronic means and includes - *(a)* voice, where the voice is used in an automated transaction; and *(b)* a stored record'.
33 See, in general, Zeffertt & Paizes 2009, p. 389 *et seq*.

(v) the reason why the evidence is not given by the person upon whose credibility the probative value of such evidence depends;

(vi) any prejudice to a party which the admission of such evidence might entail; and

(vii) any other factor which should in the opinion of the court be taken into account,

is of the opinion that such evidence should be admitted in the interests of justice.

(2) The provisions of subsection (1) shall not render admissible any evidence which is inadmissible on any ground other than that such evidence is hearsay evidence.

(3) Hearsay evidence may be provisionally admitted in terms of subsection (1)(b) if the court is informed that the person upon whose credibility the probative value of such evidence depends, will himself testify in such proceedings: Provided that if such person does not later testify in such proceedings, the hearsay evidence shall be left out of account unless the hearsay evidence is admitted in terms of paragraph (a) of subsection (1) or is admitted by the court in terms of paragraph (c) of that subsection.

(4) For the purposes of this section -

"hearsay evidence" means evidence, whether oral or in writing, the probative value of which depends upon the credibility of any person other than the person giving such evidence;

"party" means the accused or party against whom hearsay evidence is to be adduced, including the prosecution.'

Inspections *in loco* are principally intended to enable the court to follow and apply the evidence, but may also include some real evidence that is led in the trial. In *Kruger v. Ludick*[34] the practice in these matters was described as follows:

'It is important, when an inspection **in loco** is made, that the record should disclose the nature of the observations of the court. That may be done by means of a statement framed by the court and intimated to the parties who should be given an opportunity of agreeing with it or challenging it, and if they wish, of leading evidence to correct it. Another method, which is sometimes convenient, is for a court to obtain the necessary statement from a witness, who is called, or recalled, after the inspection has been made. In such a case, the party should be allowed to examine the witness in the usual way.'

34 1947 (3) SA 23 (A) at 31.

5. Conclusion

South African civil procedure is traditionally characterised by a closed pre-trial stage. This entails that the parties, at this stage, disclose to each other as little as possible of their respective cases and strategies. Part and parcel of this system is the rule that, subject to certain exceptions, a party is not entitled to be apprised, prior to the trial, of the evidence that such party's opponent intends to present at the trial. The main effect of this rule is that the statements of witnesses on factual issues (i.e. lay witnesses) are protected from being disclosed before the trial. Since they have been obtained in anticipation of litigation, they are subject to legal professional privilege. The result is that the surprise element plays a major role in the context of the presentation of oral evidence at the trial. This could, in certain instances, result in 'trial by ambush'.[35]

As a general rule, lawyers are creatures of habit and those in South Africa are no exception. Their resentment to the extension of the powers of a judge in respect of the taking of evidence and overseeing party control is clearly demonstrated in this contribution. In this regard it is significant that the Supreme Court of Appeal recently, in another context, stated:[36] 'A more active role in managing the litigation does not permit the judge to enter the arena or take over the running of the litigation.'

In the premises, there is currently no talk in South Africa of 'going forward' as far as the powers of the judge regarding the taking of evidence are concerned. The parties remain in control of the taking of evidence, and distinctly so.

35 See, De Vos 1993, p. 276.

36 *City of Johannesburg v. Changing Tides* 74 (Pty) Ltd 2012 (6) SA 294 (SCA) at 313B.

Bibliography

Bernhardt 1968
Bernhardt, W., *Das Zivilprozessrecht,* 3rd edn., Berlin: de Gruyter, 1968.

Cappelletti & Jolowicz 1975
Cappelletti, M. & Jolowicz, J.A., *Public Interest Parties and the Active Role of the Judge in Civil Litigation,* Milano: Giuffrè/Oceana, 1975.

De Vos 1993
De Vos, W.LE.R., 'Die openbaarmaking van getuieverklarings voor 'n siviele verhoor' ('The disclosure of witness statements prior to a civil trial'), *Journal of South African Law,* 1993, Vol. 2, p. 261-277.

Erasmus 1991
Erasmus, H.J., 'Historical Foundations of the South African Law of Civil Procedure', *The South African Law Journal,* 1991, Vol. 108, p. 265-276.

Hofman 2007
Hofman, J., 'Electronic Evidence in South Africa', in Mason, S. (ed.), *Electronic Evidence,* London: LexisNexis Butterworths, 2007, Chapter 18.

Hurter 2007
Hurter, E., 'Seeking truth or seeking justice: Reflections on the changing face of the adversarial process in civil litigation', *Tydskrif vir Suid-Afrikaanse Reg (Journal for South African Law),* 2007, p. 240-262.

Zeffertt & Paizes 2009
Zeffertt, D.T. & Paizes, A., *The South African Law of Evidence,* 2nd edn, Durban: LexisNexis, 2009.

Zeffertt, Paizes & Skeen 2003
Zeffertt, D.T., Paizes, A. & Skeen, A.St.Q., *The South African Law of Evidence,* Durban: LexisNexis/Butterworth, 2003.

Annex

DRAFT PRACTICE DIRECTIVE
CASE MANAGEMENT, ALLOCATION OF CASES AND
CASE MANAGEMENT CONFERENCES

1. On the commencement of this practice directive, the Registrar shall manage the flow of all cases upon the filing of an action or an application in the Registrar's office until the close of pleadings as provided in this practice directive.

2. The Registrar and his designated staff shell ensure strict compliance with the time limits laid down in the Uniform Rules of the High Court (the Rules) in respect of all notices, pleadings and the like as set out in the Schedule annexed hereto.

3. The Registrar shall notify in writing a party who fails to comply with the time limits provided for in the Rules and as set out in the accompanying schedule hereto of such non-compliance. Upon such notice by the Registrar a party shall be afforded an opportunity to remedy the default within a period of 5 days of receipt thereof failing which the Registrar shall refer the matter to the Judge-President or a Judge designated by the Judge-President.

4. The Judge-President or the designated Judge may take such steps as may be deemed necessary to enforce compliance with the Rules.

5. After the close of pleadings the Judge-President or the Deputy Judge-President or the senior Judge designated for this purpose by the Judge-President, as the case may be, shall, notwithstanding the provisions of Rule 37(1)(a), allocate the case to a Judge designated to manage the flow of the case.

6.(1) The parties must hold an initial case management conference within one month of the close of pleadings to:

(a) deal with the issues outlined in paragraph 6(4) below;
(b) attempt to agree on a case management order in accordance with Form 1;
(c) in the event of the parties reaching agreement on the case management order, they shall submit to the allocated Judge, within 7 days of the holding of the conference, both the signed minute of the conference and a draft case management order in accordance with Form 1.

(2) In the event that the parties are unable to agree on the terms of the case management order, they must forthwith inform the allocated Judge thereof and submit to the allocated Judge, within 7 days of the date of the parties' case management conference, a signed minute of that conference. The allocated Judge

shall on notice to the parties schedule a case management conference at a time set by the Judge and shall allow for sufficient time for compliance with subparagraph (3) below.

(3) At least 21 days before the case management conference before the allocated Judge, the parties shall confer about the nature and basis of their claims and defences, the possibilities for a prompt settlement or resolution of the case, and each of the issues to be addressed at the initial case management conference as set forth in subparagraph (4) below. The parties shall prepare a joint case management report concerning their discussion and shall submit the report to the Judge at least 14 days before the initial case management conference. The plaintiff or applicant, as the case may be, shall initiate contact with the defendant or respondent and shall prepare a first draft of the report. The case management report shall set forth the parties' proposals with respect to the matters identified in subparagraph (4) below. If the parties agree on proposals with respect to some or all of the issues, they shall prepare a joint proposal with respect to other issues, they shall prepare separate proposals with respect to those issues. [*sic*]

(4) The following issues shall be addressed at the initial case management conference:

(a) the need for joinder of other parties and the dates for such joinder;
(b) the need for amendments to pleadings or the filing of further particulars, and the dates for the filing of such amendments or further particulars;
(c) the need for interlocutory motions and the dates for such motions;
(d) the admission of facts and other evidence by consent of the parties;
(e) the control and scheduling of discovery, including but not limited to inspection and production of documents under Rule 35; admissions; inspection, examination and expert testimony under Rule 36p and examination of witnesses;
(f) curtailing the issues in dispute between expert witnesses by their participation in pre-trial conferences or in any other manner;
(g) the hearing and determinations of objections on points of law;
(h) any matter that might be raised as a special case for adjudication on a point of law under Rule 33(1);
(i) the giving of orders or directions for the hearing of any separate issue of law or fact under Rule 33(4);
(j) the dates for further case management conferences, if necessary, and for the final pre-trial conference;
(k) the possibilities of settlement negotiations or possible mediation of the dispute;
(l) such other matters as may facilitate the just and speedy disposal of the case, which may include the setting of trial dates.

7. The case management conference before the allocated Judge shall, save in exceptional circumstance, be completed in a single conference and shall not be adjourned.

8. Immediately after completion of the case management conference, but not longer than 14 days after completion thereof, the Judge shall issue a case management order in accordance with Form 1 annexed hereto. The case management order shall address the issues set forth in paragraph 6(4) above that are relevant to the case and shall establish a schedule for all relevant events. The case management order shall govern the subsequent conduct of the proceedings and shall be modified by the Judge only upon good cause shown.

9. The Judge may from time to time schedule, or the parties may from time to time request, additional case management conferences. Such additional conferences shall be held to facilitate the continuing judicial control of the case and may address any of the issues set forth in paragraph 6(4) above or any other issues relevant to the management or resolution of the case.

10. Prior to the trial in any case, the Judge shall hold a final pre-trial conference. The conference shall be held at a time determined by the Judge and shall be attended by the parties and their legal representatives involved in the case. The final pre-trial conference shall address the issues set forth in paragraph 6(4) above, the parties' proposed final pre-trial order and any other issues relating to a fair and efficient trial.

11. At least 14 days prior to the final pre-trial conference, the parties shall submit to the Judge a joint proposed final pre-trial order. The plaintiff or applicant, as the case may be, shall initiate contact with the defendant or respondent and shall prepare a first draft of the proposed final pre-trial order which shall identify the following-

(a) all issues of fact to be resolved at the trial;
(b) all issues of law to be resolved at the trial;
(c) all relevant common cause facts;
(d) all exhibits to be introduced into evidence during the trial, identified by the party that intends to introduce the exhibits;
(e) all objections to exhibits;
(f) the anticipated length of the trial;
(g) the trial date;
(h) any proposals for expediting the trial;
(i) prospects for settlement of the case and whether the parties have participated in mediation or other settlement efforts.

12. Immediately after completion of the final pre-trial conference, but no longer than 14 days after completion of the conference, the Judge shall issue a final pre-trial order in accordance with Form 2 annexed hereto, which the Registrar shall deliver to the parties forthwith. The final pre-trial order shall be based on the parties' proposed final pre-trial order, as modified by the Judge, shall specify the issues set forth in Paragrafph 10 above and shall set a firm date for the trial.

13. Issues and objections not specified in the final pre-trial order shall not be available to parties at the trial. Once issued by the Judge, the final pre-trial order shall be amended only to prevent manifest injustice.

14. The final pre-trial conference shall, save in exceptional circumstances, be completed in a single conference and shall not be adjourned.

15. If a party or his or her legal representative fails without lawful cause to attend an initial case management conference, additional case management conference or final pre-trial conference, fails to participate in the preparation of a case management report or proposed final pre-trial order, fails to adhere to the terms of a case management order or final pre-trial order, or fails to participate in the case management or final pre-trial processes in good faith, the Judge may issue such orders as are just, including but not limited to the following–

(a) an order refusing to allow the defaulting party to advance or oppose designated claims or defences, or prohibiting that party from introducing designated issues in evidence;
(b) an order striking out pleadings or parts thereof;
(c) an order dismissing a claim or entering final judgment;
(d) an order requiring the defaulting party or his or her legal representative to pay the other party's costs caused by the default.

16. In the case of opposed applications, where the issues are simple and no evidence is to be led, the Judge may dispense with any case management conference and may set a trial date, giving such other directions for the conduct of the hearing as he or she may deem fit.

17. This practice directive shall, as far as possible, be implemented in consonance with the provisions of Rule 37. Where necessary, directions shall be obtained from the Judge to whom a matter is allocated in order to resolve difficulties in this respect.

18. This practice directive shall come into operation on 1 October 2012.

STANDARD DRAFT CASE MANAGEMENT ORDER

IN TERMS OF PARAGRAPH 8 OF

THE CASE MANAGEMENT PRACTICE DIRECTIVE

IN THE HIGH COURT OF SOUTH AFRICA
(NORTH GAUTENG HIGH COURT, PRETORIA)

CASE NO:_____________

In the matter between:

______________________________ **Plaintiff**

And

______________________________ **Defendant**

DRAFT CASE MANAGEMENT ORDER
IN TERMS OF PARAGRAPH 8 OF
THE CASE MANAGEMENT PRACTICE DIRECTIVE

In accordance with paragraph 8 of the Case Management Directive, the following case management order is hereby issued:

1. The issues of liability and quantum are to be separated in terms of Rule 33(4), the matter proceeding to trial only on liability as encompassed by the issues outlined in paragraphs ___ to and including ___ of the Particulars of Claim, read together with the corresponding paragraphs of the Defendant's Plea.

2.
2.1 The parties are to make discovery by filing Discovery Affidavits in accordance with Rule 35 by no later than _____.

2.2 The process of copying and inspections of documents contained in the opposing parties discovery is to be completed within 1 (one) month from the date of the making of discovery.

2.3 Within 2 (two) months of the date of discovery, the Plaintiff's Attorney is to make up an indexed and paginated bundle of trial documents ("the trial bundle"), and to submit same to the Defendant's Attorney.

2.4 The Defendant's Attorney will have 2 (two) weeks from date of receipt of the trial bundle within which to supplement same by addition of other documents, and return the so-supplemented trial bundle to the Plaintiff's Attorney.

2.5 The following will apply to the trial bundle, as finalised in accordance with paragraphs 2.3 and 2.4 above:
2.5.1 The documents contained in the trial bundle are to be in chronological order or logical sequence, insofar as that is reasonably possible.

2.5.2 The status of the documents contained in the trial bundle is agreed as follows:
(a) What follows will apply to all documents contained in the trial bundle, save those in respect of which the Attorney for either party has given the opposing Attorney written notice within 2 (two) weeks of the date of finalisation of the trial bundle contesting the status of a particular document or documents.

(b) All documents contained in the trial bundle are what they purport to be, without either party necessarily thereby admitting the correctness of the content thereof, but no document may be relied on as proof of a fact or facts unless the document was pertinently referred to either in an opening address or in the course of evidence.

(c) Letters, emails and telefaxes among the documents were sent on the dates appearing thereon and received by the addressee:
(i) In the case of letters, shortly thereafter;
(ii) In the case of telefaxes and e-mails, at the times reflected thereon.

(d) Copies may be used, and the parties agree that the copies are all true copies of the originals.

2.6 Dates for delivery of Rule 36(9)(a) Notices and Rule 36(9)(b) summaries are as follows:
2.6.1 Rule 36(9)(a) Notices, 8 (eight) days before date of trial;
2.6.2 Rule 36(9)(b) Summaries, 6 (six) days before date of trial.

2.7 The Attorneys are to do everything necessary to facilitate meetings of opposing experts to be held within no more than 2 (two) weeks of the date of delivery of the opposing expert's Rule 36(9)(b) summaries, and to ensure that the opposing experts furnish joint minutes of their meetings, signed by them.

2.8 Unless a party notifies the other in writing within 2 (two) days of date of receipt of joint minutes as foresaid of non-acceptance of agreements reached between experts as contained in the joint minutes, the parties are bound by such agreements.

D. van Loggerenberg

BY ORDER

REGISTRAR

EVIDENCE IN CROSS-BORDER CIVIL LITIGATION

J. Valdhans
D. Sehnálek

THE 1970 HAGUE EVIDENCE CONVENTION, THE EUROPEAN UNION AND THE 2001 EU EVIDENCE REGULATION - INTERFACES

1. European Union - Relationships to Third Countries within the Hague Conference

On 18 March 1970 the contracting parties adopted the Hague Convention on the Taking of Evidence Abroad in Civil or Commercial Matters (hereinafter the 'Hague Convention'). In the context of the Convention, the present contribution will focus on the relationships and roles of the European Union and its Member States related to the Convention's implementation. The Hague Convention was negotiated during the Hague Conference. A majority of Member States of the European Union are currently among its parties. The EU itself is not a party to the Convention for two reasons. At the time when the Convention was negotiated the European Economic Community lacked the power to regulate aspects of private international law. Furthermore, based on the Hague Convention itself, an international organisation such as the EEC could not be among the contracting parties[1] and the Convention also excluded any later accession by an internal organisation.[2]

Since the 1970s there has been a significant shift in the division of competences between the Member States and the European Union in matters relating to aspects of private international law, as these aspects have become part of the EU's agenda.[3]

1 See Art. 37 of the Hague Convention.

2 Under Art. 39, the Hague Convention is open only to a state which is a member of the Hague Conference or of the United Nations or of a UN specialised agency, or is a party to the Statute of the International Court of Justice.

3 The scope of the European Union's competence to regulate private internal law is questionable. The legislative activities of the EU institutions indicate the intention to regulate these aspects in the future through EU law to the highest degree possible. However, Art. 81(2) TFEU stipulates that the EU institutions 'shall adopt measures, particularly when necessary for the proper functioning of the internal market'. This requirement could be understood as a certain limitation of EU competence in this area. Relationships that are not directly related to the functioning of the internal market should remain within the →

Obviously, this internal shift of competence has had an effect on the EU's relationships to third countries and international organisations. As a result, the EU was ultimately able to become a member of the Hague Conference. It took advantage of this opportunity and became actively involved in the Conference's activities.[4]

The parallel membership of the European Union and Member States in the Hague Conference also brought about an adverse consequence for third countries in terms of uncertainty as to the actual scope of the existing competences of the EU entrusted to it by the Member States in the area of private international law. Indeed, it is important to define the boundaries of competence in terms of both practical implementation of the treaties negotiated at the Conference and potential liability for their breach under international law. It is important for third countries to know who will implement a treaty and against whom they should exercise any claims based on such liability.

After acceding to the Hague Conference, the EU defined its attitude towards treaties negotiated at the Conference in a letter drafted by the European Commission. In this letter, the Commission divided the individual treaties into several groups depending on whether or not it intended to accede to them.[5] In relation to the Hague Convention, the Commission took a neutral attitude, stating that the question of the EU's approach to this treaty would be subject to further examination.[6]

No matter how clear the above division of international treaties may be, we consider that it should be supplemented with a clear and specific definition of the EU'S competences in the area of the legal relationships covered by these treaties, so as to make clear which of them fall within the exclusive competences of the EU, which are shared and which are completely outside its competence and thus remain within the discretion of the Member States. This is not indicated unequivocally by the Commission. What part of them remains within the competence of the Member States should have been specified in the international treaties that fall within the shared competences.

Accession to the Hague Conference does not cause the EU to be bound by any international treaties negotiated in this organisation. It would be bound by these treaties only if it acceded to them. In practical terms, potential accession by the EU

competence of the Member States. In particular, this could involve relationships that are in no way related to other Member States and involve only a Member State and a third country.

4 On the related problems and their solutions, *cf.* Martenczuk & Van Thiel 2008, p. 257-299.

5 The treaties were divided into four categories:
(a) Conventions which the European Community should join;
(b) Conventions requiring further reflection;
(c) Conventions which should be left aside;
(d) Conventions which should be left for the Member States to join.

6 We point out in this context that this division of treaties reflects only the Council's and Commission's understanding of the scope of the EU's involvement within the Hague Conference. It is the Court of Justice of the European Union which has the final say on whether or not the Union has competence in a certain area.

to the individual treaties is complicated by treaty provisions that allow only for accession by states. The treaties were apparently negotiated at a time when it was not envisaged that international organisations of supranational nature would be formed, having competences in aspects of private international law, i.e. those which were entrusted at that time exclusively to the competence of the individual countries themselves.[7] There are currently two possible solutions. The first, less likely approach is to change (renegotiate) the relevant treaties so that the international organisation permits accession, or the adoption of additional protocols with corresponding provisions. This, however, will be complicated particularly where the number of State Parties is high and there is a risk that the potential re-opening of the given international treaty could simultaneously initiate a debate on changes in other provisions. The second option is to adjust to the current state of affairs. In that case, the EU would call on its Member States that are not yet State Parties to enter into the treaty in its stead.[8]

The latter solution is easier and, in our opinion, more likely to be used. Nevertheless, it involves certain legal risks. However, it is a mechanism which has been tested in practice and proved feasible. This was so, for example, in the case of the European Community's membership in GATT before the emergence of the WTO.[9] Here too the Member States were parties to the treaty despite the fact that the treaty fell within the competence of the Community in terms of the internal division of competences. This approach is nonetheless conditional on acceptance by the other State Parties. Specifically, in the case of the instrument under scrutiny, i.e. the Hague Convention, the situation would be facilitated by the fact that the Convention does not *de facto* establish an international organisation as was the case with the former GATT. The Hague Convention is implemented purely at the national level through national courts and authorities. Thus, in connection with the Hague Convention, there is no need to address problems related to, for example, voting in joint bodies, or to resolve disputes through *ad hoc* tribunals as in GATT. In addition, even if the EU should accede to the Convention as a whole, it will ultimately still be implemented by the Member States and their bodies. Consequently, this argument, too, supports the second, more straightforward solution.

The only real legal issue could thus occur if the treaty was not observed for some reason. Indeed, if the European Union were a party to the treaty, the signatories would have to invoke the consequences resulting from any breach directly against the EU. This is also true in a situation where the breach was *de facto*

7 Indeed, membership of the Hague Conference as such has no direct effects in relation to individual treaties entered into at the Conference. Every such treaty stipulates its own conditions under which a certain country or international organisation may become a party. Thus, the EU is not bound by the Hague Conventions on the grounds of its membership of the Hague Conference; it would have to conclude or accede to them.

8 *Cf.* Stone 2010, p. 14.

9 See García & Garmendia 2012, p. 49 *et seq.*

committed by a Member State.[10] The Member State would subsequently not be liable under international law, as its sole liability would be based on EU law,[11] towards the EU.[12] However, this would also, in fact, mean that the consequences of a breach by a Member State could be felt by other countries through measures applied against the EU. This negative impact on all the Member States of the EU could not kick in if the relevant treaty was concluded exclusively by Member States.[13]

A treaty may also be breached by a third country. Here again, different approaches would be taken depending on who has acceded to the treaty – whether the European Union or the individual Member States. In the former case, only the EU would be permitted to draw inferences under international law, while in the latter case, in contrast, this would apply only to the Member State concerned and not to the EU. Each of these two consequences would occur under public international law. This question is currently only hypothetical in relation to the Hague Convention. The inferences drawn could be diplomatic (for example, a diplomatic note), taken and implemented by the EU itself. The suspension of obligations under the relevant treaty is another possible consequence. Once again, the decision should be made by the European Council (which approved the treaty in the first place). The decision would have to be addressed to specific Member States, which would subsequently implement it. The reason for this is practical; while the EU negotiates this kind of treaties, they are in practice implemented by the Member States.

Summarising the above, the difference between the two solutions is fundamental. If the European Union accedes to the Hague Convention, the EU itself, and not the Member States, will be the one who will be bound under the Convention.[14] However, it will be up to the Member States to provide for the actual

10 *Cf.* Verwey 2004, p. 150.

11 Indeed, international treaties are binding on the Member States only under European Union law on the basis of Art. 216(2) TFEU.

12 This is because no direct obligation has been established between the Member State concerned and a third country. A non-existent obligation cannot be breached. The only relationship established is that which is subject to the rules of public international law, namely between the European Union and the third country concerned.

13 The solution presented corresponds to the practice of public international law. Nevertheless, it is not codified. This situation is not subject to the Vienna Convention on the Law of Treaties, while the Vienna Convention on the Law of Treaties between States and International Organizations or between International Organizations, which applies to the subject matter of this problem, has yet to come into force. In addition, even the latter Vienna Convention, in its present wording, does not permit any international organisation to directly establish an obligation for its Member States.

14 Nevertheless, a direct obligation can be incurred not only by an international organisation, but also by a Member State. However, this requires an express provision to that effect. Given the absence of a general solution in the existing codified public international law, the only option is to incorporate the relevant provisions directly in the treaty being negotiated. This solution was adopted, for example, in Lugano Convention II which stipulates in Art. 1(3): 'In this Convention, the term "State bound by this Convention" shall mean any State that is a →

implementation of the treaty. It thus follows that only the EU, and not third countries, will have the right to push for observance of the treaty, doing so directly vis-à-vis the Member States.[15] On the other hand, no legal relationship whatsoever will arise between any third country and the EU in a situation where the treaty is concluded by the Member States based on EU instructions. The only conceivable option would thus be to accept this state of affairs *de facto*, as was the case with GATT. However, this ultimately will not be necessary given that treaties are implemented directly by the Member States rather than by the European Union.

2. Relationship between the Hague Convention and the Regulation

The Hague Convention also raises questions in terms of its application. In substantive terms, it regulates the same aspects as those which are provided for in the EU by Council Regulation (EC) No. 1206/2001 of 28 May 2001 on cooperation between the courts of the Member States in the taking of evidence in civil or commercial matters. Both instruments are hence part of the law applicable in the territories of the EU Member States.[16] The Hague Convention is a source of public international law and its national application is currently up to the legislation of the individual Member States. The Regulation is a source of EU law which, in view of the generally known case law of the Court of Justice of the European Union,[17] takes priority over national laws, and thus also over international treaties entered into by the Member States. This, however, could potentially result in a violation of public international law in relation to third countries. It is for this reason that the Regulation expressly stipulates, in Article 21(1), that it shall prevail only in relationships between Member States, whereby it reliably eliminates this problem. The Regulation provides for full application of the Hague Convention in any other cases. We do not consider this the optimal solution. It would be more appropriate to regulate these aspects directly in the founding treaties or within the specification of the conditions of the EU's membership in the Hague Conference or within the individual treaties. It is inconsistent with the overall approach if the relationship between an international treaty concluded by the Member States and an act adopted by the European Union is addressed in the act itself. Each of the documents is the

Contracting Party to this Convention or a Member State of the European Community. It may also mean the European Community'. Through this provision, a direct relationship is established between a third country and the European Union, as well as its Member States, under private international law on the basis of EU law.

15 The mechanism stipulated in Arts. 258 to 260 TFEU applies.

16 More precisely, those Member States that are State Parties to the Hague Convention.

17 Judgment of the Court of 15 July 1964. Case 6-64, *Flaminio Costa v. E.N.E.L.* available at: <http://eur-lex.europa.eu/legal-content/EN/TXT/?uri=CELEX:61964CJ0006&qid=1415819-372921> (last consulted in September 2014), Judgment of the Court of 17 December 1970; Case 11-70, *Internationale Handelsgesellschaft mbH v. Einfuhr- und Vorratsstelle für Getreide und Futtermittel* available at: <http://eur-lex.europa.eu/legal-content/EN/TXT/PDF/-?uri=CELEX:61970CJ0011&rid=1> (last consulted in September 2014).

source of an entirely different system of law[18] and the solution taken is unilateral;[19] fortunately, this problem is, in fact, wholly internal and does not affect third countries. On the other hand, it could be definitively resolved by the EU's accession to the Hague Convention.[20] A casuistic approach of this type, i.e. a situation where an EU Regulation provides for its relationship to international sources of law, is also common in other EU rules of private international law. However, there are considerable differences in the specific wording of the individual provisions that specify the relation of the given rules to the relevant international treaties and, without closer examination, these differences may result in doubts regarding different approaches to identical aspects.

For example, Article 69 of the Brussels I[21] Regulation provides a list of international treaties between Member States (bilateral treaties on legal aid). This solution was adopted from the predecessor of the above instrument, i.e. from the 1980 Brussels Convention on Jurisdiction and the Enforcement of Judgments in Civil and Commercial Matters. The relationship to treaties between Member States and third countries is not expressly dealt with; they remain valid and the Member

18 A closer look at the solution outlined above reveals its weaknesses. The conflict of an international treaty concluded by a Member State with EU law is addressed by Art. 351 TFEU. However, this provision applies only to treaties concluded with third countries, rather than to contractual relationships among the Member States themselves. The problem lies also in the fact that Art. 351 distinguishes between treaties concluded before and after the creation of the EEC or accession of a new Member State. The relationship of a treaty to EU law then depends on the time when, and by whom, it was concluded. The priority of European Union law over such an international treaty is not always obvious. This is confirmed, for example, by the arguments outlined in the arbitral award delivered in *Eastern Sugar v. the Czech Republic*, where the arbitration court denied EU law a priority over a bilateral treaty concluded by Member States. See Potestà 2009, p. 225-245, available at: <http://works.bepress.com/michele_potesta/1> (last consulted in September 2014). The situation is also problematic in case of bilateral treaties concluded by Member States after their accession to the European Union. Such treaties are also not subject to Art. 351 TFEU. The fact that application of such a treaty should take priority over EU law is supported by the rule contained in Art. 30 of the Vienna Convention on the Law of Treaties, which stipulates that the later treaty is to prevail. Nevertheless, the Court of Justice of the EU would not find this solution valid. *Cf.* Ghouri 2010, p. 806-830.

19 On the other hand, a suitable approach was taken in Art. 54b of the Lugano Convention (1988), which clearly defines the effect of the Convention on other competing instruments. The problem with the Hague Convention is that accession does not make it possible to amend the text of the treaty to meet the needs of the European Union. This could be resolved e.g. by a reservation.

20 Public international law allows for addressing the relationship between two international treaties by means of a subordination provision contained in one of the treaties. This option could also be used in the case at hand – given the impossibility of opening the contents of the Hague Convention, this could take the form, e.g., of a reservation to the Convention. See Manzini 2001, p. 782.

21 Council Regulation (EC) No. 33/2001 of 22 December 2000 on jurisdiction and the recognition and enforcement of judgments in civil and commercial matters.

States must proceed in accordance with them. The new Regulation, Brussels I bis,[22] uses the same solution in Article 69, with the only difference that the list of treaties is designed as a separate list prepared by the Commission. Although the procedural provisions in these rules are not universal, they do not apply to purely intra-EU relationships. The concept of rules regulating jurisdiction requires a wide range of overlaps with third countries, e.g. in situations where a person from a third country initiates proceedings before a judicial authority of a Member State towards a person with habitual residence in the territory of a Member State. We consider that if there is an international treaty between the third country and the Member State of the forum, from the viewpoint of private international law it is necessary to apply the international treaty in order for the Member State to comply with its international obligations.

The relation to international treaties is formulated more generally by EU regulations comprising conflict-of-law rules applicable to contractual and non-contractual relationships, i.e. the Rome I Regulation,[23] Article 25 and the Rome II Regulation,[24] Article 28. According to both provisions, the Regulation *shall not prejudice the application of international conventions to which one or more Member States are parties at the time when this Regulation is adopted and which lay down conflict-of-law rules*, i.e. the relevant international treaties are given priority. Only those international treaties that are *concluded exclusively between two or more of the Member States* are replaced by the Regulations. It is worth noting that the text of this provision in the Rome II Regulation (adopted before Rome I, which merely took over the previously adopted text concerning the relationship to international treaties) was written in full knowledge of the existence of the Hague Convention of 4 May 1971 on the Law Applicable to Traffic Accidents and the Hague Convention of 2 October 1973 on the Law Applicable to Products Liability, to which some (but not all) Member States of the EU are State Parties. This is thus yet again a clear attempt at replacing intra-Union relationships by EU regulation, while placing emphasis on compliance with the international obligations adopted by the Member States.

Therefore, the solutions adopted in respect of the relationship to the Convention of the Regulation on the taking of evidence in Article 21, as well as the Regulation on service of documents[25] in Article 20, which unlike the above procedural and conflict-of-law rules expressly stipulate priority of these Regulations

22 Regulation (EU) No. 1215/2012 of the European Parliament and of the Council of 12 December 2012 on jurisdiction and the recognition and enforcement of judgments in civil and commercial matters (recast).

23 Regulation (EC) No. 593/2008 of the European Parliament and of the Council of 17 June 2008 on the law applicable to contractual obligations (Rome I).

24 Regulation (EC) No. 864/2007 of the European Parliament and of the Council of 11 July 2007 on the law applicable to non-contractual obligations (Rome II).

25 Regulation (EC) No. 1393/2007 of the European Parliament and of the Council of 13 November 2007 on the service in the Member States of judicial and extrajudicial documents in civil or commercial matters (service of documents), and repealing Council Regulation (EC) No. 1348/2000.

over the relevant Hague Conventions and other bilateral or multilateral conventions, may seem surprising at first glance. We do not believe that this is so if we look at these provisions restrictively in the sense that the international conventions concerned are replaced only if the taking of evidence or service of documents takes place between Member States of the EU and hence without breach of the international obligations by individual Member States. Extensive interpretation that could perhaps be wrongly inferred from the formulation of these two articles would potentially result in breach of these obligations, on the one hand, and would be at variance with the delimitation of the scope of the two Regulations, on the other hand, as the latter are related to the taking of evidence requested by a court in one Member State for another Member State,[26] or service of a Member State's documents to another Member State. The need for strict interpretation is also confirmed by Recital 23 of the Regulation on service of documents, while Recital 17 of the Regulation on the taking of evidence is not quite so clear-cut. However, this in no way contradicts the above conclusions. This less versatile formulation more or less indicates that the aspects of territorial overlaps of unifying EU rules of private international law did not receive sufficient attention in the early period after the amendments made by the Treaty of Amsterdam.[27] These matters were not dealt with more thoroughly until around 2007; the new approach resulted in regulations providing for retroactive competences of Member States in negotiating treaties in certain selected areas.[28] Once again, however, this is a casuistic, rather than a general and systemic, solution.

3. Competence of the European Union to Accede to the Hague Convention

Having looked at the relationship between individual EU instruments regulating private international law and the international treaties concluded in this area, we shall now proceed to the aspect of accession of the European Union to the Hague Convention. It is obvious from the above that certain issues can be resolved or avoided by replacing the Member States' participation in international relations by involving the European Union. As already noted, the EU itself considers its accession possible. However, this attitude has been adopted only by the European

26 See Art. 1.

27 For more details, see, e.g., Rozehnalová & Valdhans 2009, p. 167-182.

28 Regulation of the European Parliament and of the Council (EC) No. 662/2009 of 13 July 2009 establishing a procedure for the negotiation and conclusion of agreements between Member States and third countries on particular matters concerning the law applicable to contractual and non-contractual obligations and Regulation of the European Parliament and of the Council (EC) No. 664/2009 of 7 July 2009 establishing a procedure for the negotiation and conclusion of agreements between Member States and third countries concerning jurisdiction, recognition and enforcement of judgments and decisions in matrimonial matters, matters of parental responsibility and matters relating to maintenance obligations, and the law applicable to matters relating to maintenance obligations.

Commission and the Council. Nevertheless, the actual existence of this competence can be reviewed by the Court of Justice of the EU, but only if it is asked to provide its opinion, as set forth in Article 218(11) TFEU.[29] The competence of the EU to conclude the Convention is ambiguous. The fact that the aspects of private international law have fallen within the sphere of the European Union's competences since the adoption of the Treaty of Amsterdam might suggest that this competence indeed exists. Article 81(1)(d) TFEU enables the EU to adopt legal acts regulating the taking of evidence. While it does not directly establish external competence, i.e. the possibility to also negotiate international treaties in this area, after the adoption of the Treaty of Lisbon this competence can, nonetheless, be inferred from Article 3(2) TFEU.

However, the reality is not quite so simple. In Article 3(2), the Treaty of Lisbon codified the existing case law of the Court of Justice of the EU. The foundations of the implicit competences doctrine were laid in the AETR decision[30] and were further detailed for the area of private international law particularly in Opinion 1/03.[31] Nevertheless, according to the Court of Justice of the EU, the exercise of implicit external competence is subject to its inseparability from the exercise of existing internal competence.[32] Competence is constituted if the existence of an international commitment adopted by a Member State would have an impact on EU law.[33] This requirement will not be met, for example, if the external and internal regulations are separable.[34] This, in our opinion, is true in taking evidence. The applicable Regulation pertains to mutual internal co-operation among the courts of Member States. In contrast, the Hague Convention also includes third countries and the process of taking evidence is undoubtedly separable from internal matters towards these countries. For the above reason, we consider that the implicit competence of the European Union cannot be considered exclusive, but rather only shared.

A conclusion to the contrary can be drawn from the arguments based on the ruling in *Owusu*,[35] which follows from a broad understanding of the international

[29] The existence of the European Union's competence to conclude an international treaty can be reviewed by the Court of Justice of the European Union only on application lodged by a Member State, the European Parliament, the Council or the Commission. Thus, the Member States and EU institutions might consider the competence to conclude the Convention undisputed and not apply for the review.

[30] See Case 22/70, *Commission v. Council, 'AETR'* [1971] ECR 263.

[31] Opinion 1/03 of the Court of Justice of 7 February 2006. Power of the Community to conclude a new Lugano Convention on jurisdiction and enforcement of judgments in civil and commercial matters.

[32] *Cf.* para 37 of Opinion 1/03.

[33] The problem with the condition formulated in this manner lies in its vagueness and generality. It thus opens space for a further expansion of the EU's competences through the decision-making of the Court of Justice of the EU. *Cf.* McClean 2008, p. 65.

[34] For more details on parallelism of external and internal competences, *cf.* Bourgeois 1998, p. 149 *et seq.*, available at: <http://ir.lawnet.fordham.edu/ilj/vol22/iss6/11> (last consulted in September 2014).

[35] Judgment of the Court (Grand Chamber) of 1 March 2005, Case C-281/02, *Andrew Owusu v. N. B. Jackson, trading as 'Villa Holidays Bal-Inn Villas' and Others.*

element as already taken into consideration by the Court of Justice of the EU in above-mentioned Opinion 1/03. Indeed, the rules contained in the Regulation are also applicable to legal relationships affecting only a single Member State and one or several third countries, i.e. in the area covered by the Hague Convention. From this perspective, the Regulation and the Hague Convention are not separable. The existence of exclusive competence enabling the EU to accede to the Hague Convention is a direct consequence.[36] We consider this approach extensive and hence wrong. It is likely, however, that the Court of Justice will support it if given the opportunity.

4. Content Issues

As we showed above, the question of the European Union's accession to the Hague Convention is not easy to answer. However, additional questions arise given the parallel existence of two similar bodies of legislation regulating the taking of cross-border evidence, including whether any benefit can be derived from this coexistence in the sense that these regulations might not be mutually exclusive but, to the contrary, synergic, all the more so in a situation where the more recent rule (the Regulation) does not hide the fact that it draws inspiration for its contents from the older rule.[37] Therefore, our working hypothesis for this part of the present discourse is that the Regulation replaces and supersedes the Hague Convention in matters where their respective provisions collide. The Hague Convention continues to be applicable among the Member States in matters not covered by the Regulation.

The very text of Article 21 in the Regulation on the taking of evidence provides for the priority of the Regulation over the Hague Convention only in matters of its scope, without preventing the Member States from maintaining or concluding agreements that would further facilitate the taking of evidence (provided that they are compatible with the Regulation). In terms of scope, we distinguish four basic aspects (substantive, temporal, personal and territorial) that may collide in application. Three of them are less relevant for our examination and, at the same time, very easy to assess. The temporal scope follows from the effect of the two instruments, while the territorial scope is delimited by the territories of the State Parties of the Hague Convention,[38] or more precisely the Member States of the EU with the exception of Denmark. The latter, however, is a State Party to the Hague Convention. The personal scope is not limited in any way in the Hague Convention and in the Regulation, and as such can be regarded as universal. Indeed, the

36 In cases where the EU Regulation and an international treaty apply, in substantive terms, to the same matter and both act *erga omnes*, the application of one must necessarily exclude the application of the other. The requirement of the Court of Justice of the EU for the inseparability of internal and external competences is thus fulfilled. *Cf.* Martenczuk & Van Thiel 2008, p. 296.

37 Nuyts & Sepulchre 2004, p. 306.

38 For the current list of State Parties, see: <//www.hcch.net/index_en.php?act=conventions.-status&cid=82> (last consulted in September 2014).

application of neither of the instruments is bound to personal characteristics (nationality, habitual residence, etc.) of the parties to any judicial proceedings in which the necessity arises to take evidence in another country. Thus, the substantive scope is the most interesting aspect. Differences in wording can certainly be identified between the two instruments in the specification of the substantive scope. The following text will attempt to answer the question of whether these differences in wording can be overcome by interpretation or whether they in fact constitute a difference in content. As additional topics, we shall deal with the mechanisms of taking evidence in another jurisdiction in combination with temporal, linguistic and formal aspects.

5. Substantive Scope (*ratione materiae*)

The central notions shared by both instruments are as follows:

- civil and commercial matters: this term limits the scope of the two instruments to matters of this kind; their application in proceedings on other issues is excluded;
- commenced or contemplated judicial proceedings: a phrase limiting the impact of the two instruments to application in judicial proceedings.

In addition to the above, the substantive scope is further defined by the terminology used in the two instruments - and this is where the Convention and Regulation differ. However, a different wording need not *a priori* suggest a different result in application, because the latter is influenced by the interpretation of the respective notions. We shall therefore also examine the following notions:

- competent authority vs competent court: this is a reference to the bodies which are to execute a request sent by the judicial authority before which the proceedings are held. While a Letter of Request may be addressed to a competent authority under the Hague Convention, the Regulation uses the phrase 'competent court', which appears to convey a narrower meaning.
- to obtain evidence or to perform some other judicial act vs to take evidence: as in the previous point, the formulation in the Hague Convention appears broader; another (different) judicial act may be taken under the Convention, in addition to the taking of evidence.

6. Re: Civil and Commercial Matters

Both instruments under examination use this phrase as key to the delimitation of their substantive scope. Neither of them, however, provides a definition of this central notion. The Hague Convention cannot benefit from the existence of an umbrella judicial body providing a uniform interpretation as is true of the Regulation. Therefore, the content of the said phrase is vaguer under the Hague Convention. According to the documents of the Hague Conference on Private

International Law,[39] agreement exists among the State Parties on the exclusion of criminal matters.[40] In addition to obvious civil law and commercial law matters, the matters covered also include family, labour and insolvency matters.[41] There appears to be less coherence in other matters. Tax and administrative matters seem debatable since there is consensus on the exclusion of some of these matters, but this is not true of all these issues. One of the participants involved in the negotiations at the Hague Conference even opined – quite vaguely – that a distinction between civil and commercial matters, on the one hand, and tax and administrative matters, on the other, could hardly be made.[42] It has also been repeatedly pointed out that some countries accept the systematic categorisation provided by the requesting authority, while in other countries the issue is examined by the requested authority under *lex fori*. [43] We generally consider that the Hague Convention applies to the taking of evidence in disputes following from relationships between two parties in an equal position.

We consider this aspect considerably less problematic in respect to the Regulation. The notion of a 'civil and commercial matter' has been well known in the EU environment since the adoption of the 1968 Brussels Convention on jurisdiction and enforcement of judgments in civil and commercial matters. Since it represents the cornerstone of the substantive definition of the scope of the aforementioned Convention as well as of many other, more recent legal regulations of the EU,[44] it has been repeatedly interpreted by the Court of Justice.[45] The phrase

39 See, e.g., *Explanatory report* by Ph.W. Amram, paras 20 and 22, available at: <http://www.hcch.net/upload/expl20e.pdf> (last consulted in September 2014) and particularly *Report on the Work of the Special Commission on the Operation of the Convention of 18 March 1970 on the Taking of Evidence Abroad in Civil or Commercial Matters*, 1978, p. 2, available at: <http://www.hcch.net/upload/scrpt78e_20.pdf> (last consulted in September 2014).

40 Similarly, Besso 2005, p. 13, available at: <http://www.processocivile.org/saggi-%5CARTPRO0001.pdf> (last consulted in September 2014).

41 *Report on the Work of the Special Commission of May 1985 on the Operation of the Convention* 1986, p. 2, available at: <http://www.hcch.net/upload/scrpt85e_20.pdf> (last consulted in September 2014).

42 Report 1985, *supra* n. 41, p. 2.

43 Report 1978, *supra* n. 39, p. 2-3; Report 1985, *supra* n. 41, p. 3, para 2.

44 For example, Regulation (EC) No. 44/2001 on jurisdiction and the recognition and enforcement of judgments in civil and commercial matters (Brussels I); Regulation (EC) No. 2201/2003 concerning jurisdiction and the recognition and enforcement of judgments in matrimonial matters and the matters of parental responsibility, repealing Regulation (EC) No. 1347/2000; Regulation (EC) No. 593/2008 of the European Parliament and of the Council of 17 June 2008 on the law applicable to contractual obligations (Rome I); Regulation (EC) No. 864/2007 of the European Parliament and of the Council of 17 June 2008 on the law applicable to non-contractual obligations (Rome II), and others.

45 See, e.g., Judgment of the Court of 14 October 1976, Case 29/76 *LTU Lufttransportunternehmen GmbH and Co and CO KG v. Eurocontrol* available at: <http://eur-lex.europa.eu/legal-content/EN/TXT/?qid=1415821364645&uri=CELEX:61976CJ0029> (last consulted in September 2014); Judgment of the Court of 16 December 1980, Case 814/79 *Staat der Nederlanden v. Rüffer* available at: <http://eur-lex.europa.eu/legal-content/EN/TXT/-?qid=1415821550463&uri=CELEX:61979CJ0814> (last consulted in September 2014); →

'civil and commercial matter' is defined predominantly in negative terms - the definition excludes proceedings between a public authority and a private individual where the public authority acts within its competence, or between a private individual and an entity to which the exercise of public authority has been delegated. In contrast, proceedings where a public authority (the state) acts outside the scope of its public powers, i.e. does not exercise public authority, are included.[46] Furthermore, the phrase covers proceedings on a private law matter to the extent that the matter is addressed within criminal proceedings.[47] The Regulation is also applicable in civil proceedings on the consequences of breach of competition law from the viewpoint of public law. However, we disagree with Nuyts and Sepulchre regarding the possible application of the Regulation in proceedings held before competition authorities where the authority acts as a public authority and addresses the impact of breach of competition law on competition as such.[48]

We consider that, given this interpretation, the application of the Regulation to tax and administrative matters is excluded.[49] In our opinion, this is not prejudiced by the fact that unlike many other regulations[50] constituting the European Area of Freedom, Security and Justice, the Regulation does not expressly exclude its application to tax and administrative matters.[51] We consider that our conclusion turns on the interpretation of the notion of 'civil and commercial matters' provided by the Court of Justice.[52] We believe that the addition, where application to tax and administrative matters is excluded, was included only with a view to further specification of the aforesaid. In addition, the original version of the Brussels Convention did not contain this addition; it was incorporated in its text only

Judgment of the Court of 22 March 1983, Case 34/82 *Martin Peters Bauunternehmung GmbH v. Zuid Nederlandse Aannemers Vereniging* available at: <http://eur-lex.europa.eu/legal-content/EN/TXT/?qid=1415821646822&uri=CELEX:61982CJ0034> (last consulted in September 2014).

46 Judgment of the Court (Fifth Chamber) of 15 May 2003, Case C-266/01 *Préservatrice Foncière TIARD v. Staat der Nederlanden,* available at: <http://eur-lex.europa.eu/legal-content/EN/TXT/?qid=1415821733952&uri=CELEX:62001CJ0266> (last consulted in September 2014).

47 Judgment of the Court of 21 April 1993, Case C-172/91 *Sonntag v. Waidmann,* available at: <http://eur-lex.europa.eu/legal-content/EN/TXT/?qid=1415821806005&uri=CELEX:-61991CJ0172> (last consulted in September 2014).

48 Nuyts & Sepulchre 2004, p. 310-311.

49 On the exclusion of these matters, see also Nuyts & Sepulchre 2004, p. 309-310.

50 Aforementioned Regulations Brussels I, Brussels II bis, Rome I and Rome II.

51 See, e.g., Besso 2005, p. 13.

52 Similarly also the *Practise Guide For the Application Of the Regulation On the Taking Of Evidence,* 2005, available at: <http://ec.europa.eu/civiljustice/publications/docs/guide_taking_-evidence_en.pdf> (last consulted in September 2014).

subsequently, in 1978.[53] Similarly, this addition is not part of the first version of the Service Regulation,[54] while the amended version from 2007 includes it.[55]

7. Re: Commenced or Contemplated Judicial Proceedings

Both the Hague Convention and the Regulation limit their application to the process of taking evidence in judicial proceedings. However, the possible impact on an alternative to judicial proceedings - arbitration - is not expressly addressed. The Explanatory Report to the Hague Convention refers to the clear conclusion of Commission III, which was responsible for drafting the Hague Convention, that arbitration courts should be excluded from the definition of the term 'judicial authority'. Consequently, arbitration proceedings cannot be termed as judicial proceedings. Nevertheless, other documents are not quite so strict about the impossibility of applying the Hague Convention to the taking of evidence in arbitration proceedings. The Special Commission states in the conclusions of its 2003 meeting[56] that, in accordance with the national legal frameworks of some countries, the instruments established by the Hague Convention can also be used for arbitration proceedings. However, it clearly follows from the further text that any Letter of Request must be presented by the relevant judicial authority of the state where the arbitration proceedings take place. It can be inferred that the Letter of Request must be made within the assistance role, which can be provided by common courts to arbitration tribunals under *lex arbitri*. The concept of assistance roles is based on the principle of voluntariness, by which arbitration proceedings are governed (*arbitri munus non est publicum ut iudicis*), and provides a way of avoiding the use of this principle.[57] If arbitrators have requested that evidence be taken by a common court, the court might request, under the Hague Convention, that it be taken abroad. However, this is secondary, rather than direct, application of the Hague Convention in arbitration proceedings.

The European Area of Justice legislation generally excludes its application to arbitration proceedings - typically, this is true of the 1968 Brussels Convention and the follow-up Brussels I[58] and Brussels I bis.[59] The case law of the Court of Justice

53 Art. 3 of the 1978 Accession Convention.

54 Council Regulation (EC) No. 1348/2000 of 29 May 2000 on the service in the Member States of judicial and extrajudicial documents in civil or commercial matters.

55 Art. 1(1) of the Council Regulation on the service in the Member States of judicial and extrajudicial documents in civil or commercial matters (service of documents), and repealing Council Regulation (EC) No. 1348/2000.

56 Conclusions and Recommendations of the Special Commission on the practical operation of The Hague Apostille, Evidence and Service Conventions (28 October to 4 November 2003), bod 38, available at: <http://www.hcch.net/upload/wop/lse_concl_e.pdf> (last consulted in September 2014).

57 For more on the assistance role, see Rozehnalová 2013, p. 335-340.

58 Art. 1(2) d) of Council Regulation (EC) No. 44/2001 External Link on jurisdiction and the recognition and enforcement of judgments in civil and commercial matters (the 'Brussels I Regulation').

has detailed this exclusion for various types of arbitration proceedings in relation to the possibility of making a reference for a preliminary ruling to the Court of Justice. While this option is denied to arbitrators in optional arbitration proceedings,[60] it is available to arbitrators in mandatory arbitration.[61] Provided that the arbitration institution in question is a permanent body established by law, having mandatory jurisdiction (regardless of the parties' agreement), applying the law and resolving disputes, it is regarded, from the perspective of the Court of Justice, as an equivalent of a judicial authority and is bestowed with the power to make a reference for a preliminary ruling. We consider that this concept is applicable to the legal regulations of the European Area of Justice as a whole. Therefore, an arbitration institution which meets the conditions specified above can be regarded as a judicial authority and the proceedings pursued by it can be considered judicial proceedings in the sense of the Regulation.

The existence of commenced or contemplated judicial proceedings is the subsequent precondition for the application of the Hague Convention and the Regulation. The term 'commenced judicial proceedings' probably needs no further interpretation; the procedural rules stipulate when exactly judicial proceedings commence in the given jurisdiction. The possibility of using either of the regulations in question in judicial proceedings which have not been commenced, but are contemplated, is even more complicated. Amram notes in the explanatory report to the Hague Convention that this phrasing should clearly indicate that the existence of proceedings in progress is not an essential prerequisite for the application of the Hague Convention, and that it can be used for the instruments known in common law countries as the 'perpetuation of testimony' of an aged, dying or going witness, or the civil law instruments of 'l'enquête ad futurum' or 'la procédure valétudinaire' or 'Beweissicherungsverfahren'. This provision was incorporated in the Hague Convention to cover situations where evidence must be taken for the purposes of future proceedings if there is a threat of evidence being lost and such evidence is essential for resolving the merits of the dispute.[62]

59 Art. 1(2) d) of Regulation (EU) No. 1215/2012 of the European Parliament and of the Council of 12 December 2012 on jurisdiction and the recognition and enforcement of judgments in civil and commercial matters (recast).

60 Judgment of the Court of 23 March 1982, Case 102/81 *Nordsee Deutsche Hochseefischerei GmbH v. Reederei Mond Hochseefischerei Nordstern AG & Co KG*, available at: <http://eur-lex.europa.eu/legal-content/EN/TXT/?qid=1415821896257&uri=CELEX:61981CJ0102> (last consulted in September 2014).

61 Judgment of the Court of 30 June 1966, Case 61/65 *Vaassen-Goebbels v. Beambtenfonds voor het Mijnbedrijf*, available at: <http://eur-lex.europa.eu/legal-content/EN/TXT/?qid=-1415821980528&uri=CELEX:61965CJ0061> (last consulted in September 2014), and further Judgment of the Court of 17 October 1989, Case 109/88 *Handels- og Kontorfunktionærernes Forbund I Danmark v. Dansk Arbejdsgiverforening, acting on behalf of Danfoss*, available at: <http://eur-lex.europa.eu/legal-content/EN/TXT/?qid=1415822031543&uri=CELEX:-61988CJ0109> (last consulted in September 2014).

62 Nuyts & Sepulchre 2004, p 312; similarly also the Conclusions and Recommendations of the Special Commission on the practical operation of The Hague Apostille, Service, Taking of →

However, it is obvious from the other documents of the Hague Convention and professional literature that extension of the application of the Hague Convention to also include contemplated judicial proceedings gives rise to practical issues that can be related to the specific common law institute of pre-trial discovery. The depth of the variances is further documented by the fact that this problem is addressed by every single report on the Hague Convention. Pre-trial discovery is a procedure where a party requests that the court order the other party to disclose information or submit documents. Thus, the request for evidence is authorised by the court. Evidence is not taken before actual commencement of the judicial proceedings, but rather in its initial phase, where the court or the jury become acquainted with the evidence.[63] At the request of the United Kingdom, the possibility of accepting a reservation excluding the application of the Hague Convention to pre-trial discovery of documents was incorporated in Article 23 of the Hague Convention.[64] However, the 1978 Report of the Special Commission states that as explained by representatives from the United Kingdom, the reservation was not aimed at excluding the application of the Hague Convention to all pre-trial discovery requests, but rather only of requests that do not sufficiently specify evidence to be obtained or taken.[65] Literature refers to this procedure by the parties before United States courts as 'fishing expeditions',[66] including its effect on parties other than the parties to the dispute, which served as an argument for (*inter alia*)[67] the United Kingdom to substantiate its objections and the incorporation of Article 23 providing for the adoption of a reservation. Due to the lack of a similar concept, the representatives of civil law countries repeatedly commented negatively on pre-trial discovery as a procedure which is unreasonable or overly burdensome. However, it has also been pointed out that the combination of the reasons for refusal of the taking of evidence in Article 12 and the reservation in Article 13 may be excessively limiting and result in refusal of the Hague Convention by judicial authorities in the United States.[68] A recommendation was therefore adopted in 2003

Evidence and Access to Justice Conventions (2 to 12 February 2009), para 47, available at: <http://www.hcch.net/upload/wop/jac_concl_e.pdf> (last consulted in September 2014).

63 See explanation of the USA experts in Report 1985, *supra* n. 41, p. 6.

64 The reservation applies only to documentary evidence and not to other means of evidence such as witness testimony – see *Conclusions and Recommendations* 2003, *supra* n. 56, para 35.

65 Report 1978, *supra* n. 39, p. 3. Referring to the insufficient preparatory work for the Hague Convention, the Report also contains substantiation of the United Kingdom's requirement for incorporation of a reservation (subsequently incorporated in the text of the reservation), which suggests that the reservation is to cover only those cases where a party is required:
a) to state what documents relevant to the proceedings to which the Letter of Request relates are, or have been, in his possession, custody or power; or
b) to produce any documents other than particular documents specified in the Letter of Request as being documents appearing to the requested court to be, or likely to be, in his possession, custody or power.

66 Burns 1985, p. 298; Nuyts & Sepulchre 2004, p. 313 or Report 1985, *supra* n. 41, p. 6.

67 Report 1985, *supra* n. 41, p. 6.

68 *Ibidem*, p. 7.

that the states should formulate their reservation under Article 23 as precisely as possible and avoid general formulations, or rephrase their existing reservations.[69]

Pre-trial discovery is not discussed very often in connection with the Regulation. The composition of the Member States does not suggest that this should be a problematic topic, also given the approach of the United Kingdom described above - while the UK legislation recognises this concept, it conceives its scope more restrictively than the United States. Nevertheless, as Besso points out, the Regulation does not contain any exemption equivalent to Article 23 of the Hague Convention, and therefore, in case of such a Letter of Request (e.g. the disclosure order in England), the courts in the relevant Member State should respond positively and satisfy the request.[70]

8. Re: Judicial Authority and Competent Authority

While under the Regulation a judicial authority in one state addresses the request to a judicial authority in another, under the Hague Convention the requesting authority is referred to as a judicial authority and the relevant (executing) authority in the receiving state is referred to, not as a 'judicial' authority, but as a 'competent' authority. The term 'competent' is also present in the related provisions of the Hague Convention; only Article 9, dealing with governing law, contains the term 'judicial'. The term 'competent authority' is broader, covering both judicial authorities and other persons insofar as they perform the activities of a judicial authority under the law of the forum, e.g. notaries public, commissioners and also attorneys-at-law.[71] In addition, the situation is simplified in the Hague Convention regime in that requests are sent to the Central Authority, which forwards them to the relevant authorities for execution. According to information from the State Parties, the individual Central Authorities take a quite liberal approach in that they do not consider relevant the name of the authority, but rather the character of its activities, which must be judicial by nature.[72]

The Regulation restricts itself to the term 'judicial authority'. The term 'court', or judicial authority, was again interpreted by the Court of Justice in connection with the 1968 Brussels Convention as a body deciding on its own authority on the issues between the parties.[73] Therefore, authorities acting independent of other governmental authorities, whose decisions are rendered in proceedings having the

[69] United Kingdom's reservation was recommended as a model; the text of the reservation is given above in footnote 65. For more on this, see Conclusions and Recommendations 2003, *supra* n. 56, paras 28-36.

[70] Besso 2005, p. 15.

[71] Report 1978, *supra* n. 39, p. 4-5.

[72] Report 1985, *supra* n. 41, p. 3.

[73] Judgment of the Court (Sixth Chamber) of 2 June 1994. Case C-414/92 *Solo Kleinmotoren GmbH v. Emilio Boch available at:* <http://curia.europa.eu/juris/showPdf.jsf?text=&docid=98807&pageIndex=0&doclang=en&mode=lst&dir=&occ=first&part=1&cid=420230> (last consulted in September 2014).

elements of judicial proceedings based on the principle of fair trial, can be regarded as judicial authorities notwithstanding their name, including criminal or administrative tribunals and bars.[74] In this respect we consider the approach taken by the two instruments, despite the differences in their texts, identical.

9. Re: 'To Obtain Evidence or to Perform some other Judicial Act' and 'To Take Evidence'

The Hague Convention does not provide any closer explanation of the meaning of the phrases 'to obtain evidence' or 'other judicial act'. Witness examinations and inspection of documents or other objects are the obvious means in this respect. Among all the Hague Conference documents the greatest informative value can be derived from the 1978 Report of the Special Commission,[75] which points out the tendency towards an extensive approach enabling the Hague Convention to apply to all possible means of evidence. Specific mention is made of requests concerning changes in family status or capacity, for a copy of an entry in a public register, or even to obtain the agreement or the opinion of a specialised judicial authority of the requested state in a family law matter. Thus under the Hague Convention, a request can be made to produce a document including written testimony, expert evidence or designation of a curator.[76] The judicial acts in Article 1(3) remain outside the scope of the Convention. Amram states in the Explanatory Report that the limitation of what falls under the terms 'evidence' and 'other judicial act' is also based on the fact that the act in question must be a 'judicial' act. He points out the possible refusal to execute under Article 12(a) if the execution of the given act does not fall under judicial acts in the state of execution. There have been cases in practice where the German Bundesgerichtshof ordered a blood test to be performed in Italy in a paternity acknowledgement process, the French Cour d'appel of Versailles ordered a preventive 'constatation', which included certain investigations in Spain, and the English High Court issued a search order to be executed in a Paris flat.[77] In this respect, we again refer to the above analysis of pre-trial discovery. The requesting of evidence within pre-trial discovery should not be an absolute obstacle to execution in the requested state if the evidence being requested has been sufficiently specified and the parties are not embarking on a 'fishing expedition'.

The Regulation also does not contain a definition of the phrase 'to take evidence'. In contrast to the Hague Convention, however, the text of the Regulation does not include the extension 'other judicial act'. Therefore, Nuys claims, on the one hand, that the Regulation should be interpreted extensively so as to cover all means of evidence, which would be in accordance with the Hague Convention. On the other hand, he points to the missing words 'other judicial act' in the Hague

74 Magnus, Mankowski & Wautelet 2012, p. 537. See also Briggs 2005, p. 494; Vaške 2007, p. 29.
75 Report 1978, *supra* n. 39, p. 3.
76 Nuyts & Sepulchre 2004, p. 311.
77 Besso 2005, p. 15.

Convention, which he further links to the wording of Article 4 of the Regulation and Annex A.[78] He infers that the Regulation is therefore primarily focused on two types of taking evidence: the examination of a person and the inspection of documents or objects.[79] If Nuys deals with the text of the Regulation, specifically Article 4(1)(e) and (f), and infers the possibility of the application of the Regulation to the means of evidence specified only in the above two subparagraphs, he neglects the wording of Article 4(1)(d). According to him, the request should contain a description of the taking of evidence to be performed. This is a very general wording enabling a wide interpretation. The following subparagraphs (e) and (f) then detail the contents of the request in situations where the request is for the examination of a person or for inspection of documents or other objects. We therefore do not consider that the Regulation applies only to the examination of a person and the inspection of documents or objects. Similarly, Besso does not mention any such limitation and considers that the Regulation covers both acts that can be performed by the court and those for which the involvement of a third party is required (production of documents, expert evidence, written testimony).[80]

10. Partial Conclusion

We consider that despite certain differences in the wording of the definition of the substantive scope, there are no fundamental differences between the two instruments. The differences in wording follow from the different origin and time of creation; nevertheless, the notions used in the two instruments are interpreted analogously and, consequently, there are no application differences. Although the two instruments can exist in parallel, the Regulation replaces the Hague Convention among the Member States in terms of application. Application of the Hague Convention among the Member States also lacks sense given the more flexible regulation of the mechanisms of taking evidence stipulated in the Regulation, as pointed out below.

11. Specific Aspects of Taking Evidence

While both instruments under examination can be regarded as identically designed in terms of substantive scope, differences - which are all the more significant - can be identified in the mechanisms used by these instruments to safeguard the taking of evidence in another jurisdiction. Although both instruments accept that the request of a judicial authority of one state for the taking of evidence in another state's territory represents interference with the latter's state sovereignty, each of them deals with this fact differently. This is due to the different time of creation and

78 The Annex expressly stipulates the following: 12.2.: Examination of witnesses; 12.3. Other taking of evidence - 12.3.1 Documents to be inspected; 12.3.2 Objects to be inspected.

79 Nuyts & Sepulchre 2004, p. 311.

80 Besso 2005, p. 13.

also by the envisaged territorial scope and powers of the grouping within which the regulation in question came into existence. While the Hague Conference is an international organisation with a tendency towards universal application, which is not limited to the European continent, the European Union is a community of countries that are close not just in terms of territory, but also historically, socially and culturally. While the Hague Conference is a traditional international organisation representing a platform for unification among equal parties, where the only conceivable form of co-operation consists in international treaties, the European Union represents a closely co-operating entity with coercive powers towards the Member States and the possibility to adopt its own legal regulations. It is thus obvious that the Regulation could have been designed more flexibly, or in a way which allows for a stronger ingress into state sovereignty. However, it is not our objective to concentrate on technical differences in the mechanism of taking evidence. We shall use a basic outline of the mechanisms only as a background for briefly indicating other, additional issues, such as the governing law and the use of modern technology.

The Hague Convention provides for three methods of the taking of evidence:[81]

- Letter of Request sent to the Central Authority, which forwards it to the competent authority for execution,
- inquiries by diplomatic officers, consular agents, and
- inquiries by (specially appointed) commissioners.

The key mechanism, i.e. the Letter of Request, is sent by the judicial authority in the state of origin to the Central Authority in the state of execution either directly or through its issuing authority (typically the Central Authority of the state in question).[82] This procedure is set up under the laws of the state of origin.

The Hague Convention deals unambiguously with the language aspect. The Letter of Request must be drawn up in the language of the state of execution or a translation into that language must be attached. In addition, it stipulates the obligation of the State Parties to accept the Letter of Request in English or French unless they have made a reservation in respect of this provision. Every country can also specify other languages in which it will accept the Letter of Request.

Given the procedural nature of taking evidence, it is no surprise that the competent authority in the state of execution will proceed under the law of the forum as if the evidence was being taken for the purpose of domestic proceedings.[83] Taking account of the procedural differences in the laws of the State Parties and to achieve the broadest possible application, the Hague Convention allows for making a request for the use of a special method of procedure corresponding to the law of the state of origin. The request can be rejected only if the given method or

81 Burns 1985, p. 291.

82 Explanatory report, *supra* n. 39, paras 36-38; Report 1978, *supra* n. 39, p. 4.

83 Explanatory report, *supra* n. 39, para 96.

procedure is incompatible with the internal law of the state of execution or its performance is impossible by reason of its internal practice and procedure or by reason of practical difficulties. The term 'incompatible' is not to be construed as different but, as Amram states, as referring to variance with constitutional principles – it seems to be comparable to variance with public policy. The term 'impossible' replaced the originally contemplated term 'impracticable', which in itself suggests the shift intended by the authors of the resulting text of the Hague Convention.

The grounds on which the Letter of Request can be refused are set out exhaustively and in minimalistic terms:

- in the state of execution, the execution of the Letter does not fall within the functions of the Judiciary; or
- the state addressed considers that its sovereignty or security would be prejudiced thereby.

Diplomatic officers and consular agents can take evidence in the state of their office only with respect to nationals of their home state, without coercion and only if they are authorised to do so under the laws of their state. The Hague Convention itself does not confer this authorisation on them. If the State of execution does not stipulate this, its consent is not required for this procedure. To the contrary, consent is required if evidence is to be taken with respect to a national of the state of execution or a third country. However, the state of execution may declare that permission is not required. A similar approach is used in respect of evidence taken by commissioners. Evidence can only be taken insofar as the evidence is not incompatible with the laws of the state of execution and in a manner under the laws of the State where the proceedings are being held provided that this is not prohibited by the laws of the state of execution.

It is therefore obvious that the Hague Convention permits interference in national sovereignty by allowing the taking of evidence in the territory of another country, albeit only through the Central Authority or with consent from the state of execution. Steps taken by diplomatic officers towards nationals of their country are the only exception – and this exception can also be limited.

The Regulation goes further in this respect. While it also establishes a central authority referred to as the Central Body, the function of this body is different. Rather than a body through which all requests are transmitted and which is responsible for their acceptance, forwarding and sending back the required outputs, it serves merely to deliver information to courts and, in particular, to seek solutions to any problems that may arise in connection with the requests. The Regulation is based on the principle of decentralisation, i.e. communication between the requesting court and the requested court. Mutual communication between courts in the Member States is to take place directly, without the need for any further assistance (see Article 2). The communication is to be in the language of the requested court or in other languages as identified by the state of execution.[84] In contrast to the Hague Convention, the Regulation also contains a deadline for the execution of a request, specifically not more than 90 days after receipt. For ease of communication, the Regulation provides for the use of forms for the individual acts. As under the Hague Convention, the *lex fori* of the place where evidence is taken is the law governing the taking of evidence. The requesting court can make a request for a procedure under its laws, and this procedure may be refused only if it is incompatible with the law of the state of execution or by reason of major practical difficulties. It is particularly the second reason which reveals attempts at even stronger limitations in respect of the requirement for 'gravity' than those under the Hague Convention.

The exhaustive list of reasons for refusal to execute is also markedly shorter. If we disregard the obvious reasons, i.e. that the request does not fall within the scope of the Regulation, the execution of the request under the law of the Member State of the requested court does not fall within the functions of the Judiciary (which we again consider to be non-compliant with the substantive scope of the Regulation), refusal is also possible on the grounds of failure to supplement an incomplete request and failure to provide a deposit or advance. In this respect, the Regulation comes far closer to automated execution of requests[85] than the Hague Convention, because refusal on the grounds of public policy[86] is not possible.

The most revolutionary new feature introduced by the Regulation consists in the direct taking of evidence by the requesting court. This method, applicable only on a voluntary basis, strengthens the position of the Central Body, which must give its consent to this procedure. It will not grant it when the direct taking of evidence requested is contrary to fundamental principles of law in a Member State, which corresponds to the public policy concept.

What are the effects of the above on the possibility of using modern technology in the process of taking evidence under both instruments? We refer mainly to the use of videoconferences. This is a means which has the potential of strongly accelerating and reducing the costs of the process. In the context of the Hague Conference, the first strong support for this option was provided in the wording of the 2003 Conclusions and Recommendations of the Special Commission in that no provision of the Hague Convention prevents the use of modern means of communication. Their use was placed under the regime of Article 9(2), subject to the limitations specified above.[87] A more detailed output on these aspects then provides an express analysis of the possibility of using videoconferences for the participation of the parties to the dispute (Article 7) and the judicial personnel of the requesting

84 This information, as well as information on the means of receipt of documents or manuals, which exists for ease of reference in the provisions of the Regulation, is available at the web portal of the European Judicial Atlas in Civil Matters, available at: <http://ec.europa.eu/justice_home/judicialatlascivil> (last consulted in September 2014).

85 Nuyts & Sepulchre 2004, p. 332.

86 Similarly also the Practice Guide, *supra* n. 52.

87 *Conclusions and Recommendations* 2003, *supra* n. 56, paras 42-46.

authority (Article 8) in the taking of evidence.[88] The Hague Convention does not exclude this procedure and is compatible with it; however, it does not stipulate the right to claim this method of participation, including the duty of the state of execution to respect this right. Participation through a videoconference can be refused under Article 9(2), and for judicial personnel it is also conditional on consent of the state of execution.[89] It can be expected that this option should not be refused on the grounds stipulated in Article 9(2) in those countries that use videoconferences, and it can be inferred that there exists a duty under the Hague Convention to accept requests for videoconferences, subject to availability in the specific case and technological compatibility of the systems in the state of origin and the state of execution.[90] The Commission also adopted similar conclusions in relation to the process of taking evidence by diplomatic officers, consular agents and commissioners.[91]

A positive attitude towards modern technology is also obvious in the Regulation, which expressly mentions that videoconferences and teleconferences should be enabled or encouraged both in respect of requests (Article 10(4)) and for the direct taking of evidence (Article 17(4)). The requested state may refuse to take evidence in this manner on the grounds of incompatibility with the law of the forum or by reason of major practical difficulties. The same wording is used as that for refusal of a request for a procedure under the laws of the requesting court. Again, there is an obvious effort to minimise the possibilities of refusal. Support for modern means of communication is also documented by the practical guides for the use of videoconferences in the individual Member States, available through the European Judicial Atlas in Civil Matters.[92]

12. Conclusion

The question of competence of the European Union to accede to the Hague Convention remains theoretically disputable. However, there should be no problems at the practical level. In terms of scope, there are no differences between the Hague Convention and the Regulation other than those in the wording of the two instruments. In terms of the questions of when the taking of evidence can be requested and what can be considered evidence, the Hague Convention does not impose any burden on the Member States that would go beyond what they are familiar with under the Regulation. In contrast, from the viewpoint of the methods of taking evidence, the Hague Convention provides for mechanisms ensuring

88 The Taking of Evidence by Video-link under the Hague Evidence Convention by Permanent Bureau, Preliminary Document No. 6 of December 2008, available at: <http://www.hcch.net/upload/wop/2008pd06e.pdf> (last consulted in September 2014).

89 The Taking of Evidence, *supra* n. 88, paras 12, 13.

90 *Ibidem*, paras 29, 30.

91 *Ibidem*, paras 31-35.

92 <http://ec.europa.eu/justice_home/judicialatlascivil> (last consulted in September 2014).

greater protection against interference in state sovereignty, which we regard as appropriate in relation to third countries.

Bibliography

Besso 2010
Besso, C., 'Taking of Evidence Abroad: From the 1970 Hague Convention to the 2001 European Regulation', in Nuyts, A. & Watté, N. (eds.), *International Civil Litigation in Europe and Relations with Third States*, Brussels: Bruylant, 2010, p. 365-379.

Bourgeois 1998
Bourgeois, J., 'External Relations Powers of the European Community', *Fordham International Law Journal*, 1998, Vol. 22, p. 149-173. Available at: <http://ir.lawnet.-fordham.edu/ilj/vol22/iss6/11>.

Briggs 2005
Briggs, A., *Civil Jurisdiction and Judgments*, London: LLP – Norton Rose, 2005.

Burns 1985
Burns, M.T., 'The Hague Convention on Taking Evidence Abroad: Conflict over Pretrial Discovery', *Michigan Journal of International Law*, 1985, p. 291-310.

García & Garmendia 2012
García, A.R.B. & Garmendia, R.G., 'The EU as an Actor at the WTO: Its Strengths and Weaknesses throughout History, *Eastern Journal of European Studies*, 2012, p. 49-66.

Ghouri 2010
Ghouri, A.A., 'Resolving Incompatibilities of Bilateral Investment Treaties of the EU Member States with the EC Treaty: Individual and Collective Options', *European Law Journal*, 2010, Vol. 16(6), p. 806-830.

Magnus, Mankowski & Wautelet 2012
Magnus, U., Mankowski, P. & Wautelet, P., *Brussels I Regulation, Art. 32*, Munich: Sellier, 2012.

Manzini 2001
Manzini, P., 'The Priority of Pre-Existing Treaties of EC Member States within the Framework of International Law', *European Journal of International Law*, 2001, Vol. 12, p. 781-792.

Martenczuk & Van Thiel 2008
Martenczuk, B. & Van Thiel, S., *Justice, Liberty, Security: New Challenges for EU External Relations*, Brussels: VUB Press, 2008, p. 257-299.

McClean 2008
McClean, D., 'Bilateral Agreements with Non-member States after the 'Lugano' Opinion', in Malatesta, A., Bariatti, S. & Pocar, F. (eds.), *The External Dimension of EC Private International Law in Family and Succession Matters,* Padova: Wolters Kluwer, 2008, p. 55-76.

Nuyts & Sepulchre 2004
Nuyts, A. & Sepulchre, J., 'Taking of Evidence in the European Union under EC Regulation 1206/2001', *Business Law International,* 2004, Vol. 3, p. 305-336.

Potestà 2009
Potestà, M., 'Bilateral Investment Treaties and the European Union. Recent Developments in Arbitration and Before the ECJ', *The Law & Practice of International Courts and Tribunals,* 2009, Vol. 8(2), p. 225-245.

Rozehnalová 2013
Rozehnalová, N., *Rozhodčí řízení v mezinárodním a vnitrostátním obchodním styku,* Praha: Wolters Kluwer, 2013.

Rozehnalová & Valdhans 2009
Rozehnalová, N. & Valdhans, J., 'Europejski obszar sądowy i jego wpływ na państwa trzecie, zwłaszcza wschodnie', in Zdanowicz, M. & Doliwa-Klepacka, A. (eds.), *Wybrane aspekty wpływu członkostwa Państw Europy Środkowo - Wschodniej na stosunki ze wschodnimi państwami ościennymi,* Białystok: Wydzial Prawa Uniwersytetu w Białymstoku, 2009, p. 167-182.

Stone 2010
Stone, P., *EU Private International Law,* Cheltenham: Edward Elgar Publishing, 2010.

Vaške 2007
Vaške, V., *Uznání a výkon cizích rozhodnutí v České republice,* Praha: C.H. Beck, 2007.

Verwey 2004
Verwey, D., *The European Community, the European Union and the International Law of Treaties,* The Hague: T.M.C. Asser Press, 2004.

IUS COMMUNE EUROPAEUM

A peer-reviewed book series in which the common foundations of the legal systems of the Member States of the European Union are the central focus.

The *Ius Commune Europaeum* series includes horizontal comparative legal studies as well as studies on the effect of treaties within the national legal systems. All the classic fields of law are covered. The books are published in various European languages under the auspices of METRO, the Institute for Transnational Legal Research at the Maastricht University.

Recently published:

Volume 126: *Legal Evolution and Hybridisation. The Law of Shares Transfer in England*, M. SOLINAS
Volume 127: *The Role of EU State Aid Law in Promoting a Pro-Innovation Policy. A Review from the Perspective of University-Industry R&D Cooperation*, M. CISNEROS
Volume 128: *Tradition, Codification and Unification. Comparative – Historical Essays on Developments in Civil Law*, J.M. MILO, J.H.A. LOKIN and J.M. SMITS
Volume 129: *Nobody's Perfect. Comparative Essays on Appeals and other Means of Recourse against Judicial Decisions in Civil Matters*, A. UZELAC and C.H. VAN RHEE (eds.)
Volume 130: *Legal Aid in the Low Countries*, A. TERLOUW and B. HUBEAU (eds.)
Volume 131: *State Aid and Public Procurement in the European Union*, S.L.T. SCHOENMAEKERS, W. DEVROE and N.J. PHILIPSEN (eds.)
Volume 132: *Property Law Perspectives III*, A. APERS, S. BOULY, E.L.C. DEWITTE and D. GRUYAERT (eds.)
Volume 133: *Multi-Party Redress Mechanisms in Europe: Squeaking Mice?*, V. HARSÁGI and C.H. VAN RHEE (eds.)
Volume 134: *Europe at the Edge of Pluralism*, D. GOZDECKA and M. KMAK
Volume 135: *Cooperative Agreements between Public Authorities. The Influence of CJEU Case Law on National Legal Systems*, K. WAUTERS
Volume 136: *Common Core, PECL and DCFR: Could They Change Shipping and Transport Law?*, W. VERHEYEN, F.G.M. SMEELE and M.A.I.H. HOEKS
Volume 137: *Who Does What? On the Allocation of Competences in European Private Law*, B. AKKERMANS, J. HAGE, N. KORNET and J.M. SMITS
Volume 138: *The Nature of Mutual Recognition in European Law. Re-examining the Notion from an Individual Rights Perspective with a View to Its Further Development in the Criminal Justice Area*, WOUTER VAN BALLEGOOIJ

www.ingramcontent.com/pod-product-compliance
Ingram Content Group UK Ltd.
Pitfield, Milton Keynes, MK11 3LW, UK
UKHW051926100926
8556IPUK00022B/1385

9 781780 683386